The Counterintelligence
Chronology

D1520987

ALSO BY EDWARD MICKOLUS

Terrorism, 2008–2012: A Worldwide Chronology
(McFarland, 2014)

The Counterintelligence Chronology

*Spying by and Against
the United States
from the 1700s through 2014*

Edward Mickolus

McFarland & Company, Inc., Publishers
Jefferson, North Carolina

LIBRARY OF CONGRESS CATALOGUING-IN-PUBLICATION DATA

Mickolus, Edward F., author.
The counterintelligence chronology : spying by and against the
United States from the 1700s through 2014 / Edward Mickolus.
p.   cm.
Includes bibliographical references and index.

ISBN 978-1-4766-6251-0 (softcover : acid free paper) ∞
ISBN 978-1-4766-2240-8 (ebook)

1. Spies—United States—History—Chronology.   2. Espionage, American—History—Chronology.   3. Espionage—United States—History—Chronology.   4. Intelligence service—United States—
History—Chronology.   I. Title.

UB271.U5M53 2015   327.73002'02—dc23   2015025616

BRITISH LIBRARY CATALOGUING DATA ARE AVAILABLE

Front cover image © Digital Vision/Photodisc/Thinkstock

Printed in the United States of America

McFarland & Company, Inc., Publishers
Box 611, Jefferson, North Carolina 28640
www.mcfarlandpub.com

CONTENTS

Acknowledgments

I'd particularly like to thank my colleagues in the intelligence and law enforcement communities, including staffers, contractors, and alumni, who kindly provided comments on the draft, making suggestions on sources, adding to the descriptions, and correcting details. I'm especially indebted to Cynthia Kwitchoff and several other officers still serving whose names cannot yet be disclosed. They know who they are, you don't have to, and they know that I appreciate their wise counsel. I'd also like to thank Circuit Judge Peter L. Dearing, Michael J. Hudak, Jr., C. Douglas Jones, John Nason, Jeff Riley, and George Wisnovsky for their counsel regarding FBI and defense attorney handling of foreign counterintelligence cases.

INTRODUCTION

Spying, as a profession, a second career, or just an avocation, can be traced back to Biblical times; there are more than 100 references to such activities in the Bible. Joshua, son of Nun, was probably the most famous early espionage agent, ordered by Moses to scout Canaan. Few nations have been able to survive for long without some intelligence on its enemies, not to mention its fair-weather friends. Spying has been with us since before the invention of the nation-state, as tribes, city-states, and individual gangs have sought to keep up to date on where the next challenges will come from. Alliances come and go, and leaders—of governments, corporations, or other organizations—need to keep up on what those outside of the group can do (commonly called "capabilities" in intel-speak) and are considering doing ("intentions" in the same dialect).

When I was managing new counterintelligence (CI) officers—and every intelligence officer is a counterintelligence officer—there was no one-stop-shopping book to which I could refer them that would provide thumbnails on the cases that preceded their work. There were numerous memoirs by spies, studies of individual cases, and examinations of various services, but no simple reference to the hundreds of cases that pockmark our history. This book is written to fill this gap. It is not intended to provide exhaustive detail on any case. It more mod-estly offers a quick précis of a case, with suggestions for further reading at the end. Several major espionage cases have made some spies—Aldrich Ames, Robert Hanssen, James Nicholson, for example—household names and the subjects of major motion pictures and television series. A host of others, many limned below, have popped up before, during, and after my career. While it is relatively easy to remember the major cases, the not-so-famous and fleetingly famous are more difficult, yet have important lessons for us. This chronology is designed to let the next generation of intelligence officers, as well as the American people in general, know that our enemies do not give up after a spy or two is captured, but continue their activities against U.S. interests. These thumbnail sketches are intentionally brief; further details are available in the works noted in the bibliographic essay and general bibliography that follows this list. The bibliography was written by America's foremost scholar on the literature of counterintelligence, Hayden Peake, who for many years has served as the curator of the Historical Intelligence Collection of the Central Intelligence Agency, and who has written hundreds of book reviews for *Studies in Intelligence*, publications of the Association of Former Intelligence Officers, and scholarly publications devoted to intelligence and national security.

1

During my 40-year affiliation with the U.S. Intelligence Community, there has been a depressing amount of work for counterintelligence colleagues who focus on espionage. (See Appendix A and Appendix B for a partial listing of their in-boxes.) (For purposes of this volume, "espionage" will generally refer to human penetrations of organizations to obtain secrets. Discussions of the myriad technical espionage methods, satellite or aerial reconnaissance, signals interception, cryptanalysis, and the like, while key methods of intelligence, are beyond the scope of our coverage.) Their focus is essentially on Big CI (protecting the key national security information of the country, not just limited to the files of the U.S. government, but also industrial secrets, weapons information, etc.) and Little CI (rooting out moles and other flavors of spies).

In developing these entries, I relied on descriptions offered in the books and websites in the two bibliographies that follow this chronology. I found particularly helpful—and authoritative—the websites of federal agencies with counterintelligence roles—the FBI, the USMC, the National Counterintelligence Center (NACIC), the National Counterintelligence Executive (NCIX), and the CIA—and the work of the Defense Personnel and Security Research Center (PERSEREC), the newsfeed of the Association of Former Intelligence Officers (AFIO), and the newsletter of the CI Center, plus innumerable conversations with our colleagues in these organizations.

While this chronology aims at illuminating the historical espionage threat against U.S. interests, it is not limited to cases involving Americans happening on American soil. (For a listing of the Americans cited in the chronology, see Appendix A.) Spying against Western and allied governments and firms frequently involve the theft of U.S. secrets, whether of national security or of corporate intellectual property. Hostile services look for access to American secrets, and if they cannot penetrate a U.S. organization, perhaps they can get the same information by targeting a less-well-protected third party. When appropriate, these third-party cases involving American interests are included. Moreover, while this volume focuses on spying mostly conducted by agents of the Soviet Bloc and later Russia (for a partial list of identified hostile intelligence service agents, see Appendix B), I have included mentions of spying by third countries against fourth parties to offer some context for the environment in which counterintelligence organizations operate. Credibility of these third- and fourth-party allegations, however, is frequently suspect, with regimes often using the specter of spying to whip up anti–Western and anti-dissident public opinion, rather than illuminating true espionage threats. There are also a few instances of industrial espionage involving official secrets, although most of these would otherwise be included under our earlier criteria.

For further flavor of the espionage environment, I have added major milestones in counterintelligence history, including the formation of key Western and Soviet Bloc organizations; changes in laws regarding espionage, counterintelligence, and intelligence collection; birthdates and tenures of CIA directors and deputy directors; and birthdates of other individuals who had a major impact on present-day counterintelligence practice. Also noted are defections of members of hostile intelligence services, with notes on their activities, when known. In many cases, details of their espionage work remain classified by the recipient governments.

In most cases, the main entry regarding a specific spy case is keyed to the arrest date of the individual or individuals, if known.

Second choice is the date of sentencing of the perpetrator or perpetrators. In some cases, I have had to use some other key date in the spy's career as a turncoat, such as date of walk-in, date pitched by the hostile service, or even date of death (in instances in which discovery of his or her espionage was posthumous). To permit ease of access of these cases for researchers, I have also included a brief (usually one-sentence) mention of trial dates, dates of conviction, dates of sentencing, birthdates, and any other relevant chronological material. In the charts that follow, the date(s) that appears after an individual's name refers to the date(s) his or her name appear(s) in the chronology.

Why Did They Spy?

Those who engage in counterespionage self-identify as part of a cause larger than themselves and usually cite patriotic motivations for joining an intelligence service. Colleagues who have worked in counterintelligence (CI), as well as those who have delved into other aspects of the intelligence profession, have all expressed their love of country in determining for them their choice of careers.

Alas, such altruistic motivations sometimes erode during the course of an intelligence, military or law enforcement officer's career, or during the careers of other professionals, leading them to either volunteer to hostile, and sometimes not-apparently-hostile, intelligence services (often called "walk-ins" in intelligence dialect) or exhibit vulnerabilities (exploitable problems and personality traits) that can be used by foreign intelligence services in developing a "pitch" to entice Americans to spy.

Finding sources of information has been relatively easy for intelligence organizations. Individuals commit treason for a variety of reasons, usefully summed up by the mnemonic MICE: money, ideology, compromise/coercion, and ego. There are the occasional individuals who commit treason for other reasons (psychiatric difficulties are in this category), but most of the cases noted in this chronology are attributable to MICE motivations.

Figure 1: Motivations of Spies and Would-Be Spies for Foreign Intelligence Services Against U.S. Interests, 1776–2014

	Money	Ideology	Coercion	Ego	Revenge	Adventure	Heritage	Sex
England	2	3		1	1			
Confederacy		2						
Nazi Germany	3	2		1	2	1	33	1
Imperial Japan	2							
Soviet Bloc								
USSR/Russia	70	24	9	9	14	7	3	9
Bulgaria	1							
Czechoslovakia	2			1		1		
East Germany	8	2	1	2	3	1		4
Hungary	3			1		1		
Poland	3		1					1
al Qaeda	1	2			1			
Australia		1		1				
Austria	1							
China	15	1					5	3
Cuba	1	2					1	

	Money	Ideology	Coercion	Ego	Revenge	Adventure	Heritage	Sex
Ecuador		1		1				
Egypt							1	
France	1				1			
Germany	1							
Ghana								1
Greece	1		1					
Iran						1		
Iraq	5	1		1			4	
Israel	5	3		1		1	2	
Italy	1							
Japan	1							
Jordan	1	1					1	
Liberia								
Libya	3							
Narcotraffickers	2							1
Netherlands		1						
North Korea	2						1	1
North Vietnam		1	1				1	
Philippines	1							1
Saudi Arabia		1						
South Africa	4	2						
South Korea							1	
Switzerland	1							
Syria		1					2	
Taiwan		1					1	1
Venezuela								

Methodological Note: There is some doublecounting because some individuals worked for several services or countries. Listing a service does not necessarily mean that the individual was recruited by the service. Affiliating a service with, say, a monetary motivation does not mean that the service actually paid—or even met—the spy. The entry simply indicates that the would-be spy was drawn to approach that service for the listed motivation. In many cases, the individual attempted to contact the service and was rebuffed—as far as we know.

Motivations are not vulnerabilities. I have not listed psychological or physical dependencies, such as alcohol and drug addictions, which can be used by hostile services in developing recruitment pitches, but which are not initial motivations for the spy.

The handful of cases from the Revolutionary War and Civil War are mostly tied together by ideological motivations, as To-

ries and Southerners trapped in the United States at the beginning of these respective wars were often more sympathetic to U.S. rivals.

Motivations shifted in World War II. Heritage was key in the cases of Nazi spies, most of whom were transplants from Germany. It is likely that ideology also played a part, but my sources are silent on this secondary motive. Despite the internment of Japanese U.S. citizens during World War II because of fears about possibly divided loyalties, our chronology lists no instances in which Japan recruited and ran Japanese Americans. Money, the most popular of the motivations, was the sole trigger for the two Imperial Japan spies.

In the early days of the USSR, fellow travelers sympathetic to the communist cause provided easy pickings for Soviet case officers. This pipeline of no- or low-cost communist sympathizers dried up in the

1950s. The NKVD, KGB, GRU, and other services did not rely upon ideology, however, using sexual entrapment ("What would your wife think?"), coercion ("What will happen to your family back home?"), appeals to a sense of adventure, wishes for vengeance against a country or organization that did not reward the aggrieved individual as extensively as he or she believed was warranted, and sometimes simple flattery of an enlarged ego. In virtually all instances, the Soviets paid their agents, although some ideologically-motivated sources only recouped expenses. The Soviets' reputation of being quick with a dollar for secrets led many volunteers to believe that the best place to go to get paid was the local KGB office, which often turned out to be an FBI sting operation. In some cases, this impression was warranted—longterm assets like Aldrich Ames (see Figure 3) became millionaires. In others, the Soviets sent their short-term asset packing with a hearty handshake and $8 for car fare.

The recruitment patterns established by the Soviets were mimicked by their Bloc junior partners. In virtually all instances, spies for the East European services asked for or received payment. On occasion, other motivations came into play; the East Germans were particularly adept at running Romeo operations against lonely Western secretaries with in-boxes bursting with classified memos.

The tertiary services present a mixed bag, although nearly everyone asked for and received payment. The Chinese ran a decades-long seeding operation with Larry Wu-Tai Chin and often approached American citizens of Chinese descent with calls to assist their motherland. They were not, however, beyond paying cash to the financially-motivated volunteer. The Chinese have probably led the world in adapting to new espionage technologies, developing sophisticated computer hacking operations which often do not require the use of a human source to obtain information.

Otherwise friendly services often are surprised by approaches by Americans claiming access, carrying classified documents, and offering a deal. In some cases, they happily heard the offer and accepted. In other instances, they approached the Americans. Although titularly American allies, governments often have interests that diverge from American interests, and seek to obtain their own goals, which can entail targeting Americans.

Hostile services have also been surprised by walk-ins. Even the Soviets turned some would-be volunteers away, fearing a Western provocation, a terrorist probe, or just not believing the validity of the individual's claims.

Whom Do Foreign Intelligence Services Target?

The demographics of spies illustrate a mixed bag of backgrounds. They come from all levels of society, from the scions of wealthy families and elite schools to losers carrying a dishonorable discharge throughout their lives. They roamed the halls of academe; the corridors of the White House, the Intelligence Community, and the Department of Defense; and the factory floor. Their one commonality was access, or potential access, to secrets and a willingness to use that access for their MICE motivations.

The breadth of foreign regimes and their intelligence services suggests that there would be a diversity of targeting, both of organizations and of individuals within the organizations and/or with access to information within the organizations. The interests of individual nations and individual services differ, and the types of information they need, and the likely places or individuals with access to that type of information, lead to a host of potential targets.

Figure 2: Organizations Targeted by Foreign Intelligence Services and/or Affiliations of Would-Be Spies

Targets	Rev War	Civil War	World War I	1920s–1930s	World War II	late 1940s	1950s	1960s	1970s	1980s	1990s	2000s	2010s
White House		2		1								1	
U.S. Congress		1								1	1	1	1
U.S. Army	5	2		1		1	6	7	1	13	6	4	4
U.S. Navy/ shipping				21	3		1	2	1	30	6	6	4
USMC										4	1	1	2
USAF/air			4		1		3	5	3	8	3	3	1
National Guard											1		
State/USAID			4		1	1		1	1		5	3	3
DOD			3				1				5	5	1
DOE/Manhattan					1		6				2	1	1
CIA							1		4	6	4	1	2
DIA										1	1	3	1
NSA								4		2	3	1	1
OSS					1		2						
FBI										3	1	3	
Other U.S. intel							1			1		1	
Other USG			1		1	2	2				1	1	2
U.S. journalists								1			1	1	
U.S. companies				9			3	1	4	9	6	13	6
U.S. political groups						1				3	3	2	
U.S. think tanks										1			1
U.S. universities										1		1	2
U.S. allies			1	14		2	12	8	7	9	5	4	11
United Nations										2			

Methodological Notes: Numbers show dates in which humint (human-source intelligence) cases described in the entries in the chronology came to the attention of U.S. authorities (usually the date of arrest). There is thus a slight lag between the dates of activities of the spies and this chart, which generally records the date on which the spy's activities ceased due to arrest. In instances of multiple arrests of a cell on the same date, only one case is tallied. If cell members are arrested over several days, separate tallies are used, one per date. There is some doublecounting—some individuals worked as contractors, but the target(s) were U.S. government or allied organizations and not just the contractor company.

Targets are not volunteers, but both are measures of the extent of historic security risks for these organizations.

Spying against American interests and types of interests has expanded during our history, as our foreign footprint has gotten bigger and our list of rivals has expanded. In the early days of the republic, the English were interested in defeating Washington's troops on the ground and concentrated on the fledgling army's strength. During the Civil War, the confederates tried to leverage their well-placed assets, using them as agents of influence and lethal covert action in addition to classical collectors. In the run-up to World War II, the Nazis were especially concerned about Americans shipping needed supplies to the Allies, with the bulk of their operations concentrated against U.S. shipping firms and the Navy itself. The Soviets worked the Allied target but also began getting footholds in the U.S. military and individuals involved in the Manhattan Project to build nuclear weapons. In the 1950s, foreign intelligence activity against U.S. interests expanded into more types of organizations, adding U.S. defense firms, each branch of the armed forces, and some intelligence services.

Would-be spies were watching these developments, calculating what the hostile services needed and who could fulfill their needs for money, revenge, sex, ego gratification, and the like. The 1980s saw the explosive growth of volunteers and would-be volunteers from a plethora of organizations and entities, revealing a counterintelligence problem that extended beyond classical targets. This trend has held steady in the decades following the end of the Cold War, with virtually any U.S. public or private interest a potential target of some foreign intelligence service, hostile or otherwise.

Who Collects Against American Interests?

Even before the birth of the republic, hostile intelligence services have been actively seeking to recruit Americans with access to the country's secrets. This has occurred both during major wars—the American Revolution, the Civil War, World War I, World War II, Korea, the Gulf War, Iraq-Afghan incursions, the War on Terror—and inter-war periods. Despite calls for reinvesting post-war "peace dividends" (or whatever synonym was in fashion in other eras) by Congressional leaders, the press, and pundits, the threat to American interests by foreign intelligence services has not let up. In many cases, anti–U.S. intelligence activity actually increased during apparent cessation of overt hostilities. Even if major services

took apparent "breathers" and suspended operations when counterintelligence efforts were ramped up, their activities were often replaced, or complemented, by operations by like-minded allies with different types of access and different styles of espionage.

The individuals listed in this chronology spied not just for the usual suspects—the Soviet Bloc, Cuba, North Korea, China—but also spied, or hoped to spy, for other hostile services and friendlies alike, including, inter alia, England (during the Revolutionary War), the Confederacy, Nazi Germany, Imperial Japan, Australia, Austria, Ecuador, Egypt, France, Germany, Ghana, Greece, Iran, Iraq, Israel, Italy, Japan, Jordan, Liberia, Libya, the Netherlands, North Korea, North Vietnam, the Philippines, Saudi Arabia, South Africa, South Korea, Switzerland, Syria, Taiwan, Venezuela, narcotraffickers, and terrorist groups. And that partial list is just of those who have been caught. The National Counterintelligence Executive announced in 2007 that at least 140 foreign intelligence services were spying against the U.S. Some of them probably used human-source intelligence (humint, which will be the primary focus of this study).

The ongoing nature of the intelligence threat to U.S. interests is not paralleled by the cyclic nature of the counterintelligence response, which itself is not mimicked by the response to major disasters, be they terrorist attacks, diplomatic reverses or battlefield surprises. The self-satisfied commentariat in this instance sagely calls for "better intelligence," "better penetrations of our foes," and "more human spies," as though this magic bullet had never been considered by intelligence professionals and as if "connecting the dots" were that simple in an enormously complex world. That hostile intelligence operations increase after victories (see Figure 3) is never considered by the peace dividend fandom.

Figure 3: Key Long-Term Soviet or Russian and Chinese Cases

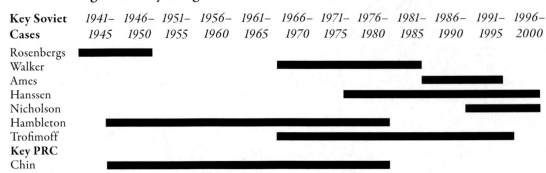

Key Soviet Cases	1941–1945	1946–1950	1951–1955	1956–1960	1961–1965	1966–1970	1971–1975	1976–1980	1981–1985	1986–1990	1991–1995	1996–2000
Rosenbergs												
Walker												
Ames												
Hanssen												
Nicholson												
Hambleton												
Trofimoff												
Key PRC												
Chin												

Since the fall of the Berlin Wall, what has become particularly troubling is not only the continuation of classical espionage operations against the West by other governments, but also the growth of espionage operations by Al Qaeda and its like-minded affiliates against the U.S. and its Western allies. Penetration of government inner sanctums by other regimes allows those regimes some insight on American decision-making. Penetration by terrorists gives them easier access to American targets as potential casualties, rather than just sources of information.

Chinese espionage has been a notable growth area in the last decade. Chinese targets and modus operandi have differed from classical Soviet or Russian styles. The Soviets tended to conduct operations aimed at government officials and corporate researchers with access to policy deliberations, official secrets, and military technology, using careful human tradecraft involving recruiting individuals over a period of years. Chinese techniques have often entailed approaches to members of the ethnic Chinese community in the United States, calling on their ancestral ties vice MICE motivations on the Soviet model.

New Paradigms

New to the espionage scene is the rise of media and public awareness of leakers and whistleblowers and new platforms, principally on the Internet, to facilitate their activities. While the motivations of spies, leakers, and whistleblowers often differ, they are similar in

- their choice of materials—generally sensitive, classified information;
- the effects of their activities—often grave damage to U.S./Western intelligence collection methods/sources; and
- the legal regimes chosen to react to their activities—reference to the Espionage Act, either in the interrogation room or in court.

While the two latter groups would bristle at being included in the same sentence—grammatically and judicially—with spies, there are a few other commonalities but also important differences:

- Classical spies act clandestinely and want the fact of their data acquisition—as well as their identities—to remain secret forever between them and their foreign handlers. Cases can continue for years, sometimes decades. The classic MICE items (money, ideology, coercion, ego) tend to be their principal motivations.
- Leakers attempt to act clandestinely, but usually for a limited period of time, and tend to self-recruit as sources for jour-

nalists or interest groups. They tend to seek to illuminate "what's really going on" for journalists and their readership, often with a policy ax to grind thrown in for good measure. Unlike spies, they often view themselves as still loyal to their government/organization, and are helping it and its clientele via nontraditional ways. As far as we know, leakers' activities have been for a limited period of time, whereas some spy cases went on for decades. (See Figure 3 for illustrative long-term Soviet or Russian and Chinese cases.)

• Whistleblowers see themselves as self-appointed guardians against waste, fraud, and abuse, and they have given up on using the system to air their concerns. Rather than spy for specific foreign intelligence services, however, they become, in effect, spies for all. They either turn into leakers or go very public with their information, hoping to stimulate dialog outside of official channels. Daniel Ellsberg's release of the Pentagon Papers was one of the watershed events of this method. The more recent revelations by former NSA contractor Edward Snowden and Private Bradley/Chelsea Manning by huge data dumps demonstrate how damaging such actions can be. Damage to national security can be the worst in these cases, with capabilities blown not just to the controlling agents of a single hostile intelligence service but to every person—friendly, neutral, or hostile—on the planet.

Whether in time of war or of peace, intelligence operations continued to be directed against American targets. Arrested long-term assets are quickly replaced by other long-term assets and supplemented by more low-key, albeit transitory, operations.

The Good News

Interservice rivalries exist across hostile intelligence services at least as much as they do across American services. While the creation of the Office of the Director of National Intelligence by President George W. Bush's signing of the Intelligence Reform and Terrorism Prevention Act of December 17, 2004, has done much to "integrate" (coordinating activities, including choice of targets, sharing budget figures, and the like) the 17 organizations that constitute the Intelligence Community, similar comity does not necessarily exist among the intelligence services in any given other country. Many overseas services were created to keep tabs on each other (the disdain depicted on televised crime dramas between police detectives and Internal Affairs is quite real among services with such conflicting roles). Lack of "deconfliction" (talking to each other about who has primacy in running what assets) often means that services trip over each other in recruiting and running the same sources, to the delight of the double-dipping assets' bank accounts. Tradecraft errors arising from such a lack of communication can lead to exposure of assets. Handoffs of assets between services can also lead to tradecraft errors that undercut the security of an operation. In addition, U.S. counterintelligence services have spoofed such handoffs, getting American traitors eager to continue from where they left off when they were suspended by a service to blab to individuals they believe are their new handlers, but are in fact undercover CI or law enforcement officers.

Moreover, the attractiveness of the American or Western way of life has led many foreign intelligence officers to rethink their allegiances and come to the American or Western side, either by directly defecting or defecting-in-place, i.e., agreeing to provide information on a short- or sometimes very long-term basis, on the activities of their erstwhile organizations. This phenomenon is likely to continue. A small sample of these successes can be seen in Figure 4.

Figure 4:
Hostile Intelligence Service Officers Who Reportedly Worked for or Defected to the West, 1900–2014

KGB and Predecessor Organizations

Georges Agabekov (June 1930)
Nikolai Artamonov (December 20, 1975)
Yuri Alexandrovich Bezmenov (February 1970)
Mikhail Bitov (1991)
Yevgeni Vladimirovich Brik (November 1953)
Aleksandr Nikolayevich Cherepanov (November 1963)
Peter Deriabin (1953)
Ilya Dzhirkvelov (1980)
Anatoli Mikhailovich Golitsyn (December 15, 1961)
Oleg Gordievsky (February 22, 1953; September 16, 1983; July 19, 1985)
Igor Gouzenko (September 5, 1945; July 21, 1955)
Anatoli Granovsky (July 31, 1946)
Reino Hayhanen (May 6, 1957)
Joseph Patrick Kauffman (April 18, 1962)
Nikolay Khokhlov (February 18, 1954)
Klementi Alekseyevich Korsakov (January 1980)
Sergei Kourdakov (September 4, 1971)
Viktor Andreevich Kravchenko (1944)
Yuri Vasilevich Krotkov (1963)
Vladimir Kuzichkin (June 2, 1982)
Stanislav Alexandrovich Levchenko (October 24, 1979)
Alexander V. Litvinenko (November 1, 2006)
Oleg Adolfovich Lyalin (March 1967; September 24, 1971)
Genrikh Samoilovich Lyushkov (June 13, 1938)
Alexei Myagkov (1972)
Yuriy Ivanovich Nosenko (February 22, 1953; February 1964)
Aleksandr Orlov (August 13, 1938)
Viktor Alekseevich Oshchenko (May 1975; July 20, 1992)
Vladimir Mikhaylovich Petrov (April 3, 1954)
Ignace Poretsky (July 17, 1937)
Yevgeni Runge (October 1967)

Valentina Rush (October 1967)
Bohdan Stashynsky (August 1961)
Dalibar Valoushek (May 1977; Spring 1981)
Gennadi Vasilenko (June 27, 2010)
Vladimir Ippoletovich Vetrov (1973; April 5, 1983)
Konstantin Dmitryevich Volkov (September 4, 1945)
Vitaly S. Yurchenko (August 1, 1985)

GRU

Walter Krivitsky (October 1937)
Oleg Vladimirovich Penkovsky (November 2, 1962)
Dmitriy Federovich Polyakov (July 23, 1963; August 1963; July 7, 1986; February 18, 2001)
Pyotr Popov (January 1953)
Vladimir Rezun (1978)
Sergei Skripal (June 27, 2010)

SVR

Sergei Olegovich Tretyakov (October 11, 2000)
Aleksandr Zaporozhsky (June 27, 2010)

Unspecified Soviet Intelligence Service and Other Soviets or Russians

Charles Lee Francis Anzalone (February 13, 1991)
Grigori Besedovsky (October 1929)
Valeriy Martynov (February 18, 2001
Sergey Motorin (February 18, 2001)
Aleksandr Ogorodnik (November 27, 1984)
Igor V. Sutyagin (June 27, 2010)
Adolf Tolkachev (June 9, 1985)
Boris Yuzhin (February 18, 2001)

Cuban DGI

Rolando Sarraff Trujillo (2001)
José Cohen Valdés (1991)

East German Stasi

Guenter Maennel (April 18, 1962)

East German Volkspolizei

Robert Bialek (August 27, 1953)

Hungarian Secret Police

Bela Lapusnyik (June 2, 1962)

Hungarian Intelligence Service

László Szabó (June 2, 1962)

Polish SB Intelligence Service

Michael Goleniewski (Autumn 1951; January 1961)

Polish UB Intelligence Service
Jozef Swiatlo (December 5, 1953)

Polish Military
Ryszard Jerzy Kuklinski (December 1981)

Romanian Securitate
Matei Pavel Haiducu (1981)
Ion Mihai Pacepa (July 1978)

North Vietnamese Intelligence Service
Yung Krall (January 31, 1978)

What Next?

The classical world of the human spy, whose exploits are described in these pages, is being replaced by that of the cyberspy. The headlines are replete with examples of private hackers, hacktivists, and government-sponsored operators. Most fictional accounts of cyberwar focus on the use of computers to damage data or seize control of key systems, such as air traffic control systems, national power grids, hospital equipment, and the like. There have been some real-world examples of this type of aggressive operation, possibly conducted by hostile intelligence services. In early 2013, the South Korean financial system was taken down by still-unidentified attackers and during the same period several U.S. banks were subjected to massive denial of service attacks by unattributed perpetrators. North Korea and Iran were frequently suggested as the respective attackers.

While this activity may well increase in the coming years, intelligence services are also likely to turn to cyberespionage as a method of enhancing their collection operations beyond that of the humint operations chronicled herein. The Mandiant Corporation in 2013 released a report outlining evidence of Chinese People's Liberation Army Unit 61398 near Shanghai conducting cyber espionage operations against hundreds of corporations, including U.S. and other Western firms. Difficulties in establishing attribution—even determining from what country the attacks originated—will make the classic find, arrest, convict, sentence, deport/trade model we saw in this book's humint cases far less likely to occur. While a second volume of this chronology will likely include a continuation of the litany of humint operations we have seen throughout history, many such operations will be supplemented, if not supplanted, by cyberspies.

The rise of cyberespionage will also make the numerical tallying, arraying, and interpretation of data in our charts more difficult. Is a cyber penetration worth the same as a human penetration of an organization? An individual cyberspy can easily penetrate hundreds, if not thousands, of organizations. Attribution of individual cyber activities is increasingly problematic as well. Cyberspies can spoof counterintelligence services, leaving breadcrumbs that appear to come from a third party.

While the rise of cyberespionage somewhat alleviates pressures to recruit human sources, humint as a profession will not wither. Hackers do not need agents in the classic sense but can still use social engineering, in which their human sources are more dupes than willing or witting collaborators.

The expansion of computer databases which store petabytes of intelligence makes it much easier for contemporary insider spies to walk off with an amount of classified data hidden on removable media that their predecessors stuffed into shopping bags. While this vulnerability has been most famously exploited by Bradley Manning, who took hundreds of thousands of documents out via a CD, and Edward Snowden, who ran off to Hong Kong with his laptops, classical spies-for-one-service cannot be far behind. An early instance occurred on

December 4, 2012, when Reuters reported that Switzerland's Federal Intelligence Service (NDB) alerted intelligence services in the UK and the U.S. that they had arrested a senior NDB IT technician who had stolen terabytes of data, including at least hundreds of thousands and possibly millions of pages of classified material onto portable hard drives.

Types of espionage work will also evolve. In addition to classic collection of intelligence, some services have also engaged in what the Soviets referred to as "active measures"—more aggressive use of staffers and agents beyond mere collection. These activities have ranged from white, gray, and black propaganda, to tampering with economic systems and political parties, to outright assassination. Although many believed that such active measures went away with the closure of the KGB, in 2006, its successor agency was accused of killing a KGB alumnus in London with polonium-210, and in 2014, a NATO official claimed that the Russians were attempting to use the anti-fracking movement in the West to keep Europe dependent upon Russian oil sales. Discovery of penetrations of governments is different from discovery of penetrations of such nongovernmental organizations.

I make no claim that this list is complete, for several reasons.

- Because of the clandestine nature of espionage, there are many cases that have not come to light in open sources. Many are still ongoing investigations.
- Public sources frequently conflict on specific cases. The news media often attempts to get insider information on prosecutions, but many reports are based upon unsubstantiated rumor or legitimate information that cannot be confirmed publicly because of defensive actions.

- In many cases, spy suspects' defense attorneys used "graymail"—unwillingness of the government to expose intelligence sources and methods in a prosecution in open court—to keep their clients off espionage annals.
- Alas, some spies haven't been caught yet. Remember, these are the famous spies. Those who are *not* famous are the successful ones, because they have not been caught—yet. The Venona files, decrypts of Soviet intelligence communications, listed 349 spies, although many were not identified by name, and many have not been discovered, or at least publicly named. The Mitrokhin Archive, material spirited out of the KGB's files by a defector in the early 1990s, refers to *thousands* of agents recruited by the KGB and its predecessors.
- Interservice cultural differences often stymie us in the search for accuracy in these cases. Law enforcement and intelligence officers handle information differently and have widely divergent views on whether, when, and how to release sensitive information to the public. Intelligence officers recruit sources who will provide secrets on the plans and intentions of adversaries; these relationships often are aimed at lasting for years. Law enforcement, including police and prosecutors, see information as evidence to be used in public court to obtain guilty verdicts and to jail criminals. The relationships with informants might be designed to last only for the duration of one case. Agreement on release of the intelligence or evidence between these two cultures is difficult at best.
- It is difficult to establish that defendants who have plea-bargained have kept up their end of the deal by fully cooperating and detailing the amount and character of the information they purloined. Spy

tradecraft is aimed at ensuring that counterintelligence officers and prosecuting attorneys will have minimal information on what really went on. It is possible that subsources of those who have been found remain active or retired from their espionage careers untouched by the law or counterespionage officers.

That said, if you are aware of missing major cases, please contact me via the publisher.

THE CHRONOLOGY

1700s

January 11, 1722: Beverly Robinson, who would become a British Army intelligence officer, was born in Middlesex County, Virginia. He was the son of a prominent Virginia family. He married into the wealthy Philipse family of New York in 1748. He retired as one of the state's wealthiest men prior to the American Revolution. He was a Tory loyalist and refused to take an American oath of allegiance. The Continental Army seized his home on the Hudson River across from West Point. He moved to British-occupied New York City, where he recruited the Loyal American Regiment, and the Guides and Pioneers. He showed valor in several battles. He also provided British General Sir Henry Clinton with intelligence regarding the West Point region. His local contacts provided information on Continental Army movements while he was in New York City. He arranged for American officers and men to defect to the British, and unsuccessfully pitched Continental Army General Israel Putnam. He became involved in Benedict Arnold's attempt to surrender West Point to the British. Arnold's headquarters was in Robinson's home. Robinson took the pretext of meeting with him regarding his property to meet with Arnold. Robinson then went to Haverstraw to meet British Major John Andre,

who in turn met with Arnold. Following American independence, Robinson settled in Bath in the UK, which repaid him for his estate's loss. He died on April 9, 1792, at his home near Bath, UK.

December 1773: Dr. Benjamin Church participated in the Boston Tea Party to protest the King's tax on tea. He later was a paid spy for British General Thomas Gage against the secret Sons of Liberty, even fooling Paul Revere. Church provided information on the plans, intentions, and capabilities of the Massachusetts rebels. His vulnerabilities included taking a mistress and maintaining a lavish lifestyle despite a meager income as a physician. A communication tradecraft error brought him to the attention of the Patriots; he sent a clandestine note to the British via his mistress, who left it with her former boyfriend. George Washington employed two teams of cryptologists to decipher the letter, which provided information on troop strength, artillery, and supplies as well as Continental Congress plans. Members of the teams included the Reverend Samuel West, Colonel Elisha Porter, and Elbridge Gerry, who would become the country's fifth Vice President. Washington's war council in October 1775 determined that there was no law against civilian espionage, thereby saving Church from the gallows. Church was released in 1780 to exile in the

West Indies, but his ship was believed to have been lost at sea. His wife moved to Great Britain, where King George III gave her a pension.

September 1, 1774: British troops raided a Cambridge, Massachusetts, arms storehouse, based on information provided by a spy network among the American patriots. The ring was established by British General Thomas Gage, commander of British forces in the area. He had also served as colonial governor of Massachusetts. The network collected military intelligence on the local militia units. The patriots in turn created a surveillance committee within the Sons of Liberty in Boston to attempt to avoid further raids against their ammunition dumps.

September 18, 1775: The Second Continental Congress created a Secret Committee with wide powers and large sums of money to obtain military supplies in secret. It was tasked with distributing supplies and selling gunpowder to privateers chartered by the Continental Congress. The Committee administered secret contracts for arms and gunpowder, funneling aid quietly sent by Spanish and French sources. Membership included Benjamin Franklin, Robert Morris, Robert Livingston, John Dickinson, Thomas Willing, Thomas McKean, John Langdon, and Samuel Ward.

November 7, 1775: The Continental Congress added the death penalty for espionage to the Articles of War. The clause was not applied retroactively, saving the life of Dr. Benjamin Church, chief physician of the Continental Army, had already been imprisoned as a British spy.

November 20, 1775: The Continental Congress received several intercepted letters. It appointed an eight-man committee that included John Adams and Benjamin Franklin "to select such parts of them as may be proper to publish."

November 29, 1775: The Second Continental Congress formed the Committee of Correspondence (soon renamed the Committee of Secret Correspondence), which became America's first intelligence organization. Committee members included Benjamin Franklin of Pennsylvania, Benjamin Harrison of Virginia and Thomas Johnson of Maryland. Later members would include James Lovell, a teacher who had been arrested by the British after the battle of Bunker Hill on charges of spying. He was exchanged for a British prisoner and was then elected to the Continental Congress. He became an expert on codes and ciphers and thus the father of American cryptanalysis. Committee intelligence operations included using overseas humint assets, running covert operations, running deception operations and double agent operations, developing codes and ciphers, funding propaganda operations, opening private mail, obtaining foreign publications for use in analysis, creating a courier system, and developing a maritime capability. The group became the Committee of Foreign Affairs on April 17, 1777, but still had an intelligence role.

June 5, 1776: The Second Continental Congress established America's first counterintelligence organization—the Committee (later called the Commission) for Detecting and Defeating Conspiracies. It tasked John Adams, Thomas Jefferson, Edward Rutledge, James Wilson and Robert Livingston "to consider what is proper to be done with persons giving intelligence to the enemy or supplying them with provisions." The group was to revise the Articles of War in regard to espionage directed against the patriot forces. It collected intelligence, captured British spies and couriers, penetrated the British intelligence service, and surveilled suspected British sympathizers, principally in New York. The Committee, led by John Jay, the first chief of American counterintelligence, examined more than 500 cases of alleged disloyalty and subversion. Washington had earlier written on March 24, 1776, "There is one evil I dread, and that is, their spies. I could wish, therefore, the most attentive watch be kept.... I wish a dozen or more of honest, sensible and diligent men, were employed ... in order to question, cross-question, etc., all such persons as are unknown, and cannot give an account of themselves in a straight and satisfactory line.... I think it a matter of importance to prevent them from obtaining intelligence of our situation."

June 28, 1776: Thomas Hickey, a former member of George Washington's guard, was hanged before 20,000 Continental troops for mutiny, sedition, and treachery in conspiring to kidnap or kill Washington. Washington wrote in his orders of the day "the General hopes will be a warning to every soldier in the Army to avoid those crimes, and all others, so disgraceful to the character of a soldier, and pernicious to his country, whose pay re receives and bread he eats." The hanging occurred seven months after the Continental Congress approved the death penalty for espionage.

August 21, 1776: The Continental Congress enacted espionage legislation, which read: "RESOLVED, That all persons not members of, nor owing allegiance to, any of the United States of America, as described in a resolution to the Congress of the 29th of June last, who shall be found lurking as spies in or about the fortification or encampments of the armies of the United States, or of any of them, shall suffer death, according to the law and usage of nations, by sentence of a court martial, or such ether punishment as such court martial may direct." The Continental Congress expanded the law on February 27, 1778, to include any "inhabitants of these states" whose intelligence activities aided the enemy in capturing or killing Patriots.

September 22, 1776: The British hanged Nathan Hale, who had attempted to infiltrate British-held territory with no backstopping for his cover story. Before his hanging, the failed intelligence officer said, "I only regret that I have but one life to lose for my country." His statue can be found at the entrance to the CIA's Original Headquarters Building. Similar statues grace Yale University and Phillips Academy in Andover, Massachusetts, his two alma maters. British General William Howe wrote in his journal, "A spy from the enemy by his own full confession, apprehended last night, was executed (this) day at 11 o'clock in front of the Artillery Park."

After graduating from Yale in 1773, he taught school before enlisting in the Continental Army, rising to Captain by September 1776. He volunteered to spy on the British, and got behind enemy lines in Manhattan. He was captured while attempting to return. The British refused him a clergyman and Bible.

September 26, 1776: The Continental Congress elected three commissioners to the Court of France, Benjamin Franklin, Thomas Jefferson and Silas Deane, counseling that "secrecy shall be observed until further Order of Congress; and that until permission be obtained from Congress to disclose the particulars of this business, no member be permitted to say anything more upon this subject, than that Congress have taken such steps as they judged necessary for the purpose of obtaining foreign alliance." Because of his wife's illness, Jefferson could not serve, and Arthur Lee replaced him. Franklin arrived in France on November 29, 1776, in effect becoming

America's first chief of station, running the country's intelligence and propaganda operations in Europe. Franklin is credited with running America's first covert action program in which he fabricated documents that led to Hessian desertions, obtained secret aid from America's allies, and conducted recruitment operations of French opinion makers, ultimately bringing France into the war.

Not all of Franklin's operations stayed clandestine. On September 8, 1821, British intelligence agent Dr. Edward Bancroft died in Margate, UK. He was born in Westfield, Massachusetts, around 1744–1745. Scholars consider him England's most important agent in the colonies during the American Revolution. The colonies-born London resident had been tutored by Deane at a Connecticut high school. Minister to France Ben Franklin hired him in 1775 as the American Legation's Secretary, where he saw all official documents and dispatches. British agent Paul Wentworth recruited Bancroft in August 1776. The British paid him a £500 bonus (worth nearly $100,000 in 2014 U.S. dollars), a £500 annual stipend, and a lifetime £200 annual pension. He used a hollow in a boxwood tree in the Paris Tuileries Gardens for impersonal communications—dead drops—to his handlers, detailing France's covert assistance to the Americans, American alliance negotiations with the French and Spanish, identities of colonial spies, and information on shipments of French aid. He also employed secret ink and ciphers. His espionage actions were not disclosed until 1889.

August 1777: American troops led by General Israel Putnam captured Tory spy Edmund Palmer, who was later hung by the patriots despite an appeal for clemency by the British governor of New York.

October 16, 1777: Captured British spy Daniel Taylor was executed. The next day, British General John Burgoyne surrendered at Saratoga. Taylor was carrying a message from commander of British forces Sir Henry Clinton to Burgoyne when he was captured at New Windsor, New York. The message was hidden in a silver ball the size of a rifle bullet. Taylor swallowed the concealment device, but a strong emetic made him vomit it up. He grabbed it, and swallowed it again. But an American general talked him into either swallowing more emetic or he would cut the message out of his stomach. Taylor was court martialed for espionage.

May 1779: American Continental Army Major General Benedict Arnold began communicating with British military intelligence chief Major John Andre via intermediaries, including his witting wife, often using codes and invisible ink. Despite a string of military victories and being wounded in battle, the Continental Congress passed him over for promotion, naming five colleagues to major general in February 1777. Some Patriot officers claimed credit for some of his accomplishments. He often was acquitted of charges by military and political foes of corruption and other malfeasance, living extravagantly in Washington and Philadelphia from business profits from the war. An arrogant and embittered Arnold decided to switch sides, even though he had moved from captain to general officer in three years. He also was facing financial difficulties as his business was foundering. After his April 1779 wedding to Philadelphia socialite Peggy Shippen, who was in touch with British intelligence officer John Andre, he volunteered to the British. By July 1779, he had provided the British with troop locations and strengths, and the locations of supply depots. He later provided information on French involvement with the Patriots, rebel information on British deployments, and Washington's comings and goings. Arnold asked for indemnification of his war-related financial losses and £10,000. He obtained command of the fortifications at West Point, New York (site of the U.S. Military Academy after 1802) in August 1780, and planned to surrender it to the British forces. The plan was exposed on September 23, 1780, when British Major John Andre was detained by three American bushwackers while carrying details of Arnold's activities to weaken West Point defenses. On the run, Arnold defected to the British, and was commissioned into the British Army as a brigadier general. In December 1780, he led British forces that captured Richmond, Virginia. He was the most senior American officer in history to defect as of the time of this writing. He died in London on June 14, 1801, at age 60.

October 2, 1780: The Americans hung British Major John Andre as a spy. Andre said, "I am reconciled to death but detest the mode. It will be but a moment's pang. I pray you bear witness that I met my fate like a brave man." Andre is one of only two known intelligence officers to have been interred at Westminster Abbey. He had been captured on September 23, 1780, when he was confronted by three Patriot irregulars, one of whom was wearing a purloined British uniform, leading Andre to believe he was with friendly forces. The trio took him to a Patriot outpost. George Washington decorated them; they received lifetime annuities.

June 8, 1783: Sergeant Daniel Bissell, of the 2nd Connecticut Regiment, received the Honorary Badge of Military Merit (which became the Military Order of the Purpose Heart), for his work as a military intelligence officer. He was one of three men in

the American Revolution to receive the honor. Lieutenant Colonel Robert Harrison, George Washington's aide-de-camp, sent Bissell into New York in August 1781 on an intelligence-gathering mission. Bissell could not make his way out of New York City, so he developed a cover story of being a Loyalist, joining Benedict Arnold's provincial regiment. He collected intelligence for more than a year, relying on his retentive memory. In September 1782, he exfiltrated through British lines and reported to Washington his eyewitness accounts on British fortifications and British methods. He refused an honorable discharge and a pension, saying that the nation could not afford losing his services and that the nation should not be saddled with annuity payments.

September 23, 1789: Silas Deane, American diplomat believed to have cooperated with British intelligence, died on board a ship bound for Canada. He was a leader of the Revolutionary movement in Connecticut when he was sent to France as an agent of the Committee of Secret Correspondence. In September 1776, he became one of three American diplomatic commissioners to France; the others were Ben Franklin and Arthur Lee. He was recalled in 1778 to answer charges of profiteering. He was not fully exonerated, but returned to France in 1780 to collect exculpatory evidence. While there, he became alienated from the American cause. Some scholars believe he cooperated with British intelligence. In 1781, letters he wrote calling for accommodation with England were published in a Tory newspaper. He became an exile in Belgium and the UK.

1800s

1861: Allan Pinkerton's team infiltrated a secessionist group planning to assassinate the newly-elected President Abraham Lincoln on his train en route to his inauguration in Washington. The detectives rerouted Lincoln to DC. Following the Confederate victory at Bull Run in July 1861, Pinkerton became the Union Army's intelligence chief, headquartered in the Army Provost Marshal's office. He led the Headquarters City Guard (which he later renamed the U.S. Secret Service), a contract intelligence and counterintelligence group reporting to General George McClellan's Army of the Potomac. The group had several counterintelligence successes in penetrating Confederate spy networks in Washington, thanks to his using law enforcement surveillance, collection and analytic techniques in his spycatching. They had fewer accomplishments in positive intelligence, having recruited no penetrations in the Richmond Confederacy. The group was disbanded shortly after Lincoln replaced General George McClellan with General Joe Hooker in November 1862.

1861–1865: Southern socialite Elizabeth van Lew ran a successful Union espionage operation in the Confederacy, working in Richmond's Libby Prison, giving Union soldiers books and food, assisting them to escape, briefing them about safe houses, and in turn collecting from them intelligence on rebel order of battle and movements. Her informants included clerks in Richmond's War and Navy Departments, a Richmond mayoral candidate, farmers, merchants, and slaves, including Mary Bowser, a household servant in the Confederate President Jefferson Davis's White House. Bowser, owner of an eidetic memory, often eavesdropped on Davis's guests, who numbered Confederate military leaders and cabinet officials. Although van Lew's socialite cover held, on occasion she would walk the streets in disguise and developed a cipher system, using invisible ink and cover letters that were de-

livered by multiple couriers. She funded her operations from her own savings, and later was reimbursed not by Washington but by sympathetic Bostonians. The Confederates investigated her family in 1864, but not thoroughly enough. Van Lew was the first person to raise the U.S. flag in Richmond at the end of hostilities. President Grant made her postmaster of Richmond. She died on September 25, 1900. She was inducted into the Military Intelligence Hall of Fame in 1993.

August 23, 1861: Allan Pinkerton arrested Confederate "stay-behind" asset "Rebel Rose" O'Neal Greenhow, who ran an espionage network in Washington, D.C. Her parents owned slaves, and a slave murdered her father. Former Vice President John Calhoun was a frequent visitor to her childhood home, speaking with her often about states' rights and pro-slavery positions. She married a wealthy State Department lawyer.

Greenhow was recruited by Confederate Captain Thomas Jordan, an assistant quartermaster in the antebellum Department of War in Washington. He was the West Point roommate of William Tecumseh Sherman, who rose to General in the Union Army and ravaged Atlanta. Jordan was promoted to Colonel and named intelligence head for General Pierre Beauregard.

She traveled in both Union and Confederate upper class circles, frequently entertaining military, legislative, and executive policymakers at her home. Following her husband's death, she became a prominent socialite, attracting Secretary of War William Seward, Senator Stephen Douglas, President James Buchanan, Senator Henry Wilson—Chairman of the Military Affairs Committee and later President Ulysses S. Grant's Vice President. She told the rebels of General Irvin McDowell's troop strength and plans to attack through Fairfax, Virginia. Pinkerton placed her under surveillance and found incriminating plain-text documents in her house. After her arrest, Confederate President Jefferson Davis said the well-connected Greenhow's information won the battle of Manassas (Bull Run) in July 1861. After a brief home detention, she was imprisoned in the Old Capitol Prison in 1862, from which she passed information by hiding messages with her eight-year-old daughter or in a woman's hair and signaling from her cell window. She was deported to the South, which sent her as an envoy to London, where she became a lobbyist for the Confederacy. Trying to sneak back into the Confederacy on the Cape Fear River in 1864, her rowboat capsized and she drowned, weighted down by the gold from her book royalties. Richmond gave her an official state funeral.

October 6, 1861: Union officials arrested Ella (or Ellie) M. Poole at Wheeling, West Virginia, for spying for the Confederacy. She had sneaked out incriminating documents in her guitar case and hidden them before the authorities arrived. She escaped Union detention four times before ultimately being released from the Old Capitol. Some scholars suggested that she switched sides and spied on the Greenhow ring.

1862: Secretary of War Edwin Stanton appointed Lafayette C. Baker to run a counterespionage organization in Washington, D.C. General-in-Chief of the U.S. Army Lieutenant General Winfield Scott had recommended him to Secretary of War Simon Cameron. He was assigned to catch Confederate blockade runners. He later moved to the staff of Secretary of State William Seward to set up and run the Department's counterintelligence service, which he called the U.S. Secret Secret (a name used by the rival group run by Allan Pinkerton). In February 1982, Baker's unit was moved to the

War Department. He was given the title of Provost Marshal, running the National Detective Bureau. His group captured such Southern spies as Belle Boyd and Wat Bowie. On July 3, 1868, Baker died of spinal meningitis.

April 29, 1862: Confederate forces hung Union intelligence officer Timothy Webster. He was born in England in 1821; his family came to the U.S. in 1834. He worked on the New York City police force, then joined Allan Pinkerton's detective agency, later moving to Pinkerton's Civil War–era counterintelligence service. He developed a cover as a secessionist sympathizer, and was accepted into the rebel Knights of Liberty. As part of his cover, he offered to work for Confederate Secretary of War Judah P. Benjamin, who used him as a courier of sensitive military documents and information on Confederate spies. Two of Pinkerton's agents, Pryce Lewis and John Scully, were spotted by the Confederates knocking on Webster's door. Under interrogation, Scully exposed Webster's espionage. The Confederacy sentenced the duo to two years. President Lincoln appealed to the Confederacy to commute Webster's death sentence, but was ignored.

September 1862: In a lucky intelligence coup, Union soldiers found Robert E Lee's "Special Order 191" which detailed Lee's plans against the North, to begin with an attack on Harper's Ferry. The sheet was wrapped around three cigars found in a field in Frederick, Maryland.

October 7, 1862: General J. E. B. Stuart awarded Antonia Ford a commission as an honorary aide-de-camp. She often reported to Stuart on Union troops who stayed in her home in Fairfax, Virginia, following the First Battle of Bull Run/Manassas. In December 1862, she also provided information to Captain John Mosby. She was arrested in

March 1862 following a raid by Mosby in which his men captured Union Brigadier General Edwin Stoughton from his bed, along with two captains, 30 privates, and 58 horses. Ford, having shown her commission to a Union female agent working for the U.S. Secret Service, was detained and held for several months before a prisoner exchange. She was arrested shortly thereafter, and held at the Old Capitol Prison.

1863: Union General Joe Hooker named Colonel George Sharpe of the 120th New York Volunteers to head the Bureau of Military Information, which collated all-source intelligence, including from open sources such as newspapers, overhead reports from balloonists, clandestine agents, reconnaissance scouts, and provided finished reports to President Lincoln and his military commanders. It was a forerunner of the *President's Daily Brief.*

June 1863: Confederate Will Talbot, left behind by his unit to spy in Gettysburg, was captured by Union forces. Union Brigadier General John Buford ordered him hanged.

September 25, 1863: Confederate authorities hanged Union soldier/sailor Spencer Kellogg Brown as a spy.

November 27, 1863: Private Sam Davis, with the 1st Tennessee Regiment but serving as a Confederate courier for the Colman's Scouts, was hanged as a spy. When offered his freedom in return for information about Confederate forces, he said, "If I had a thousand lives, I would give them all here before I would betray a friend or the confidence of my informer." (He is sometimes quoted as "I would sooner die a thousand deaths than betray a friend or be false to duty.")

1864: The Confederacy established a counterespionage service.

February 24, 1865: Union authorities at Fort Lafayette, New York, hanged Confed-

erate military officer and secret service agent John Yates Beall after he failed to free Confederate prisoners of war. Beall grew up in Jefferson County, Virginia, and studied law at the University of Virginia. He was badly wounded in the 1862 campaign in Shenandoah, and was given a disability discharge. While on bed rest, he decided to capture the Union's USS *Michigan* gunboat guarding Lake Erie; it was the sole armed vessel on the Great Lake. Confederate Naval Secretary Stephen R. Mallory turned down the plan. Beall next received approval to conduct privateering raids against Union vessels on Chesapeake Bay, beginning operations in April 1863. His band cut the telegraph cable to the eastern shore of Virginia in July 1863, blew up the Smith Island federal lighthouse in August, and captured a small flotilla of sloops and fishing schooners in September. Among them was the *Alliance*, a large sloop fitting with supplies for the Union garrison at Port Royal, South Carolina. He sent the ship on to Richmond. Maryland Volunteers captured Beall and his band, who were swapped for Union POWs. Following a short stint in the Confederate Army Engineer Corps, Beall resurrected the USS *Michigan* caper. In September 1964, he went to Toronto to pitch the idea to Jacob Thompson, the Confederate Commission and senior Confederate secret agent in Canada, and his aide, Captain Thomas H. Hines. They approved the plan as part of an effort to free Confederate POWs on Johnson's Island in Lake Erie. The operation failed and Beall returned to Canada. In December 1864, Beall was part of the operation to free senior Confederate POWs during the rail movement from Johnson's Island to Fort Lafayette in New York Harbor. Beall was arrested, convicted by a court martial of espionage and violation of the laws of war, and sentenced to death. Clemency was requested by President Lincoln, Massachusetts Governor John Andrew, Pennsylvania Representative Thaddeus Stevens, and other prominent Northerners, but he was hanged.

April 12, 1865: Union soldiers of the 1st New York Cavalry and the 12th West Virginia Cavalry in Shepherdstown, West Virginia, captured disguised Confederate spy Andrew Laypole, alias Isidore Leopold. At the start of the war, he enlisted in the 1st Virginia Cavalry, J.E.B. Stuart's first Confederate command. Laypole was initially captured by soldiers of the 2nd Massachusetts in 1862, after performing "special duty" for Stuart, but was soon freed. He then joined company D, 12th Virginia Cavalry, conducting espionage operations. Laypole was court martialed and convicted of murder. The prosecution said that while he was within U.S. lines from November 1, 1862, to April 20, 1863, he was "robbing, plundering, maltreating, wounding and killing" civilians. When he was detained, Laypole offered to serve as a double agent for the Union, and providing a list of "scouts and spies for each rebel general," according to his trial records. He was nonetheless sent to the gallows.

April 14, 1865: Noted actor with Confederate intelligence connections John Wilkes Booth assassinated President Abraham Lincoln in his booth at Ford's Theater. After a several-day search for conspirators who had plotted an abortive mission to assassinate or kidnap Vice President Andrew Johnson, Secretary of State William H. Seward, and General Ulysses S. Grant, authorities rounded up Dr. Samuel Mudd, Mary Surratt, Samuel Arnold, George Atzerodt, David Herold, Michael O'Laughlen, Lewis Paine, and Edward Spangler. At trial, Arnold, O'Laughlen, and Mudd were sentenced to life in prison. Spangler received a six-year sentence. Atzerodt, Herold, Paine and Surratt were hanged on July 7.

April 1865: Shortly after the assassination of President Abraham Lincoln, U.S. authorities arrested Confederate spy Thomas Conrad, who had used his experience as a Methodist preacher to often slip behind Union lines under cover of a federal chaplain. He was headmaster of the Georgetown College boy's school in Washington when the Civil War began. He tasked his students with sending messages by raising and lowering the shades in their dorms. After being arrested for having the school band play "Dixie" during the 1861 graduation ceremony, he began spying in earnest, acquiring information on order of battle, artillery strength and General George McClellan's battle plans from sympathetic clerks working in the Union War Department. One of his assets had penetrated the Union's counterintelligence service headed by Lafayette C. Baker, and kept him up to date on any investigations of his activities. After Booth assassinated Lincoln, Baker's team arrested Conrad, who was wearing a disguise that made him resemble the assassin. Baker released him—the war was over.

1882: The U.S. Navy established the Office of Naval Intelligence. A few years later, the Army created its Military Intelligence Division.

September 22, 1888: Congress established the military and naval attaché system, authorizing the establishment in 1889 of posts in Berlin, Paris, London, Vienna, and St. Petersburg. Within five years, attaches also went to Rome, Madrid, Tokyo, and Mexico City.

March 23, 1892: Secretary of the Navy William Hunt signed General Order 292, creating the Office of Naval Intelligence, the first federal agency dedicated to the systematic collection of intelligence on foreign military operations. ONI was placed under the Bureau of Navigation, but later became independent. ONI used information from military attaches and naval officers visiting foreign ports. ONI conducted studies on foreign passages, rivers, and other bodies of water, overseas fortifications and shipyards, and other naval-related activities.

1898: Spanish Naval Attache Ramon Carranza left Washington at the onset of the Spanish-American war to set up a spy network in neighboring Canada. U.S. Secret Service agent "Tracer" followed him into Canada and listened to his meeting an asset in a Toronto hotel. The asset, a retired naval petty officer, was arrested in Washington while mailing a letter to Spanish intelligence. The USSS broke into Carranza's Montreal house, found incriminating documents, and turned them over to Canadian authorities, who declared him *persona non grata*.

1900s

May 28, 1908: Ian Fleming was born in London. During World War II, he was an assistant to the Director of Naval Intelligence of the United Kingdom. He used this experience in writing his James Bond novels, which inspired a generation of intelligence officers to join their respective services. Fleming died of heart failure in 1964 at age 56.

1910s

July 7, 1914: Count Johann Heinrich von Bernstorff, the German Ambassador to the U.S., became the chief of Western Hemisphere espionage and sabotage for Section 3B, Military Intelligence of the German General Staff. The promotion came nine days after the assassination of Archduke Franz Ferdinand in Sarajevo. He was to be aided by Captain Franz von Papen, 35, German military attaché to Mexico, who was to transfer to the U.S. as naval attache; Captain

Karl Boy-Ed, German Naval Attache to the U.S.; and Dr. Heinrich Albert, German Commercial Attache to the U.S., who would finance sabotage operations. The spy ring concentrated on low-level sabotage targets, ignoring strategic intelligence collection.

July 18, 1914: The U.S. Congress authorized the formation of an Aviation Section within the Army Signal Corps. This opened up opportunities to conduct aerial surveillance in wartime, transforming military intelligence.

August 22, 1914: Captain Franz von Papen, chief of German espionage and sabotage in the Western Hemisphere, tasked Paul Koenig to recruit and supervise saboteurs. Koenig owned the Bureau of Investigation detective agency, handling cases for a subsidiary of Hamburg-American Line, a German shipping firm. He worked in the New York harbor dock, where he was spotted by the New York City Bomb Squad. The Squad contacted a former and now disaffected agent of the ring, who provided information on Koenig's group. Police arrested Koenig and seized a loose-leaf notebook detailing all of his agents and their assignments.

May 14, 1915: President Woodrow Wilson's executive order expanded Secret Service surveillance from clerks, technicians, and errand-runners to other staff personnel of the German Embassy. Frank Burke led the ten-man surveillance team, under the orders of USSS Director William J. Flynn. The team ran its operations from the penthouse of the Customs House at the Battery in New York City.

July 27, 1915: After Dr. Heinrich Albert, German Commercial Attache to the U.S. and a member of von Papen's spy/sabotage team, left documents on a New York elevated train in Harlem's 50th Street Station, he ran an ad in the *Evening Telegram* offering a $20 reward for their return. The U.S. Secret Service had placed him under surveillance and grabbed the bag when Albert left the train. The documents, outlining the sabotage plan, were leaked to the *New York World*. Germany recalled Von Papen and Boy-Ed.

August 1915: Captain Franz Rintelen von Kleist, a member of the German Admiralty staff, was recalled to Germany after the U.S. became suspicious of him—he had run sabotage operations, replacing Von Papen. The UK decoded a message that included Rintelen's Swiss travel alias and arrested him at a British port. The UK extradited him to the U.S., which tried and convicted him for conspiracy to instigate labor strikes under the Sherman Anti-Trust Act. He served time in an Atlanta prison. He later wrote the memoir *The Dark Invader*.

July 30, 1916: German saboteurs blew up a U.S. munitions dump on Black Tom Island, New Jersey, causing a $22 million loss.

1917: U.S. Congress enacted the Espionage Act of 1917 following U.S. entry into World War I, in a climate of fear of German subversion. Most prosecutions under the Act were not for espionage.

March 1917: German saboteurs blew up the U.S. Navy Yard at Mare Island. The attack was attributed to German Abwehr spy Kurt Jahnke.

February 13, 1917: Dutch-born Margaretha Zelle, who had become famous as exotic dancer Mata Hari, was arrested in her room at the Hotel Plaza Athénée in Paris. The courtesan allegedly had provided intelligence information to the German consul in Amsterdam, who tasked her with obtaining pillow talk. She soon came to the attention of French and UK intelligence. The French turned her as a double agent. She reportedly seduced the German military attache in Madrid. Agent H was mentioned in a German secret service telegram from Madrid to Germany, and was believed to be Mata Hari by the French. She was found guilty by a French military court and executed by firing squad on October 15, 1917, at age 41. Some historians question her guilt.

June 15, 1917: Congress passed the comprehensive Espionage Act.

December 20, 1917: Vladimir Lenin established the Cheka (Extraordinary Commission for Combating Counterrevolution and Sabotage), the forerunner of the NKVD and KGB, and put Felix Edmundovich Dzerzhinsky in charge. The Cheka could arrest, sentence and execute individuals without trial in the name of state security. By 1925, it had executed more than 250,000 Russians and had imprisoned 1,300,000 people.

April 1918: Heroin addict Madame Marie de Victorica, also known as Baroness von Kretschmann, was arrested in New York after U.S. military intelligence intercepted a letter written in secret ink to a suspected German intelligence officer. Authorities found that two of her silk scarves were impregnated with water-soluble secret inks. She was indicted on espionage charges, but was not tried after agreeing to aid the government's investigation.

August 26, 1918: The U.S. War Department issued a General Order establishing the Military Intelligence Division (MID) as one of four divisions within the General Staff. MID's first chief was Colonel Marlborough Churchill. MID was to "have cognizance and control of military intelligence, both positive and negative, and shall be in charge of an officer designated as director of military intelligence. He will be an assistant to the Chief of Staff." "Negative" intelligence is today known as counterintelligence.

June 2, 1919: An anarchist accidentally killed himself when he set off explosives at the Embassy Row, Washington, home of Attorney General Mitchell Palmer. Palmer soon created the General Intelligence Division within the Department of Justice's Bureau of Investigation, naming J. Edgar Hoover as its chief. On January 2, 1920, Hoover's agents arrested thousands of alleged subversives in 33 U.S. cities as part of the "Palmer Raids," which turned up no actual spies.

1920s

1921: The Soviets posted their first intelligence officer to the U.S.

August 10, 1921: The Soviets released former academic and international businessman Xenophon Kalamatiano from a Moscow prison. Secretary of State Robert Lansing had recruited him to report on conditions in Russia in 1916. After the Russian Revolution, he was given a confidential position in the State Department's Russian Bureau/Special Duty group. He ran several covert missions for allied forces in Murmansk and Archangel. He was arrested by the Soviets in late 1918. His death sentence was commuted on instructions from Lenin.

1924: The Soviets opened Amtorg, a front that facilitated industrial espionage against the West.

1924: The Soviet Union's fledgling foreign intelligence service, the OGPU's INO, recruited its first major penetration of the UK foreign service—Francesco Constantini, an Italian messenger in the British embassy in Rome. He provided diplomatic documents and cipher material for over a decade. His brother, Secondo, an embassy servant, also worked for the Soviets.

March 1927: A Soviet OGPU spy ring was discovered in Poland. Swiss police arrested two Soviet spies. Turkish authorities arrested a Soviet trade official on charges of espionage.

April 1927: Chinese officials raided the Soviet consulate in Beijing and found incriminating intelligence documents. The French Surete arrested members of a Soviet spy ring in Paris run by French Communist leader Jean Cremet.

May 1927: Austrian Foreign Ministry officials were caught passing classified information to the OGPU residency in Vienna. The British Home Secretary announced the discovery of an OGPU spy network. London broke diplomatic relations with Moscow.

November 16, 1927: Former UK Army intelligence officer Lt. Wilfred F. R. Macartney was arrested for spying for the USSR. He had worked in intelligence during World War I. In 1926, he paid 25 pounds to a Lloyd's of London employee for information about arms shipments to Finland. He claimed to be working for the Soviets, and asked about the Royal Air Force. The Lloyd's employee tipped off MI-5, who watched Macartney give a secret document to a member of the Soviet Trade Delegation in London. MI-5 then raided the Delegation, discovering incriminating documents. The British government broke diplomatic relations later in 1926. Following surveillance of Macartney to spot his contacts, he was arrested. He was convicted under the Official Secrets Act. He was sentenced to ten years in prison with two years of hard labor. Following his release, he joined the International Brigade in the Spanish Civil War.

August 1928: Swiss businessman Giovanni de Ry walked into the Soviet embassy in Paris with Italian codes and ciphers and requested 200,000 French francs. He offered additional Italian diplomatic ciphers. Two years later, the Soviets recontacted de Ry in Geneva and recruited him, using a false flag—the Soviet case officer claimed to be working for Japanese intelligence.

1929: Secretary of State Henry Stimson declared "gentlemen do not read each other's mail" and cut funding for the Black Chamber, a cryptographic unit run by Herbert Yardley.

August 1929: Ernest Holloway Oldham, a cipher clerk for the UK's Foreign Office Communications Department accompanying a British trade delegation to Paris, walked into the Soviet Embassy in Paris. He offered to provide the British diplomatic cipher for 50,000 British pounds. Oldham resigned from the Foreign Office on September 30, 1932. He apparently committed suicide on September 29, 1933, although the Soviets believed he had been murdered.

October 1929: Grigori Besedovsky, Soviet Charge d'Affaires of the Paris Embassy, defected to the West. The Mitrokhin archives credited him with numerous forgery operations.

1930s

January 26, 1930: Soviet OGPU agents kidnapped General Kutepov, an exiled Russian leader, in Paris. They threw him into a taxi in the seventh arrondissement. His heart gave out from the chloroform used to subdue him, and he died on board a Soviet steamer en route to Russia.

June 1930: Armenian-born OGPU officer Georges Agabekov defected in France. He was born in 1896 in Ashgabat, Turkmenistan. He joined OGPU in 1921. He was posted to Kabul in 1924, and Tehran in 1926, running intelligence operations. He ran OGPU's Eastern Section and had been in charge of the failed manhunt for Polish-born Politburo Secretary Boris Bazhanov, who had defected on a train to Iran in 1928. After his defection, the French expelled him to Belgium in August 1930. He published his English-language memoirs, *OGPU: The Russian Secret Terror*, in 1931. He was assassinated, probably by Soviet agents, in the Pyrenees Mountains in 1937.

1932: The Soviet GRU recruited Whittaker Chambers.

He was born in Philadelphia, Pennsylvania, on April 1, 1901. He was in the 1920 freshmen class at Columbia University, but was expelled in 1923 for having written and published an anti–Christian play. He then went on a youth's grand European tour, stopping in Germany, Belgium, and France. He returned to Columbia, working in the library. He joined the Communist Party in 1924, writing for the *Daily Worker* party newspaper before rising to become its editor.

In 1932, he was recruited by Soviet intelligence, working as a courier for Colonel Boris Bykov, a senior Soviet military intelligence officer in New York City whose network included agents in President Franklin Roosevelt's administration.

Chambers claimed to have undergone an ideological conversion from Communism in 1937, quitting the party in 1938. He joined the National Research Project of the Federal Works Progress Administration, and became an editor for *Time Magazine*. In September 1939, he warned Assistant Secretary of State for Latin American Affairs Adolf A. Berle that several senior government officials were communists. He fingered Alger Hiss, a Harvard Law graduate, who had served as secretary to Supreme Court Justice Oliver Wendell Holmes, and who was working in the Far East Division of the State Department. Berle took no action. Chambers made the same charges to the FBI, conveniently forgetting his earlier spying for the Soviets.

In August 1948, Chambers testified before the House Committee on Un-American Activities' Hearings Regarding Communist Espionage in the United States

Government, admitting his communist party affiliation. He said that "an underground organization of the United States Communist Party" including former Assistant Secretary of the Treasury Harry Dexter White and Alger Hiss, who was serving as the president of the Carnegie Endowment for International Peace, after having been involved in the founding of the United Nations. The duo denied the charges. Hiss filed suit for slander after Chambers echoed his charges outside the Committee.

In pretrial discovery, Chambers provided classified State Department documents from 1938 that he claimed he had received from Hiss, some of which were in Hiss's handwriting. He also gave the Committee five rolls of microfilm, two of which contained State Department documents initialed by Hiss. Chambers had hidden the materials in a hollow pumpkin, leading the media to deem them the "Pumpkin Papers."

Hiss was tried twice on two counts of perjury for having denied seeing Chambers after January 1, 1937, and giving documents to him. The statute of limitations on espionage had expired, so spying was not included in the charges. The first trial ended with a hung jury, but the second trial led to his conviction of perjury in January 1950. Hiss went on to serve 44 months in prison. In 1995, with the release of the Venona Papers, a compilation of decrypts of Soviet intelligence traffic, that showed his involvement, he nonetheless protested his innocence. He died in 1996 at age 92.

Chambers became an anti–Communist, eventually writing for the *National Review* in 1957–1958. He died on July 9, 1961. President Ronald Reagan awarded him a posthumous Medal of Freedom in 1984.

1934: The Soviets recruited Kim Philby, tasking him with infiltrating British counterintelligence.

On February 24, 1934, he married Alice "Litzi" Friedman, a Communist activist wanted by the police, in Vienna, Austria. She thereby obtained a UK passport. At the time of his marriage, he claimed to be an anti–Communist supporter of General Franco in the Spanish Civil War.

Philby later became Chief of the Soviet Section of MI-6 and also served as MI-6 liaison with the CIA and FBI. CIA Counterintelligence chief James Jesus Angleton considered him a close friend and shared sensitive materials with him, which Philby quickly provided to the Soviets. Philby remained hidden in the UK intelligence bureaucracy for another dozen years, defecting to Moscow in January 1963.

1934–1935: Soviet OGPU agents recruited Captain John H. King, who had joined the British Foreign Office Communications Department in 1934. The Irish-born King was estranged from his wife and supported a mistress on a meager salary. King was talked into providing Foreign Office telegrams, ciphers, and summaries of diplomatic correspondence.

March 5, 1936: The Office of Naval Intelligence arrested former U.S. sailor Harry Thompson on charges of spying for the Japanese during the 1930s. After serving in the Navy as a yeoman, he was recruited in San Pedro, California, by Japanese intelligence officer Toshio Miyazaki. He bought a Navy uniform to board ships, where he chatted with crewmen regarding gunnery and Pacific maneuvers. He told his Long Beach apartment roommate, William Turntine, that he could make money helping him commit espionage. Turntine intercepted a letter from Miyazaki with reporting requirements and handed it over to ONI. The FBI later spotted Miyazaki at Thompson's home. Thompson's sister told the FBI he had worked for the Japanese Embassy since

1933. Thompson was given a $500 recruitment bonus and earned $200 a month from the Japanese. Thompson was convicted in July 1936 and sentenced to 15 years for selling U.S. Navy secrets to a Japanese agent.

July 14, 1936: Former U.S. Navy Lieutenant Commander John Semer Farnsworth was arrested and charged with selling confidential information to the Japanese.

Farnsworth was born in Cincinnati and became his high school valedictorian. He graduated from Annapolis and served on destroyers during World War I. He studied aeronautical engineering at MIT and was promoted to Lieutenant Commander. He and his socialite wife were soon living beyond their means. He became heavily indebted, borrowed from an enlisted man whom he refused to repay, was court-martialed, and dishonorably discharged from the Navy in 1927 at age 34. Unemployed for years and needing money, he offered his services to the embassies of Russia, China, Peru, and Japan. He spied for the Japanese for $100 a week from 1932 to 1935, schmoozing with his former Navy associates in Washington and Annapolis. He collected information on code and signal books, tactics, diagrams, new ship design blueprints, and weapons. His aggressive questioning regarding a new destroyer alerted the wife of a lieutenant commander, who tipped the Office of Naval Intelligence and the FBI. The Bureau spotted him visiting the Japanese Embassy several times and flashing $100 bills in bars, despite his lack of a job. The Bureau also found Farnsworth had phoned Japanese Lieutenant Commander Josiyuki Itimiya several times. After reading that Harry Thompson had been sentenced, Farnsworth told a news service that he was running a double agent operation against the Japanese and requested $20,000 for the rest of the story—the amount he had re-

ceived from the Japanese. The news service alerted the ONI. The Bureau arrested him hours later.

Farnsworth pleaded *nolo contendere*. On February 26, 1937, he was sentenced to four to 12 years in prison for conspiring "to communicate and transmit to a foreign government—to wit Japan—writings, code books, photographs and plans relating to the national defense with the intent that they should be used to the injury of the United States." The information included details on the destroyers *Saratoga* and *Ranger*, firing patterns on every U.S. Navy vessel, and the comprehensive Navy handbook *The Service of Information and Security* manual, a loss which might have required major changes to U.S. naval strategy. He served 11 years. He died in Manhattan at age 59.

1937: The NKVD recruited wealthy young American Michael Whitney Straight before his graduation from Cambridge University. Returning to the U.S., he was a speechwriter for President Franklin D. Roosevelt and later worked for the Department of the Interior. In 1938, Itzhak Akhmerov became his KGB handler. He joined the U.S. Department of State's Eastern Division in 1940. He was a B-17 Flying Fortress pilot during World War II. Some accounts say that he was part of the Cambridge Spy Ring of Kim Philby, Guy Burgess, Donald Maclean, John Cairncross and Anthony Blunt. His admission during a 1963 background check about his communist leanings exposed Blunt. In 1983, his memoir *After Long Silence* explained his communist activities. He died of pancreatic cancer at age 87 in his Chicago home on January 4, 2004.

March 18, 1937: Nikolai Yezhov, head of the NKVD, denounced Genrikh Yagoda, who ran the NKVD from 1934 to 1936.

June 3, 1937: Juliet Stuart Poyntz, 51, one of the U.S. Communist Party's key leaders, disappeared after denouncing Stalin and threatening to expose a spy network she established in the U.S. Many observers believe SMERSH, the NKVD's "wet works" department, assassinated her. In 1913, she had married Dr. Frederick Franz Ludwig Glaser, a German attache in New York, so that she could spy on German operations in the U.S. for Russian revolutionaries. She conducted espionage missions in Europe and China in the early 1930s. She trained at a Soviet spy school in Moscow in 1934, and was sent back to the U.S. to establish a spy network. She recruited dozens of agents, but turned against Stalin's purges of old line Bolsheviks. She was officially declared dead in 1944.

July 17, 1937: Paris-based Soviet NKVD illegal agent Ignace Poretsky né Reiss, alias Ludwik, denounced the service. He was born in 1881 in Galicia. In 1922, Polish authorities arrested him on charges of espionage for distributing GPU/OGPU propaganda, which carried a maximum five-year sentence. En route to prison, he escaped his train in Cracow. From 1921 to 1929, he served in Western Europe, earning the Order of the Red Banner for engaging in political action operations for the Comintern. He served in Moscow from 1929 to 1932. In 1931, the Soviet Security Service recruited him to conduct industrial espionage against Germany. From 1932 until his defection, he was stationed in Paris. He watched many of his friends recalled to Moscow, where they were shot during the Great Purge. He avoided his recall in 1936 and sent his resignation and medal to Stalin the next year. He wrote a denunciation letter on July 17, 1937, to the Central Committee of the Communist Party of the Soviet Union and sent it and his medal to Stalin via the Soviet Commercial Mission in Paris. He then joined his family in hiding in Switzerland.

He was apparently abducted and assassinated on September 4, 1937, near Lausanne, Switzerland possibly by Soviet illegal Roland Abbiate, Etienne-Charles Martignat, and Italy-based OGPU agent Gertrude Schildbach. His assassins dumped his body on the side of a road in Chamblandes outside Lausanne. The assassination led Whitaker Chambers to decide to defect in April 1938.

September 22, 1937: Soviet NKVD agents kidnapped exile leader General Yevgeni Karlovich Miller, head of the White Guard ROVs, off a Paris street. The French Surete determined that he was stashed in the Soviet embassy. He was sent back to the USSR hidden in a trunk on a freighter waiting at Le Havre.

October 1937: Walter Krivitsky, Polish-born Soviet illegal resident in the Netherlands, defected in Paris following the assassination of NKVD illegal agent Ignace Poretsky. He died in the U.S. in 1941; some said of assassination made to look like a suicide. He spent nearly 20 years as a Soviet military intelligence officer before defecting to France in October 1937. He was shot to death in a Washington, D.C., hotel room on February 10, 1941.

He was born in Podwolczyska on June 28, 1899. He spent nearly 20 years as a Soviet military intelligence officer before defecting to the West. In 1920, while assigned to Danzig, he was ordered to prevent the landing of French munitions being shipped to the Polish army. In 1922, he went to Berlin to foment unrest in the Ruhr, to create the German Communist Party's intelligence service, and to form the nucleus of a German Red Army. In 1926, he became Chief of Soviet Military Intelligence for Central Europe. He was posted to The Hague in 1935 as Chief of Military Intelligence for Western Europe. In September 1937, he worried that he would be purged after one of his closest friends, Ignace Reiss, was murdered after breaking with the Soviets. The French government gave Krivitsky asylum in October 1937. During the next year, despite a French police guard force, the Soviets twice tried to kill him. He began working on a book and traveled to the U.S. in November 1938. In 1939, he testified before the House of Representatives Committee on Un-American Activities and was interviewed by UK authorities. He reentered the U.S. via Canada in October 1940, settling in New York under the alias Walter Poref. His book, *I Was Stalin's Agent*, was published in London in 1940. On February 10, 1941, he was shot to death in a Washington, D.C., hotel room. He was in transit to New York.

January 1938: British authorities arrested a spy ring operating inside the Woolwich Arsenal. They were tried and imprisoned three months later. Their ringleader was Percy Glading. One of their contacts was Latvian-born Melita Norwood, née Sernis, one of the longest-serving Soviet spies in the UK, and the KGB's most important British female agent. She was recruited in 1937 and worked for the Soviets—at times for the GRU, but mostly for the KGB—for nearly 40 years, providing them with schematics for the British nuclear bomb. She was never prosecuted. The British heard of her activities only through Vasily Mitrokhin's defection in 1992. By then, she was an 87-year-old retired grandmother in suburban London.

March 10, 1938: U.S. authorities arrested Otto Hermann Voss, a naturalized German-American employed in a Sikorsky aircraft plant in Farmingdale, Long Island, on charges of espionage for the Germans. His case officer, William Lonkowski, used Voss to recruit Werner Georg Gudenberg, an en-gineering draftsman working at an army bomber plant. The duo handed their secrets to Lonkowski, who passed them to Johanna Hofmann, 26, a hairdresser on the German liner *Europa*, who passed them to the Luftwaffe in Germany. Voss copied blueprints and plans for fighter planes, as well as for an experimental seaplane. Lonkowski ultimately penetrated most U.S. aircraft plants. Voss was sentenced to six years in prison.

Lonkowski's network fell apart when his successor, Dr. Ignatz Griebl, a prominent obstetrician who rose to a leadership position in the German American Bund, used a flamboyant agent, Guenther Gustave Rumrich, who was soon arrested and turned informant. Rumrich, born in Chicago in 1911, grew up in Europe. He enlisted in the U.S. Army upon returning to the U.S., but went AWOL, served six months in the brig, then went AWOL again. Once a civilian, he sent a letter to retired German spy chief Colonel Walther Nicolai, volunteering his services. The Nazis accepted in April 1936, communicating via the mails. Rumrich reported on events happening on the docks, chatting with sailors about ship movements, cargos, and construction. When in 1938 he contacted the State Department and Western Union, claiming to be the Secretary of State, and requested 35 blank U.S. passports for German agents to enter the USSR, he was arrested. The greedy Rumrich quickly identified other Nazi spies. He received a two-year sentence.

June 13, 1938: Japan announced that NKVD officer Genrikh Samoilovich Lyushkov had crossed the Soviet border into Manchukuo with secret documents a month earlier, defecting to the Japanese. He was the organization's most senior defector, having risen to be the Far Eastern Commander of the NKVD, in charge of 20,000–30,000 troops.

He was born in 1900 and had been part

of the Bolshevik Revolution. He joined the Cheka in 1920, serving in Moscow and the Ukraine. He joined the State Political Directorate (GPU) upon its formation and ran spy operations in Germany. He later joined the People's Commissariat for Internal Affairs (NKVD), earning the Order of Lenin and becoming a deputy of the Supreme Soviet and a member of the Central Committee. When ordered back to Moscow, he feared he was going to be part of the Great Purge in which he had enthusiastically participated, and instead defected. His family was arrested and sent to the gulag, where several died. He participated in a Russian émigré plot to assassinate Stalin that was foiled by a Soviet penetration of the hit team. He disappeared on August 7, 1945, during the Soviet invasion of Manchukuo.

July 16, 1938: Paris authorities found the headless corpse of Rudolf Klement, a German associate of the son of Leon Trotsky and secretary of Trotsky's Fourth International, on the banks of the Seine. He was believed to have died at the hands of NKVD agents, who in 1936 had created the "Administration of Special Tasks," commonly known as the Department of "Wet Operations," aimed at foreign communist dissidents and Trotskyites. The Mitrokhin archives indicated that he was abducted from his Paris home on July 13, 1938

August 13, 1938: Senior Soviet intelligence officer Aleksandr Orlov, true name Leon Lazcirevich Feldbin, defected to the U.S. He was born on August 21, 1895, in Bobrvisk, Russia. In 1916, he was drafted into the Russian Army and stationed in the Urals. In 1917, he joined the Bolshevik Party and graduated as a Second Lieutenant from the Third Moscow Military School. In September 1920, he was serving with the 12th Red Army on the Polish front, in charge of guer-

rilla activity and counterintelligence. Cheka Chief Felix Dzerzhinsky spotted him. In 1921, Orlov married while assigned to Archangel, then returned to Moscow to become an assistant to the Soviet Supreme Court. Dzerzhinsky brought him into the Cheka as deputy chief of the Economic Directorate. He later commanded the border guards in Armenia, then ran Soviet intelligence operations in France. From 1928 to 1931, he was with the Soviet Trade Delegation in Berlin, handling economic intelligence. He traveled often in Europe, directing illegals against Germany. In 1936, he went to Spain as the Soviet liaison to the Republic government regarding intelligence, counterintelligence, and guerrilla warfare. In July 1938, he was ordered to Paris. While in transit, he met with his family on the French border with Spain. He told them of his concern about the secret trials, summary executions, and terror going on in the USSR. He decided to defect. The Canadians helped the family enter the U.S. on August 13, 1938. They were granted permanent residence 18 years later. He provided extensive material to the U.S. on pre–World War II personnel and operations of the Soviet State Security Service. He wrote *The Soviet History of Stalin's Crimes*, which was published in 1953, and *The Handbook of Intelligence and Guerrilla Warfare*, published in 1963. He testified before the Senate Subcommittee on Internal Security in 1955 and 1957. He died in April 1973.

1939: The FBI arrested Russian immigrant Jacob Golos for violating foreign agent registration laws. Following a plea bargain, he received probation and a small fine. He died of a heart attack on Thanksgiving 1943. He was later identified as Elizabeth Bentley's handler.

1939: Lauchlin Currie began passing secrets to the CPUSA for sharing with the Soviets.

He was born in Nova Scotia, was an undergrad at the London School of Economics, and earned a Ph.D. in economics from Harvard, meeting fellow teaching assistant Harry Dexter White. He obtained U.S. citizenship in 1934 and joined White's Research Division at Treasury. By 1942, Roosevelt had named him a presidential adviser and head of the Foreign Economic Administration, which ran the Lend Lease program. Nine Venona messages mention his sharing FDR's foreign policy strategic plans with the Soviets. Whittaker Chambers identified him as a spy to Assistant Secretary of State Adolf Berle, who took no action. Elizabeth Bentley also warned the FBI about him. Currie had been careful to not meet with Soviet handlers while spying at the White House between 1939 and 1945. He testified before the House Un-American Activities Committee on August 13, 1948, denying that he was a spy. He traveled for the World Bank in 1950 to Colombia and ended his days there, dying in 1993. In 1995, released Venona documents identified him as Soviet agent PAGE.

June 26, 1939: Franklin Roosevelt's Presidential Directive established the authority of the FBI, the War Department's Military Intelligence Division, and the Navy Department's Office of Naval Intelligence to investigate espionage, counterespionage, and sabotage matters. The Directive read in part, "It is my desire that the investigation of all espionage, counterespionage, and sabotage matters be controlled and handled by the Federal Bureau of Investigation of the Department of Justice, the Military Intelligence Division of the War Department, and the Office of Naval Intelligence of the Navy Department. The directors of these three agencies are to function as a committee to coordinate their activities.

"No investigations should be conducted by any investigating agency of the Government into matters involving actually or potentially any espionage, counterespionage, or sabotage, except by the three agencies mentioned above.

"I shall be glad if you will instruct the heads of all other investigative agencies than the three named, to refer immediately to the nearest office of the Federal Bureau of Investigation any data, information, or material that may come to their notice bearing directly or indirectly on espionage, counterespionage, or sabotage."

October 18, 1939: Captain John H. King, a British Foreign Officer cipher clerk, pleaded guilty at a secret trial to supplying secret information to the USSR. King had served in the UK Army in World War I. He was a cipher specialist in Damascus, Paris, and Germany following the 1918 armistice, and joined the Foreign Officer's communications department in 1934. While estranged from his wife in 1935 in Geneva, he met an American woman who became his mistress. Paying for two households quickly put him into debt. He was recruited by Soviet asset Henri "Pieck" Christiaan, a successful Dutch artist, who took the couple on expensive European holidays. Pieck recruited him under a false flag while in London, claiming he needed insider information on international relations for a Dutch banker in return for money. King gave Pieck classified documents, which were photographed in a London apartment and returned to King. Some of the documents were passed to Josef Stalin. NKVD defector Walter Krivitsky in 1937 told the British that there was a highly placed mole. In 1939, two security officials met King in a Curzon Street pub, got him drunk, and listened to his boozy confession. He was arrested. He was sentenced to ten years in prison, but released after World War II with full remission for good conduct.

1940s

1940s: Under questioning by the FBI in the late 1940s, Jones York, a Northrop Corporation aeronautical engineer identified in the Venona decryptions, admitted giving the Soviets classified information on aircraft specifications. He told the Bureau that one of his handlers was Bill Villesbend, a garble of William Weisband, who was sentenced for espionage in 1950.

October 1940: George Koval entered the U.S. as a trained GRU illegal, going on to spy for eight years against the Manhattan Project. On November 2, 2007, Russian Prime Minister Vladimir Putin posthumously gave him the Hero of the Russia Federation Medal, calling him "the only Soviet intelligence officer to penetrate the U.S. secret atomic facilities producing the plutonium, enriched uranium, and polonium used to create the atomic bomb." His code name was DELMAR. Putin said he "helped speed up considerably the time it took for the Soviet Union to develop an atomic bomb of its own, thus ensuring the preservation of strategic military parity with the United States." He was the only known Soviet intelligence staff officer to obtain a security clearance and work inside a U.S. government agency.

His Jewish parents fled the tsar's persecution and settled in Sioux City in 1910. George was born on December 25, 1914. His mother, Ethel, was an underground revolutionary socialist in Russia and influenced her son's thinking. After graduating from high school at age 15, he was a delegate to a CPUSA conference. He studied engineering at the University of Iowa, but in 1932 the family returned to Russia's Birobidzhan region. In 1934, Koval studied chemical engineering at the Mendeleyev Institute of Chemical Technology, coming to the interest of the GRU. Upon his return to the U.S.,

he ran illegal operations from 1940 to 1948, working for Raven Electric. He was drafted into the U.S. Army in February 1943, then went to the Citadel for electrical engineering training. He also studied at CUNY, and moved on in August 1944 to the Special Engineer Detachment, part of the Manhattan Project in Oak Ridge. As the health physics officer, he had access to all of the facility's production of enriched uranium and plutonium and the polonium used for nuclear triggers, which he passed to the Soviets. He left on an ocean liner for Europe in 1948 and vanished from the West. In 1949, he was honorably discharged from the Red Army, and earned his doctorate from the Mendeleyev Institute in 1951. He eventually became a professor, teaching for 40 years. He died in January 2006 at age 92.

May 20, 1940: MI-5 arrested Tyler G. Kent, a code clerk in the U.S. Embassy in London and his girlfriend Anna Volkova, an anti–Semitic Russian émigré. MI-5 officials found 1,929 classified documents in his apartment, including copies of Winston Churchill's cables, a book of names of individuals under Special Branch and MI-5 surveillance, and keys to the U.S. Embassy code room. After 11 days of detention, he was fired by the U.S. Department of State, stripping him of his diplomatic immunity.

Some scholars suggest that Kent worked for the Soviets and the Germans. He was born in Manchuria in 1911, where his father served as U.S. Consul, and moved to various countries following his father's postings. He was schooled at Princeton, the University of Madrid, and the Sorbonne, picking up six languages. After he failed the Foreign Service Officer exam, he became a communications clerk in 1934. At his first assignment, Moscow, he apparently was recruited by Soviet intelligence via a Russian mistress, tasked with obtaining codebooks and classified material. He had chafed at being an upperclass individual in a job for inferiors, and became a womanizing party animal who lived beyond his means. Moved to the London embassy on June 5, 1939, he became anti–Semitic, sharing sensitive communications between Roosevelt and Churchill with isolationist U.S. legislators and later with members of the pro–Nazi Right Club in London. He was soon spotted meeting with a suspected Soviet agent who was under Special Branch surveillance. Kent met Irene Danischeivsky, who became his lover, at the Russian Tea Room. She and her husband were also under surveillance as potential Russian spies. His Russian émigré girlfriend, Anna Volkova, shared the documents with Italian Naval Attache Duco del Monte, who sent them to the Nazis. Kent brought some of the classified cables to a commercial photography store for copying. The owner contacted MI-5 after developing the film.

Kent's secret trial began on October 26, 1940, in the Old Bailey. He was charged with violating the Official Secrets Act, obtaining documents that "might be directly or indirectly useful to an enemy" and of stealing documents that were the property of U.S. Ambassador Joseph P. Kennedy. Volkova was sentenced to 10 years in prison. Kent was sentenced to 7 years but served only 5, being released in September 1945. The U.S. did not prosecute him for espionage. Kent sued the Department of State for firing him without cause; he lost. He died in 1988 as a Holocaust denier in a Texas trailer park.

August 20, 1940: Soviet NKVD agents were suspected of assassinating Leon Trotsky, founder of the Red Army, with an ice pick in Mexico City. He had been in exile since 1929.

June 1941: FBI special agents arrested 33 Nazi spies who were members of the Du-

quesne Spy Ring headed by Frederick "Fritz" Joubert Duquesne. They had been tasked with obtaining information useful for sabotage operations. Eventually, 19 pleaded guilty. The 14 men who were tried in Federal District Court, Brooklyn, New York, beginning on September 3, 1941, were found guilty on December 13, 1941. On January 2, 1942, they were sentenced to a total of more than 300 years in prison.

The ring was unraveled by William G. Sebold, born Wilhelm Debowski in Germany, who had served in the Imperial German Army in World War I as a machine gunner. He traveled to the U.S. as a sailor in 1921 and jumped ship in Galveston, Texas, where he changed his name to Sebold. He became a U.S. citizen on February 10, 1936. He became a mechanic in the Consolidated Aircraft Company in San Diego, California. During a visit with his family in Germany in September 1939, the Gestapo recruited him, threatening to expose an earlier smuggling charge that could put his U.S. citizenship in jeopardy. He was trained at a Nazi spy school, then returned to the U.S. on February 8, 1940, under the alias Harry Sawyer, an engineering consultant for Diesel Research, a Nazi front company in Manhattan. He set up a radio system to communicate intelligence to Berlin from the Nazi spy ring. However, he had visited the U.S. consulate in Cologne and agreed to become a double agent for the FBI. The shortwave communication system ran under the control of the FBI for 16 months, transmitting more than 300 messages and receiving 200. From December 1940 to June 1941, Sebold conducted 81 meetings with Nazi agents that the FBI recorded. The Bureau also gave Sebold information to share with the Nazis, enhancing his cover. Sebold in turn passed the FBI the Nazis' reporting requirements, including biological warfare, gas masks, ship movements, and anti-aircraft munitions, and how Nazi tradecraft included microdots. Most of the ring members knew each other, making the multiple arrests easier for the Bureau.

The convicted members of the Duquesne Spy ring included:

- Frederick "Fritz" Joubert Duquesne, who was born in South Africa on September 21, 1877, and became a U.S. citizen in 1913. He was a Captain in the Second Boer War. He claimed to have sunk the HMS *Hampshire*, on which Lord Kitchener was traveling to Russia in 1916. Germany awarded him the Iron Cross. By February 1940, he was running a company in New York City, when he was contacted by Sebold. Duquesne gave Sebold photographs and specifications of a new type of bomb being produced by the DuPont plant in Wilmington, Delaware. He also told Sebold how to start fires in industrial plants. He also obtained chemical warfare gas mask information. He was sentenced to serve 18 years in prison on espionage charges, as well as a two-year concurrent sentence and fined $2,000 fine for violation of the Foreign Agents Registration Act. He served his sentence in Leavenworth Federal Penitentiary in Kansas where he was beaten by inmates. In 1954 he was released due to ill health, having served 14 years. He died on May 24, 1956, at age 78.

- Paul Bante, who served in the German army during World War I. He arrived in the United States in 1930 and obtained citizenship in 1938. He joined the German-American Bund. Bante was linked to Dr. Ignatz T. Griebl, who had been implicated in a Nazi spy ring with Guenther Gustave Rumrich, who was tried on espionage charges in 1938. He told investigators that he helped German operative Paul Fehse obtain information about ships bound for the UK with war materials and supplies. Bante claimed that as a member of the Gestapo his function was to create discontent among union workers. Bante told Sebold that he was preparing a bomb fuse. He later gave Sebold dynamite and detonation caps. He pleaded guilty to violating the Foreign Agents Registration Act. He was sentenced to 18 months and fined $1,000.

- Max Blank, who entered the U.S. from Germany in 1928, working in New York City at a German library and at a book store which catered to German trade. Fehse told Sebold that Blank could obtain details about rubberized self-sealing airplane gasoline tanks, and a new braking device for airplanes, from a friend who worked in a shipyard. Blank claimed he had spied since 1936, but had lost interest, since Germany was not paying. He later pleaded guilty to violation of the Foreign Agents Registration Act. He was sentenced to 18 months and fined $1,000.

- Alfred E. Brokhoff, born in Germany, who entered the U.S. in 1923 and obtained citizenship in 1929. He worked as a mechanic for the United States Lines in New York City for 17 years prior to his arrest. He helped Fehse acquire information about the sailing dates and cargoes of vessels destined for the UK. He was sentenced to five years for violation of the espionage statutes and to a two-year concurrent sentence for violation of the Registration Act.

- Heinrich Clausing, born in Germany, who entered the U.S. in September 1934 and obtained citizenship in 1938. He served on various ships sailing from New York Harbor and was working as a cook on the SS *Argentine* at the time of his arrest. He served the ring as a courier, bringing microphotographs and other material from the United States to South American ports, from which the information was sent to Germany via Italian airlines. He set up a mail drop in South America. He was sentenced to serve eight years for violation of espionage statutes and to a 2-year concurrent sentence for violation of the Registration Act.

- Conradin Otto Dold, born in Germany, who entered the U.S. in 1926 and obtained U.S. citizenship via the Seamen's Act in 1934. Prior to his arrest, he was Chief Steward on the SS *Siboney* of the American Export Lines. He was a courier for the ring. He was sentenced to 10 years on espionage charges and to a two-year concurrent sentence and fined $1,000 for violation of the Registration Act.

- Rudolf Ebeling, who left Germany for the U.S. in 1925. He was working as a foreman in the Shipping Department of Harper and Brothers in New York City when he was arrested. He gave Paul Fehse and Leo Waalen information regarding ship sailings and cargoes. He was sentenced to five years on espionage charges and to a two-year concurrent sentence and fined $1,000 for violating the Registration Act.

- Richard Eichenlaub, who entered the U.S. in 1930 and obtained citizenship in 1936. He operated the Little Casino Restaurant in New York City's Yorkville section. The ring used it as a meeting site. He also introduced several new members into the group. He reported to the Gestapo. He obtained information from his customers who were engaged in national defense production. Bante provided dynamite to Sebold via Eichenlaub. He pleaded guilty to violation of

the Registration Act. He was sentenced to 18 months and fined $1,000.

- Heinrich Carl Eilers, who came to the U.S. from Germany in 1923 and obtained citizenship in 1932. He worked as a steward on ships sailing from New York City from 1933 until his arrest. He was unsuccessful in obtaining information from the Civil Aeronautics Authority in Washington, D.C. Customs authorities arrested him in June 1940, finding 20 letters addressed to various Europeans. He had books on magnesium and aluminum alloys which had been sent to him by cell member Edmund Carl Heine. He was sentenced to 5 years on espionage charges and a concurrent two-year sentence and fined $1,000 under the Registration Act.

- Paul Fehse, a key member of the cell, who arrived in the U.S. from Germany in 1934 and obtained citizenship in 1938. He worked as a cook on ships sailing from New York City. He arranged meetings, tasked members, correlated information, and sent the information to Germany, usually via Sebold. The Germans trained Fehse. He said he led the Marine Division of the German espionage system in the U.S. He planned to leave the U.S. on the SS *Siboney*, which was scheduled to sail from Hoboken, New Jersey, to Lisbon, Portugal, on March 29, 1941. He told arresting FBI agents that he sent letters to Italy for forwarding to Germany, and had obtained information on the movements of British ships. He pleaded guilty and was sentenced on April 1, 1941, to one year and one day for violation of the Registration Act. A later guilty plea on espionage charges yielded a 15-year sentence.

- Edmund Carl Heine, who arrived in the U.S. from Germany in 1914 and became a citizen in 1920. Until 1938, he worked in the foreign sales and service departments of Ford Motor Company and Chrysler Corporation, traveling to the West Indies, South America, Spain, and Berlin, Germany. He wrote letters from Detroit, Michigan, to Lilly Stein, one of the German spies Sebold was instructed to contact. The letters included technical data on the military, aircraft construction, and various industries. Other letters to aircraft companies asked for information about their production, number of employees, and the time required to build military planes. Heine, under the alias "Heinrich," provided the ring with aerial photographs. He sent technical books on magnesium and aluminum alloys to Heinrich Eilers, using the return address of Lilly Stein. He was sentenced to two years and fined $5,000 for violating the Registration Act.

- Felix Jahnke, who entered the U.S. from Germany in 1924, and obtained U.S. citizenship in 1930. He had studied at military school in Germany and had served in the German army as a radio operator. He and Axel Wheeler-Hill tasked radio technician Josef Klein with building a portable radio set for Jahnke, who used it to send messages to Germany. The FBI intercepted the messages. He trolled the New York docks, getting information about UK-bound vessels. He pleaded guilty to violation of the Registration Act, and was sentenced to 20 months and fined $1,000.

- Gustav Wilhelm Kaercher, who entered the U.S. from Germany in 1923, obtaining U.S. citizenship in 1931. He served in the German Army during World War I and was a leader of the German Bund in New York. He wore a German Army officer's uniform during visits to Germany. He designed power plants for the American Gas and Electric Company in New York City. Paul Scholtz had given him a table of call letters and frequencies for transmitting information to Germany by radio just before they were arrested. He pleaded guilty to violating the Registration Act. He was sentenced to 22 months and fined $2,000.

- Josef Klein, who went to the U.S. from Germany in 1925, but never became a U.S. citizen. He worked as a photographer and lithographer. He built a portable shortwave radio transmitting-and-receiving set for fellow ring members Felix Jahnke and Axel Wheeler-Hill to send messages to Germany. He was sentenced to five years for espionage and a concurrent two-year sentence under the Registration Act.

- Hartwig Richard Kleiss, who left Germany for the U.S. in 1925 and obtained U.S. citizenship in 1931. He worked as a cook on ships. He gave Sebold blueprints of the SS *America* detailing the locations of gun emplacements; how guns would be brought into position for firing; and details on the construction and performance of new speedboats being developed by the United States Navy. After pleading guilty to espionage, he was sentenced to eight years.

- Herman W. Lang, a German immigrant who participated in Adolf Hitler's Munich beer hall putsch of 1923. He went to the U.S. in 1927 and obtained citizenship in 1939. He worked as a draftsman for the Carl L. Norden Company, which produced the top secret Norden Bombsight, which gave the Allies a distinct military advantage in aerial bombing targeting. During a visit to Germany in 1938, Lang provided German military authorities with the plans for the bombsight. As an inspector for the company, he had access to the bombsight's blueprints, which he traced and handed to Abwehr agents. In October 1937, Major Nikolaus Ritter, head of the Abwehr's Aviation Section, met with Lang in New York. As part of the largest espionage trial that resulted in convictions, Lang was sentenced to 18 years in prison for espionage and to a two-year concurrent sentence for charges under the Foreign Agents Registration Act. He was deported to Germany in September 1950.

• Evelyn Clayton Lewis, who grew up in Arkansas, and lived with Fritz Joubert Duquesne in New York City, telling him of her anti–British and anti–Semitic feelings. She obtained information for Germany and helped him prepare material for transmittal to the Germans. She pleaded guilty to violating the Registration Act, and was sentenced to one year and one day in prison.

• Rene Emanuel Mezenen, a French citizen who obtained U.S. citizenship via naturalization of his father. He worked as a steward in the Pan American transatlantic clipper service. The German Intelligence Service in Lisbon, Portugal, recruited and paid him as a courier between the U.S. and Portugal on his regular commercial aircraft trips. He also spotted convoys sailing for the UK, and smuggled platinum from the U.S. to Portugal. He pleaded guilty and was sentenced to 8 years for espionage and two concurrent years for registration violations.

• Carl Reuper, who came to the U.S. from Germany in 1929 and obtained U.S. citizenship in 1936. He worked as an inspector for the Westinghouse Electric Company in Newark, New Jersey, obtaining photographs regarding national defense materials and construction. He was in radio contact with Germany via

Felix Jahnke's station. He was sentenced to 16 years on espionage charges and a two-year concurrent sentence under the Registration Act.

• Everett Minster Roeder, a Bronx-born American who worked for the Sperry Gyroscope Company as an engineer and designer of confidential materials for the U.S. Army and Navy. He was recruited in Germany as a paid agent during a visit in 1936. He obtained blueprints of the complete radio instrumentation of the new Glenn Martin bomber, classified drawings of range finders, blind-flying instruments, a bank-and-turn indicator, a navigator compass, a wiring diagram of the Lockheed Hudson bomber, and diagrams of the Hudson gun mountings. Arresting authorities found 16 guns in his Long Island home. He pleaded guilty to espionage and was sentenced to 16 years. In 1949, Roeder published *Formulas in Plane Triangles*.

• Paul Alfred W. Scholtz, who went to the U.S. from Germany in 1926 but did not become a U.S. citizen. He worked in German book stores in New York City, disseminating Nazi propaganda. He arranged for Josef Klein to construct the radio set used by Felix Jahnke and Axel Wheeler-Hill. He gave Gustav Wilhelm Kaercher a list of radio call letters and frequencies. He also encouraged members of this spy ring to secure data for Germany and arranged contacts between various German agents. He was sentenced to 16 years for espionage and a two-year concurrent sentence under the Registration Act.

• George Gottlob Schuh, a carpenter who went to the U.S. from Germany in 1923, obtaining U.S. citizenship in 1939. He sent information to the Gestapo in Hamburg from the U.S. He gave Alfred

Brokhoff information that Winston Churchill had arrived in the U.S. on the HMS *King George V*. He gave information to Germany concerning the movement of ships carrying materials and supplies to the UK. He pleaded guilty to violation of the Registration Act and was sentenced to 18 months and fined $1,000.

- Erwin Wilhelm Siegler, who arrived in the U.S. from Germany in 1929 and obtained U.S. citizenship in 1937. He was the chief butcher on the SS *America* until it was taken over by the U.S. Navy. He worked as a courier, bringing microphotographic instructions to Sebold from German authorities, bringing $2,900 from German contacts abroad to pay Lilly Stein, Duquesne, and Roeder for their services and to buy a bomb sight. He was also the ring's organizer and contact man, and obtained information about the movement of ships and military defense preparations at the Panama Canal. He was sentenced to 10 years on espionage charges and a two-year term for violation of the Registration Act.

- Oscar Richard Stabler, who arrived in the U.S. from Germany in 1923 and obtained U.S. citizenship in 1933. He worked as a barber aboard transoceanic ships. In December 1940, British authorities in Bermuda briefly detained him after finding a map of Gibraltar in his possession. He was a courier for the ring. He was sentenced to five years for espionage and to a two-year concurrent term under the Registration Act.

- Heinrich Stade, who arrived in the U.S. from Germany in 1922 and became a U.S. citizen in 1929. He was a musician and publicity agent in New York. He told Sebold he had been in the German Gestapo since 1936. He arranged for

Paul Bante's contact with Sebold. He sent data to Germany regarding points of rendezvous for convoys carrying supplies to the UK. He was arrested while playing in the orchestra at a Long Island inn. He pleaded guilty to violating the Registration Act. He was sentenced to 15 months and fined $1,000.

- Lilly Barbara Carola Stein, who was born in Vienna, Austria. She was in contact with Hugo Sebold, the German espionage instructor who had trained William Sebold (no relation) in Hamburg. She trained in this school and was sent to the U.S. in 1939. She was an artist's model and moved in New York's social circles. The Germans had told Sebold to give her microphotograph instructions. She frequently gave him items to give to Germany. Ring members used her address as a return address when they mailed data for Germany. She pleaded guilty. She was sentenced to ten years and two concurrent years for violations of espionage and registration statutes, respectively.

- Franz Joseph Stigler, who arrived in the U.S. from Germany in 1931 and obtained U.S. citizenship in 1939. He worked as a crew member and chief baker aboard U.S. ships until his discharge from the SS *America* when the U.S. Navy converted that ship into USS *West Point*. He and Erwin Siegler were couriers for the ring. He tried to recruit amateur radio operators in the U.S. as channels of communication to German radio stations. He obtained defense preparations in the Panama Canal Zone and met with other German agents to advise them in their espionage pursuits. In January 1941, he asked Sebold to tell Germany that Prime Minister Winston Churchill and Lord Halifax had arrived secretly in the U.S. on the H.M.S. *King*

George V. He was sentenced to 16 years on espionage charges and two concurrent years for registration violations.

- Erich Strunck, who arrived in the U.S. from Germany in 1927 and obtained U.S. citizenship in 1935. He worked as a seaman aboard ships of the United States Lines. He was a courier for the ring. He asked permission to steal the diplomatic bag of a British officer traveling aboard his ship and to push him overboard. Sebold said it would be too risky to do so. He was sentenced to ten years on espionage charges and to a two-year concurrent term under the Registration Act.

- Leo Waalen, who was born in Danzig when it was in Germany, jumped ship to enter the U.S. in 1935. He worked as a painter for a small boat company which was constructing small craft for the U.S. Navy. He obtained information about ships sailing for the UK, a confidential booklet issued by the FBI which contained precautions to be taken by industrial plants to safeguard national defense materials from sabotage, government contracts listing specifications for materials and equipment, and detailed sea charts of the U.S. Atlantic coastline. Prosecutors said that he had sent to Germany the sailing date of the SS *Robin Moor*, which the *U-69* sunk in the tropical Atlantic in May 1941. He was sentenced to 12 years for espionage and a concurrent two-year term for violation of the Registration Act.

- Adolf Henry August Walischewski, a German seaman who obtained U.S. citizenship in 1935. Fehse recruited him as a courier. He was sentenced to five years for espionage and a two-year concurrent sentence under the Registration Act.

- Else Weustenfeld, who came to the U.S. from Germany in 1927 and obtained U.S. citizenship in 1937. She worked as a secretary for a law firm representing the German Consulate in New York City. She delivered funds to Duquesne provided by Lilly Stein, her close friend. She lived in New York City with Hans W. Ritter, a principal in the German espionage system. His brother, Nickolaus Ritter, alias "Dr. Renken," had recruited Sebold as a German agent. In 1940, she visited Hans Ritter in Mexico, where he was serving as a paymaster for the German Intelligence Service. She pleaded guilty. She was sentenced to five years for espionage and two concurrent years on a charge of registration violations.

- Axel Wheeler-Hill, a Russian truck driver who came to the U.S. in 1923 and obtained U.S. citizenship in 1929. He obtained information regarding ships sailing to the UK from New York Harbor. With Felix Jahnke, he enlisted Paul Scholtz's help in building a radio set for sending coded messages to Germany. He was sentenced to 15 years in prison for espionage and to 2 concurrent years under the Registration Act.

- Bertram Wolfgang Zenzinger, who arrived from Germany in the U.S. in 1940 as a naturalized South African who claimed he wanted to study mechanical dentistry in Los Angeles, California. In July 1940, Siegler mailed him a pencil for preparing invisible messages for Germany. He sent several letters to Germany through a mail drop in Sweden outlining details of national defense materials. FBI agents arrested him on April 16, 1941. He pleaded guilty. He was sentenced to 18 months in prison for violation of the Registration Act and eight years for espionage.

June 21, 1941: NKVD Chief Lavrenty Beria ordered "ground into labor camp dirt" four intelligence officers who kept sending reports of an impending German invasion. He instead wrote a report to Stalin: "I again insist on recalling and punishing our Ambassador to Berlin, who keeps bombarding me with reports on Hitler's alleged preparations to attack the USSR. He has reported that this attack will start tomorrow. But I and my people have firmly embedded in our memory your wise conclusion: Hitler is not going to attack is in 1941." The Germans attacked the next day.

The Germans nonetheless continued their Haifisch deception operation, designed to convince the Russians and British that the Nazis were to conduct airborne landings against UK beachheads and airfields, not against the USSR.

July 11, 1941: Colonel William Donovan was named director of the Coordinator of Information, the predecessor of the Office of Strategic Services, which he later headed.

Donovan was born on January 1, 1883, in Buffalo, New York. He was the most decorated soldier in World War I. He became President Franklin D. Roosevelt's Coordinator of Information on July 11, 1941, then served as Director of Strategic Services from June 13, 1942, to October 1, 1945. The World War II–era OSS was the predecessor organization of the modern-day Central Intelligence Agency. Donovan was promoted to Brigadier General in the U.S. Army on March 24, 1943; and rose to Major General on November 10, 1944. Upon his release from the U.S. Army in January 12, 1946, he practiced law in New York. He was Ambassador to Thailand from 1953 to 1954. He died on February 8, 1959.

October 18, 1941: Japanese authorities arrested Richard Sorge, a GRU illegal. They had arrested his principal agent, Hotzumi Ozaki, on October 14, 1914.

He was born on October 4, 1895, in Baku, Azerbaijan. He was wounded in World War I while serving with the German Army's 3rd Guards Field Artillery. He earned a Ph.D. at Hamburg in 1919 and joined the Communist Party. He fled to the USSR and joined the Comintern. Sorge started working for the GRU in 1929, serving as an illegal in Germany, Scandinavia, the U.S., UK, and China. He developed a cover as a pro-Nazi German journalist that gave him cover to serve in Japan from 1933 until his arrest. His spy ring infiltrated the German Embassy in Tokyo, the Japanese General Staff, and the Imperial family. Ozaki was a member of a senior policy planning group of advisors to the Japanese Prime Minister, passing secrets to Sorge. In 1941, he reported on Operation Barbarossa, Hitler's plan to attack the USSR, but Stalin ignored him. He also informed the USSR that Japan did not plan to attack the USSR, allowing it to move troops to the Western Front. On November 7, 1944, Japanese authorities hanged Sorge and Ozaki. He was named a Hero of the Soviet Union in 1964.

December 7, 1941: The Japanese bombed Pearl Harbor, Hawaii, ushering the U.S. into World War II. The surprise attack led President Roosevelt to expand the activities of the Coordinator of Information, and led to the creation of the Office of Strategic Services, the predecessor of the Central Intelligence Agency.

June 28, 1942: The FBI announced the arrests within the previous fortnight of eight Nazi saboteurs who had been dropped off by submarine in Florida and New York to run sabotage operations.

In June, a German U-boat surfaced off a deserted beach at the Hamptons in Long Island, New York, leaving four Nazi saboteurs. A Coast Guardsman on beach patrol alerted the FBI, which eventually arrested this group, plus four other Nazis (team leader Edward John Kerling, 33; Werner

Thiel, 35; Herman Otto Neubauer, 32; and Herbert Hans Haupt, 22) who had gone ashore in Ponte Vedra, south of Jacksonville, Florida, on June 16 after being dropped off by the *U-584* sub. The Nazis involved in Operation Pastorius were told to cripple U.S. industry. They were believed able to blend into American society because they had lived in the U.S. earlier. The Ponte Vedra group changed out of their naval uniforms into civilian clothes, buried their sabotage equipment on the beach, walked seven miles to Jacksonville Beach, then took a bus to the Mayflower and Seminole Hotels in downtown Jacksonville before going by train to Cincinnati. Two then went to Chicago, the others met up in New York City. The saboteurs carried more than $170,000 in cash and a list of contacts and targets, including aluminum plants, hydroelectric power stations, New York City bridges, a Newark railroad terminal, and department stores. Team leader George Johann Dasch and Peter Burger, another member of the Long Island team soon fingered the rest of the group. The Gestapo had imprisoned Burger for 17 months and he never intended to conduct the operation. Burger was sentenced to life, Dasch for 30 years—but they were released and deported to Germany in 1948. A military commission tried all eight. The U.S. Supreme Court upheld the legality of the secret tribunals. Six who had not cooperated were convicted were electrocuted on August 8, 1942. President Franklin D. Roosevelt had approved the death sentences.

June 13, 1942: The Office of Strategic Services was established, taking up the mantle from the Coordinator of Information. Colonel William Donovan became the first and only Director.

July 16, 1942: The U.S. Civil Service Commission recommended that Russia-born U.S. citizen Nathan Gregory Silvermaster,

working for the Farm Security Administration and Board of Economic Warfare but later determined by Venona decrypts to be head of a Soviet spy ring, be barred from federal employment. Counterintelligence officers noted his links to various communist groups. White House advisor Lauchlin Currie and Assistant Secretary of the Treasury Harry Dexter White, both identified in Venona as Soviet assets, intervened on his behalf. Silvermaster gave the USSR information on arms, aircraft, and shipping production. Elizabeth Bentley served as one of his couriers.

February 1, 1943: The U.S. Army Signals Security Agency, the predecessor of the National Security Agency, established a pilot program to examine coded Soviet communications. Colonel Carter Clarke, Chief of the Special Branch of the Army's Military Intelligence Service, wanted to offer warning in case the Soviets and Nazis attempted to reach a separate peace. SSA analysts at Arlington Hall, Virginia, examined Soviet diplomatic messages, which, although encrypted, were sent over commercial circuits. The highly sensitive Venona program under linguist Meredith Gardner ultimately unmasked numerous Soviet agents in the U.S. The program remained classified until the 1990s.

1944: NKVD co-optee Viktor Andreevich Kravchenko, who had served as a Captain in the Soviet Army in World War II, defected to the West, requesting political asylum in the U.S. He was born on October 11, 1905. His memoir, *I Chose Freedom*, was published in 1946. His successful 1949 libel case in France against the French Communist weekly *Les Lettres Françaises* was deemed the Trial of the Century. He died on February 25, 1966, in Manhattan of a gunshot wound to the head. It was unclear whether it was suicide or KGB wet work.

January 21, 1944: The FBI arrested Velvalee Malvena Dickinson, née Blucher, alias The Doll Woman, in a bank vault where she kept her safe deposit box that contained $13,000, traced to Japanese sources. She had spied for the Japanese. Using her doll collecting hobby as a cover, she and her husband traveled to the West Coast, visiting Navy yards in San Francisco and San Diego, noting the activities of U.S. warships. Her correspondence, coded as notes about doll acquisitions, was routed through a cutout in Buenos Aires. She faked signatures of clients. When the spy ring in Argentina was wrapped up, the Japanese did not provide her with a new contact address. Her letters were sent back from Argentina, but intercepted in February 1942 by wartime censors who alerted the FBI. On February 11, 1944, a Federal Grand Jury in the U.S. District Court for the Southern District of New York indicted her for violation of the censorship statutes, conviction of which could result in a maximum penalty of ten years in prison and a $10,000 fine. She pleaded not guilty and was held in lieu of $25,000 bail. A second indictment on May 5, charged her with violating espionage statutes, the Trading with the Enemy Act, and the censorship statutes. She faced the death penalty. She agreed to a plea deal on July 28, 1944, claiming that her husband, who died in 1943, was the real spy. She pleaded guilty to the censorship violation and agreed to provide information on Japanese intelligence activities. She was sentenced on August 14, 1944, to ten years and fined $10,000. She was paroled on April 23, 1951.

June 27, 1944: French espionage officer Jacques Voyer was captured after parachuting into occupied France for the OSS and executed by German forces. He had parachuted into Chartres for the OSS in early April, and provided intelligence on German military movements and bombing targets. Four days after D-Day, he drove a motorcycle past a German convoy, and stopped to note the unit's troop strength. Two Nazi officers stopped him, but he knocked them down and fled. He was shot in the shoulder and ankle, then knocked out with a rifle butt. He was tortured for eight days, then executed and buried in a field.

October 1944: Theodore Alvin Hall né Holzberg and Harvard roommate Saville Sax volunteered their services to the Soviet intelligence services. As an 18-year-old Harvard physicist, Hall was part of developing the atomic bomb at Los Alamos, New Mexico, during World War II. They were taken seriously by NKGB agent Sergey Kurnakov, who worked under journalist cover. Hall, code named MLAD, allegedly passed secrets of his work, including a-bomb design and implosion methods, to the Soviets for nearly nine years, using Sax as his courier. Sax was replaced in 1945 by Lona Cohen, a CPUSA member recruited by her husband, Morris Cohen, for the NKVD. Hall was discharged in June 1946, joining other Manhattan Project colleagues at the University of Chicago, where he married, pursued a Ph.D., and joined the CPUSA. The Soviets via Morris Cohen recontacted Hall in 1948 and apparently recruited two other Chicago scientists who have remained unidentified. Hall ended contact with the Soviets in 1953 while he was working in microbiology at the Sloan-Kettering Cancer Institute in New York. The National Security Agency declassified a Soviet cable in 1995 that identified Hall and Sax, code named STAR, as Soviet informants. The FBI had questioned the duo in 1951, but lacked evidence to press charges. Hall had pioneered biological X-ray microanalysis while at Cambridge University. The two were never charged with espionage.

Hall was a child prodigy, entering Queens College at age 15 and later transferring to Harvard, where he roomed with Sax, also a child of Russian émigrés. On November 1, 1999, Hall, 74, died of renal cancer in Cambridge, UK.

The Cohens escaped to the UK, changing their name to Kroger. They were arrested in 1961 and sentenced to 20 years in prison. They were released in a 1969 spy exchange, and taught KGB illegals in Moscow. They were deemed Heroes of the Soviet Union. Morris Cohen died a few years before Hall did.

October 24, 1944: Simon Emil Koedel was arrested in New York for spying on American shipping for the Nazis. On March 1, 1945, he was convicted of conspiracy to commit espionage and sentenced to 15 years. He was released a year later, and deported back to Germany. He died a vagrant three years later.

November 29, 1944: A German Navy submarine dropped off Abwehr spies American-born William Colepaugh and German citizen Erich Gimpel at Frenchman Bay, Maine. Gimpel had reported to the Nazis in Peru since 1935 on Allied cargo shipments. Connecticut-born Colepaugh had failed at MIT and was dropped from the U.S. Navy for disciplinary issues. He was attracted to German militarism and traveled to Germany as a deck hand. The British torpedoed the duo's sub and tipped the FBI that spies might have landed. The duo had been tasked originally with reading American newspapers and listening to U.S. broadcasts to determine the effectiveness of German propaganda in the U.S. Presidential election. They were also to collect on aircraft, ship-building, and rockets. Colepaugh quickly decided that the task was irrelevant, and started flashing a roll of cash in New York City. He told a friend in Queens

that he was a Nazi spy, then turned himself in to the Bureau. Gimpel had tired of Colepaugh's antics, broke contact, but was picked up a week later. Some 33 days after the submarine ride, the duo was in U.S. custody. They were tried in a closed military court. President Truman commuted their death sentences to life in prison in 1945. They were released after the war. Colepaugh retired to Pennsylvania; Gimpel wrote his memoirs in Germany.

1945: Authorities arrested six people, including three government employees, involved in producing or supplying information to the magazine *Amerasia*. They were accused of espionage on behalf of the Chinese Communists. Two plea bargained convictions for unauthorized possession of government documents and were fined. The other four, including John Stewart Service, a "China Hand" expert, were cleared. On December 13, 1951, following charges of communist leanings by U.S. Senator Joseph McCarthy, the U.S. Department of State announced the dismissal of Service. In 1957 the U.S. Supreme Court ordered his reinstatement.

September 4, 1945: Konstantin Dmitryevich Volkov, Soviet Embassy Vice Consul and deputy resident of the NKVD in Istanbul, Turkey, walked into the office of the British Vice Consul in Istanbul to request political asylum. He asked for $27,000 for files and information he obtained while working at the Centre's British desk, and referred to two Foreign Office penetrations (probably Guy Burgess and Donald Maclean) and seven inside British intelligence (probably including Philby). Kim Philby tipped off the Soviets about the attempted defection. On September 24, Soviet thugs drugged Volkov and his wife and carried them on stretchers onto a Soviet aircraft bound for Moscow. Volkov told his interrogators that he intended to give the British the names of 314 Soviet agents in Turkey and 250 in the UK. He was believed to have been executed by the Soviets.

September 5, 1945: NKGB code clerk Igor Gouzenko defected to Canadian authorities in Ottawa after a suspicious GRU officer had him ordered back to Moscow for questioning. He and his wife were expecting a second child, and the family, which included a son, were enjoying the Canadian way of life. Canada offered him asylum after Gouzenko provided Canadian authorities with more than 100 documents, including details of a Soviet espionage ring in Canada, naming Colonel Nikolai Zabotin as GRU Resident in Ottawa and outing atomic scientist Alan Nunn May and other atomic spies. May and nine other atomic spies were imprisoned. He also warned that the Communist Party of Canada Member of Parliament Fred Rose, and the Party's national organizer, Sam Carr, were Soviet agents. His claim that U.S. State Department officer Alger Hiss was a Soviet agent was inconclusive. Canada prosecuted 21 citizens based upon his information.

November 1945: Soviet courier Elizabeth Bentley walked into the FBI's New York Field Office and revealed espionage by the Communist Party of the USA on behalf of the Soviets. She named more than 80 Soviet agents, 27 of them in the U.S. government. In August 1948, Bentley testified before the House Un-American Activities Committee, saying that the World War II–era Office of Strategic Services had been penetrated at the highest levels by the Soviets. Their senior most source was Lieutenant Colonel Duncan Chaplin Lee, confidential assistant to Major General William ("Wild Bill") Donovan, OSS director. Lee was also mentioned in the Venona cables. Lee headed OSS's China section of the Secret Intelligence Branch. Bentley said he provided her with information on anti–Soviet operations. Lee had attended Oxford University as a Rhodes Scholar. His classmates included OSS staffer Donald Niven Wheeler, who also was mentioned in Venona as a Soviet spy. Lee was never charged because there was no evidence supporting Bentley's allegations.

Bentley was born in 1908. A distant relative, Roger Sherman, signed the Declaration of Independence. Another relative arrived on the Mayflower. Bentley graduated from Vassar. She on occasion was referred to as the Red Spy Queen. She joined the CPUSA in 1935 while studying at Columbia University. Russian immigrant Jacob Golos served as her handler and later lover. He directed her to run a ring led by Nathan Silvermaster, a Russian-born economist who worked in federal agencies. After Golos died in 1943, he was replaced by Itzhak Ahkmerov, alias Bill, who became the head of Soviet illegals in 1941. She also ran the Perlo group of spies under the tutelage of CPUSA chair Earl Browder. The Soviets eventually weened her from her spy networks, to her distress. NKGB chief in Washington Anatoliy Gorsky gave her the Order of the Red Star, but she thought the Soviets were trying to buy her off, and she instead walked in to the FBI. She brought no back-up documentation, and the FBI was limited in how to proceed with prosecutions because of lack of corroborating evidence. She died of abominal cancer in 1963.

January 3, 1946: William Joyce, alias Lord Haw-Haw, was hanged in the United Kingdom for treason. During World War II, he broadcast Nazi propaganda into the UK from Germany. He was in contact with pro–German spies such as Annan Wolkoff, who received U.S. Embassy documents from code clerk Tyler Kent. Joyce was a member of Sir Oswald Mosely's British Union of Fascists. The Brooklyn-born Joyce moved to the UK with his family in 1921. Although Joyce was a U.S. citizen, he also had a British passport, thus subjecting him to British law.

January 12, 1946: Director of the Office of Strategic Services William Donovan stepped down and the OSS was abolished. Its staffers were dispersed to the U.S. Department of State and the War Department. The staffers later reunited when the Central Intelligence Agency was created in September 1947.

January 23, 1946: Rear Admiral Sidney Souers, U.S. Naval Reserve, was named the first Director of Central Intelligence, serving until June 10, 1946. He was not the first Director of the CIA, which came into being the next year. He later served as the Executive Secretary of the National Security Council before returning to private business. He was born on March 30, 1892, in Dayton, Ohio, and died on January 14, 1973.

February 15, 1946: Kathleen Willsher, 25, a cipher clerk, pleaded guilty in a Canadian court to passing secrets to the USSR. She was one of 18 defendants arrested based on tips from Soviet defector Igor Gouzenko. She had been based at the Soviet Embassy in Ottawa, Canada from 1943 to 1945. Gouzenko sought asylum from Canadian authorities in September 1945. His debriefing led to the arrest and conviction of Dr. Alan Nunn May on charges of passing atomic bomb data to the Soviets. Gouzenko's other information led to the formation of a Royal Commission on espionage, which generated prosecutions of 18 individuals, nine of whom were convicted. Willsher passed minor secrets, and was given only three years in prison.

March 2, 1946: Kingman Douglass was named the first Acting Deputy Director of Central Intelligence (but not DD/CIA; the

CIA was created the next year), serving until July 11, 1946. He was born on April 16, 1896, in Oak Park, Illinois. He graduated from Yale University in 1918. He was a pilot conducting aerial observation and photographic intelligence in World War I. He had been an investment banker before serving in World War II as a senior U.S. Army Air Corps intelligence liaison officer in the British Air Ministry and in the Allied Intelligence Group in the Pacific Theater. After stepping down from the DDCI position, he served in the Office of Special Operations in the Central Intelligence Group—CIA's predecessor organization—in 1946. He was the Assistant Director for Current Intelligence in the CIA from January 4, 1951, to July 11, 1952, when he returned to private business. He was married to dancer Fred Astaire's sister. Douglass died on October 8, 1971.

March 4, 1946: Scotland Yard's Special Branch arrested British nuclear scientist Dr. Alan Nunn May, who spied for the Soviets. Following a one-day trial, he was convicted of espionage and sentenced to ten years. He was released in 1952 with time off for good behavior. He became a communist while at Cambridge University. The Soviet GRU recruited him while he was working in Canada on the atom bomb. He was discovered following the defection in Canada of Soviet code clerk Igor Gouzenko, who gave authorities cables that identified May.

June 10, 1946: Lieutenant General Hoyt Vandenberg, U.S. Army (Army Air Forces) became President Harry S Truman's second Director of Central Intelligence (but not of the CIA, which was yet to be established), serving until May 1, 1947.

Vandenberg was born in Milwaukee, Wisconsin, on January 24, 1899. He became a Lieutenant General in the U.S. Army (Army Air Forces), and the second Director of Central Intelligence (the CIA was formed after he stepped down). He later served as Chief of Staff of the U.S. Air Force from 1948 to 1953 with the rank of General. He died on April 2, 1954.

July 21, 1946: MGB officer Anatoli Granovsky, under USSR Merchant Navy cover, defected in Stockholm, Sweden. He was born in 1922. The NKVD recruited him on July 20, 1939, to spy on the children of the colleagues of his prominent father, who had died in a purge. He worked behind German lines as an assassin and saboteur. He had also been trained to conduct deception operations. He tried to obtain asylum from the U.S. military attaches in Stockholm, but was turned down, and arrested by the Swedes. King Gustaf V granted him asylum on November 8, 1946, just before he was to be repatriated to the USSR, and likely execution. He later published his autobiography, *I Was an NKVD Agent*.

January 20, 1947: Brigadier General Edwin Kennedy Wright, U.S. Army, became the first Deputy Director of Central Intelligence (and later of the CIA). His predecessor, Kingman Douglass, was Acting DDCI. Wright was born on December 28, 1898, in Portland, Oregon. He had served with General Omar Bradley's 12th Army Group during World War II. He was Executive Director of the Intelligence Division of the U.S. Army General Staff in the War Department from February to June 1946. After stepping down as DDCI on March 9, 1949, he continued with his career in the Army, rising to Major General before retiring from the Army on September 30, 1955. He died on September 3, 1983.

May 1, 1947: Rear Admiral Roscoe H. Hillenkoetter became Director of Central Intelligence. He was later reappointed by President Truman on November 24, 1947, and confirmed by the Senate on December 8, 1947, as the first DCI to also serve as the Director of the Central Intelligence Agency. His tenure ended on October 7, 1950. He was promoted to Vice Admiral on April 9, 1956, and became Inspector General of the Navy on August 1, 1956. After retiring from the Navy on May 1, 1957, he entered private business. He was born in St. Louis, Missouri, on May 8, 1897. He died on June 18, 1982.

July 26, 1947: The National Security Act established the Central Intelligence Agency (formally on September 18, 1947).

September 18, 1947: The U.S. Central Intelligence Agency opened for business.

August 13, 1948: Harry Dexter White appeared before the House Un-American Activities Committee (HUAC) to answer accusations that he was part of the Ware Group of spies and had passed Treasury Department materials to the Soviets via Whittaker Chambers. Democrat Henry Wallace said that if he had been elected President, White would have been his Secretary of the Treasury. White was the Soviets' seniormost spy in the Roosevelt administration, becoming Assistant Secretary of the Treasury and being involved in creating the International Bank for Reconstruction and Development (commonly called the World Bank) and the International Monetary Fund. He was born in Boston in 1892 to Lithuanian immigrants. He served in the Army in France in World War I, then graduated from Stanford and earned an economics Ph.D. at Harvard. He joined the Treasury Department in 1934 as a banking and monetary policy analyst. He decided that the New Deal was not enough and that Soviet-style centralization was necessary for the world economy. By 1938, he had become director of monetary research, then cut ties with the Soviets for a few years when Chambers left the CPUSA. The NKVD recontacted him in 1941, adding him as agent JURIST to the Silvermaster Group under the tutelage of case officer Vitaliy Pavlov. He by then was an assistant to Treasury Secretary Henry Morgenthau, a role that allowed him access as an agent of influence. He kept the Soviets informed of U.S. plans at the conference that established the United Nations. In 1945, Elizabeth Bentley exposed him to the FBI, following Chambers tipping the FBI to him in 1942. He resigned from his position as U.S. representative to the International Monetary Fund in March 1947. A year later, Bentley and Chambers called him a spy in testimony to the HUAC. He died of a heart attack three days after his testimony.

December 15, 1948: Authorities arrested Alger Hiss, a former senior U.S. Department of State officer and Soviet GRU agent, for perjury after lying about not having given Secret State Department material to Whitaker Chambers in 1938 to pass to Soviet intelligence. On January 21, 1950, Hiss was convicted at his second trial of perjury for denying knowing Whittaker Chambers, his GRU contact. He was sentenced to five years in prison. He could not be tried for espionage because of a then-extant statute of limitations.

December 20, 1948: Laurence Duggan, former head of the Latin American Division of the U.S. Department of State, fell to his death from his New York office, ten days after being questioned by the FBI regarding his contacts with Soviet intelligence. Venona material indicated that since his recruitment by the Soviets in 1936 until his retirement in 1944, he had been "Agent 19" for the NKVD, having been recruited by Hede Massing to provide State Department documents that were photographed in the Soviets' "illegal" residency. It was unclear if his death was an accident or suicide. Democrat Henry Wallace said that if he had been elected President, Duggan would have become his Secretary of State.

1949: Alexandr Grigoryevich Kopatzky was recruited by the KGB in West Berlin as a double agent. In 1941, he attended an NKVD training school. In October 1943, the German Wehrmacht arrested him as a prisoner of war. In 1944 he was an agent of the Department of Foreign Armies against the Red Army. In 1948, he was recruited into the Gehlen Organization. As a KGB double agent, he was paid 40,000 West German marks and 2,117 East German marks for providing the identities of more than 100 U.S. intelligence officers and agents in East Germany; several were arrested, others were doubled. He was imprisoned for drunken driving in 1954, but worked for the KGB throughout the 1950s. KGB defector Anatoliy Golitzyn identified him as a double. The Mitrokhin archives indicated that he worked for the KGB in the U.S. until a few years before his death in 1982.

March 4, 1949: The FBI arrested Department of Justice employee Judith Coplon, 28, and her Soviet handler, Valentin Gubitchev, at 14th Street and 3rd Avenue in New York City after the duo tried to elude surveillance. He was carrying $125 in small bills. She reviewed FBI reports on suspected Soviet spies as a staffer at DOJ headquarters in Washington, D.C. She had a copy of a classified memo (a document faked by the FBI to use as bait), a note to her Soviet case officer, and other classified documents.

In 1942, Coplon graduated from Barnard College, where she was a member of the Young Communist League. She joined Justice's Economic Warfare Section as an analyst in New York City. One of her friends at State was a Soviet agent. In the handoff meeting, the Soviets easily recruited the 22-year-old. In February 15, 1945, she was assigned to DOJ's Foreign Agents Registration Section in Washington, D.C., which gave her access to FBI information on internal security investigations, including Soviet espionage operations. One of her Soviet handlers said that she dropped marriage so that she could concentrate on espionage. She was arrested after being identified by Venona intercepts as Soviet agent SIMA. FBI surveillance established that her trips to New York City included meetings with Russian UN employee Valentin (variant Vladimir) Gubitchev.

The Soviets tried to claim diplomatic immunity for Gubitchev, but the State Department said that he had given up his immunity when he signed the UN's oath of employment. A Washington grand jury indicted her for espionage and the theft of classified documents. A New York grand jury indicted the duo for conspiracy to convey and receive classified information. She went on trial in April 1949. She was found guilty in Washington and sentenced to 40 months to ten years. Coplon and Gubitchev were convicted of theft of government documents. He was deported a year after the arrest. The New York court sentenced her to 15 years. Her conviction in New York was overturned in December 1950 because the FBI did not have an arrest warrant. The U.S. Congress a month later passed legislation permitting warrantless arrests in spy cases. In 1951, the Washington guilty verdict was upheld by an appeals court. The Supreme Court declined to review the case. In 1967, Attorney General Ramsay Clark decided not to retry the indictments. Coplon never spent a day in prison.

She married Albert Socolov, one of her attorneys, and continued to live in the New York City area, raising four children. She earned a master's degree in education and became an expert in bilingual education. She died on February 26, 2011, in a Manhattan hospital at age 89.

October 7, 1949: Air Force Corporal Gustav Adolph Mueller was arrested while trying to hand over two secret documents to U.S. Army investigators posing as Soviet intelligence officers. Mueller, who was born in Rangoon, Burma, of an English mother and a Swiss father, became a naturalized U.S. citizen and joined the Air Force in 1947. He was assigned to the European Command Intelligence School in Oberammergau, Federal Republic of Germany. He sent a telegram to the Soviet Consulate in Bern, Switzerland, offering his services. A student who helped him send the telegram became suspicious and went to authorities. Upon his arrest, he claimed he wanted to run a double agent operation against the Soviets. Doctors determined that he was emotionally unstable and immature. On April 15, 1950, a court-martial convicted him of attempting to deliver U.S. classified information to the Soviets. He was sentenced to five years in prison, dishonorably discharged, and forfeited all pay and allowances.

1950s

1950: John Peet, the *Reuter* correspondent in Berlin, who had been recruited by the NKVD during the Spanish Civil War, defected to East Berlin.

1950: On August 12, 2014, the *Associated Press* reported that Miriam Moskowitz, 98, a Washington Township, New Jersey, woman convicted of conspiracy in 1950 as part of the atomic spy trial of Julius and Ethel Rosenberg, asked a Manhattan federal court to vacate the conviction. She had been sentenced to two years in prison on charges of conspiring with two men to lie to a grand jury investigating allegations of atomic espionage. She claimed that documents released in 2008 showed that the government withheld statements by Harry Gold that would have exonerated her.

January 24, 1950: Klaus Fuchs confessed to espionage regarding U.S. atomic bomb secrets after the British arrested him. The German-born Fuchs joined the German Communist party at age 21 in 1932 while studying at Kiel University. He fled to the UK in 1933 upon the Nazi takeover. He earned a Ph.D. in Physics at Bristol University, then joined the top secret Tube Alloys Project on the design and fabrication of the atomic bomb. In 1941, he offered to work for the GRU so that the Soviets could combat the Nazis. By 1942, he had access to U.S. nuclear research. His information led Stalin to decide to enter the nuclear arms race. He moved to the U.S. in December 1943, and contacted his U.S. controller, Harry Gold, alias "Raymond," 33, an industrial chemist who had worked as a Soviet courier and industrial spy since 1936. Fuchs began work at the top secret atomic lab at Los Alamos in New Mexico. He provided information indicating that the U.S. was using plutonium vice uranium-235 in its bombs, cutting down the Soviets' atomic bomb development time. In September 1949, the decrypted Venona intercepts led the FBI to determine that the codenames "Rest" and "Charles" both referred to Fuchs while he worked on the World War II Manhattan Project and passed information to the NKGB. UK authorities interrogated him in 1949, when he confessed. Harry Gold was arrested in Philadelphia on May 22, 1950. After a 90-minute trial on March 1, 1950, a British court sentenced Fuchs to 14 years for violation of the Official Secrets Act. He served nine years, then moved to East Germany, where he became a member of the Communist Party Central Committee.

March 1950: The Karlshorst KGB residency recruited unemployed former SS Captain Hans Clemens, who in 1951 joined the Gehlen Organization, a semi-official West German intelligence agency. He in turn recruited Heinz Felfe, a former SS comrade, who also joined the Gehlen Organization and became its counterintelligence chief in 1955. Felfe was arrested in 1961.

May 22, 1950: Authorities arrested Harry Gold, a Swiss-born chemical engineer, and charged him with espionage for working for the USSR from 1934 to 1945. His Jewish parents had fled Russia and came to the U.S. in 1913. His code name was "Raymond." He began stealing secrets for the Soviets in 1935, grabbing a dry ice formula from the Pennsylvania Sugar Company. He had served as the case officer for Klaus Fuchs, a German-born Ph.D. physicist from the UK who worked on the Manhattan project, and David Greenglass, a machinist at the Los Alamos National Laboratory. The Soviets ended the relationship in 1946 over a counterintelligence slip which led Western authorities to him. His trail led to Greenglass, Morton Sobell, and Julius and Ethel Rosenberg. On December 9, 1950, Gold was sentenced to 30 years in prison for espionage for the USSR. He was released in 1965 and settled in Philadelphia.

June 16, 1950: The FBI arrested David Greenglass, brother-in-law of Julius Rosenberg, on charges of espionage. Greenglass was the Los Alamos cutout for Soviet atomic spy Harry Gold. Greenglass was drafted into the U.S. Army in 1943 after graduating from a trade school and becoming a machinist. Although loud about his communist leanings, following technical training, he was assigned to the Oak Ridge uranium production facility and onward to the Los Alamos nuclear laboratory in a junior position related to the fabrication of the atomic bomb. He told the FBI that his wife Ruth, Soviet code-name WASP, couriered a proposal in November 1944 by Julius to spy for the NKGB. Greenglass testified against Julius and Ethel Rosenberg in an attempt to get his sentence reduced. Greenglass was sentenced to 15 years. He was freed from prison in 1960. Greenglass was born on March 2, 1922, in New York City, youngest of three children of Russian and Austrian-German immigrants Barnet Greenglass and Theresa "Tessie" Feit. He died on July 1, 2014, at age 92. He had lived at a nursing home under an assumed name.

On April 7, 2008, Ruth Greenglass, 84, died. Ruth and David Greenglass confessed to membership in the spy ring, and named the Rosenbergs as their recruiters. Ruth Greenglass had been living under an alias since the Rosenbergs were executed in 1953. Ruth Greenglass was never charged in the case.

July 17, 1950: The FBI arrested Julius Rosenberg, 33, for conspiracy to commit espionage. His wife, Ethel Greenglass Rosenberg, 35, was arrested three weeks later. They allegedly stole technical information from the atomic research center in Los Alamos. They were born and raised in New York's Lower East Side. The couple met through the Young Communist League. He graduated with a degree in electrical engineering from CUNY in 1939, married CPUSA member Ethel Greenglass, then joined the U.S. Army Signal Corps. They had two sons. In 1942, he met Soviet intelligence officer Semyon Semyonov in Central Park; Semyonov recruited Julius at their third meeting. They were involved in a spy ring that included her brother, David Greenglass, former Soviet vice consul Arkadi Yakovlev, and Philadelphia chemist Harry Gold. Julius was also run by Alexander Feklisov, who said Rosenberg passed 20,000 pages of classified documents. Rosenberg was fired by the Army Signal Corps in February 1945 for his CPUSA affiliation. Rosen-

berg's network of eight spies gave the Soviets information on conventional U.S. weapons systems, the P-80 Shooting Star jet fighter, computer technology, radar systems, blueprints for a proximity fuse, military research and development, and atomic secrets.

In addition to recruiting David Greenglass, he also recruited Russell McNutt, Soviet code names FOGEL and PERSIAN, an engineer with the Kellex Company. The firm worked in 1942 on constructing a uranium gas diffusion facility at Oak Ridge. McNutt provided information on the structural design of the facility, but refused a KGB pitch to work at Oak Ridge. Also working in his ring were Alfred Sarant and Joel Barr.

On March 6, 1951, the New York federal trial began of the Rosenbergs for conspiracy to commit espionage and passing atomic secrets to the KGB. Greenglass, who worked as a machinist at Los Alamos, told the court that the Rosenbergs asked him for information about the bomb, which they passed to Gold who in turn sent it to Russia. Gold was also a cut-out for British scientist Klaus Fuchs. Julius's Soviet code name was LIBERAL. Judge Irving R. Kaufman said their actions were "so shocking that I cannot find words to describe the loathsome offense." The Venona cables later identified Julius as a spy; they were silent on her involvement. On March 29, 1951, Julius and Ethel Rosenberg were convicted of conspiracy to commit espionage by giving atomic bomb secrets to the Soviets. On April 5, 1951, Judge Kaufman sentenced the Rosenbergs to death. The Supreme Court declined to hear the case in October 1952. The couple died in the electric chair in Sing Sing federal prison in Ossining, New York, on June 19, 1953. They were the first U.S. spies to be executed in peacetime.

July 20, 1950: Alfred Epaminondas Sarant, alias Filipp Georgievich Staros and Philip

Georgievich Staros, a CPUSA member, and Joel Barr, who recruited Sarant as part of the Rosenberg ring in 1943–1944, escaped to the Soviet Union. The electrical engineers worked on military radar in the Army Signal Corps and Western Electric. During two years, they provided 9,000 pages of classified materials on U.S. weapons, including advanced microwave radar and the M-9 gun director analog computer. The duo escaped three days after the FBI interviewed—but did not arrest—Sarant. They had forsaken their spouses and children during their complex exfiltration to the USSR. They eventually worked in the Warsaw Pact microelectronics industry and designed the USSR's first automated anti-aircraft weapon. Sarant became the scientific director of Zelenograd, the USSR's equivalent of Silicon Valley. He died of a heart attack in 1979. His Venona code name was HUGHES.

August 16, 1950: In an early rendition to the U.S. justice system, armed men kidnapped Morton Sobell and his family in Mexico, where they were hiding since June 22, 1950, after the arrests of the Rosenbergs. The kidnappers brought them to the United States border and turned him over to the FBI. The Bureau arrested him for conspiring with Julius Rosenberg to violate espionage laws. He was an American engineer with General Electric and Reeves Electronics who worked on military and government contracts. He was found guilty along with the Rosenbergs, and sentenced in 1951 to 30 years. He served 17 years and nine months in Alcatraz and other prisons until his release in 1969. In a 2008 interview with the *New York Times*, he admitted spying and implicated Julius Rosenberg. As of 2014, he was 97 years old.

October 7, 1950: General Walter Bedell Smith was sworn in as Director of Central Intelligence. Smith was responsible for the creation of the analytical and operational directorates, a distinction which remains to the present day. He had served during World War II as General Eisenhower's Chief of Staff. He was U.S. Ambassador to the Soviet Union from 1946 to 1949. He was Commanding General of the First Army from 1949 to 1950. His tenure as DCI ended on February 9, 1953, when he retired from the Army. He served as Under Secretary of State from 1953 to 1954. He was born on October 5, 1895, and died on August 6, 1961.

October 7, 1950: William Harding Jackson was sworn in as Deputy Director of Central Intelligence, serving until August 3, 1951. He was born on March 25, 1901, in Nashville, Tennessee. He earned his undergraduate degree from Princeton University and graduated from Harvard Law School. He was a lawyer and investment banker in New York before serving in the U.S. Army during World War II. He served on the intelligence staff of General Omar Bradley in 1944. After leaving the DDCI position, he was a part-time Special Assistant and Senior Consultant to the DCI from August 1951 to February 1956. He was a Special Assistant to President Dwight David Eisenhower on national security issues in 1956 and 1957. He died on September 28, 1971.

November 1950: William Weisband was convicted of contempt and sentenced to a year in prison. He was born in Odessa, Russia on August 28, 1908. His parents moved the family to the U.S. in 1924. He studied at American University. He was recruited by the NKVD (KGB predecessor) in 1934 during a trip to Russia. The 26-year-old initially was a courier and agent handler. He became a naturalized U.S. citizen in 1938. He was drafted into the U.S. Army in 1942, serving in North Africa and Italy in signals intelligence with cryptanalysts in the Armed

Forces Security Agency. At the end of the war, the agency hired him as a civilian and assigned him to Arlington Hall, Virginia. Weisband alerted the NKGB about the decryption of its list of atomic scientists in 1948. He requested asylum after his colleagues expected that a mole had tipped off the Soviets. He was discovered as a Soviet agent in 1950, having already reported on the Venona decryptions. He was never charged with espionage. However, in November 1950, he was convicted of contempt for failing to appear for a federal grand jury hearing on the Communist Party of the USA, and sentenced to a year in prison. U.S. officials believed trying him on espionage would reveal too many sources and methods to the KGB. He refused to cooperate with the FBI when questioned about espionage in 1950 and 1953. He and his wife were fired for disloyalty by the National Security Agency, the successor to the Army's Signal Security Agency. He died of a heart attack on May 14, 1967, during his family's Mother's Day visit to the Smithsonian Institution.

February 7, 1951: Authorities arrested William W. Remington, an employee of the U.S. War Production Board, who was identified by Communist Party member Elizabeth Bentley as a Soviet spy. Joseph North, a *New Masses* editor and Communist Party of the USA recruiter, introduced him to Soviet intelligence officer Jacob Golos, who recruited Remington. Remington subsequently passed information on airplane production, high octane gasoline, and synthetic rubber. Bentley said Remington ceased contact with her in 1944, when he joined the Navy. The FBI warned the White House before he could take a job as one of President Truman's special assistants in 1946. In 1947, he tried to get a job with the Atomic Energy Commission. He was convicted of perjury in 1953. He was killed in prison.

May 25, 1951: Somehow tipped off that Western intelligence was on to them, British Foreign Office employees Guy Burgess and Donald MacLean fled the UK and defected to the USSR. They were two of the Ring of Five Soviet spies inside the UK government. The five had been recruited in the 1930s at Cambridge University while undergraduates. The group included Kim Philby, who rose to become Chief of the Soviet Section of MI-6 and also served as MI-6 liaison with the CIA and FBI. Philby remained hidden in the UK intelligence bureaucracy for another dozen years, defecting to Moscow in January 1963. The Soviets put MacLean on ice in the mid–1930s but recontacted him on April 10, 1938.

August 23, 1951: Allen Welsh Dulles was sworn in as Deputy Director of Central Intelligence. He was Acting Director of Central Intelligence from February 9 through 26, 1953, when he was sworn in as DCI. (For career details, see February 26, 1953, entry.)

Autumn 1951: SIS officer George Blake, né Behar, 29, offered his services to the KGB while interned by the North Koreans. He was the cousin of Henri Curiel, co-founder of the Egyptian Communist Party. Blake said in his 1990 memoirs that he had given the KGB the names of nearly 400 Western agents. He also alerted the KGB to the Berlin Tunnel. In 1961, Polish SB defector Michael Goleniewski identified him as a KGB asset. A court sentenced Blake to 42 years in prison. After five years, he escaped from Wormwood Scrubs prison on October 22, 1966, with the assistance of three former inmates, including Irish bomber Sean Bourke and peace protesters Michael Randle and Pat Pottle. He was smuggled to East Berlin, then on to Moscow.

September 7, 1951: The CIA's Deputy Directorate for Plans (later to become the

Directorate of Operations and later the National Clandestine Service) created the 50-person Office of Technical Services. OTS served as the model for James Bond's Q Branch of gadgeteers. James H. "Trapper" Drum was named its founding chief.

September 21, 1952: U.S. Air Force Staff Sergeant Giuseppe E. Cascio, 34, was arrested on 16 counts of accepting military payment certificates from a Korean civilian. Cascio was trying to sell classified test flight data for the F-86E Sabre jet to North Korean intelligence. Cascio obtained the material from USAF Sergeant John P. Jones. Cascio was a bombardier in World War II, and had twice received the Distinguished Flying Cross. He was serving in Korea as a photo laboratory technician and occasional photographer for the 9th Air Base Group. A general court martial on June 8, 1953, found him guilty of conspiracy to pass secrets of the jet to the communists and sentenced him to 20 years of hard labor. Jones had a nervous breakdown and was deemed unfit to stand trial.

1953: KGB officer Peter Deriabin, Chief of Soviet Counterintelligence, defected in Austria. He was born in 1921. He went on to write several books about Soviet intelligence operations, including *The Secret World, Watchdogs of Terror, KGB: Masters of the Soviet Union, The Spy Who Saved the World*, and *Inside Stalin's Kremlin*. He died in 1992 at age 71.

January 1953: GRU Major Pyotr Popov threw a note into the parked car of a U.S. intelligence officer in Austria, offering military information for money. He also wanted to avenge Soviet oppression of peasants. He was later detained by the Soviets and executed.

January 14, 1953: U.S. authorities arrested Kurt Leopold Ponger and his brother-in-law, Otto Verber, for spying for the Soviets.

The duo were Jewish natives of Vienna, Austria who came to the U.S. in 1938 and secretly joined the Communist Party of the USA. They had served in U.S. intelligence during World War II because of their language skills. Ponger was an interrogator at Nuremberg. The naturalized Americans became Soviet agents in Vienna upon their return on June 15, 1949. Ponger was sentenced to 15 years in prison; Verber to ten years.

February 22, 1953: Sergeant Robert Lee Johnson, a disgruntled Army NCO who considered himself unappreciated and maltreated by the Army, and Hedy, his Austrian wife, had their first meeting with KGB officers in East Berlin. Johnson believed a promotion he deserved went to a rival sergeant, and nothing came of his accusations that another sergeant was loan sharking. He also had drinking and gambling problems. He decided to work for the Russians, seeing himself as eventually defecting and broadcasting anti–Pentagon propaganda over *Radio Moscow*. He asked his live-in girlfriend of four years, Hedy, a German prostitute, on Christmas Day 1952 to marry him "if you go over and fix me up with the Russians." He initially provided the Russians with confidential weekly summaries for Berlin Command. He obtained more sensitive material when he was reassigned to the Armed Forces Courier Center in Paris's Orly Airport. He was discharged from the Army in July 1956 at age 36. In January 1957, he was contacted by Sergeant James Allen Mintkenbaugh, a closet homosexual whom he had introduced to the KGB, and who talked Johnson into re-enlisting. He gave Johnson $500 from his previous KGB handler. Johnson rejoined the Army as a sergeant, serving in several domestic posts, including at missile installations in Texas and California, between 1957 and 1959, stealing classified documents and photographs plus a sample of rocket fuel. He moved on to the Orly Armed Forces Courier Center in March 1961. He arranged to work on weekends to have access to the classified pouches. He made a wax impression of the vault key for the KGB to copy. Johnson gave envelopes to his KGB handler, who brought them to the Soviet Embassy where KGB techs unsealed them, photographed the contents, resealed them, and returned them to Johnson the same night. His classified missile and nuclear warfare documents were given to Premier Nikita Khrushchev and other Politburo members. In 1962, the KGB awarded him the rank of Major in the Red Army. His handlers were awarded the Order of Lenin. He moved to the Pentagon in 1964 to be near Hedy, who was receiving psychiatric treatment at Walter Reed Hospital. She had violent psychotic outbursts, but he was unable to get her back into the hospital. On October 2, 1964, he withdrew $2,200 from his bank account and moved to Las Vegas. Thirty days later, the Army declared him a deserter and asked federal agencies for assistance in finding him. The FBI interviewed Hedy twice, whereupon she admitted his espionage since 1953. He was also identified via information provided by Soviet defectors Yuriy Nosenko and Oleg Gordievsky, who said Johnson had provided 17 flight bags filled with secrets, including cryptographic materials. On November 25, 1964, Johnson surrendered at a police station in Reno, Nevada; Mintkenbaugh was arrested the same month. Johnson was transferred to Washington, D.C., where he confessed to treason. On April 5, 1965, the FBI found Mintkenbaugh in a California apartment, where he confessed and fingered Johnson. On July 30, 1965, Johnson and Mintkenbaugh were sentenced to 25 years after pleading guilty to charges of conspiracy. The Soviets had paid Johnson $25,000. Johnson could not identify all of the documents he gave the Russians; the damage assessment assumed he gave them everything that went through the courier center between December 15, 1962, and April 21, 1963. In 1972 his son stabbed him to death while visiting him in prison, where he was serving on espionage charges.

February 26, 1953: Allen Welsh Dulles was sworn in as Director of Central Intelligence. He had served with the State Department from 1916 to 1926, later going on to practice law. He was Head of the Office of Strategic Services post in Bern, Switzerland, during World War II. He was the CIA's Deputy Director for Plans (operations) from January 4 through August 23, 1951. He served as Deputy Director of Central Intelligence from August 23, 1951, to February 26, 1953. After returning to private life and writing his memoirs, he served on the President's Commission on the Assassination of President Kennedy in 1963–1964. He was born on April 7, 1893, in Watertown, New York, and died on January 28, 1969. His brother, John Foster Dulles, served as Secretary of State.

April 23, 1953: U.S. Air Force General Charles Pearre Cabell was sworn in as Deputy Director of Central Intelligence, a position he held until January 31, 1962. He was Director of Air Force Intelligence from 1948 to 1951, and Director of the Joint Staff of the Joint Chiefs of Staff from 1951 to 1953. He was born in Dallas, Texas, on October 11, 1903, and died on May 25, 1971.

August 27, 1953: Robert Bialek, former Inspector General of the East German Volkspolizei, defected to West Germany. He apparently was kidnapped by the KGB's East German residency in 1955 and never seen again. Some reports said he was tortured and executed.

November 1953: Soviet illegal Yevgeni Vladimirovich Brik, 30, defected to the

RCMP Security Service in Ottawa. He had arrived in Halifax, Nova Scotia, in November 1951, under cover of a watchmaker and later photographer. He had lived in the U.S. for several years, becoming bilingual. During a love affair with the wife of a Canadian soldier, he agreed to tell the RCMP. He was run by the RCMP as a penetration of the KGB, becoming aware of at least five KGB agents. He was betrayed to the KGB on July 21, 1955, by RCMP Corporal James Morrison, who had been embezzling RCMP funds and walked into the Soviet Embassy. On August 19, 1955, the Soviets arrested Brik at Moscow Airport. On September 4, 1956, he was sentenced to 15 years in prison.

December 5, 1953: Colonel Jozef Swiatlo, deputy director of the 10th Department of the Polish Security Office (UB) intelligence service, defected during a mission in East Berlin to the U.S. military mission in West Berlin. The U.S. gave him political asylum. He reported in Radio Free Europe broadcasts an internal struggle in the Communist Party (PZPR). The UB was abolished following his defection. He died on September 2, 1994.

February 18, 1954: Soviet Captain Nikolay Khokhlov defected to the West. He said he was on a mission to assassinate prominent Soviet emigre Georgi Sergeevich Okolovich. Khokhlov instead told his target of the plot and defected with his wife. On April 20, 1954, Khokhlov gave a press conference regarding several assassination plots against Russian exiled dissidents. His 1959 book *In the Name of Conscience: The Testament of a Soviet Secret Agent* detailed other NKVD activities.

He had joined the NKVD at age 19, becoming a member of an assassination team.

On September 15, 1957, he fell ill during a conference in Frankfort, West Germany, suffering from a severe blood disorder. He was transferred to a U.S. military hospital, where he received massive blood transfusions and intravenous feeding. He had survived poisoning by thallium that had been intensively irradiated as part of a Soviet assassination attempt. He died of a heart attack in September 2007 in San Bernardino, California, at age 85.

April 1954: Aleksandr Trushnovich, Social-Democratic National Labor Union (NTS) leader in West Berlin, was kidnapped by Heinz Gleske, an undercover Stasi officer who lured him to his home. He handed Trushnovich over to the KGB residency in Karlshorst. Gleske claimed Trushnovich had voluntarily defected to East Germany. Stasi chief Markus Wolf said the KGB had assassinated Trushnovich.

April 3, 1954: Vladimir Mikhaylovich Petrov, the Soviet MVD Rezident in Australia, defected to the West with his wife, Evdokia. He began his career as a cipher clerk in the Soviet Navy in 1929. He joined the OGPU in 1933 and had NKVD tours in Moscow, China, and Sweden. One of the documents he brought with him was written in 1951 by Fergan O'Sullivan, while an employee of the *Sidney Morning Herald*. O'Sullivan had written the materials for I.M. Pakhomov, temporary MVD Rezident who was working undercover as a *Tass* journalist. O'Sullivan wrote short biographies of Australian journalists, offering assessments on their religion, political persuasion, sexual tendencies, and susceptibility to alcohol. A second document noted the location of airfields and identified individuals the author, communist journalist Rupert Lockwood, believed worked for the Australian Intelligence Service. Lockwood spent three days in the Soviet Embassy in May 1953 typing the report. Petrov became an Australian citizen in 1956. He died on June 14, 1991, at age 84.

July 20, 1954: Dr. Otto John, acting Director of the West German BfV counterintelligence agency, defected to East Germany while in East Berlin for a commemoration of the 1944 assassination plot against Hitler. He had been involved in the July 20, 1944, plot to kill Hitler; his brother was executed for participation in the plot. On July 24, 1944, he flew to Madrid and defected to UK intelligence officers. For the rest of World War II, he broadcast black propaganda for the British. Following the war, he worked with the UK in screening German prisoners and helping the prosecution of senior German military officers. In December 1950, he rose to acting director of the BfV, and was permanently appointed in December 1951. Following his defection, he spent six months in the USSR, then returned to East Berlin in December 1954 and joined the Stasi. He returned to West Berlin on December 13, 1955, claiming he had been kidnapped. A court disagreed, convicting him of treason and sentencing him to four years of hard labor. He served only 18 months. In 1958, he was freed and moved to Austria.

October 9, 1954: The FBI arrested NSA employee Joseph Sidney Petersen, Jr., who was charged with providing top secret code word documents to the Netherlands for ten years.

He was born in New Orleans in 1914. He attended Loyola and St. Louis Universities, earning an MS with concentrations in physics, mathematics, and chemistry. He joined the Signal Intelligence Service (SIS), predecessor of the Army Security Agency (ASA), in 1941, working on Japanese diplomatic and army issues. He came to the attention of counterintelligence officers in September 1953. He had made reference to having classified information in his home and often quietly associating with the head of the Dutch legation. Among his contacts was Colonel Jacobus Verkuyl, a member of the Dutch COMINT organization and liaison to the Signal Security Agency in 1942. For a time, he was Petersen's supervisor, and later friend. Verkuyl handed off Petersen to Giaccomo Stuydt of the Netherlands Legation. Verkuyl told Petersen about his problems in building up the Dutch COMINT organization. Petersen provided ideas and suggestions and later furnished information on breaking certain systems. In 1947, Verkuyl came to the U.S. on UN business and gave Petersen photostats of Dutch intercepts and introduced Petersen to his new contact. Verkuyl formally pitched Petersen, who turned down the offer. The FBI searched Petersen's residence on September 30, 1954, finding letters from his two handlers, who requested further information. Petersen was arraigned in the Northern District of Virginia and pleaded not guilty to all charges. Following a plea bargain, he pleaded guilty to a charge of "knowingly and willfully using in a manner prejudicial to the safety and interest of the United States classified [materials] concerning communications intelligence activities of the United States and foreign governments." He was sentenced to seven years in prison on January 4, 1955. He was paroled in 1959, after serving four years.

November 24, 1954: President Dwight David Eisenhower authorized the CIA to develop the U-2 spy plane. The program would allow the Agency to conduct deep-penetration flights over the USSR, during a time when the Agency had few human sources inside the Soviet Union.

1955: The KGB's SCD division used a honey trap to recruit French businessman François Saar-Demichel. He had served briefly in the DGER and its successor, the SDECE, before starting his business career in 1947 in paper manufacturing. He became a regular reporter on the de Gaulle regime and was an informal foreign policy advisor to the President in East-West relations. He was exposed by KGB defector Yuriy Nosenko.

February 21, 1955: The U.S. Department of State declared Soviet UN diplomat Maksim Grigorevich Martynov *persona non grata* in connection with his espionage activity; he left the U.S. five days later. In the summer of 1954, a Soviet Air Force officer serving as a cutout began developing a U.S. Army Colonel in East Berlin as a potential source of classified information regarding the Army Command and General Staff School at Fort Leavenworth, Kansas. The Soviet provided oral bona fides for a meeting in New York City. The American officer immediately notified the FBI, and worked with them on a sting operation in which an FBI undercover agent disguised himself as the American Colonel. The FBI noted two KGB officers providing countersurveillance for the meeting. Martynov paid the agent $250 and gave him tasking. After several meetings, the FBI confronted Martynov during an agent meeting in a New York restaurant. He waved his diplomatic passport, announced that he had diplomatic immunity, and left the scene.

March 5, 1955: Italian atomic physicist Bruno Pontecorvo, a colleague of Klaus Fuchs, told a press conference in Moscow that he had become a Soviet citizen in 1952 and now worked at the Institute of Nuclear Physics of the Soviet Academy of Sciences. Western authorities believed he had spied for the USSR from 1943 through 1948 while working on the Canadian atomic research team in Canada. In 1948, he obtained UK citizenship and a security clearance despite his association with the Communist Party. Authorities discovered in 1950 that he and his wife were communists. He agreed to be

transferred to another position without classified access. In October 1950, he fled to the USSR.

July 21, 1955: RCMP Corporal James Morrison, 39, heavily in debt, contacted Soviet KGB Resident Nikolai Pavlovich Ostrovsky to warn him that KGB illegal Yevgeni Brik (alias HART, alias GIDEON) had been doubled 18 months earlier. Morrison had been involved for several years in surveilling the Soviet Embassy in Ottawa. Morrison claimed that he had pro–Soviet sympathies and wanted to avoid a repetition of the Gouzenko case which had damaged bilateral relations. (NKGB officer Igor Gouzenko had defected to Canada on September 5, 1945.) However, he had asked the Soviets for $5,000, suggesting monetary, vice altruistic, motives. Morrison was in debt from a gambling habit. Morrison had been caught embezzling RCMP funds, but was allowed to repay the money he had stolen rather than being fired. He intended to use the money from the KGB to repay the RCMP. The Mitrokhin files indicated that he worked for the Soviets for three years, earning $14,000. He was fired from the RCMP in 1958. The government was pressed to reopen the case with the 1982 release of John Sawatsky's *For Services Rendered* that described the case. On June 9, 1983, the *Montreal Gazette* reported that he had been freed on $50,000 bail in the case that had been codenamed Long Knife. He faced three charges of violating the Official Secrets Act. He entered no plea to the charges, which each carried a 14-year sentence. On January 23, 1986, the *Philadelphia Inquirer* reported that he had pleaded guilty to selling out Brik for $2,700. He was convicted of espionage.

August 4, 1955: President Dwight D. Eisenhower signed a bill authorizing $46 million for construction of the new CIA Headquarters Building in northern Virginia.

1956: A seductive maid working for the KGB tried to blackmail the first Chief of Station/Moscow, Edward Willis Smith. Ambassador Charles Bohlen sent him home.

1956: The Mitrokhin archives claim that in 1956 the KGB recruited Thomas Edward Neil Driberg, Baron Bradwell of Bradwell, Labor MP, journalist, member of Labor's National Executive from 1949 to 1974 and party chair in 1957–1958, threatening to expose his homosexuality. While in Moscow, he obtained an interview with British defector Guy Burgess. The KGB, according to Mitrokhin, reportedly used him for active measures as well as for intelligence information on the Labor National Executive. Other individuals claimed he worked for MI-5. He was never charged, and died on August 12, 1976.

1956: The KGB contacted Yisrael Beer, Professor of Military History at Tel Aviv University and a lieutenant colonel in the Israeli Defence Force. Shin Bet arrested him for spying for the Soviets in 1961. He had been a member of the Planning Bureau of the Haganah after arriving in Palestine in 1938 and was a founding member of Mapam. He reported to the KGB Shimon Peres's attempts in 1957 to buy reconditioned German submarines. Shin Bet spotted him on March 30, 1961, giving a briefcase to Viktor Sokolov, a KGB case officer. In 1962, he was sentenced to 15 years in prison. He died in jail four years later.

March 8, 1956: The National Security Council approved the FBI's COINTELPRO (counterintelligence program) operations against the Communist Party of the United States and other radical groups. The program would become subject of media exposes and Congressional investigations years later. COINTELPRO was shut down in 1985.

April 1956: Shin Bet arrested Mossad officer Zeev Avni, born Wolf Goldstein, in Israel for spying for the KGB. He was recruited by a Czech refugee, Karl Vibrel, in 1943 in Switzerland, according to *Haaretz*. In 1948, he emigrated to Israel. He joined the Israeli Foreign Ministry in 1950. He was assigned as commercial attaché in Brussels in 1952; he was also the legation's security officer. He photographed the safe's contents for the GRU. He also joined Mossad while in Brussels, posing as a German businessman to contact former Nazis. In 1953, he was posted to Belgrade for Mossad and the Foreign Ministry, where the KGB took over his case. He provided the Soviets with Mossad communications ciphers and the identities of Mossad officers in France, Germany, Greece, Italy, Switzerland and Yugoslavia. He was sentenced to 14 years in prison. He was released in April 1963, then worked as a clinical psychologist and published some of his memoirs. He died in January 2007 at age 86.

July 8, 1957: A federal grand jury indicted Jane Foster Zlatovski, who worked in Morale Operations with OSS during World War II, and her husband George Zlatovski on charges of espionage for working as Soviet agents. She allegedly was recruited by the Soviets in 1938, joining the Soble ring in the 1940s. Some scholars believe she was SLANG in the Venona intercepts. She denied being a Soviet agent but admitted lying about her membership in the Communist Party of the USA and her marital status. FBI double agent Boris Morros had tipped authorities to her. The case was not tried as the U.S. could not obtain their extradition from France. She died in 1979. Her autobiography, *An Un-American Lady*, was published in 1980.

January 25, 1957: The FBI arrested Jack and Myra Soble for espionage, relying on a tip from double agent Boris Morros. The Soviet Secret Police recruited Jack in Berlin in 1931. He was a loyal Trotskyite, and thus of interest to Stalin. The Soviets also held Soble's wife, Myra, hostage in Moscow. Soble spied on Leon Trotsky for more than two years. Soble moved to the U.S. in 1941, where he was given several agents to run. They included Hollywood producer Boris Morros, who had been recruited in March 1941. The FBI spotted Morros in spring 1943, when the FBI saw him meeting with a Soviet intelligence officer. The FBI interviewed Morros in July 1947, when he admitting to spying for the Soviets. He agreed to become an FBI double agent. Upon their arrest, the Sobles were charged with acting as agents for the Soviets since 1947 without prior notification of the State Department and collecting and transmitting information to the USSR, and collecting and attempting to collect U.S. defense information that would be transmitted to the USSR. The duo pleaded guilty to conspiracy with others to obtain U.S. defense documents and other materials. They were convicted of conspiracy to receive and obtain national defense information and transmit same to foreign government. Jacob Abram was convicted as part of their spy ring. Myra was sentenced on August 9, 1957, to five and a half years; Jack to seven years. President George H. W. Bush pardoned her on July 5, 1991.

Jack Soble said his brother, Dr. Robert Soblen, and others were members of the spy ring. Soblen was sentenced to life in prison for espionage at Sandia National Laboratories, escaped to Israel, and apparently committed suicide in the UK while awaiting extradition.

April 5, 1957: Captain George Holmes French, a bombardier-navigator with the 60th Bombardment Squadron of Ramey Air Force Base in Puerto Rico, left a letter in a newspaper on the grounds of the Soviet Embassy. The FBI grabbed the letter, which provided contact instructions for an individual who offered to sell "valuable military information, including diagrams of weapons," for $27,500. FBI and Air Force Office of Special Investigation agents posed as Soviet intelligence officers and met him at the hotel room the letter had specified, then arrested him. His Puerto Rico residence contained 60 classified documents, which he had planned to provide to the KGB. French had earned the American Defense Service Medal and Air Medal with five oak leaf clusters during a career that included service in World War II and the Korean War. He had run up large gambling debts. On September 20, 1957, he pleaded guilty to espionage at a court martial. He was sentenced to life, later reduced to a ten-year sentence.

May 6, 1957: KGB illegal Reino Hayhanen defected in Paris. His KGB handler, Colonel Rudolf Abel, was arrested on June 21, 1957, in New York. Hayhanen had established a Finnish cover persona and served as Abel's communicator back to Moscow. Hayhanen was an alcoholic—he was arrested for drunken driving—and spouse abuser. He had misplaced a KGB concealment device with microfilm inside in 1953. The device—a hollowed-out nickel—was apparently used to purchase a newspaper. The paperboy dropped it and it cracked open, exposing the microfilm. The boy handed it to the NYPD, who shared it with the FBI.

June 21, 1957: The FBI arrested Soviet KGB Colonel Rudolph Ivanovich Abel (born Vilyam "Willie" Genrikhovich Fisher), a KGB illegal who worked in the New York City area. He had run KGB illegal Reino Hayhanen, who had defected in Paris on May 6, 1957.

Abel was born in Newcastle, England, to Russian émigré parents, who returned to

Russia with him in 1921. He studied engineering, had a working knowledge of chemistry and nuclear physics, and was fluent in English, German, Polish, Yiddish, and Russian. He joined the Young Communist League in 1922, served in a Red Army communications unit, and worked as a language teacher. In 1927, he joined the OGPU (Joint State Political Directorate, also known as the All-Union State Political Administration), the Russian intelligence service. During World War II he served as an intelligence officer on the German front, penetrating the Abwehr, using the cover of a chauffeur named Johann Weiss. By the end of the war, he had risen to Major in the NKVD. He illegally entered Canada from France in 1947, documented as Andrew Kayotis. The next year, he crossed into the U.S. By 1954, he was working as Emil Goldfus in New York City. He served as Rezident for the New York area Soviet spy network, running collection operations from such assets as former Los Alamos National laboratory scientist Theodore Hall. He was arrested partly due to Reino Hayhanen's information. On November 15, 1957, he was convicted by a federal court in Brooklyn, New York, fined $3,000 and sentenced to 30 years. He was traded on February 10, 1962, for Francis Gary Powers, the U-2 pilot earlier shot down over the USSR, on the Glienicker Bridge, which linked West Berlin with Potsdam. Following his exchange for Powers, according to a Soviet statement, he "actively participated in the upbringing of young intelligence officers." The Soviet government admitted that he was an intelligence officer in 1965. Abel died in 1971. He was one of five Soviet intelligence officers who appeared on Soviet postage stamps issued on November 20, 1990.

September 9, 1957: Authorities indicted Alfred and Martha Stern for conspiring to communicate, deliver, and transmit national security information to the USSR. They were part of a spy ring that operated in the 1940s and 1950s, targeting U.S. political groups and the U.S. government. In World War II, the group penetrated the Office of Strategic Services, the forerunner of the CIA. U.S. Embassy officers subpoenaed them at their Mexico City home in February 1957. They did not accept the subpoena, left the city, and settled in Czechoslovakia. The indictment was dropped in 1979.

October 12, 1957: KGB informer Bogdan Stashynsky assassinated Ukrainian anticommunist leader Lev Rebet in West Germany, using a poison gas sprayer. In December 1959, KGB chief Aleksandr Shelepin awarded the assassin with the Order of the Red Banner, by decree of the Presidium of the Supreme Soviet, signed November 6, 1959, for carrying out an "important government commission."

February 8, 1959: Major General William Donovan, founder and only Director of the World War II–era Office of Strategic Services, died.

February 21, 1958: A court-martial convicted U.S. Army Master Sergeant Roy Adair Rhodes of conspiracy to spy for the Soviets and falsifying a loyalty certificate. He was sentenced to five years in prison, dishonorably discharged, and forfeited all pay and allowances. In 1951, he had been assigned on an unaccompanied tour to be a mechanic in the garage of the U.S. Embassy in Moscow. By December, he had engaged in a drinking game with two Russian mechanics and two local women. The next day, he was blackmailed into revealing information, including regarding his previous job as a code specialist. He was paid between $2,500 and $3,000. He never recontacted the Soviets after he left Moscow. He was discovered in 1957 after defector Reino Hayhanen said he had been tasked with finding Rhodes.

February 28, 1959: The U.S. launched Corona, the first low-orbiting photoreconnaissance satellite. After 12 failed launches, the thirteenth succeeded, and its engineering payload was recovered.

1960s

May 1, 1960: The Soviets shot down Francis Gary Powers while he was piloting a U-2 aircraft over the Soviet Union. He was convicted after a show trial. On February 10, 1962, he was traded for Soviet KGB Colonel Rudolph Ivanovich Abel, (true name Vilyam "Willie" Genrikhovich Fisher), a KGB illegal, on the Glienicker Bridge, which linked West Berlin with Potsdam.

June 25, 1960: NSA cryptanalysts Bernon Ferguson Mitchell and William Hamilton Martin defected to Cuba and eventually to the USSR. They flew on an Eastern Airlines flight to New Orleans, took a second flight to Mexico City, then hopped the Cubana flight to Havana. They were exfiltrated to the Soviet Union the following month. On September 6, 1960, they surfaced at a press conference in Moscow, announcing that the NSA had decrypted communications of several U.S. allies, among them Italy, France, the UAE, Uruguay, and Indonesia. (Former NSA contractor Edward Snowden would make similar claims 53 years later.) They had flown secretly to Cuba in December 1959, defecting months later.

Mitchell was born in San Francisco, and studied math and science. He showed signs of deviant behavior as a teen, having sex with chickens and dogs, which he mentioned to NSA security investigators, who still hired him.

Martin was born in Columbus, Georgia, and also studied math.

The duo joined the U.S. Navy during the Korean War, serving at the Naval Radio Intercept Station at Kamiseya, Japan. The NSA picked them up in 1957 for their cryptographic experience. They soon worried that U.S. planes' intentional penetration of Soviet airspace to probe radar could start a war. In December 1959, Mitchell visited the Soviet Embassy in Mexico City, where the KGB asked him, unsuccessfully, to work in place. The duo then went to Cuba for a quick visit, defecting six months later. Eight days after they failed to report for work, security officers found a safe deposit box in Mitchell's house that included a denunciation of the U.S.

August 18, 1960: On its fourteenth (but only second successful) launch, the Corona photoreconnaissance satellite took photos of the Soviet Union. The next day, its film canister was retrieved over the Pacific Ocean by a U.S. plane. The film had 40-meter resolution. On August 19, 1960, Corona landed safely. The program gave the U.S. a technological breakthrough in collecting intelligence on the Soviet Union, large areas of which had been unknown to the West in the 1950s. The dawn of the American spy satellite system had arrived.

October 3, 1960: Authorities arrested John Gilmore, a writer, illustrator, and spy, following a series of meetings he had with Igor Melekh, a Soviet employee of the UN. The German-born Gilmore was sent to live with his U.S. relatives at age 14. He wrote for *Collier's* and the *Saturday Evening Post*, and sold drawings to *Life*. While on assignment for *Soviet Russia Today*, he traveled to the USSR. Upon return to the U.S., he collected aerial photos for the GRU, the Soviet military intelligence service, and recruited others to help him collect for the Soviets. Two were double agents who reported him to the FBI. He was indicted for espionage by a federal grand jury, but not brought to trial because Melekh was freed from federal custody on condition that he leave the U.S. Gilmore was freed and on July 21, 1961, he and his family relocated to Czechoslovakia. In return, the Soviets released two U.S. fliers whose plane had been shot down by Soviet aircraft on July 1, 1960.

January 1961: Michael Goleniewski, an officer with the Polish SBMSW intelligence service, defected to the U.S. in West Germany. He had served as deputy head of Polish military counterintelligence GZI WP, and later led the technical and scientific section of Polish intelligence. He also spied for the Soviets. Information he provided to the West after his 1959 write-in led to the exposures of George Blake and Harry Houghton and the arrests of U.S. diplomat Irvin C. Scarbeck, Swedish Air Force officer Stig Wennerström, and KGB penetrations of the BND, Heinz Felfe and Hans Clemens. A Polish court sentenced him to death. He later claimed to be Tsarevich Alexei Nikolaevich, who was believed to have been killed by the Bolsheviks on July 17, 1918. He died on July 12, 1993.

January 7, 1961: British authorities arrested Soviet KGB illegal Konon Molody, alias Gordon Lonsdale, and his agents, Harry Houghton and Ethel Gee, members of the Portland Spy Ring, as they were exchanging documents. Polish intelligence officer Michael Golienewski, alias SNIPER, tipped off Western intelligence that a KGB spy worked in the British Admiralty. MI-5 determined it was Houghton, a clerk in the Underwater Weapons Establishment at Portland, who was a former NCO in the Royal Navy. He and Gee, a filing clerk, had access to top secret materials on anti-submarine warfare and nuclear submarines. Authorities later arrested other members of the ring, including Peter and Helen Kroger, true names Morris and Lona Cohen, who

aided Molody. The American couple had spied for the Soviets in America, but fled the U.S. Later in 1961, Molody was sentenced to 25 years in prison; the Cohens to 20 years; Houghton and Gee to 15 years. In 1964, Molody was exchanged for Greville Wynne, who had served as MI-6's cutout with Oleg Penkovsky. In 1969, the Cohens were swapped for British lecturer Gerald Brooke.

March 3, 1961: Former U.S. Army Major Harold Noah Borger, 41, was arrested on charges of having spied for the East Germans since his recruitment in October 1959. He worked in an import-export business in Nuremberg. During a visit to East Berlin, he said he was led to believe that a woman he met was a Jew working for Israeli intelligence. She asked him to collect classified information from U.S. servicemen in West Germany. He was identified by a defector. He said he had fabricated his story of his recruitment. West Germany charged him with attempting to give East German intelligence an Army manual dealing with nuclear warfare, information on new protective masks, and details on plans for evacuating U.S. dependents in the event of conflict. He was the first American to be tried in West Germany on espionage charges. He claimed there had been animosity towards him in the Army after he had defended Negroes at a court martial. In May 1962, the Federal High Court in Karlsruhe, Federal Republic of Germany, sentenced him to two years and six months in prison with time spent in pretrial confinement subtracted from his sentence.

June 14, 1961: The FBI arrested Foreign Service Officer Irvin C. Scarbeck, 41, for passing classified information to Polish intelligence. He had served as Second Secretary at the Embassy in Warsaw since arriving in December 1958 with his German-born second wife and their three children. He was seduced by a 22-year-old Polish girl, then confronted by Polish intelligence officers who showed tape recordings and photographs of the affair. He had served in the U.S. Army from 1942 to 1946, rising to the rank of Staff Sergeant. He worked for the West German government before he joined the State Department in 1949. He became a Foreign Service Officer in 1956. He earned a meritorious service award in 1959 for his work on exchange student programs in San Francisco, California. In March 1961, he was due to transfer to Naples, Italy, but his replacement developed a problem, and his Warsaw tour was extended until August. On May 22, 1961, he was ordered back to Washington, D.C. In November 1961, he was sentenced to three concurrent decade-long prison terms for violation of the 1950 Internal Security Act for passing classified papers to Polish intelligence officials. On April 1, 1966, the Federal Board of Parole granted him a parole from prison after he had served a third of his sentence.

August 1961: Polish-born KGB officer Bohdan Stashynsky and his East German wife, Inge Pohl, defected in West Berlin one day before the Berlin Wall sealed off East Berlin. He admitted he had assassinated Lev Rebet and Stepan Bandera. He was tried at Karlsruhe in October 1962 and sentenced to eight years in prison.

November 29, 1961: John Alex McCone was sworn in as a recess appointee as the Director of Central Intelligence. After Senate confirmation on January 31, 1962, he was sworn in on February 13, 1962. He had been a member of the President's Air Policy Commission in 1947–1948; Deputy Secretary of Defense from March to November 1948; Under Secretary of the Air Force from 1950 to 1951; and Chairman of the Atomic Energy Commission from 1958 to

1960. At the end of his tenure on April 28, 1965, he returned to private business. He was born in San Francisco, California, on January 4, 1902, and died on February 14, 1991.

December 15, 1961: KGB Major Anatoli Mikhailovich Golitsyn defected by walking into the U.S. Embassy in Helsinki, Finland. He was born in the Ukraine in 1926. He provided leads to penetrations of Western countries, but did not name any major U.S. spies. He told Western intelligence of a Soviet master deception plan, in which any other KGB defectors who followed him would be fakes. He also said the Sino-Soviet split was part of the deception. CIA counterintelligence chief James Jesus Angleton believed him and began a mole hunt that ruined many Agency careers and wrongly imprisoned Yuri Ivanovich Nosenko, another Soviet defector. Among the cases was one highlighted on January 8, 1962, when the CIA passed to the FBI responsibility for the investigation of Peter Karlow, an Agency officer who was one of several considered to be possible moles during the 1960s by Angleton. The investigation began after Anatoli Golitsyn said that an Agency officer of Slavic background, whose name began with K and ended with "sky," was a Soviet agent known within the KGB as "Sasha." The agent allegedly had spent time in Germany. Karlow was vindicated years later and given a medal and financial remuneration for his long years of service. Sasha was later identified as CIA contract agent Igor Orlov, a Russian who had worked for the Soviets against the Nazis in World War II. He worked for the CIA in Germany, running low-level agents reporting on Soviet military personnel. Orlov died of cancer before the FBI could pursue a prosecution.

1962: The KGB recruited journalist Leopold Raymond Fletcher, who served as a

Member of the British Parliament for Ilkeston from 1964 to 1983, according to the Mitrokhin archives. He was also reporting to the Czechoslovak StB service, according to StB defector Josif Frolik. His widow denied the claim, saying that he had worked for MI-6. He died on March 16, 1991.

April 3, 1962: Lieutenant General Marshall Sylvester Carter, U.S. Army, was sworn in as Deputy Director of Central Intelligence, serving as DCI John Alex McCone's deputy through the remainder of the DCI's term, which ended on April 28, 1965. He was born on September 16, 1909, in Fort Monroe, Virginia. He had served as Special Assistant to Secretary of State George C. Marshall from 1947 to 1949, and Director of the Executive Office of Secretary of Defense George C. Marshall from 1950 to 1951. He was Chief of Staff of the U.S. 8th Army in Korea in 1959–1960. He was Commanding General of the Army Air Defense Center from 1961 to 1962. He became Director of the National Security Agency in 1965, resigning on March 28, 1969, when he retired from the Army to become a foundation executive. He died on February 18, 1993.

April 18, 1962: Joseph Patrick Kauffman, 43, a bachelor, was convicted on charges of passing U.S. defense information to the East Germans and the Soviets. After graduating from the University of Wyoming, he enlisted in the Army Air Corps in 1942. He left the military service for several years following World War II, but rejoined for a tour of active duty during the Korean conflict. In September 1960, then–Captain Kauffman began collaborating with East German intelligence officer Guenter Maennel during a holiday trip to Berlin en route from his assignment in Greenland to his new assignment at Castle Air Force Base in California. He was detained by East German police for

questioning and was held for three days in East Berlin for interrogation. In later meetings in West Berlin with East German intelligence officers, Kauffman agreed to spy.

Maennel subsequently defected to the West and identified Kauffman. Kauffman was sent to the U.S. Air Force European Headquarters in December 1961 for a preliminary hearing. He was accused of providing information to Maennel on September 29, 1960. He was charged with providing information to East Germany on U.S. Air Force installations in Greenland and Japan and providing information on fellow officers from those two locations, including their identities, descriptions, shortcomings, and weaknesses. Maennel testified that he had introduced Kauffman to Soviet intelligence and that Kauffman had signed a two-page statement in German and English that listed the information he provided to the Soviets. On April 18, 1962, Kauffman was sentenced to 20 years of imprisonment at hard labor, dismissal from the service, and forfeiture of all pay and allowances. On December 13, 1963, the U.S. Court of Military Appeals dismissed an espionage conspiracy charge while upholding his conviction for failing to report attempts by enemy agents to recruit him. Kauffman had already served almost two years of a ten-year sentence. His original sentence of 20 years had been reduced by a review board.

June 2, 1962: Bela Lapusnyik, 24, a lieutenant with the Hungarian secret police who had defected to the West, was poisoned in Austria the week before he was to go to the U.S. He was about to report details of Communist bloc operations against Western interests and Hungarian refugees. The Austrians placed him in protective custody in a maximum security cell at Vienna's police headquarters, gave him a 24-hour guard, and served him controlled meals. He nonetheless did not feel safe in Austria, and asked to be moved to the U.S. He was to fly to the U.S. on June 5, but three days earlier, he contracted a fever and became violently ill, suffering cramps and convulsions. He died on June 4. In 1965, László Szabó, a Hungarian intelligence officer who defected, said that the Czechs had employed a senior Austrian security service official in its assassination of Lapusnyik.

September 11, 1962: Dr. Robert Soblen died in the UK. He had been indicted in 1957 and convicted for conspiracy to commit espionage for the Soviets as part of a ring orchestrated by his brother, Jack Soble, who also was convicted. Soblen had been released from prison on bail, pending appeal. He fled to Israel and claimed that he had the right to citizenship as a Jew and was thus immune to deportation; no luck. U.S. Marshals arrived in the UK to escort him back to the U.S., but he slashed his wrists and stabbed himself in the abdomen. He was hospitalized in the UK, where his request for political asylum was rejected. On his way to the airport for deportation to the U.S., he ingested a concealed lethal poison.

September 12, 1962: William John Vassall, a British Admiralty clerk, was arrested for passing thousands of documents on British radar, torpedoes, and anti-submarine equipment to Moscow. The KGB recruited him while he was working in the UK Embassy in Moscow, using his homosexuality to blackmail him. He began spying, using a KGB-supplied Minox camera, upon returning to London in 1956. He was sentenced to 18 years, and served ten of them.

November 2, 1962: Colonel Oleg Vladimirovich Penkovsky, a senior GRU (Glavnoye Razeyvatelnoye Upravlenie, the Chief Intelligence Directorate of the Soviet Military Staff), was reported lost, according to a CIA/Moscow Station cable. Meanwhile,

his civilian handler, Greville Wynne, was arrested by the KGB in Budapest. Penkovsky, deemed *The Man Who Saved the World* in the book by Jerrold L. Schecter and Peter S. Deriabin, was the key Soviet asset of the CIA in Moscow during the Cold War. The Soviets arrested him in September or October 1962 after he met his UK contact in a bugged Moscow hotel room. He had provided warning intelligence to the UK and U.S. for 18 months regarding the Cuban missile crisis and the nonexistent missile gap. The Soviets executed him for espionage on May 16, 1963.

1963: NSA research analyst and Arabic linguist Victor Norris Hamilton defected to the Soviet Union shortly before the July 23, 1963, suicide of Jack Dunlap (see July 23, 1963, entry). He had resigned from the NSA following a nervous breakdown. He told the Soviet newspaper *Izvestia* in July 1963 that NSA was breaking numerous countries' diplomatic codes and ciphers. He reportedly spent the next 30 years in a Soviet mental hospital, being treated for schizophrenia.

1963: KGB officer Yuri Vasilevich Krotkov defected while serving in an undercover position in London. His information led to the exposure of John Watkins and claimed Wilfred Burchett had worked for the KGB. He later became a novelist, writing *I Am from Moscow*, *The Red Monarch: Scenes from the Life of Stalin*, and *The Nobel Prize*.

April 27, 1963: British authorities arrested Dr. Giuseppe Martelli, 39, an Italian physicist at the Culham Laboratories of the Atomic Energy Authority, at Southend Airport on espionage charges. He had been identified by a KGB defector. At his arrest, MI-5 found a record of Martelli's meetings with Nikolai Karpekov (also identified as the handler for William John Vassall, a British Admiralty spy) and other KGB officers, and partly-used one-time pads hidden in a concealment device, hollowed-heeled shoes and hollowed cigarettes, secret codes, and film. Martelli met Karpekov in Pisa in 1955, and maintained fitful contact. He pleaded guilty to nine counts of doing acts preparatory to communicating to another person, for a purpose prejudicial to the safety or interests of the State, information which might be useful to an enemy. He took the stand, testifying that he was innocent and had resisted Russian threats against his family. He claimed he took the spy gear from the Soviets to buy time. On July 14, 1963, he was acquitted of charges of essentially being ready to spy—"an act preparatory to the commission of an offense under the official secrets act."

June 20, 1963: Former Swedish air attaché Stig Wennerstrom was arrested in Sweden for serving as a double agent for Moscow for several years. He rose to become a Lieutenant Colonel in Sweden in 1941, having been recruited by the KGB while in Moscow in 1940. He also was a member of Swedish intelligence. He worked in the Swedish Embassy in Washington, D.C., in 1952–1957, reporting to the KGB on the U.S. military and NATO. He also sent information to West German intelligence. Upon his return to Sweden, he gave the Soviets the complete plans of the Swedish defense system. In 1963, his maid found films of secret Swedish documents in an urn in the Wennerstrom mansion. He claimed his spying was "in the cause of peace." He was sentenced to life in prison in February 1964.

July 23, 1963: U.S. Army Sergeant Jack Edward Dunlap, who was assigned to the National Security Agency as the driver for the Deputy Director, but also spied for the GRU, committed suicide after failing a polygraph exam. He had copied numerous classified documents, apparently since 1958.

He was paid handsomely, and bought a cabin cruiser, a Jaguar, and two Cadillacs. He was a decorated Korean War combat veteran and a husband with five children. A month after his death, his wife found classified documents in the house and turned them over to the FBI. No one had suspected him. He had received $40,000–$50,000 annually from the Soviets.

He had served for 8 years in the Merchant Marine, then earned a Bronze Star and Purple Heart for the Army in the Korean War. He ran into financial difficulties from his womanizing and trying to maintain a household with so many children. He became the chauffeur to the NSA Chief of Staff in 1958. He walked into the Soviet Embassy and offered to share the top secret documents he transported on base. During the next three years, he gave the GRU NSA manuals and cipher machine design plans, as well as CIA reports on Soviet military issues. CIA asset Dmitriy Polyakov provided a lead that identified him.

August 1963: U.S. Navy Yeoman First Class Nelson Cornelious Drummond became the first African-American convicted of espionage. He had served at U.S. Naval Headquarters in London as a clerk with top secret clearances. He had gambling, alcohol, and financial difficulties. An English barmaid who served as a Soviet spotter passed the 27-year-old's name to the KGB and GRU in 1958. The Soviets brought him in slowly, initially giving him $250 to obtain a Navy ID card to shop in the commissary, and conned him into signing a receipt for the money. Upon his return to the U.S. in 1958, he continued spying for the Soviets during his tours in Boston, Norfolk, and Newport, Rhode Island. He was initially assigned to a Mobile Electronic Technical Unit at Naval Station Newport, Rhode Island. Between 1962 and 1964, he provided classified operating manuals on naval weapons systems and antisubmarine electronics from the Newport Naval Base to Soviet UN diplomats. He came to the attention of authorities when he was spending beyond his apparent means, buying two cars and a bar outside the base. In 1960–1961, he was also arrested for drunken driving, illegal gambling, and assault. CIA asset Dmitriy Polyakov identified him in the 1960s, but the FBI decided not to use the information to protect the source. They instead surveilled him making contacts with the GRU in New York City, and monitored his growing bank account. When arrested in a Westchester County diner during a meeting with two GRU officers in 1962, he told the FBI that he was paid $20,000. He was convicted and sentenced to life in prison.

October 29, 1963: The FBI arrested an Air Force employee identified by the pseudonym Wesson for having spied for the Soviet Union since 1960. The Bureau had conducted a seven-month investigation.

October 29, 1963: The FBI arrested John William Butenko, 39, a U.S.-born son of Russian immigrants, who worked for the International Electronic Company, an ITT subsidiary which conducted classified research for the Strategic Air Command, and Igor A. Ivanov, 33, a "chauffeur" for Amtorg, the Soviet trade agency, and hence without diplomatic immunity. The arrest occurred in the parking lot of an Englewood railway station. The FBI released two Russians who had diplomatic immunity. Police found in the latters' car a brief case containing information about a secret Air Force contract and a tiny document camera. Butenko, of Orange, New Jersey, and Ivanov, of New York City, were charged with conspiracy to violate the provisions of 18 U.S.C. 794(a) and conspiracy to violate the provisions of 18 U.S.C. 951. Butenko was

also charged with violation of 18 U.S.C. 951 for spying for the USSR regarding the 465-L command and control systems of the U.S. Air Force from April 21, 1963, to the date of the arrest. Butenko earned $14,700 a year as a control administrator for the ITT subsidiary in Paramus. Butenko apparently was recruited on April 21, 1963, during a meeting at a restaurant in Norwood, New Jersey. The FBI surveilled 7 similar meetings, including those held on May 26 near Closter, May 27 at a parking lot in Fort Lee, and on September 24 between Paramus and Teaneck. Butenko enlisted in the Navy Reserve in September 1943 and was called up on October 1, 1943. On December 2, 1964, a jury found the defendants guilty on all counts; Butenko of conspiring to pass defense secrets to the Soviet Union, failing to register as an agent of a foreign government, and serving as an agent for Russia; Ivanov of conspiring to pass defense data to Russia and acting as an agent of a foreign power. On December 17, 1964, U.S. District Court Judge Anthony T. Augelli sentenced Butenko to 30 years and Ivanov to 20 on the first count; both to five years on the second; and ten for Butenko on the third. The sentences were to run concurrently. Gleb A. Pavlov, 39, an attache of the Soviet UN Mission; Yuri A. Romashin, 38, third secretary of the Soviet UN mission; and Vladimir I. Olenev were unindicted co-conspirators. They were expelled from the U.S.

November 1963: Aleksandr Nikolayevich Cherepanov of the KGB's Second Chief Directorate gave to a U.S. businessman for passage to the U.S. Embassy in Moscow 50 classified pages on surveillance and entrapment operations against diplomats and other foreigners, and offered to become a reporting source for the CIA. The Embassy returned the originals to the Russians over the objections of CIA's Chief of Station in

Moscow. KGB border guards arrested Cherepanov on the Turkestan frontier on December 17, 1963. He admitted telling the Americans about "spy dust," a substance that KGB officers would daub on suspected American intelligence officers' clothing and other items, which helped facilitate surveillance. He was sentenced to death in April 1964.

February 1964: KGB officer Yuri Ivanovich Nosenko, who had been part of the Soviet disarmament delegation in Geneva, defected to the U.S. after serving as an agent in place since June 1962. He had worked in the America Department of the KGB's Second Chief Directorate. His information led to the arrests of Robert Lee Johnson and Allen Mintkenbaugh. He also said CIA asset Pyotr Popov had been caught by the KGB. He also noted the Soviet use of tracking substances against Americans in Moscow. He later said that the KGB had determined that Lee Harvey Oswald was too unstable for them to deal with, thereby suggesting that the Soviets were not behind the assassination of President John F. Kennedy on November 22, 1963. James Jesus Angleton, head of CIA Counterintelligence, believed him to be a Soviet plant, believing the story told him by defector Anatoli Golitsyn. Nosenko was placed in solitary confinement on April 4, 1964, and faced interrogation for the next 1,277 days. He was released in October 1967 and rehabilitated in Agency eyes.

June 9, 1964: Former Private George John Gessner, 28, was found guilty in the Kansas City, Kansas, federal district court of selling information on U.S. nuclear weapons to the Soviets. He was the first person convicted under the espionage statutes of the 1954 Atomic Energy Act. He had been a nuclear weapons technician for seven years. He enlisted in the U.S. Air Force at age 17, and

was assigned to Patrick Air Force Base in Florida, working on guided missiles. He was discharged after four years. He worked as a civilian on the Titan and Atlas missile projects. In 1960, he joined the Army, working on nuclear weapons projects at Sandia, New Mexico, and Jackson, South Carolina. Ten months later, he deserted and ran off to Mexico, where he visited the Soviet Embassy. In several meetings in 1960–1961 with two Soviet colonels, he provided descriptions of the Mark VII nuclear weapon, the 280-mm. atomic cannon, and an 8-inch nuclear gun. The Soviets gave him $200 and told him to go to Cuba. While he tried to get a passport, the Soviets decided he was no longer needed, and gave him an $8 final payment. He unsuccessfully approached the embassies of Poland, Czechoslovakia, and Cuba. He meandered off to Panama City, where he was arrested because he lacked registration papers. He told an undercover U.S. agent that he had given the Soviets data on U.S. nuclear weapons. He was sent off to Fort Hood on desertion charges. On March 30, 1962, a grand jury in Kansas City, Kansas, indicted him on 5 counts of unlawfully disclosing Restricted Data to the USSR in violation of the Atomic Energy Act and one count of unlawful disclosure in violation of the Internal Security Act of 1950. The trial was delayed while authorities tried to determine his mental competence to stand trial. The sixth count was withdrawn. A jury found him guilty on the five counts. He was sentenced to life in prison.

January 7, 1965: U.S. authorities arrested Airman 2nd Class Robert Glenn Thompson, a U.S. Air Force clerk, for passing secret U.S. military information to the USSR. Also arrested was Boris V. Kaprovich, Information Counselor at the Soviet Embassy in Washington, D.C. Thompson was charged with three counts of conspiring over several years to pass military secrets to the USSR. Prosecutors said he had worked for the Soviets in Berlin from 1957 to 1963. His motivation was monetary. He admitted giving hundreds of photos of classified documents to Soviet agents while stationed in Berlin. On May 13, 1965, a court sentenced him to 30 years in prison. Air Force records said he was born in Detroit, although he later claimed he was born in Leipzig, son of a Russian father and German mother. He said he would be willing to spy for the USSR again. In 1978, he was flown to Berlin, where he was swapped for Alan van Norman, a U.S. student who had been imprisoned for trying to smuggle an East German family into West Germany.

January 24, 1965: Syrian authorities arrested Eli Cohen, a Mossad agent, in Damascus. Mossad recruited him in 1960 to infiltrate the Syrian Baath Party. He posed as a Lebanese businessman of Syrian descent, living in Argentina before moving to Syria. He befriended members of the Syrian business community, the military, the Baath Party, and Amin al-Hafez, who later became the Syrian Defense Minister. Cohen was on the short list to become the Deputy Defense Minister. Via short-wave radio, he provided Mossad information on Syrian military activities and the fortifications on the Golan Heights. Syria spotted his transmissions and arrested him. He was tortured, tried for espionage, and sentenced to death on May 18, 1965.

March 15, 1965: Frank Bossard, an employee of the UK Guided Weapons Research and Development Division of the British Air Ministry, was arrested while photographing top secret documents for the GRU, the Soviet military intelligence service. He regularly retrieved a suitcase from the Left Luggage Office at Waterloo Station, then used an alias to check into a hotel

for an hour before returning the suitcase. The MI-6 found inside the luggage a document-copying camera and a record of Russian songs. The British GCHQ signals intelligence agency discovered that the songs were transmitted from the GRU over *Radio Moscow*. The songs were codes for where dead drops were for Bossard to leave film and obtain his payments. He was sentenced to 21 years. MI5 later discovered that two decades earlier, he had served six months of hard labor for fraud.

April 28, 1965: Retired U.S. Navy Vice Admiral William F. Raborn, Jr., was sworn in as Director of Central Intelligence, a position he held until April 30, 1966.

April 28, 1965: Richard McGarrah Helms was sworn in as Deputy Director of Central Intelligence, a position he held until June 30, 1966, when he became DCI.

August 1965: U.S. Army Sergeant Glenn Roy Rohrer deserted to Czechoslovakia and requested asylum. Czech propaganda said he was a U.S. intelligence officer, but the U.S. said he was a polygraph technician. He died in suspicious circumstances in June 2003.

June 30, 1966: Richard McGarrah Helms was sworn in as Director of Central Intelligence. He was born on March 30, 1913, in St. Davids, Pennsylvania. After working as a journalist, he was commissioned in the U.S. Naval Reserve in 1942. He served with the Office of Strategic Services and its successors from 1943 to 1947. He held various posts in CIA before becoming Deputy Director for Plans from 1962 to 1965. He served as Deputy Director of Central Intelligence from April 28, 1965, until becoming DCI. His tenure ended on February 2, 1973, when he refused to assist in the cover-up of the Watergate affair that ultimately led to the resignation of Richard Nixon as President. He served as Ambassador to Iran from

March 1973 to January 1977. He was a private consultant from 1977 until his death on October 23, 2002.

July 12, 1966: Retired U.S. Army Lieutenant Colonel and military intelligence careerist William Henry Whalen was indicted for conspiracy and being an agent of the USSR. He was recruited in 1959 by GRU Colonel Sergei Edemski, Acting Soviet Military Attache in Washington, D.C., to whom he provided classified documents for cash. Whalen was on the Joint Chiefs of Staff. He was paid more than $5,000 for information on U.S. troop deployments and Strategic Air Command nuclear retaliatory strike plans. Whalen had a heart attack in July 1960 and retired from active duty the following February. He retained Pentagon access, and continued to provide classified documents to the Soviets until 1963. His name surfaced during the investigation of Stig Wennerstrom, the Swedish Air Force officer who had worked for Soviet intelligence. Soviet defector GRU Lieutenant General Dimitri Federovich Polyakov provided information leading to Whalen. The FBI began an investigation in 1966, arresting him in July 1966. Whalen confessed and was sentenced to 15 years on March 2, 1967, for selling "information pertaining to atomic weapons, missiles, military plans for the defense of Europe, information concerning the retaliation plans of the U.S. Strategic Air Command, information pertaining to troop movements, and documents and writings relating to the national defense of the United States."

October 13, 1966: U.S. Navy Vice Admiral Rufus Lackland Taylor was sworn in as Deputy Director of Central Intelligence, serving until February 1, 1969. He was born in St. Louis, Missouri, on January 6, 1910. He was Director of Naval Intelligence from 1963 to 1966. He became Deputy Director of the Defense Intelligence Agency in June 1966. He died on September 14, 1978.

October 24, 1966: U.S. Air Force radio communications specialist and Staff Sergeant Herbert Boeckenhaupt, 24, was arrested at March Air Force Base, California, for spying for the Soviet GRU from 1962 to 1966. He was stationed at March Air Force Base in California. In October 1962, while assigned to the USAF communications facility at Sidi Slimane, Morocco he offered his services to the Soviet embassy in Rabat for money, sending U.S. military secrets and top secret cryptographic data to the Soviets using secret writing. His GRU handler was Aleksei R. Malinin. He lived above his means, buying a new Avanti. Authorities found instructions for a dead drop on 35mm film and secret writing carbons in his home. He admitted communicating via an accommodation address in the UK. He was convicted in June 1967 and sentenced to 30 years in prison.

March 1967: KGB London residency officer Aleksei Nikolayevich Savin recruited Sirioj Husein Abdoolcader, 30, a Malaysian junior clerk in the Greater London Council motor licensing department, who provided registration numbers of all Security Service and Special Branch surveillance vehicles. He was the son of distinguished Malaysian attorney Sir Husein Abdoolcader. Authorities arrested Abdoolcader on September 17, 1971, following a tipoff from KGB defector Oleg Adolfovich Lyalin, who had run Abdoolcader for two years. Police found in Abdoolcader's wallet a postcard addressed to Lyalin, with registration numbers of MI-5 surveillance vehicles. Abdoolcader pleaded guilty in 1972 to violating the Official Secrets Act and received a 3-year sentence.

May 27, 1967: Helen Keenan, a typist working for British Prime Minister Harold Wilson at 10 Downing Street, and her South

African BOSS intelligence service case officer, Norman Blackburn, were arrested on espionage charges. She confessed to Scotland Yard and MI-5 that she had smuggled minutes of Wilson's cabinet meetings to Blackburn, whom she had met at the Zambesi Club. Blackburn said he gave the information to a Rhodesian intelligence officer in Dublin. The duo were tried and convicted in July 1967. He was sentenced to five years; Keenan to six months.

August 25, 1967: U.S. Army Sergeant First Class Ulysses Leonard Harris, 38, and U.S. Army Staff Sergeant Leonard Jenkins Safford, 31, were arrested on charges of conspiring to deliver to unauthorized individuals information pertaining to the national defense. Two Soviet diplomats were named as conspirators and were declared *persona non grata*. The Soviets had given a rollover camera to the duo. The two had spied between February and August 1967. Safford was an administrative supervisor in the Army Strategic Communications Command in Suitland, Maryland, at the time of his espionage activity. Safford twice gave documents to the Soviets—Nikolai F. Popov, First Secretary, Soviet Embassy, Washington, D.C., and Anatoloy T. Koreyev, a counselor of the Soviet Mission to the United Nations. Safford was court-martialed on December 5, 1967, and sentenced to 25 years of hard labor after he pleaded guilty to charges of espionage and larceny. In addition to his conspiracy, Safford had stolen a $24,076 government check. The 12-year veteran admitted that Popov gave him $1,000.

On December 15, 1967, 15-year veteran Harris was sentenced to seven years of hard labor. He had been transferred to Korea only a short time before his arrest.

August 26, 1967: U.S. Navy Petty Officer Second Class Gary Lee Ledbetter, 25, was court-martialed and sentenced to six months in prison at hard labor, and given a bad-conduct discharge for spying for the Soviets. He was working as a ship fitter on the *Simon Lake* at the U.S. submarine base at Holy Loch, Scotland. In April 1967, two British civilians approached him at a bar and asked him to provide information. Ledbetter gave them a classified training booklet about the Polaris submarine piping systems. The duo had been recruited by Peter Dorschel, a former East German bartender who was working for the Soviets. A British court sentenced him to seven years in prison.

October 1967: KGB illegal Yevgeni Runge and his wife, Valentina Rush, defected in West Germany. He was sentenced to death in absentia. He identified Leonore and Heinz Sutterlin as KGB agents. An assassination team was unable to carry out its mission against him and the operation was abandoned after 15 years.

1968: HVA "Romeo" officer Karl-Heinz Schneider using the alias Karl-Heinz Schmidt recruited Gabriele Gast, 25, a political science doctoral student at the Technical University in Aachen. She was given the code name Gisela, along with a forged passport and a concealment device in a purse. She joined a conservative think tank, providing the East Germans with materials on security issues. On November 1, 1973, Gast joined the West German Federal Intelligence Agency (BND) as an analyst on Soviet issues. She photographed confidential documents. By 1987, she had become the deputy chief of the BND's Soviet Bloc division, the BND's seniormost woman. She drafted the daily intelligence reports for Chancellor Helmut Kohl, sharing copies with the Stasi. She gave the Stasi the names of BND agents, its codes, and its analysis of the Soviet space program, economic and foreign policy, and summit meetings. She was met by Stasi chief Markus Wolf at least 7 times, initially in September 1975 in Yugoslavia. She never accepted money from the East Germans. She had tried to break off her spying during a stressful time caring for a spastic child, but was refused. She was arrested by the Criminal Investigation Department in 1990, four days before German reunification, on suspicion of treason and espionage for the GDR. On December 19, 1991, she was found guilty of espionage and treason and sentenced to six years and nine months in prison. Her handlers were given probational sentences of 12 and 18 months. She was freed on probation in 1994.

January 23, 1968: North Korea captured the USS *Pueblo*, a U.S. Navy intelligence ship operating in international waters. The sister ship, USS *Banner*, postponed operations off the coasts of North Korea and Soviet Siberia during the crisis.

September 1968: RAF chief technician Douglas Britten was arrested for providing the KGB with sensitive information from RAF signals teams in Cyprus and Lincolnshire. The KGB recruited him in 1962. While in Cyprus, he was photographed taking cash from his Soviet case officer, which was used to blackmail him to continue spying. His handler in Lincolnshire was Aleksandr Bondarenko. In February 1968, the British spotted him delivering a message to the Soviet Consulate in London. He was arrested in September and tried in November. He pleaded guilty and was sentenced in November 1968 to 21 years.

September 29, 1968: U.S. Navy employee Edward Hilledon Wine was arrested for volunteering to spy for the Soviets on August 21, 1968.

April 11, 1969: Staff Sergeant Joseph B. Attardi, 29, a six-year Army veteran, was arrested for copying top secret documents of an Army unit in Heidelberg, West Germany, and giving an acquaintance a copy of a four-page document dealing with defense measures in Europe. On August 27, 1969, Attardi was sentenced to three years in prison on charges of providing NATO defense plans to a fellow soldier.

May 7, 1969: Lieutenant General Robert Everton Cushman, Jr., U.S. Marine Corps, was sworn in as Deputy Director of Central Intelligence, serving until December 31, 1971. He was born on December 24, 1914, in St. Paul, Minnesota. He received medals for his heroism in World War II, including the Navy Cross, Bronze Star, and Legion of Merit. He commanded all Marine forces in Vietnam in 1967. He died on January 2, 1985, and was buried in Arlington National Cemetery.

1970s

1970s: The *Sydney Morning Herald* reported on August 11, 2014, that Mitrokhin Archives material released in July 2014 by the Churchill College Archive in the UK indicated that Albert James, a former NSW policeman and federal Labor MP for Hunter from 1960 to 1980, was a secret KGB informant. Declassified Australian Security Intelligence Organisation records indicated that he dealt with USSR Embassy third secretary Alexander Ekimenko, a suspected intelligence officer. He died at age 92 in 2006.

February 1970: KGB informant Yuri Alexandrovich Bezmenov, who worked as a journalist for *RIA Novosti*, defected to the U.S. Embassy in Athens, and then resettled in Canada. He had been a deputy chief in the KGB's Research and Counter-Propaganda Group, serving in India. Using the pen name Tomas D. Schuman, he wrote several books critical of the Soviet system.

July 2, 1971: Authorities arrested U.S. Air Force Master Sergeant Raymond George DeChamplin for espionage. The senior

NCO was assigned to the Joint U.S. Military Advisory Group, Thailand, from 1967 to 1971. On June 5, 1971, he volunteered his services to the KGB, offering targeting data regarding U.S. military and Thai supply depots, technical details of U.S. communication equipment, and data on U.S. order of battle. He was chronically in debt, had a history of poor work performance and had falsified destruction certificates. He was initially sentenced to 15 years, but it was overturned. He was retried and sentenced to seven years.

September 4, 1971: Soviet Navy radio officer and KGB officer Sergei Kourdakov, 20, defected to Canada by jumping ship. He was recruited for the KGB in 1969. He ran more than 150 raids on underground Christian communities in the USSR. Once in the West, he became an evangelical Christian. He died on January 1, 1973, of a gunshot wound to the head under odd circumstances. His autobiography, *The Persecutor* (also known as *Forgive Me, Natasha*), was published after his death.

September 24, 1971: The British government of Edward Heath expelled 105 KGB and GRU intelligence officers under Russian diplomatic cover for espionage-related activities. London ordered 90 Soviet officials to leave the UK and revoked the visas of another 15 officials who were abroad. The expulsions followed the defection in London of KGB Department Five Line F officer Oleg Adolfovich Lyalin, who told MI-5 that he had been sent to the Soviet trade mission at Highgate with the mission of destroying the radar station at Fylingdales on the Yorkshire moors. He also identified numerous KGB Department Five operatives in the West and KGB sabotage plans for London, Washington, Paris, Bonn, Rome, and other Western capitals. He had been an agent in place for six months before crossing over.

October 21, 1971: Authorities arrested U.S. Air Force Master Sergeant Walter Thomas Perkins for espionage. He held a top secret clearance while working as the noncommissioned officer in charge of the Intelligence Support Unit of the Air Defense Weapons Center at McDill Air Force Base in Florida. He met with the GRU in New York, New Orleans, Japan, and Mexico City. From the early 1960s to 1971, he passed classified documents regarding Chinese and North Korean defense capabilities, U.S. wartime planning, and U.S. Air Force clandestine collection operations. He was a heavy drinker, gambled, falsified documents, and had unexplained wealth. He was arrested on October 21, 1971. On August 11, 1972, Perkins was sentenced to three years in prison and reduction in grade, and dishonorably discharged for espionage.

1972: An Air Force employee identified by the pseudonym Walton was arrested for having spied for the Soviet Union since 1964.

1972: KGB Third Chief Directorate Captain Alexei Myagkov, who was attached to the 82nd Motorized Rifle Guards Regiment at Bernau, 17 miles from Berlin, offered his services to the British SIS. He provided military intelligence for two years. On January 14, 1974, he escaped to West Berlin. He published *Inside the KGB* in 1976.

February 14, 1972: FBI agents arrested Sergey Viktorovich Petrov, a Russian translator for the United Nations, after he finished meeting at a restaurant near Patchogue, Long Island, New York, with a Grumman Aerospace Corporation employee he had tasked with obtaining secrets about the F-14. The engineer had tipped off the FBI about the original espionage pitch in 1970 and had worked with the Bureau on the sting. Petrov had given the engineer a portable copying machine to use in copying sensitive technical documents and a 35 mm document camera. A federal grand jury on February 17, 1972, charged Petrov with espionage and violation of the Foreign Agents Registration Act. On August 14, 1972, the indictment was dismissed following instructions from the White House to the U.S. Department of Justice and after Petrov returned to the Soviet Union with prior court approval.

May 2, 1972: U.S. Army Lieutenant General Vernon Anthony Walters was sworn in as Deputy Director of Central Intelligence, serving until July 2, 1976. He was born in New York City on January 3, 1917. He was Acting DCI from July 2 to September 4, 1973. He was a Member of the NATO Standing Group in Washington from 1955 to 1960, with additional duties as staff assistant to President Eisenhower and interpreter to the President, Vice President, and senior State Department and Defense Department officials. He was an Army Attache in Italy from 1960 to 1962, and in Brazil from 1962 to 1967, and Defense Attache in France from 1967 to 1972. He was a private consultant and lecturer from 1977 to 1981, when he became Ambassador at Large, a position he held until 1985. He was the U.S. Ambassador to the United Nations from 1985 to 1988. He was Ambassador to the Federal Republic of Germany from 1989 to 1991. He died on February 10, 2002.

August 1972: John Symonds, former Detective Sergeant for the London Metropolitan Police, walked in to the Soviet Embassy in Rabat, Morocco and offered his services. He had been exposed in the *Times of London* on November 29, 1969, for taking bribes from London gangs. He became the KGB's first British Romeo spy, seducing women on four continents with access to intelligence information. In April 1980 he surrendered to the London Central Criminal Court. He was sentenced to two years on three charges

of accepting 150 pounds from a London criminal. No mention was made of his spying.

1973: The KGB recruited French engineer Pierre Bourdiol. From 1974 to 1979, he worked on the Ariane space project for SNIAL, the predecessor of Areospatiale, and on international ballistic missile projects. His spying career ended when the French DST arrested him on April 5, 1983, the same date that France expelled 47 Soviet diplomats. He had been exposed by KGB defector Vladimir Ippoletovich Vetrov. The Assize Court of Paris sentenced Bourdiol to five years in prison on June 16, 1987.

1973: Former CIA Latin America operations officer Philip Burnett Franklin Agee approached the KGB residency in Mexico City and offered his services as a propagandist. He joined the Agency in 1957, serving in Ecuador, Uruguay and Mexico. He had been asked to resign from the Agency in 1968 after bouts of heavy drinking, debt, and propositioning wives of U.S. diplomats. The Soviets wanted no part of what they saw as a provocation, so he began working for the more receptive Cubans. In 1975, he published *Inside the Company: CIA Diary*, in which he identified more than 250 alleged Agency officers and reporting sources. The British government deported him on June 3, 1977; he later was thrown out of the Netherlands, France, West Germany and Italy. In 1978, he co-founded the *Covert Action Information Bulletin,* designed to subvert CIA operations. In 1978–1979, he published *Dirty Work: The CIA in Western Europe* and *Dirty Work: The CIA in Africa.* The State Department revoked his passport in 1979; the Supreme Court upheld the decision in 1981. In 1980, he was granted citizenship by Grenada, where he took up residence; he later was given a Nicaraguan passport by the Sandinista regime. His autobiography, *On the Run*, appeared in 1987. He died on January 7, 2008, in Cuba from perforated ulcers.

February 2, 1973: James R. Schlesinger was sworn in as Director of Central Intelligence, stepping down on July 2, 1973.

July 21, 1973: The FBI arrested Victor Chernyshev, a First Secretary of the Soviet Embassy in Washington, D.C., on espionage charges after he was caught meeting with Air Force Office of Special Investigations Special Agent Sergeant James David Wood. Wood had sent a letter volunteering his services to the Soviets. Wood was looking for money, revenge, and adventure. He apparently did not pass any classified information. His court martial began on December 5, 1973. He pleaded guilty, was convicted and sentenced to seven years hard labor, later reduced to two years.

September 4, 1973: William Egan Colby was sworn in as Director of Central Intelligence. He was born in St. Paul, Minnesota, on January 4, 1920. He served with the World War II–era Office of Strategic Services in 1943–1945, parachuting behind enemy lines as one of the famed Jedburghs. He was an attorney in private practice in New York in 1947–1949, and with the National Labor Relations Board for a year before joining the Agency. He was Chief of the Far East Division in the Directorate of Plans from 1962 to 1967. While on leave from the Agency, he served as Director of Civil Operations and Rural Development Support in Saigon with the rank of Ambassador from 1968 to 1971. Upon return to the Agency, he served as Executive Director-Comptroller from 1972 to 1973. He was Deputy Director for Operations from March 2, 1973, to August 24, 1973, serving as well as the Executive Secretary of the CIA Management Committee. His tenure as Director ended on January 30, 1976. His

post–Agency career included law practice, consulting, writing his memoir, *Honorable Men: My Life in the CIA*, and writing a spy-fi computer game with former KGB General Oleg Kalugin. He died on April 27, 1996.

November 2, 1973: U.S. Airman First Class Oliver Everett Grunden, 20, assigned to the 100th Organizational Maintenance Squadron, Davis Monthan Air Force Base, Arizona, was arrested for attempting to sell classified information concerning the U-2 aircraft to Air Force Office of Special Investigations officers posing as Soviet agents. AFOSI agents paid him $950 for two sheets of paper, which contained classified information concerning the U-2 aircraft. Grunden additionally offered to give them a tour of the base and flight line to observe the U-2 aircraft. He was born on July 27, 1953, in Mitchell, Indiana. He joined the U.S. Air Force in 1973 at age 19 and after basic and technical training was assigned as a maintenance specialist with a Secret security clearance. He was married with a child and his wife was expecting; the couple had separated and she was living with her parents. Prosecutors said he was weak, naïve, immature, and a carouser who was motivated by money. In March 1974, he was tried by court-martial, convicted, and sentenced to five years, reduction in grade to Airman Basic, and forfeiture of all pay and allowances in excess of $300 a month, and dishonorably discharged. The U.S. Court of Military Appeals overturned his conviction based on prosecution procedural errors. He was retried in March 1977, and again found guilty, with his sentence reduced to time already served.

April 24, 1974: West German authorities arrested Gunther Guillaume, a KGB and HVA double agent who had become a personal assistant for West German Chancellor Willy Brandt, and his wife, Christel, also an

HVA agent, at their Bonn apartment. The one-time captain in the East German Army and member of the Nazi Party had denounced the communists when he was sent into West Berlin in 1956. He copied most of the secret papers that arrived on Brandt's desk, sending them on via letter drops, meetings with KGB case officers, or using his wife as a courier. In 1973, Russian defector Vadim Belotzerkovsky told French intelligence that Guillaume was a KGB spy. Brandt resigned on May 6, 1974. In December 1975, Guillaume was tried, convicted, and sentenced to 14 years in prison; Christel was sentenced to 8 years. He was released in October 1981 in a spy swap for several West German agents and political prisoners. East German leader Erich Honecker awarded him the Order of Karl Marx. He died at age 68 of kidney cancer on April 10, 1995.

October 1974: Leslie Joseph Payne, of the U.S. Army, was arrested on charges of volunteering to spy for East Germany.

1975: The Bulgarian Durzhavna Sigurnost shot to death three Bulgarian exiles—Ivan Kolev, Peter Nezamov and Besselina Stoyova—in Vienna, Austria. They had been helping other Bulgarians to defect. Austrian police identified the assassin, who had penetrated the emigree group and escaped to Sofia.

1975: James Frederick Sattler, a prominent scholar and consultant for the Atlantic Council, confessed to the FBI that he had been recruited by the East German Ministry of State Security in 1967, trained in microphotography, and had reported to the East Germans via a letterdrop in the Federal Republic of Germany. He had studied at the University of California, Berkeley, and then in Poland and East Germany. The Stasi trained him at the request of the KGB. The East Germans made him the youngest colonel in its service. He did not have access to classified information, but he frequently met with State and Defense Department officials. He taught in New Zealand, had a research fellowship in West Germany, and worked for the Atlantic Institute for Foreign Affairs in Paris. An East German defector alerted the FBI to him. Sattler had been paid $15,000 in his seven-year spying career. The *Washington Post* and *New York Times* broke the story on April 8, 1976. The FBI made him register as a foreign agent, but apparently did not pursue prosecution.

May 1975: KGB London residency Line X officer Viktor Alekseevich Oshchenko recruited Michael John Smith, a communist and an electronics engineer, who agreed to leave the Communist Party and establish less alerting credentials. In July 1976, Smith became a test engineer in the quality assurance department of Thorn-EMI Defense Electronics at Feltham, Middlesex, where he was able to provide the KGB with information on project XN-715, developing and testing radar fuses for the UK WE-177 freefall nuclear bomb. The Soviets reverse engineered the fuse for their own nuclear devices. Oshchenko defected in July 1992, providing information that led to Smith's arrest in August 1992. Police found in his Datsun documents on the Rapier missile system and Surface Acoustic Wave military radar technology. He had unexplained income of over £20,000. In 1992, he was charged with four offences under sections 1(1)(b) and (c) of the UK Official Secrets Act 1911. He was convicted on the three charges under section 1(1)(c), relating to "communicating material to another for a purpose prejudicial to the safety or interests of the State." He was sentenced to 25 years. An appeals court reduced the sentence in June 1995 to 20 years.

June 27, 1975: Authorities arrested Sadag Katcher Dedeyan, an employee of the Johns

Hopkins Applied Physics Laboratory, on espionage charges. He had access to classified information and brought home a top secret document on North American Treaty Organization defenses. Relative Sarkis Paskalian, recruited by the KGB in 1962, secretly photographed the document and sold the film to the KGB for $1,500. Dedeyan was charged with failing to report the illegal photographing of national defense information. He was convicted and sentenced to 3 years. Paskalian pleaded guilty to espionage and was sentenced to 22 years.

December 20, 1975: The KGB abducted Soviet defector Nicholas Shadrin (true name Nikolai Artamonov) in Vienna, Austria, while he was a double agent for the FBI. He was fatally chloroformed by accident while fighting his captors in the back of the getaway car. While his ship was docked in Poland in 1959, the Soviet naval officer and his mistress—later his wife—defected to Sweden, then went to the U.S. A Soviet court sentenced him to death in absentia. He changed his name to Shadrin and worked for the Defense Intelligence Agency as an analyst. The couple became U.S. citizens. Shadrin earned a Ph.D. in international affairs from George Washington University. The KGB contacted him in 1966, and the FBI told him to become a double agent.

January 30, 1976: George Herbert Walker Bush was sworn in as Director of Central Intelligence, a position he held until January 20, 1977. He was born on June 12, 1924, in Milton, Massachusetts. He served in World War II as a naval aviator in the Pacific theater. He graduated from Yale University in 1948. He represented Texas's 7th District in the U.S. House of Representatives from 1967 to 1971. He served as Ambassador to the United Nations from 1971 to 1972. He chaired the Republican National Commit-

tee in 1973–1974. He was chief of the U.S. Liaison Office (essentially an uncredentialed U.S. Ambassador) to the People's Republic of China from 1974 to 1975. The CIA campus compound is named after him. After a stint back in private business, he became Vice President of the United States from January 20, 1981, to January 20, 1989, when he became President, serving one term. To celebrate his 90th birthday, he went skydiving.

July 7, 1976: Enno Henry Knoche was sworn in as Deputy Director of Central Intelligence, a position he held until August 1, 1977. He was born on January 14, 1925, in Charleston, West Virginia. He served as a naval officer in World War II and during the Korean War. He held several positions in the CIA, including Director of the Foreign Broadcast Information Service from 1972 to 1973; Director of the Office of Strategic Research from 1973 to 1975; and Associate DDCI for the Intelligence Community from August 1975 to July 1976. He served as Acting DCI from DCI Bush's departure on January 20, 1977, until Admiral Stansfield Turner was sworn in as DCI on March 9, 1977. On July 9, 2010, he died of congestive heart failure at a Denver hospital, where he lived in retirement.

December 21, 1976: The FBI arrested Edwin Gibbons Moore, II, a retired CIA employee, a day after he had thrown a package onto the grounds of the Soviet residence in Washington, D.C. Vitaly Yurchenko, the Embassy's Security Chief (who would temporarily defect to the U.S. on August 1, 1985, but return to the Soviet Embassy in November 1985), thought the package was a bomb and turned it over to the U.S. Executive Protection Service. A U.S. Army bomb tech saw that the package contained classified CIA documents and told the Soviets that it was a bomb. He handed it over to the FBI, who found a note from a volunteer requesting for $3,000 to be dead dropped in Bethesda, Maryland. He offered to be a "penetration of the Headquarters operations of the CIA" for $250,000. He was arrested at the drop site near his home. Investigators found ten boxes of classified CIA documents at his residence. He had retired from the Agency in 1973, angry at being passed over for a promotion. He pleaded not guilty by reason of insanity, but was convicted and sentenced on December 8, 1977, to 15 years in prison. He was paroled in 1979 because of a severe heart condition.

January 6, 1977: U.S. authorities arrested Andrew Daulton Lee, alias The Snowman of "The Falcon and the Snowman," at the U.S.-Mexico border. He was initially grabbed by Mexican police who saw him throwing something onto the Soviet Embassy's grounds. They found in his clothing an envelope of filmstrips of top secret U.S. documents. Lee was a courier between TRW employee Christopher Boyce (Falcon) and the KGB. He was recruited by the KGB in Mexico City in July 1975, and was tasked to get a manual on a satellite communications system from Boyce. Lee used his spy money to fund his cocaine habit and his narcotics trafficking sideline. While high, he told his sister and a girlfriend that he and Boyce were giving the Soviets faked documents. He was also keeping from Boyce most of the money the KGB gave him. He was sentenced to life in prison. Boyce was arrested on January 16, 1977. Lee was paroled in 1998.

January 7, 1977: New Jersey authorities arrested Ivan Rogalsky, a former Soviet merchant seaman granted political refugee status, after he received a classified document from an RCA Research Center employee. The RCA employee worked on classified communications satellite and defense projects. He worked on an FBI sting after Rogalsky asked him for unclassified information about the space shuttle program. Authorities named suspected KGB officer Yevgeny P. Karpov, second secretary of the Soviet UN Mission, as a co-conspirator. Rogalsky was not tried due to questions about his mental stability after he claimed to receive instructions from disembodied voices.

January 16, 1977: Christopher J. Boyce, alias The Falcon of "The Falcon and the Snowman," an employee of the California-based defense contractor TRW, was arrested for selling classified information to agents of the USSR. For several months, he spirited classified material from TRW's communications center and brought it to the KGB in Mexico via accomplice Andrew Daulton Lee ("Snowman"). The duo earned $70,000 for their spying before Mexican police caught Lee trying to deliver classified material to the Soviet Embassy. Mexican authorities turned over top secret filmstrips to U.S. officials. Lee, who was arrested on January 6, 1977, soon implicated Boyce, who was detained in California. The duo had provided information on the Ryolite satellite surveillance system developed by TRW, as well as copies of NSA computer cards and tape from cryptographic machines. Lee had bilked Boyce, giving him only $20,000 over the years. The two former altar boys were indicted for espionage on January 26, 1977. Lee was sentenced to life; Boyce to 40 years. On January 21, 1980, Boyce escaped from prison, hiding in a drainage hole, and hid out for 19 months. After he was re-arrested, his sentence was increased by 28 years. Boyce was ultimately paroled from prison in March 2003.

Boyce's father was a former FBI agent and security director for an aircraft manufacturer.

February 27, 1977: David Henry Barnett, a former CIA officer, flew to Vienna, Austria to meet with the KGB. He was later convicted of selling details of one of the Agency's most sensitive operations. He had worked at the CIA from 1967 to 1970 as a contractor employee and later an operations officer in South Korea and Indonesia, before resigning to enter private business in Indonesia. By 1976, his seafood processing business had failed and he faced $100,000 in debts. He approached a Soviet cultural attaché in Jakarta, offering his services to the Soviets for $70,000, and provided details of Operation HABRINK, including CIA material on how to jam Soviet SA-2 surface-to-air missiles and the Whiskey-class diesel-powered submarine. He provided the names of 30 CIA intelligence officers and named agents working for the Agency. The KGB paid him $92,000 in 1976 and 1977. He returned to the U.S. in 1978, and became a trainer of operations officers as a contractor for the CIA. U.S. agents spotted him meeting the KGB in Vienna in April 1980. The FBI questioned him upon his return to the U.S. He was arrested at his CIA classroom on March 18, 1980, confessed, and was charged with espionage. He was indicted on October 24, 1980. He pleaded guilty to one charge, and was sentenced to 18 years on January 8, 1980. He was paroled on February 12, 1990.

March 9, 1977: Admiral Stansfield Turner, U.S. Navy (retired), was sworn in as Director of Central Intelligence, serving until January 20, 1981. He served until January 20, 1981. He was born in Highland Park, Illinois, on December 1, 1923. He was President of the U.S. Naval War College from 1972 to 1974; Commander of the U.S. Second Fleet from 1974 to 1975; and Commander in Chief of Allied Forces Southern Europe (NATO) from 1975 to 1977.

March 20, 1979: Authorities in Israel arrested Swedish security officer Stig Eugen Bergling on charges of turning over to the Soviet GRU thousands of documents on the location of coastal defense sites and weapon systems during the 1970s. Bergling worked for the Swedish police security service and the military. On December 7, 1979, he was sentenced to life for espionage. He escaped from prison while on leave during a conjugal visit with his wife, Elisabeth, in an apartment in suburban Stockholm on October 6, 1987, fleeing through a back door. The couple took a ferry to Finland and vanished. He apparently lived in the USSR, Hungary and Lebanon, but the homesick couple returned to Sweden in 1994. He returned to prison, but his life sentence was commuted and he was released in July 1997. The Swedish newspaper *Dagens Nyheter* reported that the Swedish tax authority recorded his death date as January 24, 2015 at age 77. He suffered from Parkinson's disease. He had changed his name to Sandberg, and later to Sydholt, according to the *New York Times*.

May 1977: The FBI arrested Dalibar Valoushek, 33, a Czech border guard recruited by the KGB and Czech StB to serve as an illegal. He worked under the control of the FBI for two years until September 23, 1979, when he was put into a witness protection program. However, his Mitrokhin Archive KGB file indicates that he had sent coded warnings to the KGB that he was under FBI control. In October 1978, an agent told the KGB that he had been turned.

August 1, 1977: John Francis Blake was sworn in as Deputy Director of Central Intelligence, serving until February 10, 1978.

December 21, 1977: Authorities arrested Gudrun Hofer, a secretary in the West German foreign intelligence service Bundesnachrichtendienst (BND), who had been recruited in the early 1970s by an East German KGB illegal. She was driving across the Austrian border to meet her controller. She confessed the next day. When she was told that her BND fiancé had broken off the engagement, she jumped through a sixth-floor window and was critically injured.

1978: The U.S. Congress passed the Foreign Intelligence Surveillance Act (FISA), under which a special court grants national security warrants secretly when the Department of Justice demonstrates that the suspect is an agent of or cooperating with a foreign entity.

1978: GRU officer Vladimir Rezun, alias Viktor Suvorov, defected to the UK while working under United Nations cover in Switzerland.

January 31, 1978: Authorities arrested Vietnamese American immigrant and antiwar activist David Truong and U.S. Information Agency GS-13 employee Ronald Humphrey on charges of conspiracy to deliver classified information to a foreign power (North Vietnam). Investigators found two top secret State Department cables in Truong's apartment. Humphrey had given classified materials to Truong, who sent them to the North Vietnamese delegation in Paris via Yung Krall, a female Vietnamese double agent working for the FBI. Humphrey was trying to obtain the release of Nguyen Chi Thieu, his common-law wife, and her five children from North Vietnam. She had tipped him off on a planned Viet Cong bombing, but was arrested by the Viet Cong. The North Vietnamese freed her and allowed her and four of her children to emigrate in July 1977. Truong's father had run for the South Vietnamese presidency. Truong founded the American-Vietnamese Reconciliation Center at Stanford. Krall's father was North Vietnamese Ambassador to the USSR. She was married to a U.S. Navy

officer and in 1977 became a double agent for the U.S. She tipped off the CIA and FBI to Truong. The Bureau bugged his phone without a warrant and installed concealed video in his office. State Department officers testified at trial that Humphrey provided details of U.S. negotiating positions. Humphrey and Truong were convicted on May 20, 1978, on six counts of espionage. They were sentenced to 15 years on July 15, 1978. Humphrey was the only known North Vietnamese penetration of the U.S. government. The Stanford-educated Truong died of cancer at age 68 on June 26, 2014, at a hospital in Penang, Malaysia.

February 10, 1978: Frank C. Carlucci was sworn in as Deputy Director of Central Intelligence, serving until February 5, 1981. He was born on October 18, 1930, in Scranton, Pennsylvania. He earned a BA from Princeton University and graduated from Harvard Business School. He was a Naval Officer from 1952 to 1954; and a Foreign Service Officer in the Department of State from 1956 to 1969. He was Assistant Director for Operations in the Office of Economic Opportunity in 1969–1970; and Director of the Office of Economic Opportunity from January–September 1971. He was Associate and later Deputy Director of the Office of Management and Budget from 1971 to 1972. He was Under Secretary of Health, Education and Welfare from 1972 to 1974. He was Ambassador to Portugal from 1974 to 1977. He later became Deputy Secretary of Defense from 1981 to 1982. He was Assistant to the President for National Security Affairs from January to November 1987. He was Secretary of Defense from 1987 to 1989. He has been a corporate executive when not in government.

March 1978: Arkadi Nikolayevich Shevchenko, Russian Under Secretary General of the United Nations, defected to the U.S.

He was the highest-ranking Soviet official to defect to the West. He told his debriefers that several KGB officers had infiltrated the UN. The Mitrokhin archive indicated that they included several personal assistants to UN Secretaries General: Viktor Mechislavovich Lesiovsky to UN Thant, Lesiovsky and Valeri Viktorovich Krepkogorsky to Kurt Waldheim, and Gennadi Mikhaylovich Yevstafeyev to Javier Pérez de Cuéllar. His wife refused to defect with him, returned to the USSR, and reportedly committed suicide two months later. He was sentenced to death in absentia in the USSR. He died in the U.S. on February 28, 1998.

May 20, 1978: The FBI arrested two Soviet employees of the UN Secretariat, Valdik Enger and Rudolf Chernyayev, in New Jersey for accepting classified information on anti-submarine warfare given then by Navy Lieutenant Commander Art Lindberg, a double agent working for the Naval Investigative Service and the FBI in Operation Lemonaid. In August 1977, Lindberg had taken a trip on the *Kazakhstan*, a Soviet cruise ship. When the ship returned to New York, he offered to sell information to one of the Soviet officers. He was later given contact instructions, the type of information to get, and locations of drop sites. The intelligence officers paid Lindberg $16,000 for his information. The FBI arrested three Soviets at a drop site—Enger, Chernyayev and Vladimir Zinyakin, Third Secretary at the USSR's UN Mission, who had diplomatic immunity. Enger and Chernyayev were the first Soviet officials to stand trial for espionage in the U.S. They were convicted and sentenced to 50 years, but were eventually exchanged for five Soviet dissidents.

July 1978: Ion Mihai Pacepa, three-star general in the Romanian Securitate and personal advisor to Nicolai Ceausescu, defected at the U.S. Embassy in Bonn, West Germany. He was acting chief of his foreign intelligence service and a state secretary of Romania's Ministry of Interior. In September 1978, the Romanians twice sentenced him to death in absentia and posted a $2 million bounty for him. Some reports indicated that the international terrorist Carlos the Jackal tried to assassinate him. He published, inter alia, *Red Horizons: Chronicles of a Communist Spy Chief*; *The Kremlin's Legacy*; and *The Black Book of the Securitate*. In 1999, the Romanian Supreme Court revoked the death sentence.

August 17, 1978: Former CIA employee William Kampiles, 24, was arrested for stealing a 68-page top secret KH-11 aerial reconnaissance manual in February 1978 and selling it to the KGB at the Soviet Embassy in Athens for $3,000. The Chicago-raised Greek-American had worked at CIA from March to November 1977, serving in the Operations Center, but resigned when told he did not have the qualifications to become an operations officer and received a negative performance evaluation. Kampiles told a friend, Anastasia Thanakos, that he had conned a Soviet official in Athens. She in turn passed the information to CIA friend George Joannides, who got Kampiles to write a letter of his exploits for passage to CIA officials. The FBI interviewed Kampiles upon his return to the U.S., arresting him on August 17, 1978, in Hammond, Indiana. He admitted committing espionage, but said that he wanted to become a CIA double agent. The FBI had already been tipped by GRU officer Sergey Bokhan, the Bureau's penetration of the GRU's Athens residency, who had met with Kampiles. Following a three-week trial in Hammond, Indiana, Kampiles was sentenced to 40 years in prison on December 22, 1978.

August 26, 1978: Bulgarian émigré Vladimir Kostov was stabbed in Paris by a device that inserted a steel pellet containing ricin in his back. Kostov had the pellet removed on September 25, after suspecting that he had been subjected to the same type of assassination attempt suffered by Georgi Markov on September 7.

September 7, 1978: An East Bloc intelligence agent fired a ricin-tipped dart from an umbrella into the ankle of Bulgarian dissident exile Georgi Markov, who was waiting for a bus on the Waterloo Bridge in London. Markov died from the poison on September 11, 1978. Bulgaria's Durzavna Sigurnost was initially suspected. In 1993, Danish authorities charged Francesco Guillino, a Dane of Italian origin, with the killing. The *Associated Press* quoted Danish authorities as saying Guillino had worked for the Bulgarian services since 1972. Guillino was freed and settled in eastern Europe. Bulgarian authorities closed the probe in September 2013, saying that statute of limitations had ended and leaving further investigation to the UK, which has no similar restriction on murder cases. As of early 2014, no one had been convicted of the murder.

July 5, 1979: French police arrested Soviet agent of influence Pierre-Charles Pathe. In May 1980, he was sentenced to 5 years but was released after a year. He admitted to receiving some amount of money from the Soviets, although the KGB file smuggled to the UK by Vasily Mitrokhin showed him receiving 974,823 francs in salary and expenses. His KGB case officer was Igor Aleksandrovich Sakharovsky, alias Kuznetsov, according to Mitrokhin. Pathe had run a weekly newsletter for the Soviets.

August 14, 1979: Authorities arrested U.S. Navy Yeoman Lee Eugene Madsen for selling 22 classified documents to an undercover FBI agent for $700. Madsen was assigned to the Strategic Warning Staff at the Pentagon and had a top secret clearance. He

smuggled classified documents hidden in his clothing. Authorities believed he intended to sell the documents to narcotrafficking organized crime figures. He said he stole the documents "to prove.... I could be a man and still be gay." He was sentenced to eight years in prison on October 26, 1979.

October 24, 1979: KGB Major Stanislav Alexandrovich Levchenko defected in Japan. He obtained U.S. citizenship 10 years later. He joined the GRU in 1966, and transferred to the KGB in 1968. He was sent under journalist cover to Japan in 1975. Upon his defection, he named 200 Japanese agents of the Soviets. A Soviet court sentenced him to death in 1981. He published his autobiography, *On the Wrong Side: My Life in the KGB*, in 1988.

1980s

1980: The U.S. Congress passed the Classified Information Procedures Act (CIPA), creating a process for determining the admissibility of classified information in espionage prosecutions.

1980: KGB officer Ilya Dzhirkvelov defected in Geneva, Switzerland. He had worked in counterintelligence in Moscow. He posed as a *Tass* reporter in Tanzania, writing propaganda against the Peace Corps. He also ran operations in Romania, Iran, India and the Sudan. He was posted to the Geneva offices of the World Health Organization from 1976 to 1979. Soviet coworkers in Geneva trumped up charges of drunk driving and hit-and-run in an accident on New Year's Day. He was recalled to Moscow in March 1980. He decided to defect. His autobiography, *Secret Servant: My Life with the KGB and the Soviet Elite*, was published in 1987 in London, where he resided.

1980: U.S. Navy photographer's mate Glenn Michael Souther offered his services to the KGB while stationed in Italy. He had held security clearances while on active duty with the Sixth Fleet in the 1970s and had access to classified photointelligence materials while with the Navy Reserve. The FBI had questioned him before his disappearance in 1986, but no charges had been placed against him. Investigators later determined that he had been paid between $50,000 and $100,000, probably by the KGB, for U.S. overhead imagery, U.S. plans on targets, NSA intercepts of Soviet communications, and H-bomb delivery routes. He was believed to have been motivated by ideology and money. He did not hide his spying from his wife and girlfriends. His wife told the Naval Investigative Service that he had confessed to her, but was ignored. A girlfriend tried to alert the FBI, but only received recorded messages. *Izvestia* announced on July 11, 1988, that he had been granted political asylum. On June 22, 1989, Souther committed suicide in the USSR.

January 1980: While undergoing training as a KGB illegal, Klementi Alekseyevich Korsakov, 32, West German son of a female KGB illegal, walked into the U.S. Embassy and provided the identities of several KGB officers, including Artur Viktorovich Pyatin, head of Line N in Washington. He was arrested at Moscow Airport and sent to the Kazanskaya psychiatric hospital. Korsakov's mother had been a KGB illegal.

1981: Romanian Securitate Foreign Intelligence Directorate agent Matei Pavel Haiducu defected to France during an industrial espionage mission. He spied on French nuclear technology beginning in 1975. He told the French Directorate of Territorial Surveillance (DST) that he had been ordered to murder two Romanian exiles. He was sentenced to death in absentia. He published his memoir, *I Refused to Kill*, in 1984. He died in 1998.

January 28, 1981: William Joseph Casey was sworn in as Director of Central Intelligence, serving until January 29, 1987. His tenure ushered in a buildup of the Agency's covert action capabilities. He was born in New York City on March 13, 1913. Casey was a prominent attorney and businessman, writing several books that were used in law schools throughout the U.S. He was commissioned into the U.S. Naval Reserve in 1943, which permitted him to join the Office of Strategic Services. He served as Chief of the Special Intelligence Branch in the European Theater of Operations from 1944 to 1945. After a long stint in private law practice, during which he created the tax shelter, he became Chairman of the Securities and Exchange Commission in 1971, serving until 1973. He was the Under Secretary of State for Economic Affairs from 1973 to 1974. He served as President and Chairman of the U.S. Export-Import Bank from 1974 to 1976. He was a member of the President's Foreign Intelligence Advisory Board from 1976 to 1977. He managed Ronald Reagan's successful campaign for President in 1980. He died on May 6, 1987.

February 12, 1981: U.S. Navy Admiral Bobby Ray Inman was sworn in as Deputy Director of Central Intelligence, a position he held until June 10, 1982. He was born on April 4, 1931, in Rhonesboro, Texas. He was Director of Naval Intelligence from 1974 to 1976; Vice Director of the Defense Intelligence Agency from 1976 to 1977; and Director of the National Security Agency from 1977 to 1981.

Spring 1981: KGB Line X Directorate T officer Vladimir Ippolitovich Vetrov offered his services to the French DST via a message he sent to a French businessman traveling back to Paris. Vetrov had worked at the Paris residency from 1965 to 1970. In 1981–1982, Vetrov gave more than 4,000 KGB S&T

collection documents to the DST. In February 1982, Vetrov stabbed to death a KGB colleague and injured a KGB secretary with whom he was having an affair. He was sentenced to 12 years for murder in Irkurtsk prison. Several months later, the KGB began to suspect him of espionage. He confessed, writing, "My only regret is that I was not able to cause more damage to the Soviet Union and render more service to France."

May 28, 1981: Authorities arrested Second Lieutenant Christopher Michael Cooke, the deputy commander of a U.S. Air Force Titan missile crew. He was charged with ten counts of failing to obey a lawful order or regulation and transmitting classified information to Soviet representatives. He walked in to the Soviet Embassy in Washington, D.C., in May 1981 and had also phoned the Embassy several times. He provided information on strategic missile capabilities during 1980–1981. He was motivated by fantasies of being a spy and financial problems. He mentioned his Soviet contacts to several Air Force associates. He had twice attempted to become a CIA employee. Air Force prosecutors thought he was part of a larger espionage ring, and offered him immunity for a full disclosure. He took the deal, and admitted to providing classified defense information to the USSR. The U.S. Court of Military Appeals ordered his release in February 1982; Cooke resigned his commission.

June 1, 1981: Authorities arrested U.S. Navy Seaman Michael Richard Murphy, 19, for espionage. The junior enlisted man made several calls to the USSR UN Mission, offering to make a deal that "would benefit both the Soviets and myself" by providing documents from the Defense Intelligence Agency and the North Atlantic Treaty Organization. After obtaining immunity in exchange for his cooperation with the investigation, he obtained an Honorable Discharge at the convenience of the government. He had received psychiatric treatment at three hospitals between 1973 and 1978, and was a drug abuser with unauthorized absences.

June 23, 1981: Authorities arrested William Holden Bell, project manager of the Hughes Aircraft Radar Systems Group in El Segundo, California, for espionage. He had been providing secret documents on "quiet radar" and other sophisticated systems to Polish intelligence officer Marian Zacharski in return for $150,000. When challenged by the FBI, Bell confessed and agreed to work with the FBI in apprehending his handler. Bell pleaded guilty and was sentenced to eight years in a federal prison and fined $10,000.

Bell, born in 1920, grew up in Seattle, joining the U.S. Navy at age 18. He served on a minesweeper at Pearl Harbor, and was twice wounded at Iwo Jima. Following World War II, he earned a physics degree from the University of California. Married with 2 sons and a daughter, he joined Hughes in 1952. While working in Belgium, he divorced his wife and married a Belgian stewardess. He soon was faced with alimony payments, back taxes, and the death of his son in Mexico. After he moved his family to California in 1976, he began playing tennis with Marian Zacharski, 26, a Polish "illegal" intelligence officer under cover as the West Coast representative of the Polish American Machinery Corporation. After a yearlong development of a father-son–like relationship, Zacharski paid Bell $5,000 for information on the U.S. aircraft industry. Another $5,000 was for unclassified Hughes documents. Bell eventually agreed to become a consultant, which earned him $7,000 to cover the purchase of his apartment. Bell eventually accepted a camera to photograph classified documents. He traveled to Austria in September 1979 to meet with Polish intelligence. He began living beyond his apparent means, buying his wife a $2,000 necklace, a new Cadillac, and a joint trip to Rio de Janeiro. He gave the Poles information on radar used in stealth bombers, F-15 lookdown-shootdown radar, the Phoenix air-to-air missile, Patriot and Hawk surface-to-air missiles, cruise missiles, and antitank missile systems.

The FBI confronted him on June 23, 1981, with a news article about a Polish UN official who had defected and named sources. He asked, "Did he mention me?"

Bell wore a wire to entrap Zacharski. On December 14, 1981, Zacharski was convicted of espionage and sentenced to life. He served nearly four years in a federal penitentiary in Tennessee.

On June 12, 1985, Zacharski was part of a spy swap, along with three other Soviet Bloc spies, who were traded for 25 persons held in Eastern Europe. Under the new post–Cold War Polish regime, Interior Minister Andrzej Milczanowski in August 1994 named him chief of the country's foreign intelligence service. He resigned 4 days later in response to a firestorm of domestic and NATO protests.

July 15, 1981: Former U.S. Army Warrant Officer Joseph George Helmich was arrested at his home in Jacksonville Beach, Florida, for selling U.S. cryptography to the Soviet Union from 1963 to 1966. He had been a cryptography custodian in France and Fort Bragg, North Carolina. While a Sergeant First Class for the 50th Signal Battalion's communications relay station at NATO headquarters, he had passed $2,500 worth of bad checks at the military commissary. His commanding officer gave him 24 hours to settle up and repay the money. Seeking to make a quick buck, he approached Soviet Embassy officials in Paris. He sold information on and the rotors to the U.S. military's KL-7 Cryptographic System to the GRU. After his promotion to Warrant Officer, he was assigned to the 82nd Airborne as the crypto officer for Fort Bragg. He soon lived above his apparent means, buying a house, two yellow Jaguars, and a swimming pool, hosting lavish parties, and buying more than 200 steaks for his colleagues at the mess hall. He provided the Soviets with KL-7 key lists, going to France and Mexico City for meetings with his handlers. He was under suspicion in 1964 after federal authorities were tipped off by a Soviet defector and questioned by Army counterintelligence investigators for his unexplained affluence. He told them that he obtained his money in the French stock market. A second defector later provided information on him. He left the Army, but kept in touch with the GRU, taking a trip to Mexico City in which he received his largest payment, $35,000. Upon returning from Vietnam, he relocated to Buffalo, New York, where the FBI began investigating him. He was again interviewed in 1980, and admitted receiving $20,000 from Soviet agents, although he claimed that no classified information was passed. In early 1981, he was spotted in Canada meeting with Soviet agents. He was arrested by FBI Special Agent C. Douglas Jones and cooperated with investigators. He told his interviewers, "My only coconspirator was the U.S. government. They made it too easy for me." He eventually admitted all of the details of his espionage over several months. The prosecution requested the death penalty, but the judge ruled the espionage statute's capital clause unconstitutional regarding civil procedure. Court-appointed defense attorney Peter Dearing, who went on to become a Circuit Judge in Florida, obtained a plea bargain under which Helmich pleaded to one count of conspiracy and one count of espionage, with consecutive sentences to run for 20 years, and the government would not have to reveal sensitive NSA equities. Helmich's was the first espionage case to be tried under the Classified Information Procedures Act, with FBI officer George Wisnovsky serving as the country's first Court Security Officer at the trial. General William Westmoreland testified as to the damage release of the tactical system would do to U.S. national security. Judge Susan Black sentenced Helmich to life in prison on October 16, 1981; he was eligible for release after 20 years. He died 19 years into his sentence. The GRU paid him $131,000 during his espionage career, the most since the Rosenberg case. Investigators recalled him as arrogant and cocky, motivated strictly by money, not affinity for the Soviets.

August 5, 1981: The Italian government expelled KGB Line X officer Anatoli Kuznetsov.

October 1981: West German Bundesverfassungsschutz (BfV) internal intelligence service officer Klaus Kuron wrote to the Staatssicherheit (HVA) residency in Bonn to offer his services. He had been a counterintelligence officer specializing in running recruited HVA agents. He was angry at missing promotions and was also in debt. He was paid 700,000 marks by the HVA over 8 years, naming double agents. He was arrested on October 8, 1980. The 54-year-old Kuron admitted on October 10, 1980, to being a double agent, saying that the KGB had tried to recruit him the previous week. He was tried and convicted of treason on February 7, 1992. The Higher Regional Court of Dusseldorf sentenced him to 12 years of imprisonment and fined him 692,000 DM. He was paroled in 1998.

October 1, 1981: U.S. Navy Ensign Stephen Anthony Baba was arrested for sending a classified electronic warfare document and two microfilm indices of key code words to the South African Embassy in Washington, D.C. He requested a down payment of $50,000. He was charged with armed robbery, extortion, and assault. He mailed the materials from the USS *Lang*, a frigate on which he had served, in September 1981, while docked in San Diego. The Embassy returned the unsolicited documents to the U.S. Baba had attempted to raise money for his Philippines-based fiancee's college education. He pleaded guilty. On January 20, 1982, he was sentenced to eight years of hard labor.

December 1981: Polish Colonel Ryszard Jerzy Kuklinski was exfiltrated to the U.S. after having reported top secret intelligence to the West for a decade following a 1970 massacre of Polish workers. He offered his services to the U.S. Embassy in Bonn via letter. Between 1971 and 1981 he passed to the West 35,000 pages of Warsaw Pact, mostly Soviet, classified documents Moscow's strategic nuclear weapons plans, technical data about the T-72 tank and Strela-1 missiles, locations of Soviet anti-aircraft bases in Poland and East Germany, methods used by the Soviets to avoid spy satellite detection of their military hardware, and plans for the establishing martial law in Poland. A Polish military court sentenced him to death in absentia on May 23, 1984; the sentence was annulled by the Polish Supreme Court, which viewed him as a hero, in 1998. He died of a stroke on February 11, 2004, in Tampa, Florida.

December 21, 1981: Bill Tanner, a double agent working for the FBI and Naval Investigative Service, began a sting operation when he walked into the East German Embassy in Washington, D.C., and offered to sell classified information he obtained as a civilian engineer working at the Naval Electronic Systems Engineering Center in Charleston, South Carolina. The operation ultimately led to the 1983 arrest of East German intelligence officer Alfred Zehe.

January 20, 1982: Norwegian authorities arrested Arne Treholt, head of the press section of the Norwegian Foreign Ministry, while he was boarding a plane for Vienna. His suitcase contained classified documents. He was charged with providing secret NATO material to the KGB. Investigators found 6,000 pages of classified material in his residence. The FBI opened an investigation of him in 1980, while he was a member of the Norwegian UN delegation, putting him under surveillance. He was motivated by ideological identification with the Soviets and blackmail. In 1985, a Norwegian court found him guilty and sentenced him to 20 years.

April 17, 1982: Authorities arrested Hungarian-born U.S. citizen Otto Attila Gilbert after he paid $4,000 to Chief Warrant Officer Janos Mihaly Szmolka, a U.S. Army double agent working for the Army, for classified documents. Szmolka had been approached by the Hungarian military intelligence service MNVK/2 while visiting his mother in Hungary in 1977. He alerted Army intelligence to the pitch, and agreed to become a double agent. In 1981, the Hungarians gave him $3,000 for 16 rolls of film of unclassified documents and offered him $100,000 for classified material on weapons and cryptographic systems. Szmolka kept his Hungarian intelligence contacts following his reassignment to Fort Gordon, Georgia, and met with Gilbert. Gilbert was sentenced in 1982 to 15 years in prison for espionage.

June 1982: The Intelligence Identities Protection Bill became law. All 13 members of the House Permanent Select Committee on Intelligence had sponsored it, in part in re-

action to Philip Agee's disclosures of the names of CIA officers.

June 2, 1982: KGB officer Vladimir Kuzichkin defected in Iran. He fled across the Turkish border using a British passport.

June 10, 1982: John Norman McMahon was sworn in as Deputy Director of Central Intelligence, a position he held until March 29, 1986. He was born on July 3, 1929, in East Norwalk, Connecticut. He joined the CIA in 1951 in a junior position. His other CIA positions included Associate DDCI for the Intelligence Community from 1976 to 1977; Acting Deputy to the DCI for the Intelligence Community from 1977 to 1978; Deputy Director for Operations from 1978 to 1981; Deputy Director for National Foreign Assessment (now called the Director for Intelligence) from 1981 to 1982; and Executive Director from January 4 to June 10, 1982. He later went into private business.

September 4, 1982: Naval Investigative Service special agents arrested Marine Corps PFC Brian Everett Slavens, who had deserted his sentry post at the USMC Modified Advanced Undersea Weapons Command in Adak, Alaska, for attempted espionage. He had confided to his sister that he was not going to return to the Marines and had visited the Embassy of the USSR in Washington, D.C., in late August or early September 1982. His father warned the Naval Investigative Service and the Marine Corps of his son's plans to desert. Slavens told investigators that he had offered the Soviets information concerning the Adak military installation, but said he had not passed any information to them. He said he had intended to sell the information for $500 to $1,000. During a polygraph, authorities determined that he did not disclose any classified information. On November 24, 1982, he pleaded guilty to one count of attempted espionage at a general court-martial held at Marine Corps Base, Camp Lejeune, North Carolina. He was sentenced to two years of confinement and forfeiture of all pay and allowances, and was dishonorably discharged.

September 30, 1982: Authorities arrested U.S. Navy Intelligence Specialist Second Class Brian Patrick Horton for failing to report contacts with the USSR Embassy in Washington, D.C., and for attempting to sell classified information to the Soviets. He was assigned to the Nuclear Strike Planning Branch at the Fleet Intelligence Center, Europe and Atlantic, in Norfolk, Virginia. Between April and October 1982, he wrote one letter to and four times phoned the Soviet Embassy, saying he could provide information on the Single Integrated Operations Plan (SIOP), the key strategic military doctrine during the Cold War. He pleaded guilty under a pretrial agreement that included a post-trial grant of immunity, thereby permitting the Naval Investigative Service to question him for six months in preparing its damage assessment. His defense attorney offered the story that Horton had approached the Soviets to determine their modus operandi because he was working on a spy novel. He was unable to pass classified information and was not paid. The prosecution countered that he had attempted to obtain between $1,000 and $3,000 from the Soviets. He was sentenced following a general court-martial on January 12, 1983, to six years of hard labor, forfeiture of all pay and allowances, a dishonorable discharge, and reduction in pay grade to E-1.

November 10, 1982: UK GCHQ translator Geoffrey Arthur Prime was convicted of spying for the USSR. He had an earlier arrest for sexually assaulting girls aged 10–15 years old; his wife then revealed his espionage. Investigators found espionage mate-

rial in his apartment. The KGB recruited him while he was on active duty with the Royal Air Force at Gatow in West Berlin; in 1968, he had handed a note to a Soviet officer at a checkpoint, asking for an intelligence contact; the KGB's Third Directorate responded. He trained at a KGB compound at Karlshorst in East Berlin for a week. Their last contact was in 1981. He had spied on Government Communication Headquarters (GCHQ) for almost nine years. Police found espionage equipment in his house. He pleaded guilty to seven counts of espionage on November 10, 1982. He was sentenced in 1983 to 35 years for espionage and three years for sexual assault. He was released from prison in March 2001, and put on the Sex Offender Register.

December 7, 1982: A British court found Hugh Hambleton guilty of spying for the Soviets for 30 years and sentenced him to ten years in prison. The Royal Canadian Mounted Police arrested him in 1979. The MGB (the KGB's predecessor) recruited him in 1947, using his need for intellectual flattery and adventure to woo him. While working for NATO from 1956 to 1961, he sent thousands of pages of defense secrets to the Soviets. Upon his return to Canada, he obtained a Laval University economics professorship, but continued to spy. Although RCMP authorities found spy gear and classified documents in his home, he was released because he did not pose a threat to Canadian security. He was arrested when he blithely flew to the UK in June 1982.

1983: The UK expelled KGB Line X officer Anatoli Alekseyevich Chernyayev, who had operated under diplomatic cover since 1979 and had obtained 800 classified items.

1983: Iran expelled the KGB Resident Leonid Vladimirovich Shebarshin and 17 other Soviet intelligence officers.

February 9, 1983: FBI agents arrested Navy Petty Officer 2nd Class Robert Wade Ellis, an antisubmarine warfare specialist, while he was trying to sell classified documents to an undercover FBI agent. He had been stationed at the Naval Air Station at Moffett Field, California. He was $13,000 in debt, but indications of financial problems were ignored by colleagues and supervisors. He was spotted contacting the Soviet Consulate in San Francisco, where he offered to sell classified documents for $2,000. He was arrested while attempting to sell photocopied documents and handwritten notes to an undercover FBI agent he thought was a Soviet officer. He was sentenced on May 2, 1983, to five years of hard labor, forfeiture of all pay and allowances, and a dishonorable discharge. His pretrial agreement led to his jail time being reduced to three years.

February 25, 1983: The KGB's Moscow Center directed its three U.S.-based residencies to begin plans for active measures to defeat Ronald Reagan in the November 1984 Presidential election. They were to contact the staffs of all potential presidential candidates in both parties. Residencies outside the U.S. were to consider sending TDY agents to assist. The Center wanted anyone but Reagan to win and use the slogan "Reagan Means War!" They were to discredit Reagan's foreign policy position by focusing on his

- militarist adventurism;
- personal responsibility for accelerating the arms race;
- support for repressive regions around the world;
- administration's attempts to crush national liberation movements; and
- responsibility for tension with his NATO allies.

The residencies were to attack his domestic policies by citing his

- alleged discrimination against ethnic minorities;
- corruption in his administration; and
- subservience to the military-industrial complex.

The plan failed.

April 1983: The U.S. charged Francisco de Assis Mira, an Air Force computer specialist stationed at Birkenfeld, West Germany, with providing classified defense information to East Germany. The Spanish-born naturalized U.S. citizen and two West Germans sold information on U.S. codes and radar to East German intelligence. In August 1982, he photographed the cover and pages of code books and maintenance schedules of air defense radar installations. He and his girlfriend asked two local drug dealers to carry the material to East Germany and contact the KGB. They made several trips between September 1982 and March 1983, each time passing information provided by Mira. They were paid between $1,136 and $1,515 per visit. On March 25, 1983, Mira told the Air Force Office of Special Investigations of his activities. He admitted wanting to become a double agent "to show the Air Force I could do more with my intelligence." He later admitted he was in it for the money and was angry over not having obtained a prized assignment. In August 1984, he was dishonorably discharged and sentenced to ten years. Under a plea bargain, he served only seven years.

April 5, 1983: French President François Mitterrand expelled 47 Soviet intelligence officers, many of them identified by KGB agent Vladimir Vetrov, who had been reporting to the DST.

April 30, 1983: Waldo Herman Dubberstein, 75, a former CIA expert on the Middle East who had worked for the Defense Intelligence Agency in later years, shot himself to death in the basement of his 32-year-old German mistress's residence. He had been indicted on seven counts for selling intelligence about military strength and capabilities in the Middle East for $32,000 between 1977 through 1980 to renegade former CIA officer Edwin Wilson, who sold them to the Libyans. (Wilson was serving a 32-year sentence for trafficking arms to the Libyans at the time of Dubberstein's indictment.) Dubberstein faced 57 years in prison and an $80,000 fine if convicted on all counts.

July 19, 1983: U.S. Navy Intelligence Specialist Third Class Hans Palmer Wold was arrested at his fiancée's residence in Olongapo City, Philippines, by NIS special agents for being absent without official leave (AWOL). He was assigned to the USS *Ranger* in San Diego, but traveled to Subic Bay in the Philippines for extended leave, then went AWOL. When he was arrested, authorities found an undeveloped roll of film. He later told investigators that the roll of film had photos from a top secret publication, "Navy Application of National Reconnaissance Systems (U)," which he covertly photographed on the *Ranger* in June 1983. He admitted that he had intended to contact the USSR. He was a substance abuser and had a record of minor security violations. He was seeking money and status. On October 5, 1983, he pleaded guilty at his general court martial to charges of unauthorized absence, using marijuana on board ship, false swearing, and "making photographs with intent or reason to believe information was to be used to the injury of the U.S. or the advantage of a foreign nation." He was sentenced to four years of hard labor, a dishonorable discharge, forfeiture of all pay and allowances, and reduction in rate to E-1.

August 1983: The U.S. arrested Navy Seaman John Raymond Maynard while he was on unauthorized absence. He had hidden 51 top secret documents in his locker. He had been an intelligence specialist on the staff of the Commander in Chief Pacific Fleet in Hawaii. A general court-martial convicted him of wrongfully removing classified material and sentenced him to ten years. The sentence was later reduced to three years.

August 18, 1983: The FBI arrested Soviet GRU (military intelligence) Lieutenant Colonel Yuriy P. Leonov, who was operating under cover as a Soviet Air Force Attache. Leonov had 60 pounds of government documents, which he had obtained from Armand B. Weiss, an editor of technical publications and a former U.S. government consultant, who was working with the FBI on a sting operation. Leonov had worked for two years to recruit Weiss, who earlier held a top secret clearance. He had paid Weiss $1,800 for sensitive but unclassified materials on weapons systems. He demanded a classified document. Weiss gave him a large number of highly technical classified publications for $500 cash. The FBI arrested Leonov outside Weiss's office. Leonov was declared *persona non grata* and expelled from the U.S.

September 16, 1983: Michael John Bettaney, a former MI-5 counterespionage officer, was arrested for trying to give classified documents to the Soviets shortly after being hired by MI-5 in 1982. Unfortunately for him, the Soviet was Embassy Second Secretary Oleg Gordievsky, an MI-6 agent reporting on the activities of Soviet intelligence in London. Bettaney had initially tried to provide material to the Soviets in the UK, but Arkadi Vasilyevich Guk, the chief of the residency, thought he was a provocation. Bettaney had drinking problems and was an admirer of Adolf Hitler. He was part of an effort to hire more "working class" officers. He was sentenced in 1984 to 23 years in prison under section 1 of the Official Secrets Act of 1911. Guk was declared *persona non grata* a few days later. Bettaney was released on parole in 1998.

October 3, 1983: U.S. Navy enlisted man Jeffery Loring Pickering pleaded guilty at a general court martial to several violations of the Uniform Code of Military Justice, including espionage. On June 7, 1983, an individual using the name Christopher Eric Loring entered the Naval Regional Medical Center in Seattle, Washington, acting very erratically and claiming that he had a large quantity of secret national security documents. He also had a plastic addressograph imprinted with the address of the Soviet Embassy in Washington, D.C. Naval Investigative Service officers found four government envelopes containing 147 microfiche cards of classified defense publications in his car and residence. Pickering had served in the Marine Corps, where he was found to be a thief, thrill seeker, and habitual liar. He left the Corps in August 1973, but couldn't make a go of civilian life, and tried to re-enlist using the Loring alias. He hid his Corps affiliation, and enlisted in the U.S. Navy on January 23, 1979. He admitted stealing classified material from the ship's office of the USS *Fanning* between July and October 1982 and noted his interest in the KGB, fantasizing about espionage. He admitted mailing a five-page secret document to the Soviet Embassy in Washington, accompanied by a letter offering his espionage services. He was convicted and sentenced to five years of hard labor, forfeiture of $400 a month for 60 months, reduction to E-1, and a bad conduct discharge. He returned to the court system on June 6, 2000, pleading guilty to making bomb threats by telephone, lying to investigators and placing two fake bombs in a roadside culvert near the Eugene Airport before President Clinton's visit of June 13, 1998. Pickering was sentenced to 13 years in prison. He had an earlier conviction for sexually abusing two teen boys. On September 22, 2000, the 51-year-old was charged with bilking taxpayers of more than $250,000 in Veteran's benefits. A federal indictment said he lied about psychological and physical injuries suffered during the Vietnam War.

October 15, 1983: The FBI arrested James Durward Harper, Jr., a Silicon Valley freelance engineer, for selling classified documents to Polish intelligence agents for $250,000. Harper was originally spotted by an American access agent of the bloc intelligence service. Although the former Marine lacked a security clearance, he obtained the documents through his girlfriend and soon wife, Ruby Louise Schuler, secretary to the president of Systems Control, Inc., a Palo Alto, California, defense contractor conducting ballistic missile research. He had worked in several companies before opening a consulting firm. Polish intelligence recruited him in Geneva in 1975. Between July 1979 and November 1981, Harper met a dozen times with Polish agents in Europe and Mexico, providing documents regarding the Minuteman ICBM and ballistic missile research. His handler was Zdislaw Prychodzien, who was given a medal by KGB chief Yuriy Andropov for the case. The couple had unexplained income, a counterintelligence warning sign. She lost her clearance in August 1981 when SCI was purchased by a UK company that shifted her to a less sensitive job. In September 1981, he tried to obtain immunity from prosecution by having his lawyer contact the CIA, but he was already under suspicion. The FBI obtained authority for a FISA wiretap, which sealed his fate. His wife died in June 1983 of cirrhosis of the liver from her alcoholism. He was unfazed, marrying two months after the funeral. The FBI confronted him on October 15, 1983, when Harper admitted, "Oh, my God! They know everything about it!" On May 14, 1984, he was sentenced to life in prison without the possibility of parole after pleading guilty to six counts of espionage.

November 10, 1983: A U.S. federal grand jury indicted East German physicist Alfred Zehe on eight counts of espionage. He was arrested on November 3, 1983, at the annual symposium of the American Vacuum Society in Boston after trying to obtain classified information from Bill Tanner, a Navy employee working under cover for the FBI. The East German government posted bail in June 1984. He pleaded guilty on February 25, 1985, and was sentenced to eight years. He and three other East German agents were part of a swap on the Glienicke Bridge linking West Berlin with Potsdam, East Germany with East Germany for 25 persons held in Eastern Europe in June 1985.

December 1983: Authorities arrested Penyu B. Kostadinov, a commercial counselor at the Bulgarian Commercial Office in New York, at a New York restaurant as he paid a graduate student for documents on nuclear energy. The student was working for the FBI. One of Kostadinov's official functions was to arrange for exchange students between Bulgaria and the U.S. A federal court ignored his claim of diplomatic immunity. In June 1985, he and 3 other Bloc agents were exchanged for 25 persons who had "been helpful" to the U.S.

March 1984: Authorities arrested Bruce Leland Kearn, a Navy operations specialist assigned as command Secret control officer for the USS *Tuscaloosa*. A general court-martial convicted him on charges of dereliction of duty and willfully delivering, transmitting or communicating classified

documents to unauthorized persons (no country was named). While AWOL, he had left behind a briefcase containing 147 classified microfiche cards (copies of nearly 15,000 pages of secret documents), seven Confidential crypto publications, and child pornography. He was sentenced to 18 months following a plea bargain.

March 19, 1984: Authorities arrested West German auto mechanic Ernst Ludwig Forbrich, 44, in the hallway of a Clearwater Beach, Florida, hotel on two counts of espionage after he paid $550 for *The Register of Intelligence Publications*, a classified military document provided by an FBI undercover agent claiming to be an Army intelligence officer. Forbrich admitted selling U.S. military secrets to East German intelligence officers for 17 years. He traveled often to the U.S., contacting former U.S. military personnel who had served in West Germany. He was convicted in June 1984 on two counts of espionage and sentenced to 15 years.

April 4, 1984: The FBI arrested former U.S. Army counterintelligence agent Richard Craig Smith, 40, at Dulles International Airport for selling information, including the identities of six double agents, to Soviet agents. He worked for the Army Intelligence and Security Command from July 1973 to January 1980, running double-agent operations. After Smith left the Army in 1980, his business ventures failed, and he faced severe financial difficulties, declaring bankruptcy on July 14, 1982. He met with KGB officers, including Victor I. Okunev, three times in 1982 and 1983 in Tokyo, and was given $11,000 for classified information. In the summer of 1983, he contacted the FBI to report that he had "conned" the Soviets out of the money, and later said that he was working for a rogue former CIA officer from Honolulu. On April 11, 1986, a federal jury acquitted him on all five counts—one of conspiracy, two of espionage and two of passing classified information to the Soviet Union. If convicted, he could have faced life imprisonment. He was the subject of Norman R. Hamilton's 1989 book *Accused: R. Craig Smith—The Spy Left Out in the Cold.*

April 12, 1984: Authorities arrested and charged U.S. Marine Corps Private Robert Ernest Cordrey with 18 counts of attempting to contact representatives of Communist countries to sell classified information about nuclear, biological, and chemical warfare. Cordrey had been an instructor at the Nuclear, Biological and Chemical Defense School at the USMC's Camp Lejeune in North Carolina. He had peddled his wares to Soviet, Czech, East German, and Polish officials. He did not contest the 18 charges. On August 13, 1984, a military court martial sentenced him to 12 years of hard labor, but a pre-trial agreement cut the jail time to two years. He was dishonorably discharged and forfeited all pay and allowances. The case was not publicized until January 1985.

April 14, 1984: USACIDC officers arrested U.S. Army PFC Charles Dale Slatten, 19, of the 8th Signal Battalion of the 8th Infantry Division, stationed at Bad Kreuznach, West Germany. He had stolen a cryptological device in February, planning to sell it to the Soviets. The two-year Army veteran had been a telephone installer at the Rose Barracks where he had access to the device. He collaborated with two friends to sell the equipment to the Russians for $1.8 million. A military court-martial convicted Slatten of espionage on August 22, 1984. He was sentenced to nine years and dishonorably discharged. He was released after serving eight years in a Kansas military prison.

He wasn't done. He moved to St. Petersburg, Florida, where he and his wife, a co-

caine addict and sometime prostitute, built up their rap sheets. In July 1994, he pleaded no contest to 11 counts of petty and grand theft for a series of thefts of pay phones from laundries, post offices, and convenience stores. During his probation six months later, Slatten's apartment manager evicted him. On February 25, 1995, Slatten made a pipe bomb and asked a friend to set it off against the front door of the manager's parents' home. The explosion damaged the house but caused no injuries. Slatten pleaded guilty to seven counts, including making, possessing, and conspiring to use a weapon of mass destruction. In August 1996, he was sentenced to another 24 years.

September 24, 1984: West German authorities, acting on a tip from FAREWELL, a French-run agent of the KGB, arrested Manfred Rotsch, head of the planning department of Messerschmitt-Bilkow-Blohm, for sharing with the KGB details of the Tornado fighter bomber, the Milan anti-tank missile, and the Hot and Roland surface-to-air missiles. He had been a Christian Social Union candidate in Bavarian local elections. The KGB recruited him in April 1954 before he left East Germany as a refugee. In 1986, he was convicted of treason and sentenced to eight and a half years in prison. He served only one year, being swapped in 1987 for an East Berlin doctor who was in prison in solitary confinement. East Germany was not for him and his wife, and they returned to their house in the Munich suburbs, to the irritation of the neighbors.

October 1, 1984: U.S. authorities arrested East German citizen Alice Michelson as she was boarding a flight from New York to Czechoslovakia. Investigators found that she was carrying tape recordings hidden in a cigarette pack. She was believed to be a courier for Soviet intelligence. She had been given the classified material by a U.S. Army

Sergeant posing as a KGB source. She and 3 other Bloc agents were exchanged in June 1985 for 25 people who had "been helpful" to the U.S.

October 1, 1984: The FBI arrested Samuel Loring Morison, a civilian analyst with the Office of Naval Intelligence. Investigators found two portions of Secret Navy documents. He had supplied Jane's Publications with classified photos of a Soviet nuclear-powered aircraft carrier under construction. The photos ran in a July 1984 edition of *Jane's Defense Weekly*. On October 17, 1985, following a seven-day trial, he became the first individual convicted under the 1917 Espionage Code for unauthorized disclosure to the press. He was also convicted of theft of government property. On December 4, 1985, he was sentenced to two years in prison. The 4th U.S. Circuit Court of Appeals upheld the conviction in April 1988. In October 1988, the Supreme Court declined to review the case.

Morison, grandson of famed naval and maritime historian Samuel Eliot Morison, was a heavy spender and unhappy with his Navy job. He was a part-time contributor to Jane's.

October 3, 1984: Authorities in California arrested GS-13 FBI Special Agent Richard William Miller and accomplices Svetlana and Nikolai Ogorodnikov. He had provided classified information to the two pro–Soviet Russian émigrés, demanding $50,000 in gold and $15,000 cash. He had financial difficulties in trying to support his 8 children and reportedly had a sexual relationship with Svetlana. He was about to travel with her to Vienna when they were arrested. Investigators found several classified documents in his residence. The Ogorodnikovs were accused of being KGB "utility agents" since 1980. Warning signs included financial difficulties, insubordination, and poor

work performance. He also was trying to get revenge against the Bureau. The romance sealed the deal for him to spy. Following a ten-week trial, the couple agreed to a plea deal on one count of conspiracy. Nikolai was sentenced to eight years; she was sentenced to 18 years. Miller pleaded innocent, and an 11-week trial ended in a mistrial. At the end of the second trial, he was found guilty on June 19, 1986, on six counts of espionage. The jury refused to believe his claim that he was trying to become a double agent against the KGB. On July 14, 1986, he was sentenced to two consecutive life terms and 50 years on other charges. The conviction was overturned in 1989 because U.S. District Judge David Kenyon had admitted polygraph evidence. Miller was granted bail in October 1989. He was again convicted on all counts of espionage in October 1990, and sentenced on February 4, 1991, to 20 years in federal prison. A federal appeals court upheld the conviction on January 28, 1993. His sentence was eventually reduced to 13 years. Miller was the first FBI employee to be indicted for espionage. He would not be the last.

November 27, 1984: Former CIA staffer and contract employee Karl F. Koecher and his wife Hana, né Pardamcova, naturalized U.S. citizens and inveterate swingers, were arrested in New York City and charged with conspiracy to commit espionage by being Czech agents. Czech intelligence had trained Koecher as an agent in 1962. He and his wife staged a fake defection to the U.S. in 1965. They were in fact illegals working for the Czech Stani tajni Bezpecnost (StB). Koecher became a spokesman for anticommunists among New York City academics. The duo became U.S. citizens in 1971. After earning a degree from Columbia University, he became a translator for the CIA's Soviet and East European Division in 1973, translating top secret materials for two years before resigning in 1975. From February 1973 to August 1983, he passed highly classified materials—including the names of CIA officers—to Czech agents. He learned about a Soviet diplomat, code named CKTRIGON. The KGB ultimately identified the CIA asset as Aleksandr Ogorodnik, a member of the Ministry of Foreign Affairs, who had begun working for the Agency in 1973 in Bogota. Ogorodnik committed suicide while writing a confession in front of KGB officers. The Koechers were planning to fly to Switzerland when they were apprehended. He was arrested after he was seen contacting KGB operatives. Less than two years after his imprisonment, on February 11, 1986, Karl, Hana, and two Czech spies were part of a nine-person exchange at Berlin's Glienicke Bridge that included Soviet dissident Anatoly Sharansky and a Czech who had been jailed for helping others leave Czechoslovakia illegally. Sharansky would go on to Israel, where he became a legislator. The Koechers returned to Czechslovakia.

December 17, 1984: Authorities in Gallup, New Mexico, arrested former Navy enlisted man Jay Clyde Wolff, 24, then an auto painter, for offering to sell for $5,000 to $6,000 classified documents regarding weapons systems on a U.S. Navy vessel to an undercover federal agent. He was discharged from the Navy in 1983. Following a tipoff, he was arrested during the meeting at a convenience store. He pleaded guilty to one count of attempting to sell classified documents. On June 28, 1985, he was sentenced to five years in prison.

December 18, 1984: Thomas Patrick Cavanaugh, a senior engineer in the Advanced Systems Division of Northrop Grumman, was arrested on charges of espionage in a hotel in Commerce, California, when he attempted to sell stealth technology to FBI undercover officers pretending to be KGB officers. He had his first meeting with the FBI agents on December 10, 1984, at the Cockatoo Motel in Commerce, California, showing them classified documents. At the second meeting on December 18, 1984, he brought B-2 stealth bomber information. He was arrested at the third meeting. He had initially phoned the Soviet Consulate in San Francisco. The FBI determined that he was separated from his wife because of his infidelity, had 25 outstanding credit accounts, had a $17,000 bill from Club Med, owed more than $41,000 in debt, and carried a $98,000 mortgage. He was also dissatisfied with his job, disliked management, and had social and political resentments. He was convicted on May 23, 1985, and sentenced to two concurrent life terms in a federal prison. He was granted parole and released from prison in 2001.

1985 is often referred to as the Year of the Spy. The number of entries that appear below offers evidentiary support for this claim, although several other years give 1985 a run for its money.

1985: Margret Hike, a secretary in the office of the West German president, was arrested for spying. She had been recruited by her lover, East German illegal Hans-Jurgen Henze, under the alias Franz Becker, in 1968. She had worked in the mobilization and security departments. Following her confession, in 1987 she was sentenced to eight years in prison and fined the 33,000 marks she had received from the KGB.

1985: Hans-Joachim Tiedge, head of counterintelligence for the West German BfV internal intelligence service, drunkenly drove up to the East German border and defected. He was a heavy gambler and had almost been charged with manslaughter after his wife died in a brawl at their home. An HVA prostitute sent to entertain Tiedge ran away.

May 17, 1985: Authorities arrested U.S. Air Force Airman Edward Owen Buchanan, 21, for attempting to transmit classified information to the USSR. The unmarried Buchanan was a student working at the 3463rd Munitions and Weapons Maintenance Technical Training Squadron at Lowry Air Force Base, Colorado. He contacted via phone and mail the East German embassy in Washington, D.C., offering his espionage services. Getting nowhere with them, he moved on to the Soviet embassy in Washington, D.C., and the Soviet Consulate in San Francisco, California. An Air Force Office of Special Investigation source tipped off the U.S. government about him. Air Force Office of Special Investigation investigators, posing as Soviet agents, paid him $1,000. He offered what he claimed were classified documents, and was arrested. He told arresting officers that although he lacked a security clearance, he was to receive one, and would be able to sell technical documents to the Soviets. He said he wanted to "sell as much classified material as he could until he made enough money to live comfortably." On August 26, 1985, a court martial sentenced him to 30 months of confinement and a dishonorable discharge.

May 20, 1985: Retired Navy warrant officer John Anthony Walker, Jr., was arrested at a Maryland motel after leaving secret documents at a KGB dead drop in Montgomery County, Maryland. Soviet Embassy official Alexei Tkachenko was spotted in the same area and returned to Moscow a few days after Walker's arrest. Walker held a top secret crypto clearance. He was charged with selling classified material to the Soviets for 18 years, beginning in December 1967, when he met with the KGB Resident in Washington, Boris Solomatin, and case officer Oleg Kalugin, who ultimately became a KGB general responsible for U.S. counter-

intelligence before resettling in the U.S. His espionage ring included his brother, Arthur James Walker (arrested on May 29, 1985); his son, Michael Lance Walker (arrested on May 22, 1985), who served on the aircraft carrier USS *Nimitz*; and former Navy friend Jerry Alfred Whitworth. Walker had received more than $1 million from the Soviets. He used the proceeds to purchase boats, airplanes, frequent travel, his own investigation firm, and expensive dinners and parties. Soviet defector Vitaly Yurchenko said the senior Walker was given an honorary rank of admiral in the Soviet Navy.

John Walker's former wife had tipped the FBI in November 1984 that the retired U.S. Navy warrant officer had spied for 18 years, compromising more than one million classified cables from the U.S. military service and U.S. intelligence agencies. A Soviet defector said Walker was the most important operation in KGB history; the Soviets would have won a hypothetical World War III because it could read U.S. military messages. Walker had contacted the KGB to get money to make up for his financial losses. Warning signals included unexplained affluence, an unstable personality, and unusual long distance travel that went unreported for years. He was sentenced in October 1986 to two life sentences plus ten years. He was scheduled for release on May 20, 2015.

Walker plea bargained for a lighter sentence for his son, Michael Lance, who received 25 years. He also agreed to testify against Whitworth.

Congress soon closed a loophole that turned up in the Walker case, permitting a death sentence for peacetime spying by military personnel.

May 29, 1985: Authorities arrested retired U.S. Navy Lieutenant Commander Arthur James Walker, 46, for illegally passing classified material to his brother, family-of-spies ringleader John Walker (see May 20, 1985, entry), in 1981–1982. Arthur Walker was an engineer for the SE Corporation in Portsmouth, Virginia, where he had a Secret clearance. He applied to VSE in 1980 at John's urging. Arthur worked on amphibious architecture and maintenance planning. He was convicted of passing classified information on ship construction and design to John. He received between $2,000 and $12,000 for his spying, much of which he returned to John to repay a debt. On August 9, 1985, Arthur was found guilty on seven counts of espionage. On November 12, 1985, he was sentenced to three life terms plus four concurrent decade-long terms and fined $250,000. He appeared to be motivated by money. He died of kidney failure at age 79 on July 7, 2014, in a federal prison in Butner, North Carolina.

June 3, 1985: Jerry Alfred Whitworth, a collaborator in the Walker spy ring (see May 20, 1985, entry), surrendered to the FBI. The retired U.S. Navy communications specialist had held a top secret clearance. The senior Walker had given him $332,000 for classified information which was given to the Soviets between 1975 and 1982. Walker told Whitworth that the information would be going to the Israelis. He was assessed as the most important asset of the Soviets in the Walker spy ring, because he gave "key lists" which allowed decoding of U.S. Navy communications. He also provided designs of cryptographic equipment. The KGB paid him $335,000. Whitworth was convicted in July 1986 on 7 counts of espionage and one count of tax evasion. On August 28, 1986, he was sentenced to 365 years in jail and fined $410,000.

June 9, 1985: The KGB in Moscow arrested Adolf Tolkachev, a Soviet defense researcher working on stealth aircraft technology. Tolkachev had dropped notes in and on the cars of American Embassy workers in Moscow, trying to offer his services. Once the CIA contacted him, he served as an asset for nearly a decade. In the fall of 1986, *Tass* reported that he had been tried, convicted, and executed. Aldrich Ames had betrayed him.

July 11, 1985: U.S. authorities arrested Sharon M. Scranage, an Operations Support Assistant at the CIA Station in Accra, Ghana, on charges of providing classified information to Ghanaian intelligence officials, including intelligence chief Kojo Tsikata, who may have shared the information with Cuba and other Marxist regimes. The Agency became suspicious following her routine polygraph. She agreed to cooperate with the FBI to arrest her Ghanaian boyfriend, Michael Soussoudis, a business consultant and permanent resident of the U.S. Scranage was charged with 18 counts of providing classified information, including the identities of CIA assets, to a foreign country. She pleaded guilty to one count under the espionage code and two counts of violating the Intelligence Identities Protection Act. The other 15 charges were dropped. On November 26, 1985, she was sentenced to five years in prison, reduced on April 10, 1986, to two years. She was paroled after serving 18 months. Soussoudis pleaded *nolo contendere* to 8 counts of espionage. He was sentenced to 20 years, suspended on the condition that he leave the U.S. within 24 hours.

July 19, 1985: KGB officer Oleg Gordievsky defected to the UK via Finland. He had earlier worked as an agent for the British SIS after the Soviet invasion of Czechoslovakia. The USSR sentenced him to death in absentia. He was spirited out of the USSR in the trunk of a British SIS car while under KGB surveillance. In October 1985, the UK expelled 31 Soviet intelligence officers Gordievsky had identified.

August 1, 1985: Vitaly S. Yurchenko, 49, Deputy Chief of the KGB's First Department of the First Chief Directorate, requested asylum at the U.S. Embassy in Rome. He had supervised KGB operations in North America and against Americans worldwide. He told debriefers, including Aldrich Ames, that there was no mole in the CIA, and provided information that led to the identification of Edward Lee Howard and NSA employee Ronald Pelton as KGB assets. He redefected to the USSR in November 1985, slipping out of the Georgetown French bistro Au Pied de Cochon when his security handler was not looking.

August 7, 1985: Authorities arrested Quartermaster Third Class Stephen Dwayne Hawkins for attempted espionage. While Hawkins was with the Commander Submarine Group 8 in Naples, Italy in June 1985, a visitor to his home saw a classified message there. Hawkins told NIS agents and polygraphers that he had taken at least 17 Secret messages home with him and was thinking of selling them to a hostile intelligence service. On January 15, 1986, a general court-martial convicted him of violating Article 92, wrongful removal of classified material and wrongful destruction of a classified message. The court sentenced him to a year in prison, reduction in grade to E-1, and a dishonorable discharge.

August 13, 1985: U.S. authorities arrested Navy Petty Officer 3rd Class Michael Timothy Tobias and his nephew, Francis Xavier Pizzo, II, on charges of stealing a dozen top secret cryptographic key cards from the USS *Peoria* when it was berthed at San Diego, California, and attempting to sell the cards to Soviet Consulate representatives in San Francisco for $100,000. The duo arrived before regular business hours, rethought their plans, and instead called the U.S. Secret Service, offering to give them the cards for amnesty and money. The U.S. also arrested Bruce Edward Tobias, Michael's brother, and Dale Vern Irene of San Diego. (Some sources say Michael was arrested on August 22, 1984.)

Pizzo pleaded guilty to five federal charges and on was sentenced to ten years in prison on October 7, 1985. Bruce Tobias and Dale Irene pleaded guilty to two counts of receiving stolen property. Michael was convicted on four counts of conspiracy and 3 of theft of government property. Two of the 12 stolen cards were not recovered. On November 12, 1995, Michael Tobias was sentenced to 20 years (some sources say August 1985). In January 1996, Bruce Tobias was sentenced to the prison time he had served (159 days). Dale Irene was sentenced to two years.

November 21, 1985: Authorities detained U.S. Navy GS-12 civilian employee Jonathan J. Pollard and his wife, Anne Henderson-Pollard, outside of the Israeli Embassy in Washington, D.C., after they failed to obtain asylum and exfiltration out of the country. They were charged under the espionage statute with selling one million classified documents to the Israelis for $50,000 during their 18 months of spying. Anne Henderson-Pollard was accused of intending to sell to Chinese representatives documents on the U.S. analysis of China's intelligence operations in the U.S. Four Israelis were named as unindicted co-conspirators.

He was ideologically motivated, believing that the U.S. was not sharing enough intelligence with its ally, although money later became a supplementary factor. There were a few tipoffs about his potential to commit treason. In 1976 while at Stanford University, he boasted of working for Mossad. He had been fascinated by espionage all his life. He was turned down by CIA. In 1979, he became a junior analyst for the U.S. Navy, following foreign ship movements. In 1984, he joined the Navy's Antiterrorism Alert Center.

Pollard volunteered to work for the Israelis during a May 29, 1984, meeting with Israeli fighter pilot Avi Sella at the Wasington Hilton Hotel. At a followup meeting, he was introduced to Yosef Yagur, Israeli Embassy science counselor and agent of Lishka Lekishrey Mada (LAKAM), the Defense Ministry's Office of Scientific Liaison intelligence service. On a biweekly basis, Pollard delivered stacks of classified documents to the apartment of an Israeli Embassy employee. Information included military and political data about Arab countries and Soviet defense systems, the Radio Signal Notations manual, and PLO facilities in Tunisia. The Israelis gave him trips to Europe and Israel, a $3,000 payment for an engagement ring, $2,500 a month, and $30,000 in a Swiss bank account.

He developed unstable work habits, had financial problems, sported a huge ego, displayed sudden wealth, and was a frequent—and inept—liar. A co-worker reported that Pollard had walked out of his office building with classified information, sparking an investigation. Beyond working for the Israelis, Pollard shared information with a South African military attaché, an Australian naval officer, two investment advisors, and a journalist.

Fellow employees had told investigators that he was seeking and copying more classified documents than were relevant to his job and documents that went beyond his account as an analyst on terrorism in Latin America and the Caribbean. He had carried full burn bags of classified documents out to the parking lot and drove away.

Surveillance cameras in his office on November 15, 1985, showed him putting 60 documents into his briefcase.

Authorities found at the Pollards' apartment a suitcase of classified materials, including many top secret items, related to military capabilities of foreign countries.

On November 18, 1985, Pollard had admitted to FBI and Naval Investigative Service investigators that he had delivered classified documents to a foreign government agent.

Pollard failed a polygraph test and alerted the Israelis that he had been spotted. LAKAM provided no exfil plan, so the couple drove his Mustang to the Embassy, which turned them away.

Under U.S. pressure, the Israelis returned some of the documents Pollard had given them, which became evidence at his trial.

On June 4, 1986, under terms of a plea agreement, Jonathan Pollard pleaded guilty to one count of conspiring to deliver national defense information to a foreign power. Anne pleaded guilty to being an accessory to possession of classified material. The Department of Justice said it would not seek a life sentence.

On March 4, 1987, U.S. District Court Judge Aubrey Robinson sentenced Jonathan Pollard to life in prison and Anne Henderson-Pollard to two concurrent five-year terms for selling classified documents to Israeli intelligence. The judge was under no obligation to follow the terms of the DOJ agreement with the Pollards.

During the next decades, Israel frequently asked U.S. Presidents to release him. Then-DCI George J. Tenet once offered to tender his resignation if Pollard was freed.

His inadvertent recruiter, Stella, was promoted to Brigadier General and given command of an Israeli Air Force base.

In 1990, Pollard divorced Anne to marry Esther Seitz, a member of the Free Pollard movement.

The Israelis granted Pollard citizenship in 1995.

November 22, 1985: Authorities arrested retired CIA/FBIS veteran Larry Wu-Tai Chin, 67, for having spied for 33 years for the People's Republic of China. He had retired in 1981 at age 63. He was born in Beijing in 1922. He worked as an interpreter during World War II at the British Military Mission and at the U.S. Army's liaison office in China, and later at the U.S. Consulates in Shanghai and Hong Kong He was recruited by communist intelligence while a college student in 1948. During the Korean War, the U.S. Department of State sent him to interview Chinese prisoners of war. He told PRC intelligence about the locations of POW camps, names of cooperative POWs, and allied questions of the POWs. He joined the CIA's Foreign Broadcast Information Service in 1952. He allegedly provided the PRC with top secret reports on the Far East written during the previous two decades. He moved to an FBIS site in California in 1951, and became a naturalized citizen in 1965. He went to FBIS headquarters in Virginia in the 1970s as a staff employee, translating materials from Chinese clandestine sources. Chin developed a gambling problem, which added to his reasons to continue spying. He was believed to have smuggled classified reports from his office between 1976 and 1982, handing them to Chinese couriers in Toronto, Hong Kong, and London. He retired in 1981, but did contract translating for the Agency. He went to Beijing in 1982, where he was given a $50,000 bonus at a Ministry of State Security banquet. He met with PRC agents in the Far East in March 1985. He might have received $1 million during his spying career. A Chinese defector tipped off U.S. intelligence to Chin. When arrested, the FBI found $564,000 in bank accounts, including $200,000 in a Hong Kong bank. His real estate investments in Virginia, Maryland, and Las Vegas came to $700,000. He

was indicted on 17 counts of espionage and income tax violations. He admitted at the start of his trial on February 4, 1986, that he had provided information to the PRC for 11 years to help the two countries reconcile. On February 8, 1986, a federal jury convicted him on all counts. Sentencing was scheduled for March 17, 1986, but he committed suicide in his cell on February 21, 1986.

November 25, 1985: Former National Security Agency communications specialist Ronald William Pelton, who had sold top secret information to the Soviets, was arrested in Annapolis, Maryland. He had agreed to talk to the FBI the previous day. He had been identified via information from Vitaly Yurchenko, Deputy Chief of the KGB's First Department of the First Chief Directorate, who temporarily defected to the U.S. in Italy on August 1, 1985. He left the NSA in July 1979 after a 14-year career. Pelton said he contacted the Soviets in 1980 because he was facing debts of $65,000 and had declared bankruptcy. He went to the Soviet Embassy in Washington, D.C., and agreed to sell classified information. The KGB debriefed him 5 times during trips to Vienna, Austria. The KGB paid him $35,000 between 1980 and 1983 for his information about U.S. collection against the USSR, including the sensitive Ivy Bells phone taps on an undersea Soviet cable in the Sea of Okhotsk. By this time, he was divorced, living with another woman, abusing alcohol and drugs, and earning little for an Annapolis boat company. Pelton was indicted on December 20, 1985, on six counts relating to espionage. He pleaded not guilty. On June 5, 1986, a court convicted Pelton on one count of conspiracy and two counts of espionage for spying for the USSR. The NSA veteran was sentenced to three concurrent life sentences for espionage on December 16, 1986. He was represented by the attorney who had defended John Walker.

December 20, 1985: Authorities arrested Randy Miles Jeffries, messenger for a private stenographic firm in Washington, D.C., and charged him with attempting to deliver national defense secrets to the USSR. The firm had transcribed closed hearings of the House Armed Services Committee. He reportedly provided 40 "sample pages" of Secret and Top Secret transcripts of hearings, offering a complete package for $5,000. U.S. agents spotted him entering the Soviet Military Office in Washington. An FBI agent posed as a Soviet representative and contacted him at his residence to set up a meeting later that day at a local hotel. The FBI arrested Jeffries at the end of the meeting. From 1978 to 1980, Jeffries was an FBI support employee with a security clearance. In March 1983, he was convicted of possession of heroin. He completed a drug rehab program in July 1985. He pleaded guilty on January 23, 1986. On March 13, 1986, a federal judge sentenced him to three to nine years in prison.

January 22, 1986: The FBI arrested Airman First Class Bruce Damian Ott, 25, an administrative clerk at Beale Air Force Base, at a Davis, California, motel as he tried to sell classified information regarding the SR-71 Blackbird spy plane to undercover agents who claimed to be USSR representatives. The documents included the SAC Tactical Doctrine for SR-71 Crews. Beale AFB was the home base of the SR-71 Blackbird reconnaissance jet. In January, Ott tried to contact USSR consular representatives in San Francisco, but his communication was intercepted. No classified material was passed. Ott wanted $160,000 for his information. After an eight-day court martial, he was found guilty and was sentenced to 25 years in prison on August 7, 1986. (Coinciden-

tally, the Soviets announced the defection of Edward Lee Howard the same day.)

March 4, 1986: The Naval Investigative Service, FBI, and local police arrested Petty Officer 3rd Class Robert Dean Haguewood after he sold part of a classified aviation ordinance manual to an undercover police officer for $360. He was stationed at the Pacific Missile Test Center at Point Mugu Naval Air Station outside Oxnard, California. He had asked around town for contacts who would pay for secret information about naval ordinance. The NIS put him under surveillance. He had serious financial difficulties. On June 20, 1986, he pleaded guilty under a plea bargain. A military court sentenced him to two years.

March 14, 1986: Israeli Army Major Yossi Amit, an AMAN intelligence officer, was arrested on charges of spying for the U.S. He had earlier served in the Israeli Defense Forces' elite paratroop unit. He was shot in the chest during a sensitive operation and was classified as partially disabled. A tribunal convicted him in 1987 and sentenced him to 12 years. The trial was conducted in camera and kept secret until 1993.

April 18, 1986: Robert Michael Gates was sworn in as Deputy Director of Central Intelligence, a position he held through the remainder of DCI Casey's tenure and well into the DCIship of William Hedgcock Webster, stepping down on March 20, 1989. After an unsuccessful confirmation hearing, he later became Director of Central Intelligence. After serving as President of Texas A&M University, he became Secretary of Defense.

May 7, 1986: Erik Sites, a U.S. Embassy-Moscow employee, was arrested, accused of espionage, and expelled from the USSR. The case was attributed to information provided by former CIA officer Edward Lee Howard, who had defected to the Soviets in September 1985.

June 19, 1986: The FBI arrested senior Soviet military attache Colonel Vladimir M. Ismaylov as he was servicing a dead drop site in rural Prince George's County, Maryland, to leave a $41,100 payment for documents he had retrieved. The Soviet Chief Directorate for Intelligence (GRU) agent attempted to buy secret Air Force documents. He was the highest-ranking Soviet Air Force officer at the Soviet Embassy in Washington, D.C. An Air Force officer pretended to be willing to sell USAF secrets after the Soviets asked the officer to photograph documents relating to the Strategic Defense Initiative (the "Star Wars" nuclear missile defense system) and other programs including cruise missiles, stealth bombers and a hypersonic passenger jet. The U.S. expelled Ismaylov for activities incompatible with his diplomatic role.

July 7, 1986: The KGB arrested GRU Lieutenant General Dmitriy Federovich Polyakov, codenamed TOPHAT by the FBI and BOURBON by the CIA. Following an extensive interrogation, he was executed in 1988 and buried in an unmarked grave. While stationed in New York in January 1962, he had volunteered his services to the U.S. He was handled by the FBI while still serving at the United Nations in New York. When he was reassigned to Rangoon, Burma in 1965, the CIA took over the case. He provided thousands of documents on weapons systems, S&T, military/political strategy, and intelligence. He worked for the U.S. for 18 years, possibly making him the most productive Soviet spy in American history. He was exposed to the KGB by Aldrich Ames. He had celebrated his 65th birthday the day before his arrest.

July 29, 1986: *Bild Zeitung*, a West German daily newspaper, revealed a KGB forgery operation involving an alleged speech by U.S. Secretary of Defense Caspar Weinberger. The journalist asked the U.S. government for comment on the document, which stated the opposite of the real U.S. position on the Strategic Defense Initiative, saying it was an offensive system to be used to control NATO. The document also claimed that the Soviets did not have an SDI program.

August 7, 1986: *Tass* announced that fired CIA officer Edward Lee Howard had been granted political asylum in the USSR. He had been scheduled to go to Moscow as a first tour case officer before being fired. While under FBI surveillance, Howard escaped from his car and fled the U.S. in September 1985.

Howard joined the CIA in January 1981 as an operations officer trainee. He had a BA in international relations from the University of Texas, had worked for the Peace Corps in Colombia, and for the Agency for International Development in Peru. Howard was fired by the CIA in May 1983 after he failed four polygraphs that had turned up petty theft and drug abuse.

On February 5, 1984, authorities in New Mexico arrested Howard after he fired a .44 caliber Magnum revolver during a drunken brawl. He received five years of probation on charges of illegal gun possession and aggravated assault. He had been working as an economic analyst with the New Mexico state legislature.

In September 1984, he met with KGB officers in Vienna, Austria. He was paid for classified information that led to the expulsion of five U.S. diplomats from Moscow.

On September 24, 1984, a former CIA supervisor and psychologist interviewed Howard at his home. He told them that in October 1983, he had paced in front of the Soviet Consulate in Washington, D.C., wondering whether he should offer his services to the Soviets.

On August 1, 1985, KGB defector Vitaly Yurchenko identified him and NSA officer Ronald Pelton as moles who sold classified information to the KGB. On August 3, 1985, the CIA informed the FBI that a Soviet agent identified in traffic as ROBERT was Edward Lee Howard. The Bureau began surveillance of Howard, but within a month, Howard spotted the surveillance and apparently began making plans to flee.

On September 19, 1985, FBI agents confronted Howard with evidence that he had been spying for the USSR, attributing the information to Oleg Gordievsky, rather than the real source, Vitaly Yurchenko. Howard refused a polygraph and denied the charges. The next day, he told the FBI that he would get a criminal attorney and would meet with them the next Monday. Instead, he had his wife drive him on a countersurveillance route, use a "jack in the box" popup that looked like a passenger remained in the car while he jumped out, and vanished.

On May 7, 1986, Erik Sites, a U.S. Embassy-Moscow employee, was arrested, accused of espionage, and expelled from the USSR. The case was attributed to information provided by Howard.

After his defection, he attempted to resettle in Hungary and Sweden, but both expelled him.

In July 2002, a Russian news service announced the death of Howard, 50, from a broken neck from a fall. Howard had been drinking heavily since defecting to the Soviet Union in 1985.

CIA counterintelligence officers attributed the exposure of CIA Soviet asset Adolf Tolkachev to Howard, who would have run him during his abortive Moscow posting. In September 1985, the Soviet media announced that Tolkachev, an electronics engineer at the Moscow Aviation Institute, had been executed for spying.

September 12, 1986: The U.S. and USSR swapped prisoners. Gennadiy F. Zakharov, a Soviet employed by the UN and arrested for espionage in New York, and U.S. journalist Nicholas Daniloff, who had been arrested for espionage in Moscow, were freed to their Ambassadors. The FBI had arrested Zakharov on August 30, 1986, for conspiracy to commit espionage by recruiting an agent on a U.S. campus using his cover as an international civil servant. The agent was under FBI control, working for a defense contractor. The Soviets retaliated on September 2, 1986, by picking up Danilov on charges that his Soviet contact, Misha, had given him classified information. The U.S. had earlier announced that the Russian, Byelorussian, and Ukrainian UN missions should be downsized by 105 individuals in four increments: 25 on October 1, 1986; 25 in April 1987; 25 in October 1987; and 30 in April 1988. Soviet UN Ambassador Belogonov refused to comply. Daniloff was released without charge on September 23. As part of the resolution of the case, the Russians released dissident Yuri Orlov to the West, and Zakharov flew back to Moscow after pleading *nolo contendere*.

October 27, 1986: Former Air Force Sergeant Allen John Davies, who was working as a lab technician at a Silicon Valley defense contractor at the time of his arrest, was charged with trying to pass classified information to Soviet agents. Authorities believe his first contact was on September 22, 1986. He had been on active duty for a decade for the U.S. Air Force as an avionic sensor system technician, but was separated in 1984 for poor job performance. He was spotted trying to contact a Soviet diplomatic facility, and was arrested after passing a drawing and giving detailed oral information relating to U.S. reconnaissance technology to an FBI undercover agent posing as a Soviet officer in Golden Gate Park in San Francisco on September 22, 1986. He provided detailed information and a hand drawing regarding U.S. reconnaissance technology. In October, he provided more classified information. He told interrogators he acted "out of revenge because of the unfair way he was treated" by the Air Force. He wanted to "embarrass the U.S. government and to interfere with the effectiveness of U.S. reconnaissance activities." The UK-born spy obtained U.S. citizenship at age 11. On May 27, 1987, he pleaded guilty to espionage and attempting to communicate classified information to an unauthorized person. On August 27, 1987, he was sentenced to five years in prison for attempting to communicate secrets to an unauthorized person.

December 2, 1986: As part of a sting by the Naval Investigative Service and Canadian intelligence, Navy Lieutenant Donna Geiger walked onto the *Akademik Boris Petrov*, a Soviet scientific research vessel, while it was docked at St. John's, Newfoundland. She said she was a "disgruntled female naval officer ... working in a world dominated by men ... assigned to an isolated duty station." She brought classified information to establish her bona fides. Two months later, she received a contact letter. The operation eventually led to the arrest of Stephen Joseph Ratkai. On February 6, 1989, he pleaded guilty to one charge of attempted espionage. On March 9, 1989, the Newfoundland Supreme Court sentenced him to two concurrent nine-year prison terms.

December 4, 1986: Navy security agents arrested retired Navy Senior Chief Radioman Michael Hahn Allen, who worked at the Cubi Point Naval Air Station in the Philippines, on suspicion of espionage. He had retired from the Navy in 1972 and was working as a civilian clerk. He admitted giving classified U.S. documents to Philippine intelligence officers after investigators showed him a video of him stuffing documents in his pockets. At the time of his arrest, he was carrying a photocopy of a Secret page. Authorities found six other classified documents at his residence. He was charged with removing and photocopying classified material from the communication center between July and December 1986. Prosecutors said he wanted to promote his local used car dealership, bar, and cockfighting ring. On August 14, 1987, he was found guilty of 10 counts of espionage, sentenced to eight years in prison, and fined $10,000. He forfeited his retirement annuity.

December 14, 1986: At a Christmas party at the U.S. Embassy in Vienna, Austria, U.S. Marine Security Guard Sergeant Clayton John Lonetree, 26, told CIA Chief of Station James Olson that he had been involved in espionage while an MSG at the U.S. Embassy in Moscow and had been given a new Soviet handler on December 12. On January 1, 1987, Lonetree was arrested after admitting to involvement with a female KGB agent, Violette Seina (or Sanni). She had been a telephone operator and translator for the U.S. Embassy in Moscow, where Lonetree began his affair with her after they met at the November 1985 Marine Ball. She introduced him in January 1986 to her "Uncle Sasha," later determined to be a KGB officer, Alexi Yefimov. Investigators determined that Lonetree had provided sensitive information to the Soviets and had allegedly given them access during evenings to the U.S. Embassy in Moscow. He later provided an Embassy/Vienna phone book and floor plans. A turnover meeting in December 1986 did not go well, and he decided to admit his spying. Soviet chiding of the treatment of his fellow Native Americans did not sway him.

While he initially was romantically involved, he also had anti-government attitudes and developed a close friendship with his Soviet handler. He was also paid $3,500.

Corporal Arnold Bracy was arrested for collaboration with Lonetree. He also was romantically involved with Soviet women. Five other Marine Guards were later detained on suspicion of espionage, lying to investigators, or improper fraternization with foreign nationals.

On January 27, 1987, the Naval Investigative Service charged Lonetree with espionage.

Lonetree was tried on 13 counts, including espionage, conspiring with Soviet agents to obtain names and photographs of U.S. intelligence officers, providing personality data on U.S. intelligence officers, and providing information concerning the layout of the U.S. Embassies in Moscow and Vienna.

On August 21, 1987, a military court convicted Lonetree of the 13 counts. He thus became the first U.S. Marine convicted of spying against the U.S. On August 24, 1987, he was sentenced to 30 years in prison, fined $5,000, loss of all pay and allowances, demoted to the rank of private, and discharged dishonorably. Espionage charges against Bracy and the other Marines were dropped after investigations determined that they had not permitted Soviet agents to enter the U.S. Embassy in Moscow.

Lonetree's sentence was reduced in May 1988 to 25 years; in 1992 to 20 years; and later to 15 years. He was freed for good behavior in February 1996 from Fort Leavenworth.

May 1987: Japan discovered a spy ring working for Soviet intelligence that had supplied secret documents on AWACS technology. The Japanese government expelled a member of the Tokyo KGB residency. Moscow in turn expelled the Japanese naval attaché and a Mitsubishi executive.

May 26, 1987: William Hedgcock Webster was sworn in as Director of Central Intelligence, a position he held until August 31, 1991. He was born in St. Louis, Missouri, on March 6, 1924. He had served as a Lieutenant in the U.S. Navy in World War II and the Korean War. He worked in private law practice, also serving as the U.S. Attorney for Missouri's Eastern District in 1960–1961. He was a Judge for the U.S. District Court for Missouri's Eastern District from 1970 to 1973, rising to become Judge of the U.S. District Court of Appeals for the 8th Circuit from 1973 to 1978. He served as Director of the Federal Bureau of Investigation from 1978 to 1987. He is the only individual to have served as the Director of both the FBI and CIA. He was the only DCI to be referred to as "Judge."

July 31, 1987: Zaire expelled three KGB Line PR officers—a First Secretary and two technical personnel—for "infiltration and disinformation activities." France had expelled the First Secretary in 1983.

August 20, 1987: The Japanese government expelled Soviet trade representative Yuri Pokrovsky after he was detained while trying to purchase documents relating to military aircraft. Several months earlier, three Soviet diplomats working in Tokyo were part of a spy ring seeking information on Japanese-based U.S. Air Force F16s and Airborne Warning and Control System aircraft.

September 28, 1987: West German authorities arrested Estonia-born U.S. citizen Svetlana Tumanova, a secretary at the U.S. Army Foreign Language Training Center in Munich. She married a Soviet émigré. Soviet intelligence recruited her in 1978 to provide information through coercion based on threats against her parents who still lived in the USSR. She was convicted of providing biographical information on personnel at the Language Center for nine years. She was sentenced to five years of probation.

December 21, 1987: FBI agents detained Hou Desheng, a PRC military attaché, and Zang Weichu, a PRC consular official, at Tony Chang's restaurant in Washington, D.C., after Hou accepted what he believed were classified NSA documents from a federal employee, who was an FBI double agent. The U.S. expelled them for "activities incompatible with their diplomatic status"—the first Chinese diplomats expelled since the opening of diplomatic relations in 1979.

January 14, 1988: Authorities arrested U.S. Army Sergeant Daniel Walter Richardson, who was stationed at the Aberdeen Proving Ground, and charged him with attempting to spy for the USSR. He planned to sell national defense information to the Soviets. He was detained at the Holiday Inn in Aberdeen, Maryland, while carrying an unclassified military manual and circuitry from the M-1 tank while trying to meet with an undercover FBI agent who posed as a Soviet representative. Although he had a Secret clearance, the Army said that he had "no ready access to classified materials" and no classified information was passed. He had been trained as an instructor, but instead his duties consisted of issuing tools to students at the Ordinance Center School at Aberdeen. Prosecutors said he was motivated by money and revenge against the armed services. The mediocre soldier had been demoted in August 1987 for repeated tardiness. Upon arrest, he was charged with espionage, failure to report contacts with a foreign government, theft, and unauthorized disposition of government property. On August 26, 1988, a military jury sentenced him to ten years, fined him $36,000, and discharged him with a bad conduct record on charges of espionage, failure to

report contacts with a foreign government, theft, and unauthorized disposition of government property.

January 22, 1988: Navy Master-at-Arms 1st Class Wilfredo Garcia was convicted at a general court-martial of espionage, conspiracy to commit espionage, larceny, conspiracy to commit larceny, sale of government property, and violations of military regulations. In late 1985, Naval Investigative Service and FBI agents were tipped off that a civilian businessman in Vallejo, California, was trying to sell classified Navy documents to representatives of a foreign government. Garcia, who was stationed at Mare Island Naval Shipyard, was the source of the documents, which dealt with submarine activities. He had sold the documents to the civilian for $800,000, with a promise of more money when they were resold to a foreign government, probably from the communist bloc. Several classified documents were taken on commercial aircraft and cached in a residence in Manila, the Philippines, for sale to a foreign power there. He was sentenced to 12 years of confinement, reduced in rank to E-1, forfeited all pay and allowances, and received a dishonorable discharge from the Navy. He had served in the Navy for 15 years.

February 9, 1988: Authorities arrested Chinese-born Douglas S. Tsou, a former translator for the FBI. He had written a letter to a Taiwan government representative naming a Chinese intelligence officer who had unsuccessfully offered his services to the FBI. Tsou was a naturalized American citizen, coming to the U.S. in 1969 after fleeing to Taiwan during the Communist takeover of China in 1949. He worked for the FBI from 1980 to 1986 in San Francisco and Houston. He was believed to have begun spying in March 1986. He was found guilty of espionage on February 9, 1988. On January

2, 1992, a federal court sentenced him to 10 years for espionage.

April 16, 1988: Authorities arrested and charged Thomas Joseph Dolce, a civilian research analyst at the Aberdeen Proving Ground, with committing espionage for the Republic of South Africa. He held a secret clearance at the U.S. Army Material Systems Analysis Activity at Aberdeen since 1973, but resigned on September 30, 1987, for "personal reasons." He said he was motivated for ideological reasons, having a long-term interest in the Republic of South Africa. He had moved to the country in 1971, but returned to the U.S. for better job prospects. Before 1971, he had been a U.S. Army clandestine warfare specialist. He had sent an unclassified paper on the topic to South African representatives. The FBI began investigating him in April 1988.

On October 11, 1988, he pleaded guilty in federal court to one count of espionage and said between 1979 and 1983, he passed scores of secret documents on 40 or more occasions by mail or in person to military attaches at the Embassy of South Africa in Washington, D.C., and at South African missions in London and Los Angeles. The documents related to Soviet military equipment. He apparently never received money from them. On April 20, 1989, he was sentenced to ten years in prison and fined $5,000.

June 11, 1988: Canadian authorities arrested Stephen Joseph Ratkai on espionage charges arrested following a double agent operation begun in 1986 by Canadian intelligence and the U.S. Naval Investigative Service after he met with U.S. Navy Lieutenant Donna Geiger to pick up classified documents she had offered to provide. He had attempted to obtain classified U.S. military documents related to the operation of the U.S. Naval installation at Argentia,

Newfoundland, where Geiger was stationed. She was working with the Naval Investigative Service and Canadian intelligence. She walked onto *Akademik Boris Petro*, a Soviet scientific research vessel, docked in the St. John's Newfoundland harbor. She claimed to be a "disgruntled female naval officer, working in a world dominated by men ... assigned to an isolated duty station." She brought classified information to establish her bona fides. Two months later, a letter indicated she would be contacted soon. In May 1987, after receiving contact instructions in a letter, she met "Michael" in the parking lot of the Hotel Newfoundland in St. John's, where she was paid and given collection tasking. A week later, she met Michael in a restaurant, where he paid her for classified information. He told her to collect on the classified Sound Underwater Surveillance System and the Argentia facility. Following several more meetings, investigators determined that Ratkai was Michael. In their final meeting on June 11, 1988, Geiger led Ratkai to a room at the Hotel Newfoundland, where surveillance equipment recorded the exchange of money for classified information. Upon leaving the room, Canadian authorities arrested him. On February 6, 1989, he pleaded guilty to a charge of spying for the USSR from May 1987 to June 1988 and to one charge of attempted espionage. On March 9, 1989, the Newfoundland Supreme Court sentenced him to two concurrent nine-year terms.

Ratkai was born in Canada, but raised in his father's native Hungary after the death of his Canadian mother. He returned to Canada as an adult to work as a short order cook, but frequently returned to Hungary.

August 23, 1988: Retired U.S. Army Sergeant First Class Clyde Lee Conrad was arrested in West Germany and charged with copying and transmitting classified NATO and U.S. documents to the Hungarian and Czechoslovak intelligence services between 1976 and 1988. Swedish authorities arrested two Hungarian-born doctors believed to have been couriers for Conrad. He was believed to have recruited a dozen U.S. Army employees to supply classified information. He provided the Hungarians with descriptions of nuclear weapons and plans for the movement of troops, tanks, and aircraft. An Army friend of Conrad's, Danny Williams, agreed to serve as a double agent to collect evidence for a prosecution. With the fall of the Berlin Wall, the next Hungarian government apologized to West Germany for Conrad's actions. West Germany's Koblenz State Appellate Court convicted and sentenced him to life in prison for treason and espionage on June 6, 1990. He died at age 50 on January 8, 1998, in a German prison.

He had a host of tipoffs, including making monetary offers to co-workers (who did not report it); unexplained wealth after severe monetary problems; possession of espionage equipment; gambling problems; and overspending on fast cars. Investigators said he was motivated by egotism, adventure, and money.

In setting up his spy ring, he paid a dozen Army employees to supply classified information, for which he received $1.2 million. His ring reportedly included Roderick James Ramsay, sentenced in August 1992 to 36 years in prison; Jeffrey Rondeau and Jeffrey Eugene Gregory, sentenced in June 1994 to 18 years each; and Kelly Therese Warren, arrested on July 10, 1987, and sentenced on February 12, 1999, to 25 years in prison. Imre Kercsik and Sandor Kercsik, two Hungary-born doctors who lived in Sweden, acted as couriers for the ring. The doctors were convicted in Sweden in 1988 of participating in illegal intelligence activity.

Conrad had been recruited for the Hungarians in 1976 by his supervisor in the 8th Infantry Division, Sergeant First Class Zoltán Szabó, a decorated Vietnam vet who spied for the Hungarians for 16 years. Szabó was convicted by Austria of espionage in 1989, and received a ten-month suspended sentence.

October 4, 1988: A military court convicted Navy Chief Petty Officer David Fleming of the theft of 16 Secret photographs and four classified training manuals. He had been arrested in October 1987 while serving as chief photographer on the submarine *La Jolla*, based at San Diego, California. Federal agents found the materials at his apartment. He claimed he had to develop photos at home because of the cramped quarters on the sub. The court convicted him on espionage statutes, although no evidence was presented that he intended to provide them to foreign powers. He was sentenced to four years of confinement and was given a bad conduct discharge. In April 1989, a Navy parole board in San Diego recommended that the remainder of his sentence be commuted. He was paroled in 1990.

November 17, 1988: Authorities in Arkansas arrested former U.S. Navy radio operator Henry Otto Spade for unauthorized possession of two top secret documents, one of which was a cryptographic key card. He stole the items while on active duty, but apparently never tried to sell them after his discharge from the Navy in April 1988. He had served on the USS *Midway* and the USS *Bristol County*. He was charged with one count of espionage, which carried a ten-year prison sentence. On March 14, 1989, he was sentenced to three months of probation.

December 21, 1988: Authorities in Savannah, Georgia, arrested U.S. Army Warrant Officer James Michael Hall, III, after he bragged to an undercover FBI agent that over 6 years he had sold top secret signals intelligence to East Germany and the Soviets.

After his daughter was born in 1982, he began experiencing financial problems, and decided to spy. He offered his services to the KGB in 1985; he was soon found by the KGB to be double-dipping with the East Germans. He dropped contact with the KGB upon returning to the U.S. He apparently received more than $300,000 for his spying from the Hauptverwaltung Aufklarung (HVA: Main Reconnaissance Administration, the Stasi's foreign intelligence wing) and other bloc services. Stasi chief Erich Mielke presented him with a medal for distinguished service. His unexplained spending included purchase of a house and two expensive vehicles and flying lessons. In his mortgage application, he listed "$30,000 in a shoebox." He was also identified by "Canna Clay" (a pseudonym), an East German academic who had served as a translator for HVA meetings with Hall. Hall also was assisted by Huseyin Yildirim, a Turkish-American cutout, who was convicted on July 20, 1989. In a sting operation, Hall agreed to meet Canna Clay in the U.S., where he would be introduced to a Soviet intelligence officer (actually an undercover FBI agent). Hall was arrested at the meeting. On March 9, 1989, he was sentenced to 40 years in prison, fined $50,000, and dishonorably discharged. After 18 years in prison, he said, "I'm a treasonous bastard, not a Cold War spy." As of 2013, he remained in prison. (Some sources list him as James William Hall.)

1989: German authorities arrested Elke Falk, who was contacted in the 1970s by KGB illegal Kurt Simon, alias Gerhard Thieme, after she had advertised in an In Search Of singles column. She was a secretary in the FRG Chancellor's office in 1974, using a miniature camera to copy documents. She later worked for the transport ministry and the economic aid ministry. The KGB paid her 20,000 marks. Her pros-

ecutors said she worked for the HVA. She was sentenced to six and a half years, but after a few months, she was swapped in an East-West exchange.

January 10, 1989: U.S. authorities arrested former Navy Chief Petty Officer Craig Dee Kunkle, a specialist in anti-submarine warfare, as he tried to sell classified information for $5,000 to FBI undercover agents claiming to be Soviet diplomats at a Williamsburg, Virginia, motel. When he had tried to contact the USSR Embassy in December 1988, the FBI and Naval Investigative Service opened a case on him. He had been a Navy anti-submarine squadron member for 12 years in the Atlantic and Pacific Fleets, holding a Secret clearance. Yet he was less than honorably discharged in 1985 for multiple incidents, including exposing himself. He was an alcohol and drug abuser, and had financial and marital problems. After leaving the Navy, he worked as a hospital security guard. On December 9, 1988, he mailed diagrams, photos, and information on anti-submarine warfare tactics to a post office box in Alexandria, Virginia, he had been led by the FBI to believe was a Soviet site. The FBI had been in contact with him on six previous occasions. He told arresting officers that he was angry with the Navy and cash-strapped, so he offered to sell classified information. He was indicted on one count of attempted espionage, to which he pleaded not guilty, and ordered held without bond. He faced life in prison and a $250,000 fine. In a plea agreement, he pleaded guilty to one count of espionage on May 4, 1989, because he did not want his family to go through a trial. He was sentenced to 12 years without parole and fined $550. He was placed on three years of probation following the jail time.

February 20, 1989: Michael Peri, 22, a U.S. Army electronic warfare signals specialist, fled to East Germany with U.S. military secrets on a laptop computer. The "good clean-cut soldier with a perfect record" had twice been nominated as Soldier of the Month. He returned to the West on March 4, 1989. He was arrested on March 16, 1989. He pleaded guilty to espionage and was convicted in 1989 of passing classified information to East Germany, and ultimately was sentenced to 25 to 30 years in a military prison. He said he had made an impulsive mistake because he was overworked and unappreciated.

March 3, 1989: A British court convicted Erwin van Haarlem, a Czechoslovakian illegal agent, of spying and sentenced him to ten years. He was arrested in 1988 in his Hertfordshire apartment while transmitting an intelligence message to Prague.

March 9, 1989: Assistant military attache Yuri N. Pakhtusov, 35, a lieutenant colonel in the Soviet army working for the Soviet Military Mission since June 1988, was ordered out of the U.S. and declared *persona non grata* for "engaging in activities incompatible with his diplomatic status." In August 1988, he approached a U.S. employee of a defense contractor to obtain information on how the U.S. government conducts cyber security in its classified systems. The American reported the pitch and agreed to be part of an FBI sting. Pakhtusov was caught with the documents he had received.

March 20, 1989: Richard J. Kerr was sworn in as Deputy Director of Central Intelligence, relinquishing the position on March 2, 1992. He was born on October 4, 1935, in Fort Smith, Arkansas. He was a CIA intelligence analyst from 1960 to 1972, then served as Deputy Director and Director of several CIA analytical offices from 1976 to 1982. He was Associate Deputy Director for Intelligence from 1982 to 1985, Deputy Director for Administration from January to April 1986, and Deputy Director for Intelligence from 1986 to 1989. He served as Acting DCI upon the end of the tenure of DCI William Hedgcock Webster on September 1, 1991, until Robert Michael Gates was sworn in as DCI on November 6, 1991.

May 5, 1989: The FBI arrested former Air Force pilot Ronald Craig Wolf in Dallas, Texas, after he sent top secret documents to an FBI undercover officer posing as a Soviet intelligence agent. He was trained by the Air Force as a Russian language voice-processing specialist with a top secret clearance, flying intelligence missions on reconnaissance aircraft in the Far East. He was discharged in 1981 because of "unsuitability for service due to financial irresponsibility." He worked as an auto salesman, but was unemployed when arrested. The FBI began to investigate him in March 1989, when it learned that he wanted to sell secrets to the Russians. Wolf met with an FBI undercover agent claiming to be "Sergei Kitin," a Soviet Embassy official. He told "Kitin" about his military background and interest in defecting. He said he wanted to trade Air Force secrets for money and to get revenge against the U.S. government. He was told to mail letters to a Maryland post office box, detailing the type of information he had. He sent "Kitin" top secret signals intelligence. In a plea deal, the government reduced his potential life sentence to ten years. On February 28, 1990, Wolf pleaded guilty to federal charges of attempting to sell classified information. In June 1990, he was sentenced to ten years without parole.

May 21, 1989: Austrian authorities arrested Zoltán Szabó, a Hungarian-born immigrant to the U.S., for conducting espionage while with the U.S. Army. On September 29, 1989, an Austrian court convicted him of espionage. He apparently began his espionage career in 1971, when he agreed to a pitch by the Hungarians. During his 20 years in the army, he earned a silver star for bravery in Vietnam combat, and had several assignments in Germany. He recruited Clyde Lee Conrad while with the Eighth Army Infantry Division's war plans staff.

July 6, 1989: Navy Airman Donald Wayne King and Navy Airman Apprentice Ronald Dean Graf, both assigned to the Naval Air Station in Belle Chasse, Louisiana, were sentenced after they pleaded guilty to conspiracy to commit espionage and theft of government property. The Naval Investigative Service arrested them at a New Orleans motel on March 3, 1989, after they gave $150,000 worth of sensitive and classified aircraft parts and technical manuals to an undercover NIS agent posing as a foreign government representative. The stolen government property and manuals dealt with the Navy's P-3 anti-submarine aircraft. In January 1989, an informant tipped the New Orleans NIS office about the duo. They were also charged with selling cocaine. King was sentenced to ten years, reduction in rank to E-1, forfeiture of all pay, and a dishonorable discharge. Graf was sentenced to five years, reduction in rank to E-1, forfeiture of all pay, and a dishonorable discharge. Graf said he was trying to pay off a $1,000 debt.

July 20, 1989: Turkish-American Huseyin Yildirim was convicted of cooperating with U.S. Army Warrant Officer James Michael Hall in the conduct of espionage for the communist bloc. He was the cutout between Hall and the East German service in passing top secret data to the East Germans and Soviets from 1982 to 1988 and obtaining money in return. Hall had told an undercover FBI agent that over 6 years he had sold top secret data to those countries. He was believed to have received more than $100,000. Yildirim had been thrown out of the Turkish military for assaulting an officer. He had volunteered his services to the East Germans in 1978. He was rebuffed, but recruited the next year when he developed better access, working as a mechanic in the U.S. Army's auto repair shop in West Berlin. After a two-day trial that heard 32 prosecution witnesses, he was sentenced to life in prison. He was released on parole in 2004 after serving 14 years.

July 25, 1989: U.S. Navy Petty Officer Third Class (E-4) Russell Paul Brown, stationed on the USS *Midway*, was arrested for espionage. He used his secret clearance to obtain classified information, which he passed to shipmate James Rodney Wilmoth, an uncleared individual who failed to sell sensitive information to the KGB in Japan. Brown pulled top secret documents out of a burn bag and gave them to Wilmoth, who was arrested on the same date. Brown was convicted of conspiracy to commit espionage and lying to Navy investigators. He was sentenced to a decade in prison and dishonorably discharged. On September 24, 1989, a court martial convicted U.S. Navy Airman recruit James Rodney Wilmoth of attempting to sell classified information to a Soviet agent in Japan and possession, use, and distribution of hashish. Wilmoth worked in food services on the aircraft carrier USS *Midway*.

October 14, 1989: The FBI arrested former Marine and Air Force communications officer Frank Arnold Nesbitt, a Memphis resident, for delivering unauthorized information to Soviet agents. In June 1989, he had left a note for his family on his weed trimmer reading "I'm gone. Don't look for me." He failed to settle in Belize, so he moved to Guatemala City to study Spanish. In August, he was on a tourist bus in Sucre, Bolivia, and met a group of Russian ballet dancers. Following his attendance that evening at the ballet, the next day he met a Soviet official traveling with the group. He then went to La Paz, where another Soviet embassy official set up his flight to Moscow. He claimed he stayed at a Moscow safehouse for 11 days, where he wrote from memory 32 pages about U.S. defense communications and was polygraphed. He was given a tour of the city, and met more KGB officers. His request for Soviet citizenship was denied because a check of his autobiography "led to suspicion of his possible connections with the criminal underworld," according to the Soviet Foreign Ministry. He returned to Guatemala, where he contacted U.S. authorities, who in turn escorted him to Washington, D.C. The FBI met him there, then arrested him 11 days later. He offered to be a double agent, claiming he did not give the KGB anything useful. The National Security Agency determined that the information he provided was classified. He had served in the military between 1963 and 1966, and 1969 and 1979.

He was indicted on November 8, 1989, for conspiring with a Soviet agent to pass sensitive national defense information to the USSR. He initially pleaded innocent to espionage and conspiracy charges, facing a life sentence and $500,000 in fines. His lawyer said he "wanted to have some excitement in his life." He agreed to a lowered sentence in a plea bargain and pleaded guilty on February 1, 1990, to delivering unauthorized information to Soviet agents. On April 27, 1990, U.S. District Court sentenced him to 10 years in a psychiatric treatment facility at a federal prison. His psychiatric evaluation had turned up severe personality disorders.

December 1, 1989: Navy Petty Officers 3rd Class Charles Edward Schoof and John Joseph Haeger were arrested on the tank landing ship USS *Fairfax County* on charges of conspiracy to commit espionage. The two operations specialists, assigned to the Norfolk area, were trained in radar communications, electronic countermeasures, and navigational plotting. Schoof was believed to be the instigator, although Haeger had the combination to the safe. Schoof phoned the Soviet Embassy in Washington, D.C., to ask for someone to come to Norfolk to take the classified material, but it was outside the 25-mile limit for Soviet travel. Schoof then trolled several bars, hoping to get a ride to the Embassy. A shipmate reported Schoof to the ship's commanding officer. On April 24, 1990, Schoof was sentenced to 25 years in prison, stripped of all rank, forfeited all pay and allowances, and dishonorably discharged. Haeger was sentenced to 19 years in prison, forfeited all pay and allowances, and dishonorably discharged.

December 21, 1989: An Italian court sentenced former U.S. Army paratrooper Tommaso Mortati on charges of passing top secret documents to Hungarian military intelligence. He had been arrested in Vincenza, Italy. The Italian-born U.S. citizen admitted disclosing secrets about U.S. and NATO bases in Italy and claimed he belonged to an espionage network, believed to be the Conrad spy ring in Bad Kreuznach, Germany. Mortati left the Army in 1987 but remained in Italy as his American wife continued to work for the U.S. Army base in Vincenza. He was recruited by Zoltán Szabó in 1981, who sent him to Hungary for a fortnight of espionage training in Budapest. Mortati told Italian investigators that he tried to bribe several Italian officers in 1984 and 1985. Investigators found in his home a hidden two-way radio used to transmit his coded reports. He had received a $500 monthly retainer from the Hungarian Intelligence Service plus a payment for every report filed. The court convicted him and sentenced him to 20 months, suspended.

Late 1980s: West German hackers offered to steal U.S. government defense and technology secrets for the KGB.

1990s

February 7, 1990: The U.S. Department of State dismissed Felix Bloch, Director of its Bureau of European and Canadian Affairs, for being a security risk. His clearances were revoked. He had served as deputy chief of the U.S. mission in the Vienna Embassy when Marine Sergeant Clayton Lonetree had confessed to espionage. Investigators believed Bloch contacted the KGB in the mid–1970s, when he was an economics officer in East Germany. In Paris, he was photographed meeting Reino Gikman, a Finn who turned out to be a Soviet illegal. Bloch received a mysterious phone warning—tapped by the FBI—saying that he and Gikman had been spotted. The Department was unable to develop sufficient evidence to prosecute him for espionage, although it was aware of his illegal contact with Soviet intelligence officers.

June 8, 1990: Authorities in Tampa, Florida, arrested former U.S. Army Sergeant Roderick James Ramsay and charged him with conspiracy to commit espionage. U.S. Army Sergeant Clyde Lee Conrad had recruited Ramsay in June 1983, when he was transferred to 8th Army Headquarters in the Federal Republic of Germany. Ramsay used a videotape machine to copy more than 45 hours of classified information, for which he received $20,000. He pleaded guilty and cooperated with investigators. He was sentenced to 36 years.

June 14, 1990: Authorities arrested Science Applications International Corporation general manager Ronald Joshua Hoffman for violations of the Arms Export Control Act and the Comprehensive Anti-Apartheid Act. He was irritated with his SAIC salary at his job in Century City, California, so he branched out to create a home business he named Plume Technology. He stole a classified software program, CONTAM, which SAIC had developed for the Air Force, which had applications for the design of spacecraft, guided missiles, and launch vehicles. In 1986, he approached Japanese firms working on Japan's space program and offered to sell them CONTAM "data, components and systems, expertise in the field, and training for employees in use of the system," according to the charges. Nissan, Mitsubishi, and two other firms paid Hoffman more than $750,000. He also approached firms in Germany, Italy, Israel, and South Africa. Late in 1989, his secretary alerted SAIC's chief counsel to his suspicious behavior. Hoffman resigned, but returned to his office that evening and stole boxes of CONTAM documents. Customs and Air Force investigators posed as South African buyers and caught him trying to sell them CONTAM modules without an export license. Hoffman was convicted in 1992. He was sentenced on April 20, 1992, to 30 months in prison and fined $250,000.

1991: John Cairncross admitted being the Fifth Man in the Soviet espionage ring that included Kim Philby, Donald Maclean, Anthony Blunt (who worked for MI-5 and was later knighted for his work in art history), and Guy Burgess. The latter two recruited him to communism during their days at Cambridge University in the 1930s, then turned him over to their KGB handler, Samuel Cahan. He joined the British Foreign Office in 1936. During World War II, he worked at the Government Code and Cipher School at Bletchley, giving the Soviets all of the code information he came across.

He told MI-6 that he would fill the back seat of a Soviet-provided car with several cases of decoded German documents. Later in World War II, he worked in the London headquarters of MI-6, passing to the Soviets the Allied plans for post-war Yugoslavia. In 1967, MI-5 confronted him with evidence of his espionage. He agreed to cooperate, and was not prosecuted. He was given a "safe" job at the UN Food and Agricultural Organization in Rome. In 1990–1991, KGB defectors Yuri Modin and Oleg Gordievsky identified him. Cairncross died on October 8, 1995.

1991: KGB agent Mikhail Bitov defected to the UK.

February 13, 1991: Authorities arrested Marine Corporal Charles Lee Francis Anzalone, 23, stationed in Yuma, Arizona, on suspicion of attempted espionage. The investigation had lasted for four months after Anzalone, working as a telephone lineman in November 1990, called the USSR Embassy in Washington on the pretext of asking about a college scholarship. He actually wanted to offer his services as a spy. An FBI agent posed as a Soviet intelligence officer when he contacted Anzalone, who gave him two technical manuals about cryptographic equipment, a security badge, and guard schedules. Anzalone, of partly Mohawk heritage, said he hated capitalism, the U.S. government, and the country's treatment of Native Americans. He said his call was only a ruse to get money from the Soviets. On May 3, 1991, he was convicted of attempted espionage, adultery with the wife of a Marine stationed in the Persian Gulf, and possession and use of marijuana. He was sentenced to 15 years in prison.

April 22, 1991: Air Force Office of Special Investigation agents detained Jeffrey M. Carney, a former intelligence specialist and Sergeant with the U.S. Air Force in Berlin.

Carney enlisted in the U.S. Air Force in December 1980. He feared that the military would discover his homosexuality. From April 1982 to April 1984, he was stationed at Berlin's Tempelhof Central Airport, working as a linguist in support of U.S. signals intelligence collection at the Electronic Security Command. He had intended to defect during an October 1983 visit to East Berlin, but the East Germans talked him into working in place to "earn" his defection. He copied classified documents which he gave to the East German Ministry for State Security (MfS). In 1984, he was transferred to Goodfellow Air Force Base in Texas, working as an instructor, but also continued to spy for the East Germans, providing top secret materials in Air Force electronic intercept plans and capabilities, and a program to disrupt Soviet air-to-ground communications. He defected in 1985 after he found his gay lover dead with a plastic bag over his head in their apartment's bathtub. He also feared being detected in his next polygraph, so he ran to the East Germans in Mexico City. The East German HVA brought him to Cuba and then East Berlin. He later translated intercepted official telephone communications of U.S. military commanders and U.S. Embassy officials in Berlin. He also provided assessments of many individuals. He eventually became a subway conductor. A former HVA handler gave his name to the media for money. After his arrest in the reunified Berlin, he pleaded guilty to charges of espionage, conspiracy, and desertion. On December 2, 1991, a general court martial in the U.S. sentenced him to 38 years in prison, forfeiture of all pay and allowances, reduction in grade to E-1, and a dishonorable discharge. His sentence was reduced to 25 years in exchange for his full cooperation with investigators. He served 11 years of his sentence before being released.

August 1991: Crowds pulled down the bronze statue of Felix Dzerzhinsky in Moscow's Lubyanka Square in front of KGB headquarters. He had founded the Cheka, the Bolsheviks' first internal security service.

October 11, 1991: The USSR State Council abolished the KGB. Its First Chief Directorate was renamed the Sluzhba Vneshney Razvedki (SVR), the foreign intelligence service of the Russian Federation. Its first director was Academician Yevgeni Maksimovich Primakov, previously Director of the Institute of World Economics and International Relations, who had been a key foreign policy advisor to Gorbachev. Primakov later became Boris Yeltsin's Foreign Minister in 1996 and Prime Minister in 1998.

November 6, 1991: Robert Michael Gates was sworn in as Director of Central Intelligence, serving until January 20, 1993. He was born on September 25, 1943, in Wichita, Kansas. He worked as an intelligence analyst in CIA's Directorate of Intelligence from 1966 to 1974, when he earned his Ph.D. from Georgetown University. From 1974 to 1979, he served on the National Security Council Staff, returning to the Agency in late 1979. He was Director of the DCI/DDCI Executive Staff from 1981 to 1982. He became Deputy Director for Intelligence in 1982, serving until 1986. In 1983, he also picked up the portfolio of Chairman of the National Intelligence Council. On April 18, 1986, he became Deputy Director of Central Intelligence, serving until March 20, 1989 (this included a stint as Acting Director of Central Intelligence from December 18, 1986, to May 26, 1987). He went to the White House in March 1989, where he served as Deputy Assistant to the President for National Security Affairs, and was promoted in August 1989 to Assistant to the President and Deputy for National Security

Affairs, serving until 1991. After his Agency career, he served as President of Texas A&M University before becoming Secretary of Defense on December 18, 2006.

December 3, 1991: Army artillery Specialist 4th class Albert T. Sombolay was sentenced by a military judge in Baumholder, Germany to confinement at hard labor for 34 years, reduction to E-1, forfeiture of all pay and allowances, and dishonorable discharge. When the Zaire-born U.S. citizen was arrested on March 29, 1991, he admitted to providing Desert Shield deployment information, military identification cards, and chemical protection equipment to Jordanian officials for money. In July 1991, he pleaded guilty to espionage and aiding the enemy. He had joined the Army in 1985 as a cannon crewman. In December 1990, while with the 8th Infantry Division in Baumholder, he contacted the Iraqi and Jordanian embassies to volunteer his services for the "Arab cause." He passed information to the Jordanian Embassy in Brussels on U.S. troop readiness and promised more information, such as videotapes of U.S. equipment and positions in Saudi Arabia. He told the Jordanians that he would be deployed to Saudi Arabia and could provide them useful information. He offered the same services to the Iraqi Embassy in Bonn, Germany, but was ignored. On December 29, 1990, Sombolay's unit was deployed to Saudi Arabia, as part of Desert Shield, unaccompanied by Sombolay. He continued to contact Germany-based Iraqi representatives and provided a Jordanian official with chemical warfare equipment, including a chemical suit, boots, gloves, and decontamination gear). U.S. Army Military Intelligence spotted him.

1992: GRU officer Stanislav Lunev defected to the West and reported on locations of KGB stay-behind weapons caches.

1992: KGB officer Sergei Illarionov defected in Italy.

April 9, 1992: KGB archivist Vasily Mitrokhin defected in Riga, Latvia, to the British Embassy, bringing with him thousands of KGB documents, later dubbed the Mitrokhin Archives. He worked with British intelligence scholar Christopher Andrew, releasing two volumes to the public: Christopher Andrew and Vasili Mitrokhin, *The Sword and the Shield: The Mitrokhin Archive and the Secret History of the KGB* (New York: Basic Books, 1999), 700 pp., and Christopher Andrew and Vasili Mitrokhin, *The World Was Going Our Way: The KGB and the Battle for the Third World, Newly Revealed Secrets from the Mitrokhin Archive* (New York: Basic Books, 2005), 677 pp.

April 9, 1992: U.S. Navy Admiral William Oliver Studeman was sworn in as Deputy Director of Central Intelligence, serving the remainder of DCI Gates's and DCI Woolsey's tenures and stepping down on July 3, 1995. He was born on January 16, 2940, in Brownsville, Texas. He was Commanding Officer of the Navy Operational Intelligence Center from 1982 to 1984, Director, Long-Range Planning Group, and Executive Director of the Advanced Technology Panel of the Chief of Naval Operations Executive Board from 1984 to 1985, Director of Naval Intelligence from 1985 to 1988, and Director of the National Security Agency from August 1988 to April 1992. He served as Acting DCI from January 21 to February 5, 1993, and January 11 to May 9, 1995.

May 22, 1992: Virginia Jean Baynes, a former CIA secretary, pleaded guilty to espionage in federal court and went on to serve a 41-month prison term. Baynes was born on August 6, 1947. She joined the Agency in 1987 as a secretary (she worked for the author for a time), and went to Manila in 1989. The FBI opened an investigation of her in April 1991. She passed two or three classified documents to former U.S. airman and now martial arts instructor Joseph Garfield Brown, whom she had met while enrolled in the karate class he taught at an embassy annex. She said he asked her for information on assassinations planned by insurgents in the Philippines. (See December 27, 1992, entry for additional information on Brown.)

July 20, 1992: KGB science and technology officer Viktor Oshchenko defected at the UK Embassy in Paris with his wife, Natalie, and 14-year-old daughter. His cover was councellor at the Russian embassy in Paris. He exposed Michael John Smith, a member of the Communist Party of Great Britain and the Young Communist League, whom he had recruited while serving at the Soviet Embassy in the UK in 1975.

In 1992, Smith faced 4 charges under the UK Official Secrets Act 1911. He was convicted of three counts of "communicating material to another for a purpose prejudicial to the safety or interests of the State." He was sentenced to 25 years in prison. His sentence was reduced to 20 years on appeal in June 1995.

October 22, 1992: U.S. Army Sergeant Jeffrey S. Rondeau, who was stationed at Bangor, Maine, was arrested in Tampa, Florida, on espionage charges. He was accused of passing Army and NATO defense secrets, including tactical nuclear weapons plans, to Hungarian and Czech intelligence from 1985 to 1988. He was believed part of the Clyde Lee Conrad spy ring, which ran out of the 8th Infantry Division, Bad Kreuznach, German, in the mid–1980s. Roderick James Ramsay assisted with the investigation into Rondeau. In 1991, the former Army sergeant in Germany was sentenced to 36 years for his involvement in the ring. Ramsay gave Rondeau a torn dollar bill as a recognition signal. Rondeau was indicted on three counts of conspiring with Conrad, Ramsay and others to "copy, steal, photograph and videotape" documents to sell to the Hungarians and Czech for an unspecified amount of money. On March 28, 1994, Rondeau pleaded guilty to espionage and was sentenced to 15 years. In June 1994, a military court sentenced Rondeau and Sergeant Jeffery Eugene Gregory, another member of the Conrad ring, to 18 years in prison.

December 27, 1992: FBI agents arrested former U.S. airman and martial arts instructor Joseph Garfield Brown at Dulles International Airport on charges of spying for the Philippine government. He had provided an official in Manila with Secret CIA documents on Iraqi terrorist activities during the Gulf War and plans by Philippine insurgent assassination squads. Undercover FBI agents lured him back to the U.S. on the promise of a job teaching self defense tactics to CIA officers. On December 28, 1992, a federal court indicted him on 3 counts of espionage. He was accused of obtaining classified documents in 1990–1991 in Manila from CIA secretary Virginia Jean Baynes, then passing them to a local government official. She had pleaded guilty to espionage in federal court on May 22, 1992, and began a 41-month prison term. She had met him at the karate class he offered at the embassy annex. She said that in 1990, he asked her to obtain the CIA information.

He enlisted in the U.S. Air Force in 1966, leaving in 1968. He stayed in the Philippines, working as a martial arts instructor for the country's Department of Tourism until his arrest.

He pleaded guilty in April 1993 to a charge of conspiring to commit espionage and was sentenced to six years in prison.

February 5, 1993: Robert James Woolsey was sworn in as Director of Central Intelligence, a position he relinquished on January 10, 1995. Woolsey was born in Tulsa, Oklahoma, on September 21, 1941. He earned a BA at Stanford University in 1963, was a Rhodes Scholar at St. John's College, Oxford University, earning a second BA in 1965 and MA in 1970, and earned his law degree from Yale University in 1968. He was a U.S. Army Captain from 1968 to 1970, serving as a Program Analyst in the Office of the Secretary of Defense. He was an advisor with the U.S. Delegation to the Strategic Arms Limitation Talks (SALT I) in Helsinki and Vienna in 1969 and 1970, later moving to the National Security Council Staff. He was General Counsel for the U.S. Senate Committee on Armed Services from 1970 to 1973. He was affiliated with the Shea Gardner law firm between stints with the government since the 1970s, making partner in 1979. He was Under Secretary of the Navy in 1977 to 1979. He was a Delegate-at-Large to the U.S.-Soviet Strategic Arms Reduction Talks (START) and Nuclear and Space Talks (NST) in Geneva from 1983 to 1986. He also was on the President's Commission on Strategic Forces from 1983 to 1984; the President's Commission on Defense Management from 1985 to 1986; and the President's Commission on Federal Ethics Law Reform in 1989. He was Ambassador and U.S. Representative at the negotiations on Conventional Armed Forces in Europe in 1989–1991. He was blamed in the press for the Aldrich Ames case, which was brought to light during his tenure.

February 5, 1993: Former Defense Intelligence Agency analyst Frederick Christopher Hamilton pleaded guilty to two counts of unlawfully communicating classified information to a foreign country when he gave classified U.S. intelligence reports on the military readiness of Peruvian security forces to Ecuadoran officials. From 1989 to 1991, he worked as a research technician in the Defense Attache's office in Lima, Peru. He apparently believed such leaks could avert a conflict between Peru and Ecuador, which had been disputing their border for 50 years. Hamilton, who had advanced degrees in Spanish and Portuguese, was working as a language instructor at a Virginia military academy at the time of his arrest. He met Ecuadoran representatives in their Lima embassy on February 13, 1991, and May 20, 1991. He shared information on U.S. intelligence operations and the identity of U.S. sources in the area, passing five Secret intelligence reports and orally summarizing four other classified reports. He received no money for his efforts. His attorney said, "What he thought he was trying to do was prevent a war. The purpose of disclosing the documents that he did was to show the country was concerned about being attacked, that the other country had neither the intent nor the ability to attack." Under the terms of his plea agreement, he could not appeal the 37-year sentence he received on April 16, 1993. In turn, the Department of Justice agreed not to prosecute him on charges of espionage.

May 3, 1993: Former State Department communications officer Steven J. Lalas, 40, was arrested in Northern Virginia on charges of passing sensitive military information to Greek officials. Lalas claimed he had been recruited by a Greek military official in 1991, worried about the welfare of his Greek relatives if he did not cooperate. U.S. authorities disagreed, saying that he began spying after his recruitment by a Greek military intelligence officer in 1977 while Lalas was with the U.S. Army. Prosecutors said he passed 700 classified documents on such topics as plans and readiness for U.S. mili-

tary strategy in the Balkans, and the U.S. assessment of Greek intentions toward the former Yugoslavia. He sold DIA documents about troop strength, political analysis, and military discussions. He also threw in FBI counterterrorism communications and the names and positions of CIA officers overseas. He had served in Belgrade, Istanbul, and Taiwan before he served at the U.S. Embassy in Athens. The Greeks reportedly paid him $20,000 for 240 documents between 1991 and 1993. The U.S. became suspicious in February 1993 when a Greek Embassy official made a statement to a State Department officer suggesting that he knew the contents of a secret U.S. Embassy/Athens cable. A video monitoring system showed Lalas stealing documents that had been marked for destruction. He failed two FBI polygraph exams. In June 1993, he pleaded guilty to one count of conspiracy to commit espionage. On September 16, 1993, he was sentenced to 14 years in federal prison without parole.

August 3, 1993: Department of State Bureau of Political Affairs secretary Geneva Jones was arrested for theft of U.S. government property; she was carrying classified documents when arrested. She held a top secret clearance while working for the Bureau of Political-Military Affairs. She was indicted on August 31, 1993, for receiving stolen property and transmitting national defense information to unauthorized persons. She said she had passed classified documents for 18 months to Dominic Ntube, a West African journalist who lived in Washington, D.C. A search of his apartment after his arrest on August 4, 1993, found thousands of classified cables and 39 Secret CIA documents, including materials regarding U.S. military operations in Iraq and Somalia. Some of the material was run in West African magazines. Her phone was tapped for several months after classified documents were found in the West African command post of Charles Taylor, who was attempting to overthrow the Liberian government. FBI agents said that in one month, they had watched her take a total of 130 documents on 16 occasions from the State Department and hide them in newspapers or a grocery bag. On August 31, Ntube and Jones were indicted for receiving stolen property and transmitting national defense information to unauthorized persons. In June 1994, she pleaded guilty to 21 counts of theft and two counts regarding unlawful communication of national defense information. U.S. District Judge Harold H. Greene sentenced her to 37 months in prison, more than what the prosecution had requested, saying, "Somebody would have to be a complete moron not to know that when you work for the State Department you can't take documents out and give them to anybody."

December 3, 1993: Yen Men Kao, a Chinese citizen living in Charlotte, North Carolina, and who owned two restaurants there, was arrested after a six-year investigation into a spy ring that sought secrets on advanced naval weapons and technology. He was charged with violating U.S. immigration laws. Chinese intelligence agents had offered him $2 million to obtain U.S. weapons technology. His ring hoped to illegally export the Navy's MK 48 Advanced Capability (ADCAP) torpedo, two F 404-400 General Electric jet engines used in the Navy's F/A-18 Hornet fighters, and fire control radar for the F-15 Eagle. Kao did not get those systems, but he did transfer embargoed oscillators used in satellites, for which he paid $24,000 to an undercover FBI agent. On December 22, 1993, an immigration judge ordered Kao's deportation to Hong Kong for overstaying his visa and

for espionage. Prosecution was declined so that counterintelligence sources and methods would not have to be made public, and to avoid offending the Chinese. He reportedly had a gambling problem and had lost the proceeds from his espionage. He feared reprisal from the PRC, and asked to be deported to Hong Kong. He left behind a naturalized citizen wife and their two children.

1994: Cuban intelligence officer José Cohen Valdés defected to the U.S. In 2002, the Institute for Cuban and Cuban-American Studies in Coral Gables, Florida, published his monograph, *El servicio de Inteligencia Castrista y la comunidad Académica.*

February 7, 1994: Former National Security Agency staffer employee and Russian agent Robert Stephen Lipka sent a letter to an FBI agent posing as a Russian intelligence officer. He had met several times with the alleged Russian to talk about Lipka's spying for the USSR from 1964 to 1967. Lipka included a magazine article about the printing of counterfeit $100 bills by Syrians and Iranians, with the annotation, "An interesting story, imagine the damage that converting this stuff to gold coins and silver coins would do???? 60-/40????" Lipka had ceased contact with the KGB in 1974.

Lipka was born in 1945 and joined the army out of high school. He was detailed by the Army to NSA headquarters in NSA's central communications room in 1964, and soon began spending beyond his salary. He volunteered to the KGB at the USSR's Washington Embassy, agreeing to provide photographs of NSA documents. He was 19 years old when he began passing information to the KGB via dead drops along the C&O Canal near the Potomac River. He provided copies of top secret reports sent by the NSA to the White House and also gave the KGB communications on U.S. troop movements around the world. The

KGB paid him between $500 and $1,000 per delivery. He received $27,000 from the KGB while a spy. James Bamford, who has written extensively on the NSA, said in the *Los Angeles Times* that Lipka may have been responsible for the loss of U.S. lives during the Vietnam War.

He left the Army and NSA in 1967 to pursue a degree and lost access to classified materials. The FBI became aware of an illegal married couple sent in 1968 to recontact him in Lancaster, Pennsylvania, but never found them.

At the end of the Cold War, Vassily Mitrokhin's purloined KGB files included Lipka's name. Following the defection of KGB officer Vitaly Yurchenko, Lipka came under suspicion in 1993. Lipka might have been the mid–1960s walk-in described in the autobiography of KGB Major General Oleg Kalugin, who said a soldier was seeking money. In December 1993, FBI undercover officers posed as KGB contacts willing to pay him owed money, saying his case had been transferred from the GRU. He told the agents about his earlier activities.

On February 23, 1996, authorities arrested Lipka at his home in Millersville, Pennsylvania. He was charged with committing espionage while working as an NSA communications clerk from 1964 to 1967. Lipka had told his first wife, Patricia, about his espionage, bringing her to drop sites in the woods. She agreed to immunity and cooperated with the Bureau. On May 23, 1997, Lipka pleaded guilty to one count of espionage. His plea agreement called for a jail term not to exceed 18 years. On September 24, 1997, Lipka, now 51, was sentenced to 18 years and fined $10,000.

February 21, 1994: The FBI arrested CIA GS-14 case officer Aldrich Hazen Ames, 52, and his wife, Colombia-born Maria del Rosario Casa Ames, on charges of providing classified information to the Soviet KGB, and its successor, the Russian SVR, over nine years. The case was the most damaging spy case involving the CIA up to that time, and generated numerous calls for changes in Agency and Intelligence Community counterintelligence procedures.

Ames joined the CIA on June 17, 1962, as a clerk-typist in the Directorate of Operations. He served tours in Istanbul and Mexico City. He married a fellow CIA officer, Nancy Segebarth, but the marriage soon failed. He met Maria Del Rosario Casa Dupuy, a Colombian cultural attaché, who was reporting to an Agency colleague on Soviet bloc diplomats during his Mexico City tour. He and Nancy separated in 1983. Rosario followed him to the U.S. and became a U.S. citizen. From 1983 to 1985, Ames led the counterintelligence branch of CIA's Soviet/Eastern Europe Division of the Directorate of Operations, directing analysis of Soviet intelligence operations. The job gave him access to U.S. penetrations of the KGB and Soviet military intelligence (GRU). During this period, Ames's financial problems blossomed from the expensive divorce and Rosario's lavish lifestyle.

As part of a joint FBI-CIA unit targeting Soviets in the U.S., he developed access to Soviets, which would help him explain meetings with them.

On April 16, 1985, he walked into the Soviet Embassy in Washington, D.C., and provided classified information to the KGB, including the names of two Soviet agents. He asked for, and soon received, $50,000. At a June 13, 1985, meeting with Sergey Chuvakhin, he provided the KGB with the "Big Dump," a collection of operational data that included information on ten CIA assets who were later executed. Ames had stuffed the data into plastic bags and carried them out of Agency headquarters. Among those identified were GRU general Dmitriy Polyakov, KGB London resident Oleg Gordievsky, and a dozen other Soviets working for the CIA and FBI, including Valeriy Martynov and Sergey Motorin, who worked for the KGB in Washington, D.C. He continued providing information to the Soviets during tours in Rome and at headquarters. His contact in Rome was Alexander Khrenkov, whom he was supposedly developing for the CIA-FBI CI unit. His information allowed the Soviets to close down 100 intelligence operations and execute U.S. and allied agents.

Several unexpected deaths or disappearances of U.S. agents overseas led to an opening of an investigation, but Ames was not yet discovered. A second investigation involving Paul Redmond, Sandy Grimes and Jeanne Vertefeuille ultimately found Ames by digging through financial records, inter alia. Their investigation was showcased by the TV series *The Assets* in 2014.

Ames was extravagant in his use of the $2.5 million he received from his Russian handlers. He paid cash for his $500,000 Arlington home, threw in $100,000 in improvements, ran up a $455,000 credit card bill, and purchased a Jaguar sedan. He claimed that the money came from his wife's wealthy Colombian family.

Rosario found his spy notes in 1992, but looked the other way as she enjoyed their expensive KGB-funded lifestyle, which included 500 pairs of shoes.

A search of his office unearthed 144 classified intelligence reports not related to his work in the Counternarcotics Center. A search of his house and trash offered spy notes and texts on his computer disks.

On April 28, 1994, Ames and his wife pleaded guilty to conspiracy to commit espionage and to evade taxes. He was sentenced to life without parole. Under the plea agreement, she was sentenced on October 21, 1994, to five years and three months in prison on the espionage charge and to evading taxes on the $2.5 million Ames received from the Russians.

Ames's father, Carleton, had earlier served in the nascent CIA. He eventually washed out, partially due to drinking problems which he passed on to three of his four children, including Aldrich.

May 1994: President Clinton issued a presidential directive establishing the National Counterintelligence Center. The chief of counterespionage at CIA was to come from the FBI.

May 10, 1995: John Deutch was sworn in as Director of Central Intelligence, a position he relinquished on December 15, 1996. He was born in Brussels, Belgium, on July 27, 1938, the only foreign-born DCI. He earned a Ph.D. in Chemistry from the Massachusetts Institute of Technology, where he was a professor. He became a U.S. citizen in 1945. His career oscillated between academe and government. He served as a systems analyst with the Department of Defense from 1961 to 1965. He taught at Princeton University as an Assistant Professor of Chemistry from 1966 to 1969. He was part of the MIT faculty in 1970–1977 and served there from 1980 to 1993, as Professor of Chemistry, Chairman of the Chemistry Department, Dean of Science, and Provost. He was the Director of Energy Research, Acting Assistant Secretary for Energy Technology, and Under Secretary at the U.S. Department of Energy in 1977–1980. He was the Under Secretary of Defense for Acquisition and Technology from 1993 to 1994. He was Deputy Secretary of Defense from 1994 to 1995. Upon leaving the Agency, he became Institute Professor of Chemistry at MIT. The Agency's Office of Security investigated his misuse of his computer, which he took home with classified information. While DCI, he instituted an "asset scrub" to ensure that human sources of intelligence were not violating human rights standards.

May 25, 1995: Authorities arrested retired Lockheed Corporation engineer John Douglas Charlton for attempting to sell secret documents he had stolen from the firm when he retired. He was charged with ten counts of espionage. On October 17, 1995, under the terms of a plea agreement, he admitted to selling two classified schematics regarding the anti-submarine program, and to knowing that the Captor Project material was highly classified. Prosecutors said "the documents would have enabled any nation to discover some of the workings of the program." Charlton began working for Lockheed in Sunnyvale, California, as a research specialist. He took early retirement in 1989, but apparently was disgruntled and took classified documents on U.S. defense projects. His Lancaster, California, residence contained illegal guns and documents on the Sea Shadow Navy stealth project and the Captor Project on mines which release anti-submarine torpedoes. He tried to sell the information to an undercover FBI agent for $100,000 five times between July and September 1993. He believed the agent was a French official. On April 8, 1996, a federal court sentenced him to two years and fined him $50,000 for his guilty plea to two counts of attempted transfer of defense information. He was to be placed on probation for five years after his release and was not eligible for parole.

July 3, 1995: George John Tenet was sworn in as Deputy Director of Central Intelligence, a role he held throughout the tenure of DCI John Deutch, who left the position on December 15, 1996. He served as Acting DCI from December 16, 1995, until he became DCI on July 11, 1997. He was born in Flushing, New York, on January 5, 1953.

After graduation from Georgetown University's School of Foreign Service, he obtained a Master's degree from Columbia University. He was senior staffer for the Senate Select Committee on Intelligence, and intelligence director on the National Security Council.

October 8, 1995: Indian businessman Aluru Prasad and naturalized U.S. citizen Kota Subrahmanyam (the latter was arrested on October 18, 1995) were arrested for passing classified defense information to the KGB in Bermuda, Portugal, Switzerland, and Cyprus, the latter in 1990. Kota Subrahmanyam was president of the Boston Group computer consulting firm in Massachusetts. They were believed to have met in Cyprus with KGB officer Vladimir Galkin, who was arrested by the U.S. at JFK Airport in October 1996 on charges of conspiracy to commit espionage. Galkin was released on November 13, 1996; he did not commit espionage on U.S. soil, but was charged for involvement in the conspiracy.

October 14, 1995: U.S. Navy Lieutenant Commander Michael Stephen Schwartz agreed to a plea bargain regarding charges of passing Department of Defense classified documents and computer diskettes to Saudi Navy officers between November 1992 and September 1994, while he was assigned to the U.S. military training mission in Riyadh. The U.S. Navy surface warfare officer had served in the Gulf War. He was charged with four counts of espionage and five counts of violating federal regulations for removing classified material to his home. The Naval Criminal Investigative Service began its case in September 1994. The documents reportedly included classified messages to foreign countries, military intelligence digests, intelligence advisories, and tactical intelligence summaries. He apparently was not paid, but was trying to be helpful to the Saudis. The plea bargain allowed him to avoid a court martial and imprisonment. He received an "other than honorable" discharge, and lost all retirement benefits and other military privileges.

1996: The U.S. Congress passed the Economic Espionage Act, under which theft or misappropriation of trade secrets became a federal offense.

1996: Karl Wienand, a West German SDP parliamentary whip during the government of Chancellor Willi Brandt and an associate of Herbert Wehner, leader of the party's parliamentary delegation, was sentenced to two and a half years in prison and fined the million marks he had received from the HVA for spying. He had been recruited in 1970 and spied for the Stasi through 1989. He was in the inner circle of Brandt, Chancellor Helmut Schmidt, and Wehner.

January 24, 1996: Robert Chaegon Kim, 56, a civilian computer technician of the Office of Naval Intelligence, wrote to naval attaché Back Don-Il, a South Korean Navy captain, offering to spy for him and another South Korean official. The FBI found a draft of the letter on Kim's workplace computer. He was arrested on September 24, 1996. He was charged with supplying classified information to an employee of the office of the South Korean military attaché. On May 7, 1997, under a plea agreement, Kim pleaded guilty to one count of espionage. He was sentenced to nine years.

Kim was born in Seoul, Republic of Korea. His family emigrated to the U.S. in the mid–1960s, and he obtained U.S. citizenship in 1974. In 1978, he worked for the Maritime Systems Directorate of the Office of Naval Intelligence.

On October 4, 1999, the U.S. Supreme court unanimously rejected without comment Kim's appeal. He claimed in his appeal that his civil rights had been violated and

that he had received a tougher sentence because he was a naturalized, rather than native-born, U.S. citizen.

January 24, 1996: Polish Prime Minister Jozef Oleksy resigned after a military prosecutor began an investigation of claims that Oleksy had passed information to the KGB from the 1980s until 1995. Oleksy said he had social contact with two senior KGB members, but said he had not spied.

February 5, 1996: The Russian Federal Security Service arrested retired Russian Navy Captain Alexander Nikitin on espionage charges. He was a consultant for a Norwegian environmental group, studying the hazardous waste emanating from Russian nuclear submarines. The Russians claimed he had given the group classified information.

April 3, 1996: Authorities in Orlando, Florida, arrested Navy Petty Officer Kurt G. Lessenthien and charged him with attempted espionage. He had offered information about nuclear submarine technology to a Russian government official. After he phoned the Russian, he was contacted by undercover FBI and Naval Criminal Investigative Service officers posing as Russians. Lessenthien, an instructor at the Navy Nuclear Power School in Orlando, Florida, asked for thousands of dollars in exchange for Top secret information about the movement of U.S. submarines. He had run up nearly $25,000 in credit card debt, chasing a woman he'd hoped to marry. A Navy psychiatrist said his personality flaws drove him to ruin his military record. A prosecutor said Lessenthien spied for excitement and money and had squirreled away classified materials since 1991. On October 18, 1996, a military court sentenced him to life in prison on espionage charges, but allowed him to serve 27 years under a plea agreement. He was dishonorably discharged and ordered to forfeit all pay and benefits.

August 7, 1996: Former Pentagon civilian employee Phillip Tyler Seldon pleaded guilty to passing classified materials to a Salvadoran Air Force officer while on active duty as a U.S. Army officer in El Salvador. After he left the Army, he took a civilian DOD job. Between November 1992 and July 1993, Seldon gave the Salvadoran three packets of documents, none of which was Top Secret. He said the duo met while he was an intelligence advisor, and thought the Salvadoran had the proper clearances. He mentioned this during a CIA polygraph during his applicant processing. On November 8, 1996, a U.S. District Court sentenced him to two years in prison.

August 21, 1996: Army PFC Eric O. Jenott, 20, was charged with espionage, damaging military property, larceny, and unauthorized access to government computer systems. He worked as a communication switch operator at the 35th Signal Brigade at Fort Bragg, North Carolina, since June 26, 1996. He was accused of providing a classified system password to a Chinese national located at Oak Ridge, Tennessee. Jenott claimed that the password was not Secret, and charges related to his penetration of defense computer systems stemmed from his attempt to be helpful when he discovered a weakness in an encoded Army computer system. He nonetheless revealed that he had hacked into Navy, Air Force, and the Defense Secretary's systems before he joined the Army in 1994. On January 3, 1997, a court martial found him not guilty of espionage, but guilty of lesser offenses in his original charge. He was sentenced to three years in prison, less the six months already served awaiting trial.

November 16, 1996: Authorities at Dulles International Airport arrested CIA GS-15 operations officer Harold J. Nicholson prior to his scheduled departure for Switzerland.

He marked his 45th birthday the next day. He was the most senior CIA officer to be arrested for espionage. He was carrying several rolls of film of Top Secret documents. He was charged with passing biographic information on hundreds of CIA case officers trained between 1994 and 1996, and counterintelligence information including the summary of interviews with Aldrich Ames, in return for $300,000.

He joined the Agency on January 26, 1982. He served as an operations officer in Manila, Bangkok, Tokyo, and Bucharest. He began spying for the Russians in June 1994 while serving as Deputy Chief of Station in Kuala Kumpur, Malaysia. In late 1995, he failed a series of polygraph examinations. Investigators found him to be an extravagant spender with unusual foreign travel patterns which were followed by large bank deposits. Nicholson was in the middle of a messy divorce and child custody fight. He claimed he began spying to pay his bills and get money for his three children, volunteering to spy for Russian SVR officer Yuri Vlasov in exchange for $25,000. He soon made it more than a one-time episode, accepting tasking on Chechnya, searching CIA databases and asking colleagues for information on a topic not within his account back at CIA headquarters.

Surveillance spotted him getting into a car with Russian diplomatic plates during a visit to Singapore in July 1996. Investigators followed his money trail—he made large bank deposits after overseas trips which netted him $180,000.

On November 21, 1996, he was indicted on one count of conspiracy to commit espionage for the Soviet Union. He pleaded innocent to espionage charges on December 20, 1996. He reversed himself on March 3, 1997, pleading guilty under a plea agreement in which he admitted to having been a Russian spy. On June 6, 1997, a federal judge sentenced him to 23 years and seven months in prison, reduced because of his cooperation with investigators. He was sent to the federal prison in Sheridan, Oregon. A decade later, he faced becoming the first U.S. intelligence officer convicted twice of betraying his country.

On January 29, 2009, Nicholson, now 59, and his son, Nathaniel Nicholson, 26, a U.S. Army veteran, pleaded not guilty to charges of conspiracy, money laundering and acting as a foreign agent in which Oregon U.S. Attorney Karin Immergut deemed "a sinister and continuing scheme." Nathaniel had been indicted on January 27, 2009. The father had asked his son, via personal meetings, phone calls, and letters, to travel around the world to collect cash from the Russians as a "pension" for his earlier spying. Nathaniel reportedly met with Russians in San Francisco, Mexico City, Lima, and Cyprus (the latter on December 10, 2008). Nathaniel reportedly obtained $47,000 between June 2006 and December 2007, giving the money to siblings and grandparents. Prosecutors said Harold had tried to recruit inmates and their relatives and associates to contact the Russians. An inmate tipped authorities to the scheme. On April 9, 2009, U.S. District Judge Anna J. Brown granted Nathaniel's motion for pre-trial release. He agreed to testify against his father, and was sentenced to five years of probation. She also ordered him to volunteer 100 hours of service to military veterans and to obtain advance approval for any contact with his father. Nathan had been an Army Ranger, but was injured in a parachuting accident at Fort Bragg and was released with an honorable discharge. On November 8, 2010, Harold Nicholson pleaded guilty to conspiracy to act as an agent of a foreign government and laundering money from inside the federal prison in Sheridan, Oregon. Harold's guilty plea netted him 8 more years

in prison, but ensured that Nathan would not need to testify against his father.

December 18, 1996: Edwin Earl Pitts, 43, who had joined the FBI on September 18, 1983, was charged in Alexandria, Virginia, with attempted espionage, conspiracy to commit espionage, and other counts. He had worked in counterintelligence in the FBI New York Field Office in the 1980s. Financial pressures from the high cost of living in New York led him to volunteer to the KGB in 1987. Pitts allegedly spied for the USSR and Russia from 1987 to 1992, for which he was paid more than $224,000. He lost access when he was assigned to the FBI's Legal Division in Washington. However, the FBI ran a sting operation, featuring a supposed recontact by the KGB, which had new tasking. He passed more classified information until the Bureau had enough evidence for a case, arresting him in December 1996. The evidence against him included a computer disk that contained a letter he wrote to the KGB in February 1990. He pleaded guilty to two counts of espionage on April 30, 1997. He was sentenced to 27 years in prison on June 23, 1997. He told FBI investigators that he suspected that fellow FBI agent Robert P. Hanssen was also spying.

February 24, 1997: An undercover FBI agent, posing as a South African intelligence officer, received a letter from Theresa Marie Squillacote, 39, who said that she had resigned from her position as senior staff attorney in the office of the Deputy Undersecretary of Defense for Acquisition Reform. She earlier worked for the House Armed Services Committee. Her boss had been asked by the White House if she would like to be Undersecretary of Defense. Squillacote said she was "thrilled ... in terms of your and my joint efforts (which was my primary motivation for this politicking anyway)." She went on to say that because her boss instead resigned, "while I no doubt could be of value to our efforts at DOD, in virtually any slot, if I stayed under these new conditions I could easily turn into some staff nonentity buried in the bowels of the Pentagon not of any particular strategic value.... I hope you will not be disappointed." She detailed her 15–20 years of work for East German intelligence: "My primary occupation—my career, in effect. I wanted to do political work full time, and view these anti-imperialist efforts as such." She wrote about her tradecraft, handlers, travels, training, and code names. She had written a 1995 letter to the communist Deputy Defense Minister of South Africa, offering her services. The positive replies came from the FBI, not the South African.

She was among three former University of Wisconsin student radicals who were arrested on October 4, 1997, and charged on October 6, 1998, with spying for Bloc intelligence services, the Russians, and the South Africans since the 1970s. They had met in the Communist Party chapter of the University of Wisconsin while students. After graduation from the Catholic University Law School, she served at the National Labor Relations Board, the House Armed Services Committee, and as senior attorney to the Deputy Undersecretary of Defense for Acquisition Reform. Kurt Alan Stand, 42, a regional representative of the International Union of Food, Agricultural, Hotel, Restaurant, Catering, Tobacco and Allied Workers Association, recruited Squillacote about the time he married her in 1980. Stand was recruited in his teens by his father, an East German intelligence officer who emigrated to New York and who introduced his son to Lothar Ziemer, an officer of the East German Ministry of State Security HVA foreign intelligence service. Stand and Squillicote named their two chil-

dren Rosa and Karl after German revolutionaries Rosa Luxemburg and Karl Liebknecht. Also in the ring was James Michael Clark, 49, a private investigator from Falls Church, Virginia, who had worked for a defense contractor at the Rocky Mountain Arsenal in Boulder, Colorado, and who had access to classified information on chemical warfare. The HVA trained the trio in espionage, secret writing, photography, and radio communications. They used fake UK passports for travel to East Germany.

Squillacote gave the FBI false flag agent four secret DOD documents in October 1996.

Clark admitted in court on October 16, 1998, that he had passed 24 classified documents to East Germany. The documents covered chemical warfare defense, analyses of Soviet leadership, nuclear doctrine, and the Warsaw Pact.

Clark was convicted on June 3, 1998, on a charge of conspiracy to commit espionage. He was sentenced on December 4, 1998, to 12 years and seven months in prison. He had received a reduced sentence for having provided evidence on his fellow conspirators.

Squillacote and Stand were convicted on October 23, 1998, of spying for the Soviet bloc. HVA documents naming them as agents sealed their fate. On January 20, 1999, Squillacote was sentenced to 21 years and ten months; Stand received 17 years and six months. On April 16, 2001, the U.S. Supreme Court rejected their appeal.

July 11, 1997: George John Tenet was sworn in as Director of Central Intelligence, a position he held for seven years, stepping down on July 11, 2004. He was Legislative Assistant, rising to Legislative Director, for Senator John Heinz from 1982 to 1985. He was a staff member of the Senate Select Committee on Intelligence from 1985 to 1988, serving as its Staff Director from 1988 to 1993. He was a member of President-elect William Jefferson Clinton's national security transition team from 1992 to 1993. From 1993 to 1995, he served as Special Assistant to the President and Senior Director for Intelligence Programs at the National Security Council. He became Deputy Director of Central Intelligence on July 3, 1995. After leaving the Agency, he wrote his memoirs, taught at Georgetown University (his alma mater) and was on the Board of QnetiQ, a consulting firm. Tenet oversaw the Agency's role in the Global War on Terrorism.

October 31, 1997: U.S. Air Force General John Alexander Gordon was sworn in as Deputy Director of Central Intelligence, a position he held until June 29, 2000. He was born on August 22, 1946, in Jefferson City, Missouri. He earned a BS in physics from the University of Missouri in 1968, an MS in physics from the Naval Postgraduate School in Monterey in 1970, and an MA in business administration from New Mexico Highlands University. He entered the Air Force in 1968 via the Reserve Officer Training Corps. He was a long range planner for the Strategic Air Command. He later served at the U.S. State Department's Bureau of Politico-Military Affairs. He commanded the 90th Strategic Missile Wing, which controlled the Peacekeeper ICBM. He served on the National Security Council, the Secretary of Defense's staff, and as Director of Operations for Air Force Space Command. He was Associate Director of Central Intelligence for Military Support. He retired from the Air Force on August 1, 2000. He became the first Administrator of the National Nuclear Security Administration, and Under Secretary of Energy. He next became Deputy National Security Advisor for Combating Terrorism, and Homeland Security Advisor in the White House. In post-government life, he served on corporate boards.

December 7, 1997: Under terms of a plea bargain, Dr. Peter H. Lee admitted to passing classified defense secrets to China in 1985 while he was a research physicist at Los Alamos National Laboratory (He later worked at Livermore.). The naturalized U.S. citizen was born in Taiwan. He had conducted classified research on laser stimulation of nuclear detonations for the Department of Energy. He also admitted to lying to a government regarding his 1997 trip to the PRC to lecture on his work for TRW, Inc., denying that he had given technical information to the Chinese. TRW fired him on the day of his plea. The U.S. government said he had been compensated by the PRC via travel and hotel expenses. On March 26, 1998, Federal District Judge Terry L. Hatter sentenced Lee to one year in a community corrections facility, three years of probation, and 3,000 hours of community service, and fined $20,000.

January 24, 1998: Cuban illegal officer Gerardo Hernandez, alias Giro, re-entered the U.S. at Memphis, Tennessee, under the alias Manuel Viramontez. Hernandez and other Cuban "Wasp" network members provided Cuba with information on U.S. military installations, government functions, and private political activity. The FBI soon wrapped up the group.

On June 8, 2001, a federal jury in Miami convicted five Cuban agents of espionage against the U.S. Ringleader Gerardo Hernandez was found guilty of contributing to the death of four fliers from the Brothers to the Rescue exile group who were shot down in 1996 in international airspace by Cuban MiGs; he had tipped Havana to the flights.

In 2011, Wasp member Rene Gonzalez

finished his sentence. He returned to Cuba in 2014 after serving part of a judge-imposed period of supervised release and renouncing his U.S. citizenship.

On February 28, 2014, *AP* reported that Fernando Gonzalez, 50, another member of the "Cuban Five," returned to a hero's welcome in Havana, a day after finishing 15 years in a U.S. prison on espionage-related charges. Gonzalez and four others were arrested in 1998 and convicted in 2001 in Miami for conspiracy and failure to register as foreign agents in the U.S. Prosecutors said they tried to infiltrate military bases and spy on anti–Castro Cuban exile groups. Fernando Gonzalez was sentenced to 19 years, but reduced on appeal, as were the sentences of two others.

Antonio Guerrero was scheduled to be released in September 2017.

CNN reported on December 17, 2014, that President Barack Obama sent three members of the Cuban 5 Wasp Network of intelligence agents convicted in 2001 in exchange for an unnamed U.S. intelligence source (soon identified by *AP* as Cuban Directorate of Intelligence cryptologist Rolando Sarraff Trujillo, now 51) held for 20 years and U.S. contractor Alan Gross, who had been held since 2009. The freed Cubans included Gerardo Hernandez, who was serving two life sentences; Luis Medina, aka Ramon Labanino; and Antonio Guerrero. They had a few years left on their sentences. Fellow Cuban 5 members Rene Gonzalez and Fernando Gonzalez had been released earlier after serving most of their 15-year sentences. The same day, President Obama announced that the countries would begin normalization of relations and open embassies.

April 3, 1998: Douglas F. Groat, a former CIA officer, was arrested and charged with four counts of espionage and extortion for passing sensitive intelligence information to two foreign governments regarding the targeting and compromise of their cryptographic systems in March and April 1997 and attempting to extort over $500,000 from the CIA in return for not disclosing additional secrets. Groat had been placed on a three-year paid administrative leave in the spring of 1993 after the Agency determined that he posed a security risk regarding a discipline/job performance issue. His ex-wife said he had refused to take a polygraph exam. He initially tried to extort money from the Agency in May 1996 and was fired in October 1996, following a 16-year career in cryptography. He pleaded guilty to one count of attempted extortion on July 27, 1998, and was sentenced on September 27, 1998, to five years in prison, followed by three years of probation.

May 1, 1998: Donald Charles Lieber, a clerk at the U.S. Department of State's South Africa desk, pleaded guilty to a violation of Title 18, U.S. Code 641, Theft of Government Property (classified documents). The FBI and Department of State's Bureau of Diplomatic Security determined that from June 1990 to March 1993, he had removed numerous classified documents from State's headquarters. Lieber said he had given the documents to an intelligence officer working at the African National Congress (ANC) mission to the United Nations in New York City. He said he was recruited while a college student in New York in 1986 and was trained by the ANC in intelligence operations in Zambia for three months in 1988. On July 30, 1998, he was found guilty and sentenced to ten months in prison, followed by three years of probation. Because the ANC was not yet a "foreign government," he could not be charged with a more serious violation under the Internal Security Act of 1950.

September 12, 1998: U.S. authorities arrested ten members of a Cuban spy ring collecting information on U.S. military installations and anti–Castro groups in Florida. The number of arrests in this case eventually reached 14; authorities said it was the largest Cuban spy ring uncovered in decades, involved in attempting to penetrate U.S. Southern Command, infiltrate anti–Castro exile groups and manipulate U.S. media and political organizations. In October 1998, Joseph Santos, 38, and his wife Amarylis Silverio Santos, 37, plus several other defendants, pleaded guilty to charges downgraded from espionage to acting as unregistered agents of a foreign government. On February 4, 2000, he was sentenced to years; she to three and a half years. Also arrested were Nilo Hernandez and his wife Linda, and Alejandro M. Alonso, who agreed to cooperate with federal authorities.

October 10, 1998: Authorities arrested former NSA analyst and retired U.S. Army Sergeant David Sheldon Boone, 46, at an airport hotel after he flew to the U.S. from Germany to meet his Russian intelligence contact, who was really an FBI undercover agent. A grand jury indicted him on November 5, 1998, on one count of conspiracy to commit espionage and two counts of passing two Top Secret documents to his Soviet handler. On December 20, 1998, Boone pleaded guilty to conspiracy to commit espionage for the former Soviet KGB. He admitted that from 1988 to 1991, he gave "highly classified documents" to the KGB, including a 600-page manual describing U.S. reconnaissance programs, details of U.S. targeting of tactical nuclear weapons and the U.S. military's use of signals intelligence. He had worked for the Army for 21 years, serving in Vietnam from 1971 to 1972. His career included stints at NSA headquarters and an October 1988–June

1991 posting at the U.S. Army intelligence station in Augsburg, Germany. In October 1988, the same month that he separated from his wife and children, he walked into the Soviet Embassy in Washington, D.C., and offered to spy, providing a classified document to establish his bona fides. The FBI said he was under "severe financial and personal difficulties," as his former wife had garnished his Army sergeant's pay, leaving him with only $250 a month. The Soviets gave him $300. At a second meeting, he agreed to work for the KGB in Augsburg, and was given $1,500. KGB officer "Igor" contacted him in Augsburg and met him quarterly until June 1990, when his Top Secret/SCI clearance was suspended because of "his lack of personal and professional responsibility." Boone retired from the Army as a Sergeant First Class in 1991. He was believed to have been paid $50,000–$60,000 for his espionage. He stayed in Germany, working on computer jobs. In September 1997, an FBI agent contacted Boone, claiming to be a Russian spy. After two recruitment meetings, Boone resumed spying. On December 18, 1998, under terms of a plea deal, Boone pleaded guilty to conspiracy. On February 26, 1999, he was sentenced to 24 years and four months in prison, and agreed to forfeit $52,000, including his retirement annuity, and a hand-held scanner he used to copy documents.

May 15, 1999: Authorities arrested Australian citizen Jean-Philippe Wispelaere, a former Defense Intelligence Organisation analyst, as he arrived at Washington, D.C.'s Dulles International Airport on a flight from London, where he met an undercover FBI agent. On May 17, he was charged with espionage and attempted espionage by trying to sell more than 700 classified U.S. national defense documents to the FBI agent. In the six months he had worked at ADIO, he had stolen more than 900 sensitive documents and photographs. On November 19, 1999, he was declared mentally incompetent to stand trial because of bouts of schizophrenia while in custody. On March 8, 2001, he pleaded guilty to attempted espionage. The next day, he was sentenced to 15 years.

November 5, 1999: First Class Petty Officer Daniel M. King was arrested after failing a routine polygraph. He had been assigned to the National Security Agency. The 18-year-veteran was accused of mailing a computer diskette containing classified information about U.S. submarine operations to the Russian Embassy in Washington in 1994, when he was working in a Navy unit of the NSA. He said he was angered by personal problems, and received no payment. On March 17, 2000, the Court of Appeals for the Armed Forces suspended jury hearings to review allegations that the Navy had violated King's constitutional rights. On March 10, 2001, the Navy dropped the charges after the military judge questioned the evidence and doubted the validity of King's confession.

December 9, 1999: The FBI arrested Russian SVR technical intelligence officer Stanislav Borisovich Gusev, 54, while he was loitering outside the State Department headquarters building, conducting a weekly remote-controlled technical operation against a sensitive 7th floor conference room. He had recorded between 50 and 100 conversations. He had been spotted in the summer of 1999, at which time State and the FBI began providing him with disinformation. He claimed diplomatic immunity. He was ordered out of the U.S. within ten days.

December 10, 1999: Los Alamos National Laboratory Chinese American nuclear scientist Wen Ho Lee, 59, was arrested on 59

counts of mishandling classified information; most of the charges were under the Atomic Energy Act. He was placed in solitary confinement without bail for 278 days. He faced a life sentence. He was not charged with passing to the Chinese secrets about the W-88 nuclear warhead because the FBI could not make the case.

Lee, born in Taiwan in 1939, earned a Ph.D. in engineering from Texas A&M University. He obtained U.S. citizenship in 1974. He became a specialist in hydrodynamics at the Argonne National Laboratory and later moved to Los Alamos. FBI phone taps in December 1982 indicated that he had contacted Guo Bao Min, fellow Chinese American scientist who had been fired from Lawrence Livermore National Laboratory after he came under FBI suspicion of providing nuclear weapons information to the Chinese (the Department of Justice declined prosecution in the Tiger Trap case). He initially denied the contact when confronted by the FBI, but later said he had shared Los Alamos materials subject to export controls with Taiwanese scientists.

During a visit to China in 1988, Lee was visited in his hotel room by Hu Side, head of Chinese nuclear physics, who peppered him with questions about nuclear bomb detonation math formulas.

Beginning in 1988, Lee copied codes and files from his classified computer onto his unclassified computer. In 1993, the downloading was flagged by the Network Anomaly Detection and Intrusion Reporting system, but otherwise unreported.

The FBI in August 1997 intended to request FISA surveillance, but was turned down by the Department of Justice.

Lee passed a polygraph in 1998, but admitted the Side meeting in 1988. He was moved to a less sensitive job, but not before returning to his classified computer and deleting downloaded files.

On March 6, 1999, the FBI conducted a hostile interrogation, but he denied conducting espionage. Los Alamos fired him on March 8, 1999, for not reporting his foreign contacts, not safeguarding secrets, and deceiving lab security officials.

On September 13, 2000, Lee accepted a plea bargain from the federal government. He pleaded guilty to a felony count of mishandling classified information and agreed to cooperate with the FBI. Lee was released on time served in the Sante Fe jail after the government's case against him regarding Chinese acquisition of the W-88 Trident D-5 nuclear warhead trigger could not be proven. He was not charged with espionage.

Lee later sued the U.S. government and five news organization for violating his privacy during the investigation. In June 2006, the U.S. government and the media organizations agreed to a $1.6 million settlement.

December 31, 1999: Former KGB officer Vladimir Putin was appointed acting president of Russia. He was later elected, twice. He had headed the FSB.

2000s

February 17, 2000: In a sting codenamed Operation False Blue, the FBI arrested Cuban-born Mariano M. Faget, 54, an Immigration and Naturalization Service official in Miami, on espionage charges. On February 19, 2000, the State Department ordered the expulsion of Jose Imperatori, a second secretary at the Cuban Interests Section in Washington, D.C., who was linked to Faget. Cuba refused to allow his expulsion, but on February 26, 2000, the FBI took him into custody and put him on a Bureau plane to Montreal. Canada ordered his expulsion on February 28, 2000; Imperatori left on March 2. Faget pleaded not guilty on March 6. On May 29, 2000, Faget was convicted on four counts of disclosing classified information, converting it for his own gain, lying to the FBI and failing to disclose foreign-business contacts on his security clearance application. The 34-year veteran of federal service was sentenced to 5 years on June 29, 2001. He also lost his federal pension.

April 8, 2000: Federal prosecutors filed espionage charges against Timothy Steven Smith, 37, a civilian Department of Defense employee assigned as an ordinary seaman on the USNS *Kailua*, an ammunition ship moored at the Puget Sound Naval Shipyard in Bremerton, Washington. They said that on April 1, he tried to steal classified computer disks and documents from an officer's cabin in an attempt to get revenge on shipmates who mistreated him. One of the five classified documents he stole detailed the transfer of ammunition and the handling of torpedoes on U.S. Navy ships. He said he wanted to steal "valuable, classified materials" and sell them via the Internet to terrorist groups.

June 14, 2000: The FBI arrested retired Army Reserve Colonel George Trofimoff, 74, in Tampa, Florida. He was charged with conducting espionage by giving the USSR documents, photographs, negatives, and other data related to U.S. national defense. Trofimoff was born in Germany in 1927, the child of Russian emigrees, and obtained U.S. citizenship in 1951. He enlisted in the U.S. Army, from which he was honorably discharged in 1953 while remaining in the Army Reserves. He rose to become chief of the Army section of the Nuremberg Joint Intelligence Center in Germany, a storehouse of classified information and the place where defectors and refugees were debriefed by the German, French, UK and U.S. military regarding life and military operations in East Germany. He was recruited in 1969, heavily in credit card debt. He worked there from 1969 to 1994, spiriting out of the facility 50,000 pages of classified documents, which he photographed in his home. The Soviets paid him $250,000 for the documents that provided insights on intelligence requirements, NATO order of battle, and NATO knowledge of Warsaw Pact capabilities. They also awarded him the Order of the Red Banner for "bravery and self-sacrifice in the defense of the socialist homeland."

Igor Vladimirovich Susemihl, a childhood friend who became a Russian Orthodox priest, recruited him for the KGB. Susemihl had served as the Archbishop of Vienna and Austria and temporary Archbishop of Baden and Bavaria. Trofimoff and Susemihl, who died in 1999, were arrested by the German government in 1994 on espionage charges, but were freed because the statute of limitations had expired.

With the defection of Vassili Mitrokhin, the FBI had information that led them to Trofimoff. After he retired to Florida, the FBI approached him in a sting operation in which an undercover Russian-speaking FBI agent posing as an SVR intelligence officer offered payment for past services. Secret video equipment recorded him regaling the "Russian" with stories of his past work for the KGB, and identifying photographs of KGB officers he had known. During Trofimoff's trial, former Soviet KGB General Oleg Kalugin said Trofimoff's code name was Marktiz. Trofimoff was convicted of espionage on June 26, 2001. On September 27, 2001, he was sentenced to life in prison.

July 7, 2000: Ruth Werner, who had worked for the Soviets during World War II, died in her native Berlin at age 93. The lifelong communist had provided atomic bomb secrets, and worked with Klaus Fuchs, the World War II–era Red Orchestra, and the Lucy Soviet networks in Switzerland.

She began spying when she and first husband Rudolf Hamburger, an architect and Soviet agent, went to live in Shanghai, where he worked for the UK-administered municipal council. She was approached by German communist agent Richard Sorge, the USSR's key spy in the Far East (who was later executed by the Japanese in 1944). Sorge codenamed her Sonya, and sent her for espionage and radio communications training at the Red Army's intelligence headquarters, the 4th Department, later to become the GRU. She organized Chinese Communists battling the Japanese on the Manchurian border, and served in Poland and Switzerland. In 1942, Fuchs contacted Hamburger, who put him in touch with Werner, who passed Fuchs's information to the Soviet residency in London or by radio to Moscow. Moscow broke contact in 1946. The next year, two Special Branch officers visited, but could not arrest her. She departed the UK for East Germany in 1950, the day before Fuchs's trial began.

October 11, 2000: Russian SVR colonel Sergei Olegovich Tretyakov defected to the U.S. He was born in Moscow on October 5, 1956. He was deputy chief of the Russian SVR's residency in New York. From 1995 to 2000, he ran all Russian covert operations in New York City, supervising more than 60 officers. He shared more than 5,000 SVR cables and wrote some 400 papers for various U.S. government agencies. He worked in place for the U.S. for 3 years. His grandmother was a typist for the KGB processor organization. His mother worked in the KGB's financial office. He died at age 53 from a heart attack at his home in Osprey, Florida, on June 13, 2010. He was the subject of Peter Earley's *Comrade J: The Untold Secrets of Russia's Master Spy in America After the End of the Cold War* (2007).

October 19, 2000: John E. McLaughlin was sworn in as Deputy Director of Central

Intelligence, a position he held throughout the remainder of DCI George J. Tenet's tenure. He went on to serve as DCI Porter Goss's deputy from September 24, 2004, to January 21, 2005. He was born in McKeesport, Pennsylvania June 15, 1942. He earned a BA from Wittenberg University in 1964, and an MA in international relations from the Johns Hopkins School of Advanced International Studies. He was a U.S. Army officer from 1966 to 1969, serving a tour in South East Asia from 1968 to 1969. He joined CIA in 1972, serving as an analyst on various European, Russian, and Eurasian issues. He served a rotational tour at the State Department's Bureau of European and Canadian Affairs, where he followed European relations with the Middle East, Central America, and Africa from 1984 to 1985. He was Deputy Director and later Director of the Office of European Analysis from 1985 to 1989. He was Director of Slavic and Eurasian Analysis from 1989 to 1995. He was Vice Chairman for Estimates, and Acting Chairman of the National Intelligence Council from 1995 to 1997. He was Deputy Director for Intelligence from 1997 to 2000. He later joined the faculty of Johns Hopkins University and was a frequent commentator on national security issues for national news media outlets.

2001: The National Counterintelligence Executive became the successor organization of the National Counterintelligence Center.

February 18, 2001: Authorities arrested 25-year FBI veteran Robert P. Hanssen after he had left his 22nd package containing classified material in a public park near his home in Vienna, Virginia. Hanssen was charged on 21 federal counts of committing espionage and related offenses.

Hanssen, abused by his father as a child, joined the FBI on January 12, 1976. He

began spying for the GRU in 1979 while assigned to the FBI's New York Field Office on Soviet counterespionage cases. New York City was expensive, especially for a father of six. He volunteered to the Soviets, and never revealed his name to them nor met them, trying to ensure that he could not be exposed because of moles in the KGB. He principally used mail and dead drops, which he, not the Soviets, selected. The Soviets paid in cash and diamonds during his 20 years in which he gave up the names of CIA and FBI penetrations of the Russian intelligence services. He initially betrayed GRU General Dmitriy Polyakov, but the Soviets took no actions until June 1985, after Aldrich Ames confirmed the reporting.

His wife, Bonnie, found him writing a note to the GRU. He claimed he was swindling the Soviets. She reported the activity to her priest, who persuaded Hanssen to stop and give the proceeds to charity. He returned to FBI headquarters in 1981, and cut off the Soviet connection.

In October 1985, he volunteered to the KGB, sending a note to Viktor Cherkashin, chief of KGB counterintelligence at the Washington Embassy, requesting $100,000 and exposing agents Sergey Motorin, Valeriy Martynov, and Boris Yuzhin, whom Ames had earlier exposed. Notes of praise from the KGB included one from Chairman Vladimir Kryuchkov. He used an FBI phone in 1986 to contact the KGB, and often used the same drop sites. He dropped contact in 1991 when the USSR collapsed.

In 1993, he approached a GRU officer and said he was an FBI agent who had worked with the Russians.

After checking the FBI's Automated Case System to see what the FBI was surveilling, he contacted the Russian SVR, successor to the KGB, in 1999. He went on to give the Russians 26 diskettes, 27 letters, and 22 packages of classified materials, for which he was paid $600,000 in cash and diamonds and $800,000 in an escrow account he never touched. He provided information on the FBI's double agent program, names of personnel targeted for recruitment, information on a tunnel built under the Soviet Embassy in Washington, NSA reading of Soviet satellite communications, a U.S. assessment of Soviet estimates of the U.S. nuclear capability, and continuity-of-government operations.

While friends said he was a devoted and conservative Catholic—a member of Opus Dei—who was devoted to his family, investigators also discovered bizarre sexual behavior and a relationship with stripper Priscilla Sue Galey, whom he gave a Mercedes and a trip to Hong Kong. He gave a friend clandestine videotapes of Hanssen making love to his wife, Bonnie.

He was never polygraphed, and underwent only one minor reinvestigation before coming under suspicion.

On February 5, 2001, the FBI searched Hanssen's office in FBI Headquarters, finding an 8MB Veersa Card Flash Memory Adaptor storage card that contained letters associated with the "B" operation, identifying him as KGB source B.

When arrested, he asked the agents, "What took you so long?"

On July 6, 2001, he pleaded guilty to 15 counts of espionage, attempted espionage, and conspiracy, via a plea deal arranged by defense attorney Plato Cacheris in which his wife would receive a portion of his government pension and retain the family home. He escaped the death penalty in exchange for his cooperation. On May 10, 2002, he was sentenced to life without the possibility of parole. His case was featured in the 2007 movie *Breach*.

August 23, 2001: The FBI arrested retired U.S. Air Force Master Sergeant Brian Patrick Regan as he attempted to board a flight to Frankfurt and Zurich. He had worked on signals intelligence and air defense systems during his 20-year military career. He had worked as a TRW, Inc. contractor at the National Reconnaissance Office in Chantilly, Virginia. He had access to satellite images of missile facilities and foreign launch preparations. He came under suspicion when it was discovered that Libya had classified U.S. documents and Libyan officials had received encrypted messages suggesting they contact an e-mail address for Steve Jacobs. The FBI found that the e-mail account was accessed from Washington, D.C., area public libraries and spotted Regan at a terminal. He was carrying coordinates of missile sites of two foreign countries and the locations of Chinese and Iraqi Embassies in Europe. He was believed to have spied for the Libyans. On October 23, 2001, he was indicted on a single count of attempted espionage. A federal grand jury in Alexandria, Virginia, added to the charges on February 14, 2002, charging him with attempted espionage for Iraq, Libya and China, noting that he wrote a letter to Saddam Hussein offering to sell top secret defense information for $13 million. He admitted stealing 800 pages of classified documents. Investigators cracked codes found on some of the documents he was carrying at arrest, as well as in his cell, and ultimately found that he had buried more than 20,000 pages of documents, CD-ROMs, and videotapes at 19 secret caches at state parks in Maryland and Virginia. The documents contained information about U.S. satellites, early warning systems and weapons of mass destruction. On February 20, 2003, a federal jury convicted Regan of three counts of attempted espionage. On March 20, 2003, Regan accepted a life sentence in exchange for an agreement not to prosecute his wife, who authorities said might have obstructed justice to help her husband.

August 31, 2001: Authorities arrested George and Marisol Gari on charges of conspiracy to act as agents of a foreign government without proper identification or notice to the Attorney General. Prosecutors said they were members of the largest Cuban spy ring ever detected, the Wasp Network (la Red Avispa), five members of whom were convicted in June 2000 of conspiring to spy on the U.S. for the Cubans. They included Fernando Gonzalez Llort, Rene Gonzalez Sehwerert, Antonio Guerrero Rodriguez, Gerardo Hernandez Nordelo, and Ramon Labanino Salazar. They were targeted with collecting information on the Southern Command in Florida, the naval base of Boca Chica in Key West, and McDill Air Force Base in Tampa. The five had been arrested by the FBI in 1998; another four escaped to Cuba. An appeals court panel later overturned the conviction, but the full court upheld the original guilty verdict.

September 11, 2001: Al Qaeda crashed four hijacked airliners into the World Trade Center, the Pentagon, and a Pennsylvania field, killing nearly 3,000 people. In reaction, the Bush Administration in November 2004 announced the creation of the Director of National Intelligence structure to oversee the Intelligence Community.

September 21, 2001: The FBI arrested Ana Belen Montes, 44, a senior Defense Intelligence Agency analyst, at her DIA office on Bolling Air Force Base for conspiracy to commit espionage by delivering highly classified U.S. national defense information to Cuba's Direccion General de Inteligencia (DGI).

She was born on February 28, 1957, on a military base in Germany to parents of Puerto Rican background. Her father was a U.S. Army psychiatrist; her mother was a federal investigator; her brother and sister worked for the FBI. Her sister worked in the FBI Miami Field Office, where she was part of the investigation of the Wasp Network of DGI agents. Ana's mother divorced the father because he abused the children.

Ana had worked for DIA since 1985, and had worked on Cuba since 1992. She was a member of the 1993 Director of Central Intelligence Exceptional Analyst Program, a prestigious sabbatical granted to only a handful of analysts in the Intelligence Community each year. As part of the EAP, she traveled to Cuba in 1993 to study the Cuban military. She lived alone in a co-op in Washington, D.C., and had few social contacts. She graduated from the University of Virginia in 1979 and Johns Hopkins's School of Advanced International Studies' MA program in 1988, majoring in foreign affairs and international studies, with concentrations on the Caribbean.

She apparently started working for the Cubans in 1984 while a staffer at the Department of Justice. During the next 16 years, she communicated with Cuban case officers by passing diskettes, using pagers and pay phones, and employing high frequency shortwave broadcasts with encrypted messages. She worked for ideological motives. During those years, she provided the names of intelligence officers, information on a sensitive collection project, and defense contingency planning regarding Cuba.

The FBI searched her apartment in May 2001, finding clandestine communications procedures on her laptop. FBI surveillance spotted her using surveillance detection routes before using pay phones.

In March 2002, Montes pleaded guilty to one count of conspiracy to commit espionage. On October 16, 2002, she was sentenced to 25 years in prison with another five years of supervised release. She told the court she acted because of her opposition to U.S. policy on Cuba and admitted that she had worked for Cuban intelligence for 16 years. She agreed to cooperate with investigators.

Montes claimed former State Department employee Marta Rita Velázquez helped recruit her by introducing her to Cuban intelligence in New York, went with her to a clandestine trip to Cuba for operational training, and helped her obtain her DIA job. She resigned from USAID in June 2002 after Montes's arrest but months before Montes pleaded guilty. On April 25, 2013, the U.S. Department of Justice unsealed a grand jury indictment in 2004 against Velázquez, 55, for spying for Cuba. She was living in Stockholm, Sweden, which does not extradite people accused of espionage.

February 4, 2003: John Joungwoong Yai, 59, a South Korean-born naturalized U.S. citizen living in Santa Monica, California, was arrested on charges of spying for the North Koreans since 1995. The FBI said that the North Koreans had passed him $100 bills in return for information he collected from newspapers and other public sources. He was charged with one count of failing to register as a foreign agent and two counts related to his bringing $18,179 in cash into the U.S. after a trip to Vienna, Austria and failing to declare the money on a customs form. His wife, Susan Youngja Yai, who worked at a Los Angeles bank, was charged, but not arrested, for failing to declare the cash. He eventually was sentenced to two years after pleading guilty to lesser felony charges regarding the cash non-declaration.

April 9, 2003: Authorities arrested Los Angeles businesswoman Katrina M. Leung on charges of obtaining a classified national security document for the Chinese govern-

ment. The FBI said she had a 20-year affair with James J. "J.J." Smith, 59, a former FBI senior China counterintelligence agent who believed he had recruited her as an informer, code named Parlor Maid, in 1982 against the Chinese. She had been working in a firm suspected of illegally sending tech insights to the Chinese. Smith had worked for the Bureau for 30 years before retiring in 2000. He was arrested and charged with negligence. The next day, William Cleveland, Jr., resigned as head of security at Lawrence Livermore National Laboratory after his security clearances were revoked and authorities began investigating his nine years in the position since he retired from the FBI in 1993. Court papers indicated that Cleveland admitted having a sexual relationship with Leung from 1988 to 1993, and that the affair resumed in 1997 and 1999, even after he found that she had unauthorized contact in 1991 with Chinese intelligence. Prosecutors said she sometimes copied classified documents Cleveland had left unattended at her house.

Leung, born Chan Man Ying in Guangdong Province on May 1, 1954, moved to Hong Kong and later the U.S. (in 1970). She graduated from Cornell in architecture and engineering in 1976, having joined pro–China organizations. She later earned a University of Chicago MBA. In 1980, she began work in California for Sida International, which promoted trade with the Chinese. She and her husband, Kam, became members of the local political elite, serving on boards.

She came to the attention of authorities several times, but was not stopped for years. When Cleveland was investigating Lawrence Livermore National Laboratory scientist Guo Bao Min, he interviewed, and soon began an affair with, her. In 1987, the FBI found that Leung had asked the Chinese Consulate in San Francisco to call her back at a phone booth. In April 1991, a woman using a code name called a Ministry of State Security officer in China to say she was discussing a visit to Beijing by Cleveland. In May 1991, Smith confronted Leung about the call. She admitted passing information to Chinese intelligence, but continued to do so. In 1992, a source told the U.S. that a Chinese double agent named "Katrina" was working for the FBI. In 2000, a second source said she was working for the MSS. The Bureau finally built a case and interviewed her in December 2002, admitting that she filched classified documents from Smith's briefcase.

On May 12, 2004, Smith pleaded guilty to falsely concealing the affair from the Bureau in return for prosecutors dropping two counts of gross negligence in handling of national security documents. As part of his plea bargain, he was released on probation for three years and fined $10,000. He was prohibited by the Department of Justice from sharing further information relating to the case with Leung or her attorneys.

Leung had been charged with unauthorized access, retention, and copying of national defense information; lying to federal investigators; and tax evasion for not reporting the $1.7 million she had received as an FBI informant. A federal judge ruled that the DOJ prohibition on Smith violated her constitutional rights and dismissed the case.

On December 16, 2005, Leung pleaded guilty to a tax violation and lying to authorities about her affair with Smith. She was given three years of probation, ordered to complete 100 hours of community service, fined $10,000 and ordered to participate in FBI debriefings for 18 months.

July 17, 2003: Walter Zapp, the inventor of the Minox camera that was used frequently in espionage operations, died in Switzerland.

September 10, 2003: Army Islamic Chaplain Captain James J. Yee, 35, also known as Youssef Yee, was taken into custody and held on suspicion of espionage and treason, although he was not immediately charged on those counts. He ultimately was charged with mishandling classified information, adultery and keeping pornography on his government computer. The Army dropped all charges on March 19, 2004. He had earlier served as the Muslim Chaplain at Guantanamo Bay.

September 23, 2003: Senior Airman Ahmad I. Halabi, a U.S. Air Force translator who worked with Al Qaeda and Taliban detainees at the Guantanamo Bay prison, was arrested on charges of spying for Syria. Military authorities said he "attempted to deliver sensitive information to Syria, including more than 180 notes from prisoners, a map of the installation, the movement of military aircraft to and from the base, intelligence documents and the names and cellblock numbers of captives at the prison in Cuba." He was eventually charged with five counts of espionage, three counts of aiding the enemy, nine counts of giving false statements to interrogators, 11 counts of failing to obey a lawful order and one count of bank fraud. The Army admitted a year later that only one of the 200 documents he was alleged to have plotted to smuggle to Syria was classified. He pleaded guilty to four lesser crimes.

September 29, 2003: Ahmed Fathy Mehalba, a civilian translator for the Titan Corporation who worked at Guantanamo Bay military base, was arrested after immigration officials at Logan Airport in Boston said they found classified materials in his possession. On January 10, 2005, Mehalba pleaded guilty to lying to government agents and removing classified documents. He was believed contemplating spying for Egypt.

January 12, 2004: Former NSA computer expert Kenneth Wayne Ford, Jr., was indicted in U.S. District Court in Greenbelt, Maryland, on charges of illegally possessing secret information relating to the national defense. His updated May 23, 2005, indictment included charges of unlawfully possessing classified national defense information and making a false statement in a submission to Lockheed Martin for a security clearance. He was convicted on those charges on December 15, 2005.

February 12, 2004: Ryan Gilbert Anderson, 26, a Specialist and tank crewman in the Washington National Guard, was arrested on five counts of attempting to provide aid and information to Al Qaeda. Anderson converted from Lutheranism to Islam while studying Middle Eastern military history at Washington State University, where he graduated with a B.A. in 2002. He served at Fort Lewis. In late 2003, as his National Guard unit was preparing to deploy to the war in Iraq, Anderson tried to contact Al Qaeda cells in the U.S. via Internet chat rooms. He was spotted by Shannen Rossmiller, a Montana city judge who monitored jihadi sites. She traced his Arab pseudonym, Amir Abdul Rashid, and tipped off the Department of Homeland Security, which notified the FBI. In January 2004, the DOJ and FBI videotaped him offering to what he thought were Al Qaeda representatives sketches of M1A1 and M1A2 tanks, a computer disk with his identifying information and photo, and information about Army weapons systems, including "the exact caliber of round needed to penetrate the windshield and kill the driver of an up-armored Humvee." A court martial convicted him on all five counts. On September 3, 2004, he was sentenced to life in prison without the possibility of parole, demotion to the rank of private, and a dishonorable discharge.

March 11, 2004: Susan Lindauer, a former Congressional aide and journalist whose father had been Alaska's Republican nominee for governor, was arrested on charges of being an unregistered agent of Iraq in a conspiracy to spy for the Iraqi Intelligence Service and engage in illegal financial transactions with the Saddam Hussein regime. Prosecutors said she had accepted $10,000 from the Iraqis. She faced 25 years in prison. She was declared incompetent to stand trial when mental health professionals determined that she suffered from delusions of grandiosity and paranoia. Judge Loretta A. Preska upheld the incompetency ruling on September 16, 2008. On January 16, 2009, the federal government dropped its case, saying that prosecution would no longer be in the interests of justice. Lindauer said that she would sue.

August 2004: Dohuk, Iraq-born U.S. citizen Sami Khoshaba Latchin was arrested on charges of making false statements to immigration officials regarding his employment as a deep cover "sleeper agent" for the Iraqi Intelligence Service and membership in Iraq's Baath Party. He moved to the U.S. in 1993, and became a naturalized U.S. citizen in 1998. In 2007, he pleaded innocent. He was convicted on April 16, 2007, and sentenced on November 26, 2007, to four years in prison.

September 15, 2004: Donald W. Keyser, former Principal Deputy Assistant Secretary of State for East Asian and Pacific Affairs, was arrested on charges of concealing a trip to Taiwan. He was suspected of improperly passing documents to Taiwanese intelligence agents. On December 12, 2005, he pleaded guilty in a plea agreement to mishandling classified documents and lying about his relationship with a Taiwanese intelligence officer. He admitted having a personal relationship between 2002 and 2004 with Isabelle Cheng, an employee of Taiwan's intelligence agency, the National Intelligence Bureau. In January 2007, he was sentenced for possessing secret documents and lying to investigators; he was to serve one year and one day in jail, and pay a fine of $25,000.

September 24, 2004: Porter Johnston Goss sworn in as the last Director of Central Intelligence. He was born on November 26, 1938, in Waterbury, Connecticut. He earned his BA from Yale University in 1960 and was in the same class as Ambassador-to-be John Negroponte, who became the first Director of National Intelligence, subsuming many of Goss's responsibilities as DCI. Goss served as a U.S. Army intelligence officer in 1960–1962, and later was an operations officer with the CIA's Directorate of Operations from 1962 to 1972. He was a small business owner, founded a newspaper, and was a member of the city council and later mayor of Sanibel, Florida, from 1974 to 1983. He was a Commissioner of the Lee County (Florida) Commission from 1983 to 1988, serving as its Chair from 1985 to 1986. He was a Member of the U.S. House of Representatives for Florida's 14th District from 1989 to 2004. He chaired the House Permanent Select Committee on Intelligence from 1997 to 2004. He co-chaired the joint Congressional inquiry into the 9/11 attacks. Upon the creation of the Director of National Intelligence in the wake of the 9/11 Commission Report, he became the first Director of the Central Intelligence Agency (DCIA), reporting to the DNI. He resigned as DCIA on April 21, 2005.

December 17, 2004: President George W. Bush signed the Intelligence Reform and Terrorism Prevention Act, which restructured the Intelligence Community, creating the positions of the Director of National Intelligence, and a separate Director of the Central Intelligence Agency.

May 1, 2005: Authorities arrested Jordanian-born Palestinian Hafiz Ahmad Ali Shaaban, 52, a truck driver, in Greenfield, Indiana, on charges of traveling to Iraq prior to the 2003 U.S. invasion and offering to sell for $3 million the names of U.S. intelligence operatives in that country to agents of Saddam Hussein's intelligence service. He also wanted Iraqi support to set up an Arabic TV station in the U.S. that would broadcast pro–Iraqi material. He also said he would organize volunteers to act as human shields in the coming war. He obtained U.S. citizenship via faked ID. Authorities suggested he had entered the U.S. in 1993. In 1972, he had lived in Moscow, marrying his first wife. While in Moscow, Russian intelligence agents trained him. News reports said he had been a Soviet-trained mining engineer and had obtained Russian citizenship. Shaaban was convicted of conspiracy against the U.S., acting as a foreign agent without notification to the U.S. Attorney General, violation of sanctions against Iraq under the International Emergency Economic Powers Act, unlawful procurement of an identification document, fraudulently acquiring U.S. naturalization, and tampering with a witness. On May 27, 2006, he was sentenced to 13 years and four months in prison and incarcerated in the maximum-security prison in Colorado, far from his second wife and son. He was stripped of his U.S. citizenship.

May 4, 2005: In a case on the legal border between leaks and espionage, Pentagon Near East and South Asia Bureau analyst Lawrence A. Franklin was arrested and charged with illegally disclosing highly classified information about possible attacks on American forces in Iraq to two employees of the American Israel Public Affairs Committee

(AIPIC), Keith Weissman and Steven J. Rosen, who were believed to have relayed the information to Israeli intelligence. He had earlier worked at the Defense Intelligence Agency before moving to the office of Under Secretary of Defense for Policy Douglas Feith. On May 24, 2005, prosecutors added a charge of possession of classified documents. On August 4, 2005, Rosen and Weissman were indicted on charges of illegally receiving and passing on classified information to foreign officials and reporters over 5 years. On October 5, 2005, Franklin pleaded guilty to 3 counts of improperly retaining and disclosing classified information. On January 20, 2006, Franklin was sentenced to 12 years and seven months in prison; the sentence had been reduced because he had cooperated in the investigation against the two former AIPIC employees.

July 2005: U.S. Navy Vice Admiral Albert M. Calland, III, was sworn in as the Deputy Director of the Central Intelligence Agency, serving until July 2006. He was born in 1952. He graduated from the U.S. Naval Academy in 1974 and earned an MS in national resource strategy from the Industrial College of the Armed Forces in 1996. He served as command officer of the Special Operations Command Center, Naval Special Warfare Command, and Associate Director of Central Intelligence for Military Support. After CIA, he was Deputy Director for Strategic Operational Planning at the National Counterterrorism Center. He retired from the Navy on July 1, 2007, later become Executive Vice President for Security and Intelligence Integration with CACI International, Inc.

October 2005: Maui resident and former Northrop Grumman scientist Noshir Sheriarji Gowadia was arrested. In November 2005, he was indicted on charges of selling

secrets about the B-2 stealth bomber to China for $110,000. He was deemed a flight risk. A grand jury added to the charges a year later, accusing the Bombay-born naturalized U.S. citizen of trying to sell more U.S. classified military information to individuals in Israel, Germany, and Switzerland. Prosecutors said at least eight foreign countries—among them China, Israel, Germany, Switzerland, and Austria—were shown documents relating to the B-2's stealth technology. He had been a lead engineer on the B-2 project. The indictment said he "spent more than two years working with China's military to design and test a radar-evading component for a new Chinese cruise missile as part of an espionage conspiracy" and that he "worked closely with a Chinese government agent and missile technicians to illegally supply the stealth-missile technology during six visits to China between 2003 and 2005." He was also charged of money laundering and making false statements. He had worked at Northrop Corporation from 1968 to 1986. On October 26, 2007, he was charged in Hawaii with providing information to China on how to make cruise missile exhausts hard to detect. He had traveled to China six times. His trial lasted four months. On August 9, 2010, Gowadia, now 66, was convicted in the U.S. District Court for the District of Hawaii on 14 of 17 charges of conspiracy, violating the arms export control act, and money laundering, by selling military secrets to China, which was trying to design a stealth cruise missile. On November 22, 2010, he was sentenced to life in prison. On January 26, 2011, the Department of Justice reported that he had been sentenced to 32 years.

October 5, 2005: Former FBI intelligence analyst and retired United States Marine Corps gunnery sergeant Leandro Aragoncillo, 45, a naturalized Filipino-American, was indicted and arrested in New Jersey for espionage and with leaking classified information to Filipino oppositionists. It was the first case of an arrest for espionage in the White House. From 1999 to 2001, he worked in the Office of the Vice President for VPOTUS Al Gore and VPOTUS Dick Cheney. He began sending classified documents to his contacts in January 2005. He was also believed to be in contact with French intelligence from 2002 to 2004. In May 2006, he pleaded guilty to four charges. On July 18, 2007, he was sentenced to ten years in prison.

October 28, 2005: Chi Mak, an engineer working for the California-based Power Paragon, a subsidiary of L-3 Communications, and his wife were arrested at their home. Chi's brother, Tai Wang Mak, was detained at Los Angeles International Airport while waiting to board a plane for the People's Republic of China while carrying computer disks containing encrypted technology related to the Navy's Quiet Electric Drive for warships and submarines. Chi and three relatives were also held for conspiracy to export articles involving Navy technology. FBI agents also arrested a Chinese Ministry of State Security intelligence official, but later released him. Tai refused to cooperate. Chi admitted passing material, but said it was all unclassified.

Chi's spy ring had operated since 1985, according to Assistant U.S. Attorney Deidre Z. Eliot. The spy ring included Rebecca Lai-wah Chiu Mak (his wife), Tai Wang Mak, Fuk-heung Li, and Tai's son Yui "Billy" Mak. The FBI said Chi Mak took computer disks from his company, where he was the lead engineer on a project involving naval warship propulsion.

Chi Mak was born in Guangzhou, China in 1940. He began his espionage career in the 1960s, when he and spouse Rebecca

moved to Hong Kong and monitored U.S. ships bound for Vietnam. The couple came to the U.S. and obtained U.S. citizenship in 1985. He joined Power Paragon, and obtained a security clearance in 1996. He initially flew to Hong Kong to hand the firm's naval secrets to his brother, Tai, who worked for Chinese military intelligence.

In 2001, Tai and his spouse, Fuk Heung, came to the U.S. as permanent resident aliens. He became a broadcast engineer for a California-based Chinese television station.

The FBI began its investigation of the network in 2004. In February 2005, the FBI found in Chi's trash a list of Chinese intelligence requirements on early warning systems, submarine propulsion, missile launching procedures, destroyer technology, and communications. They also found classified information in his e-mails and a briefcase with compact disks from his office. In October 2005, the Bureau learned of a planned trip by Tai and his wife to China, apparently to deliver information Chi had acquired on the Quiet Electric Drive silent propulsion systems for U.S. warships, for which he was lead engineer.

In June 2006, the government indicted Tai's son Yui "Billy," a UCLA student who helped him to encrypt the information. He pleaded guilty was sentenced to 11 months.

In October 2006, the government indicted all five spy family members on charges of conspiracy to export U.S. defense information.

Chi Mak was convicted by a federal grand jury in May 2007 of two counts of conspiring to smuggle sensitive material regarding U.S. Navy submarines, acting as a foreign agent without notifying the U.S. government, and making false statements to federal agents. Chi Mak, 65, was sentenced in federal court on March 24, 2008, to 24 years and six months in prison for exporting U.S. defense articles to the People's

Republic of China. U.S. District Judge Cormac Carney said he wanted to send China a message not to "send agents here to steal America's military secrets." Chi Mak was also fined $50,000. He was never charged with espionage because the data was not deemed classified, although it was marked NOFORN. Information he sent included materials on the Aegis antimissile system.

Tai Mak pleaded guilty and was sentenced to ten years.

Rebecca Lai-wah Chiu Mak pleaded guilty and was sentenced to three years.

Fuk-heung Li pleaded guilty and was given three years of probation.

May 30, 2006: U.S. Air Force General Michael Vincent Hayden was sworn in as the Director of the Central Intelligence Agency. He was born on March 17, 1945, in Pittsburgh, Pennsylvania. He entered active duty in 1969 as a distinguished graduate of the Reserve Officer Training Corps program of Duquesne University, where he earned a BA and MA. He held senior staff positions at the Pentagon, the National Security Council, and the U.S. Embassy in Sofia, Bulgaria, as well as serving as Deputy Chief of Staff for the UN Command and U.S. Forces in Korea. From May 1993 to October 1995, he was Director of the Intelligence Directorate, U.S. European Command, in Stuttgart, Germany. He was Commander of the Air Intelligence Agency and Director of the Joint Command and Control Warfare Center, both headquartered at Kelly Air Force Base, Texas, from January 1996 to September 1997. From March 1999 to April 2005, he was the Director of the National Security Agency and Chief of the Central Security Service at Fort George C. Meade, Maryland. In April 2005, he became the first Principal Deputy Director of National Intelligence under DNI John Negroponte. With the PDDNI appointment came his fourth star, making him the highest-ranking intelligence officer in the Armed Forces.

June 21, 2006: Ronald N. Montaperto, 66, a former Defense Intelligence Agency analyst, pleaded guilty in a plea agreement to one count of illegally retaining classified documents. He had passed top secret information to Chinese intelligence officials. He served as a China specialist at a U.S. Pacific Command research center until 2004. His case officers included Chinese attaches and other Chinese officers.

He had taught at Indiana University and the U.S. Army War College before joining DIA in 1981 as a China analyst. He moved to to the China Analysis Center of the National Defense University, and later was Dean of the Asia-Pacific Center for Security Studies of the U.S. Pacific Command in Hawaii. In 1982, in a DIA program, he met with Chinese military attaches. He kept quiet about maintaining contact with two attaches, Colonels Yang Qiming and Yu Zhenghe, sharing top secret information for a decade. In 1989, he applied to the CIA. An FBI investigation of his links to Chinese intelligence in 1991 was dropped for lack of evidence, even though he admitted to passing unspecified classified information orally to the Chinese.

The FBI recontacted Montaperto in 2003, offering a sham position with DIA that required a polygraph. He admitted to giving the Chinese information about Chinese military sales in the Middle East. The Bureau found classified documents in his home. He admitted to more than 60 contacts with Chinese military intelligence.

On September 9, 2006, he was sentenced to three months, after the intervention of numerous senior defense and intelligence officials.

July 24, 2006: Stephen R. Kappes was sworn in as Deputy Director of the Central

Intelligence Agency. He was born on August 22, 1951, in Cincinnati, Ohio. He earned a BS in pre-med from Ohio University and an MS in pathology from Ohio State University. He joined the Marine Corps in 1976, and joined the CIA in January 1981. He was based in the Near East and South Asia Division until joining the Senior Intelligence Service in July 1995. He served overseas for 12 years in the Middle East, Asia, and Europe. He spoke Farsi and Russian. From 2000 to 2002, he was Associate Deputy Director of Operations for Counterintelligence, concurrently serving as Chief of the Counterintelligence Center, leading operations and technical programs against foreign espionage threats. He was Associate Deputy Director for Operations and Deputy Director for Operations from 2002 to 2004. He retired from federal service and entered the private sector in 2005, serving as Chief Operating Officer and on the Board of Directors of ArmorGroup International until he was called back to become DDCIA. He retired from the position on April 14, 2010.

September 18, 2006: William Shaoul Benjamin, 64, of Los Angeles, pleaded not guilty to charges that he worked for the former Saddam Hussein–led Iraqi regime, failure to notify the U.S. government, and lying to immigration officials when he applied for U.S. citizenship. He communicated with Iraqi Da'irat al-Mukhabbarat al-'Amma intelligence officers, who gave him the code name 9211 and tasked him with infiltrating anti-regime exile groups in the U.S. The indictment said that he was paid for his service from 1993 through 2001. He faced 20 years in prison.

November 1, 2006: Dissident former KGB officer Alexander V. Litvinenko, who lived and worked in the UK, was poisoned in London. Polonium-210 is a rare and highly toxic radioactive isotope. British pundits blamed former KGB bodyguard Andrei K. Lugovoi for putting the polonium into a teapot at the Millennium Hotel in London's Mayfair district where he met Litvinenko on November 1, 2006. The Crown Prosecution Service filed criminal charges against Lugovoi, who had since become a member of the Russian parliament; he denied the charges. Russia denied London's extradition request.The UK expelled four Russian diplomats after Moscow refused to hand him over for trial. Litvinenko died of polonium-210 poisoning on November 23, 2006.

December 4, 2006: U.S. Naval Petty Officer 3rd Class Ariel Jonathan Weinmann pleaded guilty to espionage, desertion and other charges regarding his alleged theft of a Navy laptop and trying to sell its classified contents to an undisclosed foreign government. He was arrested on March 25, 2006, at the Dallas–Fort Worth International Airport while traveling from Mexico City, Mexico en route to Vancouver, British Columbia. In March 2005, in Manama, Bahrain, he attempted to deliver classified information relating to national defense to a Russian representative. He deserted on July 3, 2005, while his submarine, the USS *Albuquerque*, was in port in Groton, Connecticut. Weinmann provided secret information to a foreign, probably Russian, representative in Vienna, Austria, circa October 19, 2005, and circa March 19, 2006, near Mexico City. He claimed he had downloaded classified biographies of Austrian government employees and technical manuals on the Tomahawk cruise missile, which he hoped to provide to the Austrian government. He pleaded guilty to espionage, desertion and related charges. In December 2006 he was sentenced by a military court-martial at Norfolk Naval Station to 12 years in prison and a dishonorable discharge for desertion and turning over classified information to a foreign agent. He was demoted to seaman recruit.

December 19, 2006: Former Florida International University professor Carlos Alvarez pleaded guilty to conspiring to be an unregistered agent who informed on the Cuban exile community for the Cuban government. His wife, Elsa, a counselor for the university, pleaded guilty in Miami federal court to being aware of his illegal activity, harboring him and failing to disclose it to authorities. Prosecutors said he became involved with the Cuban intelligence service in 1977; she apparently joined him in 1982. He was arrested in January 2006. On February 27, 2007, he was sentenced to five years in prison.

February 14, 2007: A U.S. Army contract translator known variously as Abdulhakeem Nour, Abu Hakim, Noureddine Malki, Almaliki Nour, and Almalik Nour Eddin, pleaded guilty in federal court in New York to charges of possessing classified national defense documents. In 1998 he used a false identity on forms applying for U.S. citizenship. He used the alias in August 2005 to get hired as an Arabic translator for the L-3 Titan Corporation, which provides translation services in Iraq for U.S. military personnel. He was granted secret and top secret security clearances. In 2004, while serving with an intelligence unit of the 82nd Airborne Division at Al Taqqadam Air Base in Iraq in the Sunni Triangle, he took several classified documents from the U.S. Army without authorization. The documents noted coordinates of insurgents' locations which the U.S. Army was targeting and plans for protecting Sunnis on their pilgrimage to Mecca. He photographed a classified battle map of a base near Najaf. In September 2005, the FBI and military investigators interviewed Nour in Iraq. A search of his

apartment in September 2005 yielded a computer file with a photograph of the Empire State Building with a bull's-eye on it, and a faked shipping company ad showing a 9/11 plane flying toward a World Trade Center tower with the words "We fly things straight to your office." He was arrested later that month at his Brooklyn apartment and was charged in October 2005 with lying to federal officials. He originally said he was born in Lebanon in 1960, was unmarried, and that his parents died in Beirut. He later said he was a Moroccan born in 1959, married, and that his parents were living in Morocco. He pleaded guilty in December 2005 to using a false identity to acquire U.S. citizenship. On February 14, 2007, he pleaded guilty to unauthorized possession of classified documents. On May 19, 2008, he was sentenced to ten years and one month in prison; his U.S. citizenship was revoked.

August 1, 2007: Former Chinese national Xiaodong Sheldon Meng, 42, pleaded guilty in a court in California to two counts of conducting economic espionage for the Chinese Navy Research Center by exporting source code for simulation software developed by Quantum3D, a San Jose company, for fighter pilot training. This was the first U.S. conviction involving source code under the Arms Export Control Act and second conviction under the Economic Espionage Act of 1996. Under the terms of the plea agreement, he could be sentenced to only two years and fined $500,000 on the Economic Espionage Act conviction and $1,000,000 on the Arms Export Control Act conviction, and a three-year supervised release.

September 26, 2007: Authorities in California charged Lan Lee and Yuefei Ge with economic espionage and stealing trade secrets from two firms on behalf of the Chinese military.

February 11, 2008: Authorities arrested naturalized U.S. citizen Dongfan "Greg" Chung, 72, a former Rockwell International and Boeing engineer, after he was indicted for stealing 24 B-1 bomber manuals, documents about the space shuttle, F-15 fighters, helicopters, the Delta IV rocket, and the Air Force C-17 Globemaster cargo plane, and providing it to the Chinese as an unregistered agent. He traveled often to China, meeting with Chinese officials and giving lectures. He apparently had spied for China since 1979, when he sent a letter volunteering his services and received a note from Professor Chen Lung Ku of the Harbin Institute of Technology, who told him, "We are all moved by your patriotism. We'd like to join our hands together with the overseas compatriots in the endeavor for the construction of our great socialist motherland."

Chung was born in China and emigrated to the U.S. in 1962. Chung worked for Rockwell from 1973 until Boeing bought its defense space unit in 1996. He retired from Boeing, but worked as a contractor until September 2006. He held a secret security clearance. China started tasking him via letters in 1979. His letters mentioned sending 24 manuals on the B-1 bomber. Investigators discovered Chung during the espionage investigation of fellow engineer Chi Mak. Between 1985 and 2003, Chung visited China for meetings with government officials. In 2006, FBI and NASA agents found in his home more than 250,000 pages of documents from Boeing, Rockwell and other defense contractors.

On July 16, 2009, in America's first economic espionage trial, Chung was convicted of economic espionage and acting as an agent of China. U.S. District Judge Cormac J. Carney found him guilty of conspiracy to commit economic espionage; six counts of economic espionage to benefit a foreign country; one count of acting as an agent of the People's Republic of China; and one count of making false statements to the FBI, which had arrested him in February 2008.

Each economic espionage charge carried a maximum sentence of 15 years in prison and a $500,000 fine. The charge of acting as an agent for a foreign government carried a maximum penalty of ten years in prison and a $250,000 fine. The charges of conspiracy to commit economic espionage and making false statements to federal investigators each carried a maximum sentence of five years in prison and a $250,000 fine.

On February 8, 2010, he was sentenced to 15 years and eight months in prison.

February 11, 2008: The U.S. arrested Gregg William Bergersen, 51, a former Defense Department employee, and Tai Shen Kuo, a naturalized U.S. citizen who was a PRC agent, on espionage charges. On March 30, 2008, Bergersen pleaded guilty in U.S. District Court in Alexandria, Virginia, to one count of conspiracy to communicate national defense information to people not entitled to receive it. Saddled with gambling debts and eager for income after his retirement, he had passed classified information on projected U.S. military sales to Taiwan and communications security to Tai Shen Kuo, a New Orleans businessman of Taiwanese descent, but said he was not aware that the material would reach the mainland Chinese government. He thought Kuo worked for the Taiwanese. Bergersen also provided details of Po Sheng, a Taiwanese military communication system. Bergersen resigned as a weapons systems policy analyst at the Defense Security Cooperation Agency in Arlington, Virginia. He pleaded guilty to conspiracy to disclose national defense information. He was sentenced to 57 months in prison.

Kuo was also charged. On May 13, 2008,

Tai Shen Kuo, 58, admitted in U.S. District Court in Alexandria, Virginia, to giving the Chinese government highly sensitive military information he obtained from Bergersen. He was tasked by PRC intelligence in the 1990s with spotting and cultivating individuals with access to U.S. defense information. Kuo got Bergersen's interest with the prospect of a consulting partnership on defense issues. He gave Bergersen cash for casino bets, a box of cigars, concert tickets, and dinners in exchange for information on U.S. military sales to Taiwan for the next five years. The two met in restaurants in Alexandria and Loudoun County, Virginia, Las Vegas, and Charleston, South Carolina. The PRC paid Kuo $50,000. In July 2007, FBI agents videotaped Kuo putting $3,000 in cash into Bergersen's shirt pocket while they were in a rental car on the way to Dulles International Airport. He pleaded guilty to conspiracy to deliver national defense information to a foreign government. He was later sentenced to 15 years and eight months in prison and fined $40,000.

Kuo used the services of Yu Xin Kang, 33, a permanent resident alien in love with Kuo, as a courier from New Orleans to Chinese intelligence back in China. She received 18 months in prison.

Kuo was also running former U.S. Air Force Colonel James Wilbur Fondren, Jr., at whose Virginia home he was staying when he was arrested. (See May 13, 2009, entry.)

March 3, 2008: Werner Franz G., 44, a German engineer who worked for EADS's Eurocopter unit, was charged as a foreign agent. German prosecutors accused him of receiving $20,000 from a Russian intelligence agent in return for documents, handbooks, and other information for "technical products." He was accused of meeting several times with the intelligence officer in Germany and Austria, using anonymous e-mail accounts to set up the meetings, in May 2004–December 2006. He pleaded guilty in a Munich court on April 12, 2008, to charges of being a foreign agent. He faced one to ten years in prison.

April 15, 2008: The FBI arrested U.S. Navy civilian contractor Randall G. Craig, Jr., 41, during a sting operation. Craig thought he was selling personal information about thousands of military personnel and reservists to an undercover officer he thought was an intelligence officer of a foreign government. He was indicted for aggravated identity theft and using authorized computer access for personal gain.

April 22, 2008: Federal authorities arrested New Jersey resident Ben-Ami Kadish, 84, on four counts of conspiracy. He told the FBI that he gave Israeli intelligence 50–100 classified documents between 1979 and 1985, including information about U.S. nuclear weapons, F-15 fighter jets, and the U.S. Patriot missile defense system. A criminal complaint filed in Manhattan said that he had been a mechanical engineer at the U.S. Army's Armament Research, Development and Engineering Center in Dover, New Jersey. He had worked for the Army's Picatinny Arsenal for 27 years. Authorities said he was run by Yosef Yagur, the same Israeli Scientific Relations Office case officer who ran Jonathan Pollard. Prosecutors said Kadish would check secret documents out of the library and then allow Yagur to photograph them in Kadish's basement. One of the documents was classified "restricted data." On March 20, 2008, in a phone conversation, Yagur reportedly told Kadish to lie to FBI interviewers, saying, "Don't say anything. Let them say whatever they want.... What happened 25 years ago? You didn't remember anything."

Kadish could face the death penalty. He was released on $300,000 bail, secured against his home in Monroe Township, New Jersey. He was charged with single counts of conspiracy to disclose documents related to the national defense of the U.S. to the government of Israel, conspiracy to act as an agent of the government of Israel; conspiracy to hinder a communication to a law enforcement officer; and conspiracy to make a materially false statement to a law enforcement officer.

On December 30, 2008, Kadish pleaded guilty to a criminal charge of serving as an unregistered agent for Israel. He faced five years in prison; sentencing was scheduled for February 2009. He claimed he only wanted to help Israel, and had received only nominal gifts and family dinners from his case officer in return for classified documents he had taken from a U.S. Army research and engineering center at the Picatinny Arsenal in Dover, New Jersey, between 1980 and 1985. Judge William H. Pauley, III fined him $50,000 on May 29, 2009, but chose not to jail him, given his advanced age.

April 23, 2008: Rodolfo Edgardo Wanseele Paciello, 40, a Miami resident, pleaded guilty in federal court to being an illegal agent by providing countersurveillance for a Venezuelan DISIP intelligence official who traveled to south Florida in October 2007 to organize an alleged coverup of Venezuela's $800,000 campaign donation to Christina Fernandez de Kirchner, an Argentine presidential candidate. Wanseele and four others, including two wealthy oil executives, an attorney, and a DISIP official, were trying to silence Guido Alejandro Antonini Wilson, a Key Biscayne man caught with the money in Argentina in August 2007, who was assisting the FBI's investigation. On November 3, 2008, a federal jury convicted Franklin Duran of acting as an agent for Venezuela in the plot. In December

2007, Duran, 41; Moises Maionica, 36; Antonio J. Gomez, 37; Paciello; and Carlos Kauffmann, 36, had been charged on two counts.

May 28, 2008: Yu Xin Kang, an accomplice of Tai Shen Kuo, a naturalized U.S. citizen from Taiwan who was a PRC agent, pleaded guilty in the Eastern District of Virginia to aiding and abetting an unregistered agent of the PRC. Kang, who was arrested on May 13, 2008, admitted assisting Kuo by periodically serving as a conduit for the delivery of information from Kuo to a PRC official. She was later sentenced to 18 months in prison.

October 15, 2008: A South Korean court sentenced Won Jeong Hwa, a North Korean woman, to five years in prison in an espionage case involving sex and poisoned needles. She was arrested in July 2008 on charges of giving classified information to Pyongyang, including the locations of key military installations, lists of North Korean defectors, and personal information on South Korean military officers.

October 28, 2008: A Japanese court sentenced a 35-year-old Navy Lieutenant Commander to a two-and-a-half-year suspended sentence for passing classified information about the Aegis radar system to an unauthorized colleague. It was the first conviction under a 1954 law regarding leaking confidential information about weapons and ships given to Japan by the U.S.

November 5, 2008: A London court convicted Iranian-born former British Army Corporal Daniel James, a former interpreter, of spying for Iran by sending e-mails to a diplomat while serving in Afghanistan. Prosecutors said he had eccentrically fantasized about being a hero. Instead, he was convicted of communicating information to an enemy.

December 22, 2008: Saubhe Jassim al-Dellemy, 67, an Iraqi who came to the U.S. in the 1980s as a student on scholarship from the Iraqi Baath Party and became a permanent resident in 2000, pleaded guilty to a federal conspiracy charge and admitted to secretly serving for more than a decade for the Saddam Hussein regime. His code name was Adam. He provided information to Iraqi intelligence about the identities and activities of anti-regime groups. The Maryland resident hosted meetings of Iraqi intelligence officers and government officials at a restaurant near National Security Agency headquarters. He was the manager of Gourmet Shish Kebab in Laurel, Maryland; his wife owned the restaurant. He was charged with conspiring to act as an unregistered agent of a foreign government, which carried a five-year term. In addition to his intelligence collection, he also helped Iraqi intelligence officers in the Iraqi Interests Section's Washington Station to shred documents that would have identified Iraqi intelligence agents.

January 18, 2009: Najib Shemami, 60, of Sterling Heights, Michigan, pleaded guilty in court to spying for Saddam Hussein's regime. He admitted he had aided Iraq without U.S. government approval by sharing information with the Iraqi intelligence service, reporting on U.S. and Turkish military activities and providing information about Iraqi exiles in the U.S. He was represented by attorney Ed Wishnow. Sentencing was scheduled for May 2009. He faced four years in prison.

February 13, 2009: Leon Edward Panetta was sworn in as the third Director of the Central Intelligence Agency, serving until June 30, 2011. He was born on June 28, 1938, in Monterey, California. He earned a BA from the University of Santa Clara in 1960, returning for his JD in 1963. He served in intelligence as a Captain in the U.S. Army, earning the Army Commendation Medal. In 1969, he was Special Assistant to the Secretary of Health, Education and Welfare. In March 1969–February 1970, he headed the U.S. Office for Civil Rights. In 1976, he was elected to the U.S. House of Representatives, and was re-elected eight times. He had extensive experience in the House of Representatives, chairing the House Committee on the Budget. He later was Director of the Office of Management and Budget. He was President Bill Clinton's Chief of Staff. On July 1, 2011, he was sworn in as Secretary of Defense, stepping down on February 25, 2013.

April 2009: Computer forensic investigators traced penetrations of the Joint Strike Fighter project back to Internet addresses in China.

April 3, 2009: The U.S. District Court in Connecticut sentenced former U.S. Navy signalman second class Paul Raphael Hall, alias Hassan Abujihaad, 31, of the naval destroyer USS *Benfold* to ten years in prison for providing Al Qaeda supporters in London with secret information about planned ship movements. The sentence was to be followed by 3 years of supervised release for the Phoenix native. Abujihaad had leaked the Navy aircraft carrier battle group's movements and a drawing of its formation when it was to pass through the Strait of Hormuz on April 29, 2001. He provided computer files to Babar Ahmad, a terrorist supporter in London who ran the Azzam Publications jihadi website before he was arrested in 2004. The FBI arrested Abujihaad in March 2007. On January 31, 2008, a New Haven, Connecticut, judge ruled that prosecutors could claim that Abujihaad made coded references to terrorist plots. He was convicted of leaking details of the ship movements to terrorists on March 5, 2008.

On March 4, 2009, U.S. District Judge Mark Kravitz overturned his 2008 conviction on providing material support to terrorists, but upheld his conviction for disclosing classified national defense information, noting his deeming the bombing of the USS *Cole* as a "martyrdom operation."

May 13, 2009: James Wilbur Fondren, Jr., 62, was charged in a criminal complaint unsealed in the Eastern District of Virginia with conspiracy to communicate classified information to an agent of a foreign government. The complaint said that from November 2004 to February 11, 2008, Fondren had conspired to give classified information to the Chinese. He had worked at the Pentagon and was the Deputy Director, Washington Liaison Office, of the U.S. Pacific Command, since 2001. He was put on administrative leave in February 2008. He faced a maximum five years in prison and a $250,000 fine. He retired from active duty as an Air Force Lieutenant Colonel in May 1996. In February 1998, he began providing consulting services Via Strategy, Inc. from his Virginia home; his sole client was Tai Shen Kuo, a naturalized U.S. citizen from Taiwan who had business interests in the PRC. Apparently unbeknownst to Fondren, Kuo worked for the PRC and was running a separate spy network (see February 11, 2008, entry on the Bergersen case). Fondren nonetheless knew that Kuo was working for a foreign government, but thought it was Taiwan. Fondren wrote "opinion papers," eight of which included classified DOD information, which he sold to Kuo for $350–800 per paper. When Kuo was arrested, he had a copy of *The National Military Strategy of the United States of America 2008* which Fondren had provided. On September 25, 2009, a federal jury in Alexandria, Virginia, convicted him of providing classified documents, including a report on

Chinese military power, to a Chinese government agent and lying to the FBI about it. On January 22, 2010, the U.S. District Court in Alexandria sentenced Fondren to three years in prison.

June 4, 2009: Walter Kendall Myers, 72, a retired State Department officer, and his wife, Gwendolyn Steingraber Myers, 71, were charged at U.S. District Court in Washington, D.C., with conspiracy to act as illegal agents, to commit wire fraud, and to communicate classified information to the Cuban government. They pleaded not guilty. They reportedly had been spying for Cuba since 1978, using shortwave radios and brush passes, sending encrypted e-mails from Internet cafes, and deploying grocery carts as deaddrops. They had traveled to Brazil, Ecuador, Jamaica, Italy, and Mexico for operational meetings and used the code names 202 and 123, respectively, because they believed it was too risky to meet their Cuban handlers in the U.S.

Walter Myers was born on April 15, 1937, to a prominent Washington family. His mother, Elsie Alexandra Carol Grosvenor Myers, was the granddaughter of Alexander Graham Bell and daughter of Gilbert Grosvenor, director of the National Geographic Society. Myers attended a Pennsylvania prep school, graduated from Brown, and obtained his Ph.D. from Johns Hopkins. He served in the U.S. Army. He separated from his first wife in 1974 after a decade of marriage, losing custody of their two children. In 1975, he was convicted of reckless driving when he lost control of his car and killed a teenage girl and injured her two friends, receiving three years of unsupervised probation.

Gwendolyn Steingraber was born in Sioux City, Iowa, and grew up in rural South Dakota. She worked on the McGovern presidential campaign and in the Senate office of James Abourezk. The couple met in the 1970s and began marching for various liberal causes. A police raid turned up marijuana plants in their basement. The couple married in 1982.

Walter Myers began working for the State Department as a contract instructor at the Foreign Service Institute in 1977. He visited Cuba for two weeks in December 1978, guided by a Cuban intelligence officer working at the United Nations. Six months later, a Cuban official visited the couple in their South Dakota home, where he recruited them. Walter resumed working for the State Department, figuring that he could not get employment at the CIA because he could not pass a CIA polygraph. He obtained a top secret clearance and worked at State's Bureau of Intelligence and Research on European issues from 1988 until retiring in October 2007. Their last meeting with the Cubans appears to have been in Guadalajara, Mexico, in 2006.

The Bureau spotted them in an intercept of Cuban intelligence communications that mentioned a penetration of the U.S. government. Agent E-634 reportedly had a shoulder tumor; Gwendolyn had such surgery 9 days after the intercept. The Cuban service was also to surveil an area around the agents' new home; the Myers couple moved within the month. The Bureau also discovered that the duo used the same brand of shortwave as Cuban asset Ana Belen Montes.

The FBI sent an undercover agent, posing as a Cuban agent, to meet with the couple in Washington in April 2009. Myers told the FBI officer during three meetings that the couple had visited Fidel Castro in 1995 during a secret trip. The duo agreed to provide information on the Summit of the Americans in 2009 and on USG personnel involved in Latin American policy. The couple had wanted to take their yacht "to sail

home" to Cuba in 2009. The FBI arrested them on June 4, 2009, at the Capital Hilton Hotel before their next ops meeting with the undercover officer. FBI officials found more than 200 sensitive or classified intelligence reports concerning Cuba on his computer.

U.S. Magistrate Judge John M. Facciola denied them bail on June 10, 2009, saying they were likely flight risks. The couple faced 14–17 years in prison if convicted.

Walter Myers pleaded guilty in federal court on November 20, 2009, to conspiring to commit espionage and wire fraud, having spied for Cuba over the previous three decades. His wife pleaded guilty to conspiracy to gather and transmit national defense information. Under their plea agreement he faced a mandatory life sentence; she faced six to seven and one half years. They were also to cooperate with investigators and forfeit $1.7 million—his U.S. government salary over the years—along with their 37-foot Malo sailboat.

On July 16, 2010, U.S. District Judge Reggie B. Walton sentenced Walter to life in prison and Gwendolyn to six years and nine months in prison. They also forfeited $1.7 million in cash and property, including all of his federal salary. They kept their sailboat. They asked to be imprisoned near each other.

October 19, 2009: The FBI arrested Stewart David Nozette, 52, of Chevy Chase, Maryland, a former government physicist who worked for the White House's National Space Council, Executive Office of the President, Defense Department, and Department of Energy's Lawrence Livermore National Laboratory on charges of attempting to spy for Israel in exchange for $11,000 in cash and an Israeli passport. He allegedly tried to give U.S. top secret nuclear and space secrets to an FBI agent posing as a Mossad agent. He faced life in prison. He had worked for the past decade for Israel Aerospace Industries, an Israeli parastatal firm. The Chicago native had developed a radar experiment that detected water on the moon's south pole in 1994; the Clementine bistatic radar experiment is on display at the National Air and Space Museum. The technology can also be used to track ballistic missiles. In a series of dead drops in which he was passed questions, he provided envelopes filled with classified information about U.S. satellites, early warning systems and American abilities to retaliate against a large scale attack. He was alleged to have traveled overseas on January 6, 2009, and dropped off two computer thumb drives. He was also being investigated over allegations that he criminally defrauded NASA via his Alliance for Competitive Technology firm. In January 2009, he had secretly pleaded guilty to overbilling NASA and DOD more than $265,000 for contracting work. Nozette earned a Ph.D. in planetary sciences from MIT in 1983. After his arrest, the FBI seized his safe deposit box in La Jolla, California, that contained 55 gold Krugerrand coins worth $50,000 and $30,000 in savings bonds.

On October 29, 2009, Nozette pleaded not guilty in U.S. District Court to attempted espionage for Israel. He was ordered held without bond until a jury trial. He apparently planned to leave behind his wife, Wendy McColough, if he had to flee the U.S. for Israel or India, where he planned to "tell everything." He had told an undercover FBI agent posing as a Mossad agent that he wanted "only a percentage of the development cost, roughly $2 million, as compensation."

Authorities added two more counts of attempted espionage in November 2010.

On September 7, 2011, he pleaded guilty to one count of attempted espionage. He was represented by attorneys Robert L.

Tucker, John C. Kiyonaga and Bradford Berenson. On March 21, 2012, U.S. District Judge Paul L. Friedman adhered to a plea deal and sentenced Nozette to 13 years in prison on the espionage conviction and three-plus years for unrelated fraud and tax evasion convictions. The sentences were to run concurrently. Nozette was also to pay $217,795 in restitution.

December 30, 2009: Jordanian Humam Khalil Abu-Mulal al-Balawi, alias Abu Dujana Khorasani, 36, a Jordanian doctor who became a double agent for the Taliban and Al Qaeda, set off his explosives belt at Forward Operating Base Chapman in Khost Province, Afghanistan, killing seven CIA officers, including Chief of Base/Khost, and a Jordanian and wounding eight people, including six Americans, among them the Deputy Chief of Station/Kabul. Al-Balawi had led the Jordanian intelligence service and the CIA to believe that he was a penetration of Al Qaeda's leadership. An officer in the Jordanian Dairat al-Mukhabarat al-Ammah (General Intelligence Department) had driven him to the CIA base at the camp for debriefing. Al Qaeda said it was avenging the death in an August drone strike of Baitullah Mehsud, leader of the Taliban in Pakistan, and Al Qaeda terrorists Abu Saleh al-Somali and Abdullah Said al-Libi. Several jihadi websites later ran confessor videos by al-Balawi.

The CIA publicly identified the dead as Chief of Base Jennifer Lynne Matthews, 45; Daren James LaBonte, 35; Scott Michael Roberson, 39; Harold E. Brown, Jr., 37; Elizabeth Hanson, 30; and security contractors Jeremy Jason Wise, 35; and Dane Clark Paresi, 46.

Al-Balawi had frequently posted on jihadi websites under the name Abu Dujana al-Khorasani, making him an attractive Al Qaeda recruit.

Al-Balawi's Istanbul-based wife was Defne Bayrak, 31, Turkish journalist who wrote *Osama bin Laden: Che Guevara of the East*. Her husband had provided medical aid to Hamas in Gaza during an Israeli assault and was in contact with the Jordanian Muslim Brotherhood. He had run the al-Hesbah Forum, a major Al Qaeda website. He told a high school classmate he sought jihadi martyrdom against the U.S. and Israel.

The Jordanian GID arrested al-Balawi in 2009 for his jihadi postings. "Abu Dujana" had posted on a jihadi website on December 29, 2008, that after seeing a photo of two dead Islamic women, "anyone who sees such painful picture and does not rush to fight should consider his manhood and masculinity dead. I have never wished to be in Gaza, but now I wish to be a bomb fired by the monotheists or a car bomb that takes the lives of the biggest number of Jews to hell."

Sometime in 2008–2009, he offered his double agent services to the Jordanians to find Al Qaeda deputy chief Ayman al-Zawahiri, according to the *Washington Times*.

On August 20, 2010, federal authorities in U.S. District Court in the District of Columbia charged Pakistani Taliban leader Hakimullah Mehsud with conspiracy to murder a U.S. national while outside the U.S. and conspiracy to use a weapon of mass destruction against a U.S. national while outside the U.S. The charges were unsealed on September 1, 2010.

May 6, 2010: Michael Joseph Morell was sworn in as the Deputy Director of the Central Intelligence Agency. He was born in Cuyahoga Falls, Ohio, on September 4, 1958. He earned a BA in economics from the University of Akron and an MA in economics from Georgetown University. He joined CIA's analytic ranks in 1980. He pro-duced the *President's Daily Briefing* and became President George W. Bush's briefer. During 2006–2008, he was CIA's first Associate Deputy Director. In 2008, he became Director for Intelligence. He twice served as Acting Director of the CIA. He announced his CIA retirement on June 12, 2013. After government, he became *CBS News*'s Senior Security Correspondent.

June 8, 2010: Federal officials arrested Army SPC Bradley E. Manning, 22, an intelligence analyst with the U.S. Army, for sharing classified material with Wikileaks. He took credit for leaking a video of a helicopter attack. He was believed responsible for ultimately sharing more than 700,000 classified Secret Internet Protocol Router Network (SIPRNET) documents with Wikileaks, which he downloaded from his classified computer system onto a Lady Gaga CD between March 28 and May 4, 2010. It was the biggest leak, by volume, of classified material in U.S. history. In addition to Iraq and Afghanistan battlefield reports, he also leaked video of a 2007 U.S. Apache helicopter attack in Baghdad that killed nine people, including a *Reuters* photographer. In July 2010, military prosecutors said he would be charged for "delivering national defense information to an unauthorized source."

The *Washington Post* reported on February 2, 2011, that a Fort Drum, New York, mental health specialist had deemed Manning, who hailed from Crescent, Oklahoma, unfit for deployment to Iraq, but his commanders sent him anyway. He had balled up his fists and screamed at higher-ranking officers in his unit, been demoted a rank for assaulting a fellow soldier, and worried his sergeant so much that his supervisor disabled Manning's weapon.

On March 2, 2011, the Army added 22 more charges, including "aiding the enemy";

wrongfully causing intelligence to be published on the Internet, knowing that it was accessible to the enemy; multiple counts of theft of public records; transmitting defense information; violating Army information security regulations; and computer fraud. He was also charged with "adding unauthorized software" once between February and April 2010 and once on May 4, 2010, "to extract classified information." He faced life in prison; the prosecution said it would not request capital punishment. He also faced forfeiture of all pay and allowances, reduction in rank to the lowest (E-1) pay grade, and a dishonorable discharge.

Among the charges was violation of the Espionage Act for providing national defense information to "persons not entitled to receive it."

During a hearing on December 17, 2011, to determine whether he would be court-martialed, witnesses noted that Manning claimed to be suffering from a gender identity disorder and had a Facebook page under the name Breanna Manning.

On February 28, 2013, Manning pleaded guilty to 10 lesser charges and said that he wanted to start a national debate about "killing and capturing people." "I believed that if the general public, especially the American public, had access to the information ... this could spark a domestic debate over the role of the military and our foreign policy in general." He was expected to receive a 20-year sentence for pleading guilty to misuse of classified information. Trial was set for June 2013 on 21 charges of aiding the enemy and violating the Espionage Act, which could result in a life sentence. He claimed he had approached the *Washington Post* and *New York Times* before settling on Wikileaks. The prosecution rested on July 2, 2013; the defense rested eight days later. Prosecutors requested a 60-year sentence. Manning did not take the stand.

On July 30, 2013, Manning was convicted on 20 of 22 charges but acquitted of aiding the enemy under Article 104 and one count under the Espionage Act for a video of an airstrike in Afghanistan's Farah Province. Army Colonel Denise Lind convicted him of six espionage counts (including under the Espionage Act the Iraq airstrike video, classified memos, military records, database files, and Army records), five theft charges (Article 134, stealing government property, including military records, database files, State Department records, and a server address list), two computer fraud charges (under the Computer Abuse and Fraud Act of State Department records and classified cables) and other military infractions (including Article 134 wanton publication of intelligence on the Internet, and Article 92 failure to obey a lawful order or regulation, among them bypassing security, unauthorized software, unintended system use, and storing classified information). He faced 136 years in prison. A sentencing hearing was scheduled for July 31.

On August 21, 2013, he was sentenced to 35 years in prison, demoted, and was to be dishonorably discharged.

He announced that he would like to be known as a woman named Chelsea E. Manning. He became the first transgender military inmate to request hormone treatments.

June 27, 2010: The U.S. arrested 10 individuals serving as members of a Russian "illegal" espionage ring. The FBI said that some of the spies were sent to the U.S. by the SVR (the KGB successor agency) in the mid–1990s. Some of them served as ostensible couples, with children, living in the suburbs and driving minivans in Yonkers, Arlington, and Rosslyn, Virginia. They used encrypted computer systems to communicate with their handlers. Others in New Jersey and

Boston used steganography, hiding messages in images. Still others in Boston and Seattle used burst transmissions. Cash was passed via brush passes. The FBI said the group had not acquired any classified or sensitive U.S. government information. Two separate criminal complaints filed in the U.S. District Court for the Southern District of New York charged 11 defendants with conspiring to act as unlawful agents of the Russian Federation within the U.S., which carries a five-year term. Nine (not Chapman and Semenko) were also charged with conspiracy to launder money, which carries a 20-year term. Some of them were told to visit universities to find CIA recruits, investigate changes in CIA leadership, make contacts at senior levels of policymaking councils and in political parties, and follow nuclear sciences.

Anna Chapman, maiden name Anya Kushchenko, 28, of New York City, was arrested in Manhattan. The "sexy spy" divorcé claimed to have founded an online real estate company worth $2 million. She said she had a master in economics. She figured out the plot had been compromised by the FBI. She had accepted a fake passport from an undercover FBI officer claiming to be a Russian case officer. She was represented by attorney Robert Baum. The Russian citizen had lived in the U.S. fulltime since 2009. She had 181 Facebook friends and 150 LinkedIn connections, with five recommendations. Her Twitter feed was @nycrentalsnews. She was denied bail on July 1. London quickly revoked her British citizenship, which she had obtained by marrying a Briton, Alex Chapman; they divorced in 2006. Her father had worked in the KGB.

Richard Murphy, 39, and Cynthia Murphy, 35, were arrested at their home in Montclair, New Jersey. He was an architect; she had recently earned an MBA. He claimed Philadelphia roots. She said she was from New York and worked as a vice president at Manhattan's Morea Financial Services. They entered the U.S. in the mid–1990s, settling in New Jersey, from which they were to investigate the U.S. position on a new strategic arms reduction treaty and the Iranian nuclear program. They had two young children. They told Judge Kimba Wood that their true names were Lydia and Vladimir Guryev.

Juan Lazaro, 66, and Victoria Palaez, 55, were arrested at their home in Yonkers, New York. He was an adjunct economics professor at Baruch College in New York; he admitted that Lazaro was an alias and that he had not been born in Uruguay, as he had earlier claimed. She was a Peruvian-born columnist for New York's Spanish-language newspaper, *El Diario La Prensa*. They had two sons. The FBI said she traveled to a South American country to shuttle cash for other Yonkers-based agents. In 2002, she brought eight bags each containing $10,000. She was granted $250,000 bail on July 1, 2010.

Michael Zottoli, 40, who claimed to be a U.S. citizen, and Patricia Mills, 31, who claimed to be Canadian, were arrested at their Arlington, Virginia, home. The married couple had earlier lived in Seattle and other locales until their October 2009 move. The FBI searched their Seattle apartment in February 2006, finding an SVR-provided steganography program. Prosecutors said they were Russian citizens; Zottoli is named Mikhail Kutzik and Mills is named Natalia Pereverzeva. She was a stay-at-home mother; they had two small children.

Donald Howard Heathfield, 48, and Tracey Lee Ann Foley, 47, were arrested at their Cambridge, Massachusetts, apartment. The "Boston Conspirators" lived with their two teenage boys in Harvard Square. He earned an MPA from Harvard in 2000 and from 2000 to 2006 worked for the Cambridge-based Global Partners, Inc. consulting firm, from which he contacted a former senior U.S. national security official. He had used the Heathfield alias to discuss "research programs on small yield, high penetration nuclear warheads" according to charging documents. The real Heathfield died at six weeks old in 1962. He was the CEO of Future Map Strategic Advisory Services. She worked at Redfin Real Estate. They had two boys, aged 16 and 20.

Mikhael Semenko, 28, a travel specialist at Travel All Russia LLC in Arlington, Virginia, since 2009, was arrested at his nearby residence. He spoke Russian, English, Spanish, and Mandarin Chinese. His LinkedIn profile cited his graduate study at Seton Hall University; he had interned for the World Affairs Council. He met with an undercover FBI agent blocks from the White House on June 26, 2010, responding to code words.

The 11th member of the group, alleged ringleader Christopher Metsos, 55, was captured in Cyprus on June 29, trying to board a flight to Budapest, Hungary while carrying a Canadian passport. He was freed on bail but denied permission to leave the country and faced extradition to the U.S. He buried cash in New York, which was dug up by two Seattle-based members two years later. He vanished the next day.

Russia confirmed that they all were Russian citizens.

The ten pleaded guilty in a U.S. court on July 8, 2010, to being unregistered agents of Russia as part of a spy trade. The ten agreed to not return to the U.S. without the permission of the Attorney General, and remit any money made from publication of their spy stories. Several forfeited U.S. assets and real estate. They were flown out of the U.S. to Vienna, Austria, later that day. Nine of them flew on to Russia; Palaez went to Peru.

Four Russian men accused of being spies were pardoned by President Dmitri A. Medvedev and released to the West in Vienna. They were identified as arms control research Igor V. Sutyagin, who had been imprisoned for 11 years; GRU colonel Sergei Skripal, sentenced in 2006 to 13 years for spying for the UK; Aleksandr Zaporozhsky, a former SVR agent who had served seven years of an 18-year sentence; and former KGB major Gennadi Vasilenko, who was arrested in 1998, released, but rearrested in 2005 and convicted on weapons charges.

July 12, 2010: The U.S. announced the detention of Alexey Karetnikov, a 23-year-old Russian. The FBI had been surveilling him since he entered the U.S. in October 2009 to live in Seattle and work at Microsoft. He was deported on July 13. Some officials said he was not part of the 10 SVR illegals case of the previous month. The U.S. did not have enough evidence to charge him with espionage, so he was detained for immigration violations.

July 13, 2010: Iranian nuclear scientist Shahram Amiri, 32, flew back to Tehran from Washington, D.C. He had claimed in Internet videos to have been kidnapped by the CIA, but also had claimed that he had chosen to come to the U.S. to study for a Ph.D. Media observers suggested that he had shared Iranian nuclear secrets with the U.S. since defecting in Saudi Arabia on June 3, 2009, but became worried about how his family was being treated back home. He said he worked at Iran's Malek-e-Ashtar Industrial University, which observers believed was connected to the Revolutionary Guards Corps.

August 26, 2010: Scotland Yard detectives were investigating the murder of MI-6 officer Gareth Williams, 31, whose body was stuffed in a holdall bag and dumped in his bathtub. Williams was on rotation to MI-6

Headquarters from the GCHQ headquarters in Cheltenham, Gloucestershire. His phone and SIM cards were laid out in a "ritual" manner. He apparently had been killed two weeks earlier in his two-bedroom, top floor apartment at 36 Alderney Street, Pimlico, central London. The cause of the "boffin's" death remained to be determined; the coroner denied earlier reports that he had been stabbed. Williams had joined GCHQ in 2001 after dropping out of the St. Catharine's College, Cambridge master's program in advanced mathematics.

September 17, 2010: Pedro Leonardo Mascheroni, 76, and his wife, Marjorie Roxby Mascheroni, 67, appeared in federal court in Albuquerque, New Mexico, following a sting operation. They were charged with conspiracy to help develop a nuclear weapon for Venezuela. The couple had worked at Los Alamos National Laboratory. Pedro told an undercover FBI agent that he could help Caracas develop a bomb within 10 years, using a secret underground nuclear reactor to produce and enrich plutonium, and an open, above-ground reactor to produce energy. They were indicted on 22 counts. They pleaded guilty in 2013 to trying to help Venezuela develop a nuclear weapon. On January 28, 2015, *AP* reported that he was sentenced to 5 years in prison and 3 years of supervised release. Pedro was a naturalized U.S. citizen from Argentina. She was sentenced to a year and a day for conspiring with her husband to sell nuclear secrets.

October 22, 2010: Glenn Duffie Shriver, 28, of Grand Rapids, Michigan, admitted in the U.S. District Court in Alexandria, Virginia, to accepting $70,000 from two Chinese intelligence officers while he tried to get hired by the CIA and U.S. Department of State. He planned to sell classified information to Beijing. He pleaded guilty to one count of conspiracy to provide national defense information to the People's Republic of China. Prosecutors and defense attorneys agreed to recommend a four-year sentence, followed by supervised release of three years.

After traveling to China for study 3 times between 2001 and 2004, he was approached by Chinese intelligence while living in Shanghai in 2004. He had studied Mandarin at East China Normal University in Shanghai in 2002–2003 as a Grand Valley State University international relations student, then answered an ad for someone to write a paper on U.S.-PRC relations for $120. The Chinese then recruited him. He failed the Foreign Service exam in 2005 and 2006, but was given $10,000 and $20,000, respectively, for the attempts. He applied to the CIA's National Clandestine Service in 2007, traveled to China, and was paid $40,000 in cash. He met with Chinese agents at least 20 times between 2004 and 2007. He was tripped up during the CIA's recruiting process, and was arrested in June 2010 while trying to board a plane in Detroit bound for South Korea. He was charged in June 2010 with making false statements in his CIA application when he said he had no contact with foreign agents and failed to list a trip to China in 2007. On January 21, 2011, U.S. District Judge Liam O'Grady sentenced Shriver to four years in prison and two years of supervised release, per his plea agreement.

November 20, 2010: Russia issued five postage stamps commemorating the exploits of five intelligence officers, including Colonel Rudolph Ivanovich Abel, who was exchanged for U-2 pilot Francis Gary Powers in 1962.

December 2, 2010: British authorities arrested Katia Zatuliveter, 25, a researcher for Mike Hancock, 64, a Liberal Democrat in the House of Commons, on suspicion of espionage. She was subjected to a deportation order after MI-5 decided that she was a Russian SVR "sleeper" agent who was targeting Hancock. Hancock sits on Parliament's defense select committee and on the All-Party Parliamentary Group for Russia. She had worked for him for two years. Zatuliveter earlier worked for the UK Defense Forum.

December 6, 2010: The Naval Criminal Investigative Service announced the arrest the previous week of Petty Officer Bryan Minkyu Martin, 22, native of Mexico, New York, and Navy intelligence specialist training with the Joint Special Operations Command at Fort Bragg, for taking top secret documents from military networks and offering to sell them to an undercover FBI investigator posing as a Chinese intelligence agent. The two met at a Hampton Inn in Spring Lake, North Carolina, on November 15, where Martin allegedly offered to bring two classified documents to their next meeting in return for "long-term financial reimbursement." He accepted $500 in cash. Over the next several days, he handed over several secret and top secret documents, and was paid $3,500 for documents involving naval operations and intelligence assessments regarding military operations in Afghanistan and Iraq. Martin enlisted in 2007. He was charged on March 3, 2011, with attempting to forward classified information to a person not authorized to receive such information. His court martial was held at the Region Legal Service Office at Norfolk Naval Station. He was assigned to the Expeditionary Combat Readiness Center at Joint Expeditionary Base Little Creek–Fort Story in Virginia Beach. He was preparing to deploy to Afghanistan in support of the Army and had been training at Fort Bragg before deployment. On May

19, 2011, Martin pleaded guilty to four counts of espionage and seven other charges and admitted to taking $11,500 from the FBI agent he knew as "Mr. Lee." He said he wanted to sell the documents to China because they would pay the most. He faced a life sentence. On May 20, 2011, he was sentenced to 48 years in prison, with 14 suspended, and was dishonorably discharged.

December 22, 2010: British Foreign Secretary William Hague expelled a Russian diplomat following "clear evidence" of spying. The case was unrelated to that of Ekaterina Zatuliveter, expelled earlier in December.

March 1, 2011: A German court sentenced Harald Sodnikar, 54, a helicopter technician in Austria's armed forces, to a one-year suspended sentence after he admitted to spying for the Russian Foreign Intelligence Service (SVR). He had been arrested in 2007. He apparently did not provide any classified information to the Russians. The Munich court ruled that he had aided the SVR in obtaining technical documentation about Eurocopter helicopters in exchange for 6,500 British pounds.

March 17, 2011: Captain Chris V., 37, a former Dutch F-16 pilot, was arrested in The Hague on charges of spying for Belarus. The case was made public on April 28, 2011. He had left the Air Force in 2010. The Dutch secret service said he was on the verge of revealing "one or more state secrets" before his arrest.

September 1, 2011: Bryan Underwood, 31, a contract security officer at the U.S. Consulate in China was arrested a day after being indicted with two counts of making false statements. He did not appear at his scheduled September 21 status hearing in a federal court in the District of Columbia. The FBI arrested him on September 24 in Los Angeles. Federal authorities issued a superseding indictment that charged him with one count of attempting to provide U.S. defense information to a foreign government, two counts of making false statements, and one count of failing to appear in court after he ignored the conditions of his release. He faced a sentence of life without parole. The former Indiana resident had worked as a guard from November 2009 to August 2011. In March 2011, in debt from bad investments, he was turned away from a Chinese government building. On August 30, 2012, Underwood pleaded guilty in U.S. District Court in Washington to one count of attempting to communicate national defense information to a foreign government by trying to pass details on the new Guangzhou Consulate's security systems to the Chinese Ministry of State Security for $3–5 million. He also was to provide access to the construction site so that the MSS could install listening and other monitoring devices. Sentencing guidelines called for a 15–20 year prison term. Sentencing was scheduled for November 19, 2012. He decided to sell the information after he incurred losses in the stock market. On March 5, 2013, Judge Ellen Huvelle of the U.S. District Court for the District of Columbia sentenced him to 9 years in prison.

September 6, 2011: General David Petraeus was sworn in as the 4th Director of the Central Intelligence Agency. He was born on November 7, 1952, in Cornwall, New York. After graduating from the U.S. Military Academy in 1974 with a BS, he earned an MPA in international relations in 1985 and a Ph.D. in international relations in 1987, both from Princeton University. He became the Army's chief theoretician and practioner of counterinsurgery, leading U.S. troops in Iraq and Afghanistan as Commander of U.S. Central Command and Commander of U.S. Forces in Afghanistan

and of the International Security Assistance Force. He resigned on November 2, 2012, after revealing an extramarital affair.

October 2011: German special forces police commandoes stormed the Marburg home of Andreas and Heidrun Anschlag (the name means "attack") near Stuttgart in the southwest. The couple had come from South America with fake Austrian passports in 1988. He started work as an engineer; she appeared to be a housewife. When the German police raided the house, they caught Heidrun sitting at her radio equipment communicating with Moscow. She fell off her chair, dragging wires out of the wall with her. He was arrested elsewhere in Germany. A contact inside the Dutch Foreign Ministry passed them secret information via a dead drop each month. The duo was charged with espionage by stealing information on NATO and EU strategy and passing it to the SVR, the Russian foreign intelligence agency, which had paid them 100,000 euros annually. Their Stuttgart trial began on January 15, 2013. They were believed to have spied for 23 years, passing thousands of European Union, NATO, and UN secrets to the then–USSR and successor Russian service via dead drops, satellite phone calls, and the Internet. The information reportedly covered the relationship between the West and Eastern European and Central Asian regimes. At the time of the trial, he was 54; she was 48. Their daughter, a medical student, was unwitting of their activities. The court did not know their true names, although they were believed to be Sasha and Olga; their code names were Pit and Tina. Heidrun used the alias Alpenkuh1 (alpine cow 1) in sending coded messages via Youtube. She received coded radio messages from Moscow twice per week. Their attorney was Horst-Dieter Potschke, who had earlier defended 1970s Stasi spy

Gunter Guillaume. The duo faced ten years in prison.

The Dutch source, Foreign Ministry official Raymond Valentino Poeteray, 60, was arrested in March 2012 and was to be tried in 2013 in the Netherlands. He was deeply in debt. Poeteray had begun his diplomatic career in 1978 and served in the Dutch embassies in Hong Kong and Indonesia. The court said the Russians paid him at least €72,000 ($94,000) in cash alone between January 2009 and August 2011. On April 23, 2013, the *Associated Press* announced the Poeteray was sentenced by a Hague court to 12 years for spying for the Russians, providing information about the civil war in Libya, EU fact-finding missions in Georgia, and Dutch peacekeeping missions in Kosovo and Afghanistan. The court granted his one request, ordering the investigators return his watches: an Omega, a Graham, a Breitling, a Bulgari, and a Corum. All were fakes.

On July 2, 2013, a German court convicted the couple; he was sentenced to six and a half years in prison; she was sentenced to five and a half years. *Die Welt* reported that the Russians had rejected a German offer of a spy swap—the duo for Valery Mikhailov, a retired Russian intelligence official arrested in 2010 and sentenced to 18 years. On November 22, 2014, German authorities announced the release and deportation of Heidrun after she served half of her prison sentence.

October 2011: Authorities at Joint Base Elmendorf-Richardson arrested Spc. William Colton Millay. On November 6, 2011, the U.S. Army charged Millay, an Alaska-based military policeman, with communication and transmitting national defense information to a person he believed was a foreign intelligence agent. He hailed from Owensboro, Kentucky. On April 10, 2013,

the 24-year-old pleaded guilty before a military judge in Anchorage, Alaska, to attempted espionage, failing to obey regulations and communicating national defense information. He had given the information to an undercover FBI agent posing as a foreign intelligence agent. He was angry that his unit had deployed to Afghanistan without him. Authorities said he lied to counterintelligence officials about the communications he had made to a foreign nation. He also got another soldier to give him classified information. The investigation was conducted by the FBI, Army Counterintelligence, and the Air Force Office of Special Investigations.

Millay joined the Army in 2007. He served in Korea and Fort Stewart, Georgia. He had one tour of Iraq from December 2009 to July 2010 during Operation Iraqi Freedom. He went to the Anchorage base in May 2011. He was assigned to the rear detachment of the 164th Military Police Company, 793rd Military Police Battalion, 2nd Engineer Brigade.

October 12, 2011: A federal grand jury indicted Mohamad Anas Haitham Soueid, 47, a Syrian-born naturalized U.S. citizen living in Leesburg, Virginia, of seeking to "undermine, silence, intimidate and potentially harm" those protesting the regime of Syrian President Bashar al-Assad and its crackdown on demonstrators. The indictment said he worked for the Syrian Mukhabarat intelligence service since March 2011 in collecting audio and video recordings of people protesting the regime in Syria and the U.S. The indictment said that between April and June he e-mailed 20 audio and video recordings to a Syrian intelligence official, listed as an unindicted co-conspirator. He also was alleged to have sent a coded message to the agent in April 2011 regarding a meeting of protestors in Virginia. His written note to a Syrian official stated that "violence against protesters was justified, raiding of homes of protestors was justified, and that any method should be used to deal with the protestors," according to the indictment. On October 27, 2011, U.S. District Court Judge Claude Hilton overturned a magistrate's decision to free Soueid on home detention, deemed Soueid a flight risk, and ordered him to remain in jail until trial in March 2012. Soueid pleaded not guilty.

December 6, 2011: Syed Ghulam Nabi Fai, 62, pleaded guilty in federal court in Alexandria, Virginia, to one count of conspiracy to defraud the U.S. and one count of impeding the administration of tax laws in a decades-long operation by Pakistan's spy agency to influence U.S. policy on Kashmir through unregistered lobbying and campaign contributions to members of Congress. U.S. District Judge Liam O'Grady set a March 9, 2012, sentencing date; Fai faced 8 years in prison for helping send at least $3.5 million from Pakistan's government through the Washington-based Kashmiri American Council to sway the attitudes of Congress.

January 13, 2012: Canadian Navy Sub-Lieutenant Jeffrey Paul Delisle, 40, who was working at a high-security naval intelligence and communication center in Halifax, Nova Scotia, and earlier served at the military's main clearing house in Ottawa, was arrested for spying for Russia. Canada quietly requested that two Russian diplomats leave the country; another four were dropped from the diplomatic list by the end of the month. He had access to "Five Eyes" (U.S., UK, Canada, Australia, New Zealand) shared intelligence. He was the first person charged under the Security of Information Act. He was denied bail on March 30, 2012.

He was raised in Lower Sackville, a Hal-

ifax suburb. He joined the military as a reservist in 1996 and was assigned to 3 Intelligence Company, an army training group in Halifax, in a low-level clerical position. In 1998, he filed for bankruptcy. He joined the regular forces in March 2001 as a private, and made sergeant in November 2006, while stationed in the office of the Chief of Defense Intelligence in Ottawa. His apparent spying began the next year. His wife had cheated on him, and he was bringing up his 4 children by himself. He apparently had walked into a Russian Embassy in 2006 and offered his espionage services at C$3,000 a month (circa U.S. $3,060). He had been plagued by bankruptcy filings and a messy divorce. He used a memory stick to spirit out secrets. In 2008, he was sent to the Royal Military College of Canada in Kingston, Ontario, was commissioned as an officer, and graduated with a BA. He returned to Halifax in 2010 to the Trinity intelligence center, but financial difficulties continued. Court documents said one of the alleged offences happened between July 6, 2007, and January 13, 2012, while the other was alleged to have happened between January 10–13, 2012. Delisle also faced a breach of trust charge under the Criminal Code for an incident that allegedly occurred between July 6, 2007, and January 13, 2012. He faced life in prison if convicted. He had met with the SVR in Brazil. Customs officers were suspicious when he returned from overseas with large amounts of cash. According to press reports, he was believed to have provided military signals intelligence from such databases as Stone Ghost, which is available to the Five Eyes allies. He pleaded guilty on October 10, 2012, to one count each of communicating safeguarded information, attempting to communicate safeguarded information, and breach of trust. On February 8, 2013, Nova Scotia's Chief Judge of the Provincial Court Patrick Curran sentenced

Delisle to 20 years in prison and fined him $111,817. Delisle had claimed a bad marriage had led him to his spying. Later in the month, he was expelled from the military, and stripped of his service decorations and commission. The government also sought to recover the salary he was paid since his arrest.

August 7, 2012: German authorities arrested Manfred K., 60, a German civilian who worked at NATO's air command headquarters at the U.S. Ramstein air base, charging him with obtaining state secrets and transferring the data to his private computer with the intent to provide them to an unidentified third party.

November 12, 2012: James F. Hitselberger, 55, a former Arabic linguist for the U.S. Navy in Bahrain, was charged on two counts under the Espionage Act of copying classified national defense information documents and shipping them back to the U.S., including to Stanford University's Hoover Institute, which holds the "James F. Hitselberger collection 1977–2012." The documents contained sensitive information about troop positions in Iraq, gaps in U.S. intelligence and commanders' travel plans. An FBI agent wrote that he had access to "all communications with sensitive sources in highly sensitive locations, including communication procedures, true names and tradecraft used by the sources." He earlier lived in Wisconsin. He was caught with classified documents in April 2012, but was not arrested. He flew home from Bahrain, but traveled throughout Europe for eight months. He was arrested in Kuwait and handed over to the U.S. in October 2012. He was held without bail. He wrote to an archivist that a March 2005 document would stay classified until 2015, but "regardless of the case, this material seems to warrant archival preservation. I will leave the

matter up to you to determine when researchers can have access to these items, as I am fully confident that your institution balances national security concerns with the needs of researchers of original source material." He was a student in Arabic and history at Georgetown University in the 1980s, then attended graduate school in politics and government at the University of Texas at Austin in the early 1990s. From October 2004 to February 2007, he was a contract linguist with a Secret clearance for Titan Corporation, a subsidiary of L3 Communications, working in several military camps in Iraq. In June 2011, he joined Global Linguist Solutions LLC and went to Bahrain in September 2011 working for a naval warfare group under a joint special operations task force. He pleaded not guilty and faced 20 years in prison.

December 4, 2012: *Reuters* reported that Switzerland's Federal Intelligence Service (NDB) intelligence service alerted intelligence services in the UK and U.S. that they had arrested a senior NDB IT technician who had stolen terabytes of data, including at least hundreds of thousands and possibly millions of pages of classified material onto portable hard drives he hid in his backpack. He was arrested in the summer but released from prison during an investigation by the Federal Attorney General office of Switzerland as to whether he had intended to sell the data to foreign officials or companies. He became disgruntled when his advice on using the data was ignored by Defense Ministry officials; NDB is part of the Defense Ministry. He had administrator rights, giving him access to most of the NDB's networks. Investigators seized portable storage devices, possibly before he was able to sell them. He had quit showing up to work, and was spotted when UBS, the largest Swiss bank, alerted authorities about a suspicious attempt to set up a new numbered bank account.

December 6, 2012: Former U.S. Navy submarine warfare specialist Robert Patrick Hoffman, II, 39, living in Virginia Beach, Virginia, was arrested on charges of trying to provide classified information on tracking U.S. submarines to FBI undercover agents posing as Russian intelligence officers. On October 21, the Navy veteran tried to give to the agents classified national defense information. The government said he intended to harm the U.S. and give an advantage to the Russian Federation. The court documents did not state whether he sought payment, but a law enforcement official told the media he asked for money. He had trained in cryptology. He retired from active duty in November 2011 as a petty officer first class. He faced life in prison. He pleaded not guilty on May 17, 2013. A jury found him guilty on August 21, 2013, of one count of attempted espionage. On February 10, 2014, Senior United States District Court Judge Robert Doumar in an Eastern District of Virginia sentenced Hoffman to 30 years in federal prison.

Hoffman was born in Buffalo, New York. He served in the U.S. Navy for 20 years before retiring with the rank of Petty Officer First Class on November 1, 2011. His Navy Military Occupation Specialty (MOS) was Cryptologic Technician—Technical (CTT). He served on U.S. nuclear submarines for most of his career, operating sensors and systems designed to collect data and information about potential enemies, scanned the environment for threats to the submarine, and provided technical and tactical guidance to the submarines' commanding officers.

The FBI began investigating him in 2012, sending undercover agents posing as SVR members to meet with him. Three times in September-October 2012, he filled a drop site with encrypted thumb drives containing secret and top secret/sensitive compartmented answers to the questions posed to him by the agents.

February 2013: The Mandiant Corporation, a U.S. information technology firm, released a report outlining evidence of Chinese People Liberation Army Unit 61398 near Shanghai conducting 141 cyber espionage operations against hundreds of corporations, including U.S. and other Western firms.

March 8, 2013: John O. Brennan was sworn in as Director of the Central Intelligence Agency. He was born on September 2, 1955, in North Bergen, New Jersey. He graduated from Fordham University in 1977 with a BA in political science. While at Fordham, he studied at the American University in Cairo in 1975–1976. In 1980 he earned a master's degree in government with a concentration in Middle Eastern studies from the University of Texas at Austin. He worked at the CIA from 1980 to 2005. In the Directorate of Intelligence, he covered the Near East and South Asia before directing counterterrorism analysis in the early 1990s. In 1994 and 1995 he was the Agency's intelligence briefer to President Bill Clinton. After serving as a Chief of Station in the Middle East, in 1999 to 2001 he was Chief of Staff to DCI George Tenet. He served as Deputy Executive Director of the CIA until 2003, when he began leading the Terrorist Threat Integration Center, a multiagency effort to establish what would become the National Counterterrorism Center. In 2004, he became NCTC's Interim Director. After retiring from the CIA in 2005, Mr. Brennan worked in the private sector for three years at The Analysis Corporation. He served in the Obama White House for four years as Assistant to the

President for Homeland Security and Counterterrorism.

March 15, 2013: Benjamin Pierce Bishop, 59, a U.S. defense contractor who worked in Pacific Command intelligence in Hawaii, was arrested at PACOM Headquarters at Camp H.M. Smith in Hawaii on charges of handing classified national security information to a 27-year-old Chinese woman he was dating. The indictment in U.S. District Court in Honolulu said he sent her an e-mail in May 2012 with PACOM's war plans, nuclear weapons, and U.S. relations with various countries. In September 2012, he told her in a phone call about the deployment of U.S. nuclear weapons and U.S. ability to find hostile short- and medium-range ballistic missiles. He met her at a conference in Hawaii on international military issues; they began their sexual relationship in June 2011. She was in the U.S. on a J-1 student visa. He was charged with concealing his relationship with the woman in violation of his security clearance and faced one count of communicating national defense information to a person not entitled to receive it and another count of unlawfully retaining national defense documents and plans. Authorities searching his home in November 2012 found a dozen secret documents. In February 2013, she asked him what the West knew about "the operation of a particular naval asset of the PRC," which he researched for her. Bishop was also a Lieutenant Colonel in the U.S. Army Reserve. His court-appointed attorney, Birney Bervar, said he had served for 29 years.

March 16, 2013: The FBI and DHS arrested Bio Jiant, a contractor at the National Institute of Aerospace (NIA) who worked at NASA-Langley. He was carrying hard drives, flash drives, and computers that contained confidential military secrets and rocket technology from NASA Labs and had a one-way ticket from Dulles International Airport.

March 25, 2013: A federal grand jury in Newark, New Jersey, on September 26, 2012, convicted Sixing Liu, alias Steve Liu, 49, a Chinese citizen employed by L-3 Communications/Space and Navigation Division, a major defense contractor, of nine of 11 counts of violating the Arms Export Control Act and the International Traffic in Arms Regulations, one count of possessing stolen trade secrets in violation of the Economic Espionage Act of 1996, one count of transporting stolen property in interstate commerce, and one count of lying to federal agents. He was acquitted on 2 counts of lying to federal agents. The court sentenced him on March 25, 2013, to five years and ten months for taking thousands of files about a disk resonator gyroscope and other defense systems to China in violation of a U.S. arms embargo. The stolen files included information on the performance and design of guidance systems for missiles, rockets, target locators, and UAVs. A Department of Justice bulletin said he stole the information "to position and prepare himself for future employment in the PRC. As part of that plan, Liu delivered presentations about the technology at several PRC universities, the Chinese Academy of Sciences, and conferences organized by PRC government entities." David Smukowski, President of Sensors in Motion, which developed the technology with L-3, said loss of the gyroscope technology alone could cost the U.S. military hundreds of millions of dollars. Liu earned a doctorate in electrical engineering, then came to the U.S. in 1993. He joined L-3 in 2009. He traveled to China in 2009 and 2010 to make the presentations without the permission of L-3.

April 25, 2013: The U.S. Department of Justice unsealed a 2004 grand jury indictment against former State Department employee Marta Rita Velázquez, 55, for spying for Cuba. She was living in Stockholm, Sweden, which does not extradite people accused of espionage. She was a graduate of Princeton University and Georgetown University Law School. She had been outside the U.S. since 2002. Ana Belen Montes, a former DIA analyst who admitted spying for Cuba for 17 years, said Velázquez helped recruit her. They met while graduate students at the Johns Hopkins University School of Advanced International Studies. The Puerto Rico–born Velázquez introduced Montes to Cuban intelligence in New York in 1984, went with her to a clandestine trip to Cuba for operational training, and helped her obtain her DIA job. Velázquez had worked at the Department of Transportation and for 13 years as a legal officer with the U.S. Agency for International Development, where she held a top secret clearance and was posted to U.S. embassies in Nicaragua and Guatemala. She traveled to Panama for an operational meeting with Cuban intelligence. She resigned from USAID in June 2002 after Montes's arrest but months before Montes pleaded guilty. The indictment charged her with one count of conspiracy to commit espionage by "spotting, assessing, and recruiting U.S. citizens who occupied sensitive national security positions or who had the potential of occupying such positions in the future." If convicted, she faced life in prison. The case is *United States v. Velázquez*, 04-cr-00044, U.S. District Court, District of Columbia (Washington).

June 6, 2013: The *Guardian*, and later the *Washington Post*, revealed that Booz Allen Hamilton contractor Edward Snowden, 29, had leaked that the National Security Agency had arrangements with several major Internet and telephony providers to grant access to the metadata of all phone records. Snowden, a former CIA staffer on contract with NSA, later turned up in Hong Kong, saying that the U.S. had been behind hundreds of hacking operations against Chinese systems. On June 14, 2013, federal prosecutors charged Snowden with espionage and theft of government property. Snowden flew to Moscow's Sheremetevo airport, hoping to fly from there to asylum in one of 20 countries he contacted. The U.S. revoked his passport, and the Russians said that because he lacked legitimate travel documents, he could not leave the transit lounge. On July 2, the plane carrying Bolivian President Evo Morales to Bolivia from Russia was diverted to Austria when France, Portugal, Spain and Italy denied access to their airspace due to suspicions that Snowden was on board. He remained stuck in Moscow, but Nicaragua, Bolivia, and Venezuela offered him asylum if conditions warranted and he could get there. He said he would accept temporary asylum in Russia, although President Vladimir Putin had said that Snowden would have to quit damaging its partner, the U.S. On August 1, 2013, the Russians provided Snowden with temporary asylum documents, good for a year. Snowden left the airport that day to stay with Americans in Moscow he met online. Snowden said in July 2014 that he would like to extend his stay in Moscow for another year. Meanwhile, the *Washington Post* in July 2014 revealed that Snowden had provided it with the full content of 160,000 individual intercepts. On August 1, 2014, Russia extended Snowden's asylum for three years.

August 9, 2013: Avril Dannica Haines was named Deputy Director of the Central Intelligence Agency, the first woman to hold the job. Haines was born on August 29, 1969. She earned received a bachelor's degree in Physics from the University of

Chicago and a J.D. from Georgetown University. From 2001 to 2002, she was a Legal Officer at The Hague Conference on Private International Law. From 2002 until 2003 she served as a law clerk for Judge Danny Boggs on the U.S. Court of Appeals for the Sixth Circuit. She worked in the Office of the Legal Adviser at the Department of State from 2003 to 2006, in the Office of Treaty Affairs and then in the Office of Political Military Affairs. From 2007 to 2008, she worked for the United States Senate Committee on Foreign Relations as Deputy Chief Counsel for the Majority. In 2010, she became the Deputy Assistant to the President and Deputy Counsel to the President for National Security at the White House since 2010. On January 9, 2015, CIA Director John Brennan announced that the President intended to nominate David Cohen to replace Haines, who would become the President's Deputy National Security Advisor.

November 30, 2013: The Royal Canadian Mounted Police arrested Canadian citizen Qing Quentin Huang, 53, on charges of attempting to sell classified information about the Canadian ship building procurement strategy to the Chinese government. He worked for Lloyd Register, a subcontractor to Irving Shipbuilding. He was charged under the Security of Information Act in trying to provide information on Canada's strategy in building patrol ships, frigates, naval auxiliary vessels, science research vessels and ice breakers.

January 31, 2014: Authorities arrested Marine Intelligence Officer and Gunnery Sergeant Jose Emmanuel Torres, 37, on charges of federal bribery, exceeding authorized access to a government computer and extortion. The Puerto Rican native from Cooper City enlisted in 1999, serving in Iraq from September 2009 to January 2010. He had

money and marriage problems. He drove to the 200 Gulf Stream Way, Dania Beach, Florida, parking lot outside Bass Pro Shops to pick up a duffel bag containing $235,000 in cash, but was instead arrested. Authorities had been building the sting operation against him for two years. He thought he had recruited an immigrant seeking U.S. residency who was going to help him steal the money from Colombian drug smugglers. Torres was serving at U.S. Southern Command in Doral, Florida, on assignment to the Defense Intelligence Agency, tracking drug smugglers and terrorists. He often worked with DOD and Homeland Security/Immigration and Customs Enforcement. He appeared in federal court on February 3; the case was continued until February 5 so he could find an attorney. Torres faced 40 years in prison and a $250,000 fine.

The criminal complaint alleged that in January 2012, Torres met a man at Miami's Krome Dentention center in Miami who was attempting to obtain U.S. residency. A year later, the detainee had been freed, and Torres asked him for $10,000, saying he was not earning enough as an E-7 Marine with 14 years of service (this normally is a $40,000 annual paycheck). Officials said Torres indicated that the man would be rearrested if he did not pay. The man instead reported the threat and became an FBI informant. The FBI recorded text messages, telephone calls, a hidden email account and Skype calls between Torres and the informant. In November 2013, the informant paid Torres $6,000. The charge sheet said Torres met the informant in several Broward County parking lots, including those outside T.G.I. Friday's in Davie, Walmart Supercenter in Cooper City, a medical plaza in Weston and a Publix in Plantation.

At their penultimate meeting outside Publix on January 29, Torres gave the informant a four-page Drug Enforcement Agency seizure report to show Colombian drug smugglers that agents had intercepted $500,000 of their money. Torres planned to get $250,000 for passing the report. On January 31, at 10:30 a.m., the duo met outside the Bass Pro Shops alongside I-95, where the informant gave Torres the duffle bag. The FBI promptly arrested him, according to the *South Florida Sun-Sentinel*.

March 2014: *CNN* and the *New York Times* reported on July 10, 2014, that federal authorities discovered that in mid–March Chinese hackers, possibly working for the PRC government, broke into the Office of Personnel Management network that stores sensitive information about federal workers, including material on background checks for anyone working with the federal government, employee hiring, wages, pensions and security clearances.

March 17, 2014: Lithuanian State Security Department officials told *Naharnet* that Russian diplomat Valery Katula at the Russian Embassy in Vilnius worked undercover for the GRU military intelligence service, targeting European Union ties with former Soviet states. The Lithuanian State Security Department told the press, "Katula attempted to recruit a Lithuanian civil servant to provide classified and other sensitive information about Lithuania's presidency of the European Union.... There were promises of money in exchange for information." The Lithuanians said Katula tried to recruit the Lithuanian official in late 2013. Lithuanian Foreign Minister Linas Linkevicius said the country was not expelling Katula from the country because "the fact that it has been made public is a sufficient measure at this moment."

May 19, 2014: The U.S. Department of Justice filed 31 criminal counts against five hackers in Unit 61398 of the Third Department of the People's Liberation Army, headquartered in a building in Shanghai, accusing them of stealing American trade secrets via a cyber-espionage campaign that ran from 2006 to 2014 against American companies in the nuclear power, metals and solar products industries, specifically Westinghouse Electric, U.S. subsidiaries of SolarWorld AG, U.S. Steel, Allegheny Technologies and Alcoa, plus the the United Steel, Paper and Forestry, Rubber, Manufacturing, Energy, Allied Industrial and Service Workers International Union. The formal charges accused the five of counts of conspiring to commit computer fraud; accessing a computer without authorization for the purpose of commercial advantage and private financial gain; damaging computers through the transmission of code and commands; aggravated identity theft; economic espionage; and theft of trade secrets.

Attorney General Eric Holder told a press conference, "This is a case alleging economic espionage by members of the Chinese military and represents the first-ever charges against a state actor for this type of hacking." Justice identified the hackers as Wang Dong, Sun Kailiang, Wen Xinyu, Huang Zhenyu, and Gu Chunhui, all officers with the PLA. DOJ listed their aliases as

- Wang Dong: Jack Wang, UglyGorilla;
- Sun Kailiang: Sun Kai Liang, Jack Sun;
- Wen Xinyu: Wen Xin Yu, WinXYHappy, Win_XY, Lao Wen;
- Huang Zhenyu: Huang Zhen Yu, hzy_lhx; and
- Gu Chunhui: Gu Chun Hui, KandyGoo.

Authorities said the hacking aided state-run competitors of U.S. firms and cost American jobs. The indictment said that the hackers

- stole cost, pricing and strategy information from SolarWorld;
- stole specifications for Westinghouse power plant pipes being built in China and examined executives' e-mails regarding Chinese ventures in 2010;
- used phishing e-mails to install malware on U.S. Steel computers, allowing them to exploit servers in 2010; and
- stole e-mail about union strategies regarding Chinese trade practices.

The Department of Justice separately charged the makers of malicious software used by hackers.

Some reports estimated that the costs to the U.S. of commercial cyber-espionage had reached $120 billion annually.

June 28, 2014: Canadian authorities arrested Su Bin, Chinese owner of Chinese aviation company Lode Tech, which was based in Canada. On July 11, 2014, the U.S. Department of Justice announced that he had hacked into Boeing Aerospace computers for several years and stole information about U.S. military aircraft and weapons, working with two contacts in China to sell the information to Chinese state-owned companies. DOJ said it did not have indications of Chinese government involvement in the hacking, nor of theft of classified information. The U.S. sought his extradition to face charges of unauthorized computer access. The FBI said the hacking began in 2010, and that more than 65 gigabytes of data were stolen over the next two years. The trio stole information on Boeing's C-17 military cargo plane and Lockheed Martin's F-22 and F-35 jets.

July 2, 2014: *CNN* reported that computer security firm Symantec had issued a report indicating that Russian hackers possibly affilitated with the Russian intelligence services had conducted highly-sophisticated computer attacks on U.S. oil and gas companies in a caper entitled Energetic Bear. The firm said the group had introduced malware into computers at power plants, energy grid operators, gas pipeline companies and industrial equipment makers in the United States and Spain, with other attacks elsewhere in Europe. The programs steal documents, usernames and passwords. The Crowdstrike firm had reported the Energetic Bear at work in 2012. The malware was later found inside the networks of European and U.S. defense contractors and health care providers, manufacturers, construction companies and universities doing nuclear energy research.

July 7, 2014: The Churchill Archives Centre at Cambridge University released 19 boxes of the Russian-language materials that KGB senior archivist Vasili Mitrokhin spirited out of Russia in 1992. The Mitrokhin Archives exposed numerous KGB agents, including Melita Norwood, 87, the "great-granny spy," who had passed UK atomic secrets to the Soviets for years. Her file said she was a "loyal, trustworthy, disciplined agent" who was awarded the Order of the Red Banner of Labour for her service. The papers included a list of 1,000 KGB agents in America.

July 7, 2014: The *Washington Post* reported that Chinese Deep Panda hackers believed affiliated with the Chinese government had been attacking U.S. Middle Eastern experts at American think tanks, according to Dmitri Alperovitch, chief technology officer of the CrowdStrike firm. He said the group shifted its targeting on June 18, when Sunni extremists seized Iraq's largest oil refinery. It had earlier gone after Asian experts at American research firms.

September 8, 2014: U.S. District Judge Beverly Reid O'Connell sentenced Brian Scott Orr, 42, of Marina del Rey, to 37 months in prison, a fine of $10,000, and three years of supervised release for providing sensitive information about a network used to control and communicate with military satellites to an undercover officer he believed worked for the Chinese government. From 2009 to 2011, he identified and evaluated vulnerabilities of the Air Force Satellite Control Network computers that control military satellites. After his 2011 resignation, he illegally kept training materials on how to operate the computer network. From September to November 2013, he met several times with an undercover FBI agent posing as a representative of a Chinese intelligence service, selling two thumb drives of sensitive military data for $5,000. He claimed to be the "foremost expert on attacking the computer network" who could destroy or disrupt U.S. military satellites for the Chinese government, or show the Chinese how to do so for a "big reward." The FBI arrested him in November 2013. He pleaded guilty to retention of stolen government property on March 17, 2014.

October 14, 2014: The *Washington Post* quoted iSight Partners, a cybersecurity firm, indicating that since 2009, SandWorm, a Russian hacking group, probably working for the government, had exploited a flaw in Microsoft Windows that they used to spy on NATO, the Ukrainian government, a U.S. university researcher, a Polish energy firm, a Western European government agency, a French telecommunications firm and other national security targets. The group's command server was in Germany.

October 15, 2014: Polish officials announced that a Polish army colonel and a Polish-Russian civilian attorney with Polish and Russian passports were detained on suspicion that they spied for Russian military intelligence. The suspects had some access to lawmakers and to energy security issues. Leonid Sviridov, 48, a Russian journalist

who worked for the *Rossiya Segodnya* news agency, was stripped of his right to work in Poland. In 2006, the Czech Republic imposed the same sanction against him for suspected spying. On November 14, Poland expelled several Russian diplomats for suspected espionage. Russia retaliated by PNG-ing four Polish diplomats. On November 26, the *Associated Press* reported that Sviridov was fighting expulsion.

October 27, 2014: *Yahoo News* and *UPI* reported that the FBI was investigating a "second Snowden" who was believed to have passed sensitive Terrorist Identities Datamart Environment intelligence secrets to *The Intercept*, a news website associated with Edward Snowden. The FBI searched the Virginia home of a government contractor as part of a criminal investigation.

November 6, 2014: The FBI found classified information in a search of the home of retired U.S. Ambassador Robin L. Raphel, 67, the previous month as part of a counterintelligence investigation. They also searched her State Department office. *CNN* reported that at the time of the search, she was an adviser on Pakistan under a contract to the State Department's Special Representative for Afghanistan and Pakistan. Her clearance was pulled in October 2014 and she was placed on administrative leave. Her contract lapsed on November 2 and was not renewed. She had earlier served as assistant secretary of state for South Asia and ambassador to Tunisia. She earlier worked as a CIA analyst before joining the Foreign Service for 30 years. She retired in 2005, and became a lobbyist for the Pakistani government. She returned to State in 2009 to work as an adviser to the late Richard Holbrooke at the U.S. Embassy in Islamabad, disbursing aid money. On November 20, 2014, the *New York Times* reported that the investigation stemmed from an intercepted conversation in which a Pakistani official said his government was obtaining U.S. secrets from a prominent retired U.S. diplomat. Raphel was represented by attorney Amy Jeffress of Arnold and Porter. In 1988, her former husband, Arnold L. Raphel, then U.S. Ambassador to Pakistan, died in a plane crash with Pakistani President General Mohammad Zia ul-Haq.

November 17, 2014: *Der Spiegel* reported that Moscow expelled a German diplomat in retaliation for the earlier PNGing of a Russian diplomat accused of espionage.

December 5, 2014: *Business Insider* reported that the Defense Department indicted Saudi-born Mostafa Ahmed Awwad, 34, a civilian engineer in the Nuclear Engineering and Planning Department at the Navy's shipyard in Norfolk, Virginia, for attempting to send schematics for the U.S.'s newest nuclear-powered aircraft carrier to an undercover FBI agent who he believed was working for Egyptian intelligence. Awwad worked at the department since February 2014. One night in September, an Arabic speaker called Awwad to set up a meeting the next day, posing as an Egyptian intelligence agent. The Justice Department said Awwad claimed "it was his intention to utilize his position of trust with the U.S. Navy to obtain military technology for use by the Egyptian government, including but not limited to, the designs of the USS *Gerald R. Ford* nuclear aircraft carrier." Justice said Awwad set up dead-drops, giving his handler "four computer-aided drawings of a U.S. nuclear aircraft carrier downloaded from the Navy Nuclear Propulsion Information system," photos of blueprints for the vessel, and suggestions for the best places to strike the carrier in order to sink it. Awwad allegedly brought a handgun to one of his meetings. Awwad faced 20 years in prison. Awwad married in Cairo. He had a Secret

clearance. FBI.gov reported on June 15, 2015 that Awwad pleaded guilty to charges of attempted espionage. Sentencing was scheduled for September 21, 2015. He faced life in prison, but the plea agreement suggested 8–11 years.

December 14, 2014: Estonian police charged former State Security Services (CAPO) agent Uno Puusepp with treason after Russian state broadcaster *NTV*'s laudatory documentary *Our Man in Tallinn* quoted the Russian Federal Security Service saying that he had been a double agent since 1996. He had retired from CAPO and moved to Moscow three years earlier. He told *NTV*, "After 20 years of knowing you can be found out and taken away, you get used to the pressure slowly and quietly." He was recruited by former KGB officer Nikolai Yermakov, who said Puusepp's motivation was not money but dislike of working for the Estonian establishment. The two met while Puusepp was working for USSR/Estonia's KGB as a wiretapping expert in the 1970s. The Estonians had earlier arrested and sentenced to a 15-year prison term KGB agent Vladimir Weitman. Also appearing on the *NTV* documentary was former Estonian intelligence operative Karl Pax, who was suspected of working with Puusepp.

December 31, 2014: Authorities near NATO's Zoknai air base in Siauliai, Lithuania, detained several alleged members of a Russian spy ring suspected of infiltrating the Lithuanian army. Lithuanian Lieutenant Colonel Vidmantas Raklevicius said that one of the detainees was one of his officers, who had been in the Lithuanian air force for ten years.

January 9, 2015: CIA.Gov reported that CIA Director John Brennan announced that President Obama had selected David S. Cohen to be the new CIA Deputy Director. Cohen became the Department of

Treasury's Under Secretary for Terrorism and Financial Intelligence in June 2011, leading policy, enforcement, regulatory, and intelligence functions aimed at identifying and disrupting the lines of financial support to international terrorist organizations, proliferators of weapons of mass destruction, narcotics traffickers, and other illicit actors posing a threat to U.S. national security, and overseeing the Department's efforts to combat money laundering and financial crimes. During 2009–2011, he was Assistant Secretary for Terrorist Financing, where he was responsible for formulating and coordinating the Department's counterterrorist financing and anti-money laundering efforts. He was in private law practice for seven years. He initially joined the Treasury Department in 1999, working in the Office of the General Counsel as Senior Counsel to the General Counsel, where he was involved in crafting legislation that formed the basis of the Title III of the USA Patriot Act, and the 2001 update to the Bank Secrecy Act. He earlier practiced law for nine years in the private sector. He earned his law degree from Yale Law School and his undergraduate degree from Cornell University. He was scheduled to become CIA Deputy Director in February 2015.

January 26, 2015: *ABC News* reported that federal officials arrested Evgeny Buryakov, Deputy Representative in the U.S. for Russia's Vnesheconombank, in Manhattan. A criminal complaint accused him of working for the Russian SVR's Directorate ER as a "non-official cover" agent. The Department of Justice said his spy ring involved Igor Sporyshev and Victor Podobnyy, had worked in the U.S. before on behalf of Russia and were protected by diplomatic immunity. Sporyshev worked as a Trade Representative for Russia in New York until late 2014 and Podobnyy was an attaché to Russia's Permanent Mission of the Russian Federation to the United Nations. Federal officials said the ring was to obtain information on potential sanctions against Russia and U.S. efforts to develop alternative energy resources.

APPENDIX A:
ALLEGED AMERICAN SPIES

The following is a list of Americans or long-term resident aliens investigated (including some who were arrested, charged and convicted, and others who were cleared) for espionage or espionage-related activities or who defected to foreign intelligence services or mishandled classified materials between 1900 and 2014.

Soviet or Russian Services

Jacob Abram (January 25, 1957)
Aldrich Hazen Ames (February 21, 1994)
Maria del Rosario Casa Ames (February 21, 1994)
David Henry Barnett (February 27, 1977)
Joel Barr (July 17, 1950; July 20, 1950)
Elizabeth Bentley (November 1945)
Felix Bloch (February 7, 1990)
Herbert Boeckenhaupt (October 24, 1966)
David Sheldon Boone (October 10, 1998)
Christopher J. Boyce (January 16, 1977)
Arnold Bracy (December 14, 1986)
Russell Paul Brown (July 25, 1989)
Edward Owen Buchanan (May 17, 1985)
John William Butenko (October 29, 1963)
Thomas Patrick Cavanaugh (December 18, 1984)
Whittaker Chambers (1932)
Lona Cohen (October 1944; January 7, 1961)
Morris Cohen (October 1944; January 7, 1961)
Christopher Michael Cooke (May 28, 1981)
Judith Coplon (March 4, 1949)
Robert Ernest Cordrey (April 12, 1984)
Lauchlin Currie (1939)
Raymond George DeChamplin (July 2, 1971)
Sadag Katcher Dedeyan (June 27, 1975)
Nelson Cornelious Drummond (August 1963)
Laurence Duggan (December 20, 1948)
Jack Edward Dunlap (July 23, 1963)
Robert Wade Ellis (February 9, 1983)

George Holmes French (April 5, 1957)
George John Gessner (June 9, 1964)
John Gilmore (October 3, 1960)
Harry Gold (January 24, 1950; May 22, 1950)
Jacob Golos (1939; February 7, 1951)
David Greenglass (June 16, 1950)
Ruth Greenglass (June 16, 1950)
Oliver Everett Grunden (November 2, 1973)
John Joseph Haeger (December 1, 1989)
Robert Dean Haguewood (March 4, 1986)
James Michael Hall, III (December 21, 1988)
Theodore Alvin Hall né Holzberg (October 1944)
Victor Norris Hamilton (1963)
Robert P. Hanssen (December 18, 1996; February 18, 2001)
Ulysses Leonard Harris (August 25, 1967)
Joseph George Helmich (July 15, 1981)
Alger Hiss (1932; December 15, 1948)
Robert Patrick Hoffman, II (December 6, 2012)
Brian Patrick Horton (September 30, 1982)
Edward Lee Howard (August 7, 1986)
Dale Vern Irene (August 13, 1985)
Randy Miles Jeffries (December 20, 1985)
Robert Lee Johnson (February 22, 1953)
William Kampiles (August 17, 1978)
Tyler Kent (May 20, 1940)
Daniel M. King (November 5, 1999)
Craig D. Kunkle (January 10, 1989)
Gary Lee Ledbetter (August 26, 1967)
Andrew Daulton Lee (January 6, 1977)
Duncan Chaplin Lee (November 1945)

Kurt G. Lessenthien (April 3, 1996)
Patricia Lipka (February 7, 1994)
Robert Stephen Lipka (February 7, 1994)
Clayton John Lonetree (December 14, 1986)
William Hamilton Martin (June 25, 1960)
Russell McNutt (July 17, 1950)
Richard William Miller (October 3, 1984)
James Allen Mintkenbaugh (February 22, 1953)
Bernon Ferguson Mitchell (June 25, 1960)
Edwin Gibbons Moore, II (December 21, 1975)
Boris Morros (January 25, 1957)
Miriam Moskowitz (1950)
Gustav Adolph Mueller (October 7, 1949)
Michael Richard Murphy (June 1, 1981)
Frank Arnold Nesbitt (October 14, 1989)
Harold J. Nicholson (November 16, 1996)
Nathaniel Nicholson (November 16, 1996)
Nikolai Ogorodnikov (October 3, 1984)
Svetlana Ogorodnikov (October 3, 1984)
Bruce Damian Ott (January 22, 1986)
Sarkis Paskalian (June 27, 1975)
Ronald William Pelton (November 25, 1985)
Walter Thomas Perkins (October 21, 1971)
Jeffery Loring Pickering (October 3, 1983)
Edwin Earl Pitts (December 18, 1996)
Francis Xavier Pizzo, II (August 13, 1985)
Kurt Leopold Ponger (January 14, 1953)
Juliet Stuart Poyntz (June 3, 1937)
William W. Remington (February 7, 1951)
Roy Adair Rhodes (February 21, 1958)
Daniel Walter Richardson (January 14, 1988)
Ivan Rogalsky (January 7, 1977)
Ethel Greenglass Rosenberg (July 17, 1950)
Julius Rosenberg (July 17, 1950)
Leonard Jenkins Safford (August 25, 1967)
Alfred Epaminondas Sarant (July 17, 1950; July 20, 1950)
Saville Sax (October 1944)
Charles Edward Schoof (December 1, 1989)
Hafiz Ahmad Ali Shaaban (May 1, 2005)
Nathan Gregory Silvermaster (July 16, 1942)
Charles Dale Slatten (April 14, 1984)
Brian Everett Slavens (September 4, 1982)
Richard Craig Smith (April 4, 1984)
Morton Sobell (August 16, 1950)
Jack Soble (January 25, 1957)
Myra Soble (January 25, 1957)
Robert Soblen (January 25, 1957; September 11, 1962)
Glenn Michael Souther (1980)
Alfred Stern (September 9, 1957)
Martha Stern (September 9, 1957)
Michael Whitney Straight (1937)

Kota Subrahmanyam (October 8, 1995)
Robert Glenn Thompson (January 7, 1965)
Bruce Edward Tobias (August 13, 1985)
Michael Timothy Tobias (August 13, 1985)
George Trofimoff (June 14, 2000)
Svetlana Tumanova (September 28, 1987)
Otto Verber (January 14, 1953)
Arthur James Walker (May 20, 1985; May 29, 1985)
Michael Lance Walker (May 20, 1985; May 22, 1985)
John Anthony Walker, Jr. (May 20, 1985)
First name unknown Walton (1972)
Ariel Jonathan Weinmann (December 4, 2006)
William Weisband (November 1950)
First name unknown Wesson (October 29, 1963)
William Henry Whalen (July 12, 1966)
Donald Niven Wheeler (November 1945)
Harry Dexter White (July 16, 1942; August 13, 1948)
Jerry Alfred Whitworth (May 20, 1985; June 3, 1985)
James Rodney Wilmoth (July 25, 1989)
Edward Hilledon Wine (September 29, 1968)
Hans Palmer Wold (July 19, 1983)
Ronald Craig Wolf (May 5, 1989)
James David Wood (July 21, 1973)
Huseyin Yildirim (December 21, 1988; July 20, 1989)
Jones York (1940s)
Jane Foster Zlatovski (July 8, 1957)

Soviet Bloc Services

Czechoslovakia

Jeffrey M. Carney (April 22, 1991)
Clyde Lee Conrad (August 23, 1988)
Robert Ernest Cordrey (April 12, 1984)
Jeffrey Eugene Gregory (August 23, 1988; October 22, 1992)
Roderick James Ramsay (August 23, 1988; June 8, 1990)
Glenn Roy Rohrer (August 1965)
Jeffrey Rondeau (August 23, 1988; October 22, 1992)
Kelly Therese Warren (August 23, 1988)

GDR (East Germany)

Harold Noah Borger (March 3, 1961)
James Michael Clark (February 24, 1997)
Robert Ernest Cordrey (April 12, 1984)
Francisco de Assis Mira (April 1983)
Leslie Joseph Payne (October 1974)

Michael Peri (February 20, 1989)
James Frederick Sattler (1975)
Theresa Marie Squillacote (February 24, 1997)
Kurt Alan Stand (February 24, 1997)
Huseyin Yildirim (December 21, 1988; July 20, 1989)

Hungary

Clyde Lee Conrad (August 23, 1988)
Otto Attila Gilbert (April 17, 1982)
Jeffrey Eugene Gregory (August 23, 1988; October 22, 1992)
Tommaso Mortati (December 21, 1989)
Roderick James Ramsay (August 23, 1988; June 8, 1990)
Jeffrey Rondeau (August 23, 1988; October 22, 1992)
Zoltán Szabó (August 23, 1988; May 21, 1989)
Kelly Therese Warren (August 23, 1988)

Poland

William Holden Bell (June 23, 1981)
Robert Ernest Cordrey (April 12, 1984)
James Durward Harper, Jr. (October 15, 1983)
Irvin C. Scarbeck (January 1961; June 14, 1961)
Ruby Louise Schuler (October 15, 1983)

Chinese Services

Gregg William Bergersen (February 11, 2008)
Benjamin Pierce Bishop (March 15, 2013)
Larry Wu-Tai Chin (November 22, 1985)
Dongfan "Greg" Chung (February 11, 2008)
James Wilbur Fondren, Jr. (February 11, 2008; May 13, 2009)
Yuefei Ge (September 26, 2007)
Noshir Sheriarji Gowadia (October 2005)
Anne Henderson-Pollard (November 21, 1985)
Eric O. Jenott (August 21, 1996)
Yu Xin Kang (February 11, 2008; May 28, 2008)
Yen Men Kao (December 3, 1993)
Tai Shen Kuo (February 11, 2008)
Lan Lee (September 26, 2007)
Peter H. Lee (December 7, 1997)
Wen Ho Lee (December 10, 1999)
Katrina M. Leung (April 9, 2003)
Fuk-heung Li (October 28, 2005)
Sixing Liu (March 25, 2013)
Chi Mak (October 28, 2005)
Rebecca Lai-wah Chiu Mak (October 28, 2005)
Tai Wang Mak (October 28, 2005)
Yui "Billy" Mak (October 28, 2005)

Rian Minkyu Martin (December 6, 2010)
Xiaodong Sheldon Meng (August 1, 2007)
Guo Bao Min (December 10, 1999)
Ronald N. Montaperto (June 21, 2006)
Brian Scott Orr (2014)
Brian Patrick Regan (August 23, 2001)
John Stewart Service (1945)
Glenn Duffie Shriver (October 22, 2010)
Bryan Underwood (September 1, 2011)

World War II Axis Services

Nazi Germany

Paul Bante (June 1941)
Max Blank (June 1941)
Alfred E. Brokhoff (June 1941)
Heinrich Clausing (June 1941)
William Colepaugh (November 29, 1944)
Conradin Otto Dold (June 1941)
Frederick "Fritz" Joubert Duquesne (June 1941)
Rudolf Ebeling (June 1941)
Richard Eichenlaub (June 1941)
Heinrich Carl Eilers (June 1941)
Paul Fehse (June 1941)
Dr. Ignatz Griebl (March 10, 1938)
Werner George Gudenberg (March 10, 1938)
Edmund Carl Heine (June 1941)
Felix Jahnke (June 1941)
Gustav Wilhelm Kaercher (June 1941)
Tyler Kent (May 20, 1940)
Josef Klein (June 1941)
Hartwig Richard Kleiss (June 1941)
Simon Emil Koedel (October 24, 1944)
Herman W. Lang (June 1941)
Evelyn Clayton Lewis (June 1941)
Rene Emanuel Mezenen (June 1941)
Carl Reuper (June 1941)
Everett Minster Roeder (June 1941)
Guenther Gustave Rumrich (March 10, 1938)
Paul Alfred W. Scholz (June 1941)
George Gottlob Schuh (June 1941)
Erwin Wilhelm Siegler (June 1941)
Heinrich Stade (June 1941)
Oscar Richard Staler (June 1941)
Lilly Barbara Carola Stein (June 1941)
Franz Joseph Stigler (June 1941)
Erich Strunck (June 1941)
Otto Hermann Voss (March 10, 1938)
Leo Waalen (June 1941)
Alfred Henry August Walischewski (June 1941)
Else Weustenfeld (June 1941)
Alex Wheeler-Hill (June 1941)
Berram Wolfgang Zenzinger (June 1941)

Imperial Japan

Velvalee Malvena Dickinson née Blucher (January 21, 1944)

John Semer Farnsworth (July 14, 1936)

Harry Thompson (March 5, 1936)

Other Services/Entities Approached and/or Spotting, Assessing, Developing, Recruiting and Running Human Sources

Al Qaeda

Ryan Gilbert Anderson (February 12, 2004)

Paul Raphael Hall/Hassan Abujihaad (April 3, 2009)

Timothy Steven Smith (April 8, 2000)

Austria

Noshir Sheriarji Gowadia (October 2005)

Ariel Jonathan Weinmann (December 4, 2006)

Australian Military

Jonathan P. Pollard (November 21, 1985)

Cuba

Philip Burnett Franklin Agee (1973)

Alejandro M. Alonso (September 12, 1998)

Carlos Alvarez (December 19, 2006)

Elsa Alvarez (December 19, 2006)

Mariano M. Faget (February 17, 2000)

George Gari (August 31, 2001)

Marisol Gari (August 31, 2001)

Linda Hernandez (September 12, 1998)

Nilo Hernandez (September 12, 1998)

Ana Belen Montes (September 21, 2001)

Gwendolyn Steingraber Myers (June 4, 2009)

Walter Kendall Myers (June 4, 2009)

Joseph Santos (September 12, 1998)

Amarylis Silverio Santos (September 12, 1998)

Marta Rita Velázquez (September 21, 2001; April 25, 2013)

Ecuador

Frederick Christopher Hamilton (February 5, 1993)

Egypt

Mostafa Ahmed Awwad (2014)

Ahmed Fathy Mehalba (September 29, 2003)

El Salvador

Philip Tyler Seldon (August 7, 1996)

France

Leandro Aragoncillo (October 5, 2005)

John Douglas Charlton (May 25, 1995)

Germany

Noshir Sheriarji Gowadia (October 2005)

Ghana

Sharon M. Scranage (July 11, 1985)

Michael Soussoudis (July 11, 1985)

Greece

Steven J. Lalas (May 3, 1993)

Iraq

Saubhe Jassim al-Dellemy (December 22, 2008)

William Shaoul Benjamin (September 18, 2006)

Sami Khoshaba Latchin (August 2004)

Susan Lindauer (March 11, 2004)

Abdulhakeem Nour (February 14, 2007)

Brian Patrick Regan (August 23, 2001)

Hafiz Ahmad Ali Shaaban (May 1, 2005)

Najib Shemami (January 18, 2009)

Albert T. Sombolay (December 3, 1991)

Israel

Noshir Sheriarji Gowadia (October 2005)

Anne Henderson-Pollard (November 21, 1985)

Ben-Ami Kadish (April 22, 2008)

David Nozette (October 19, 2009)

Jonathan J. Pollard (November 21, 1985)

Steven J. Rosen (May 4, 2005)

Keith Weissman (May 4, 2005)

Italy

Ronald Joshua Hoffman (June 8, 1990)

Japan

Ronald Joshua Hoffman (June 8, 1990)

Jordan

Albert T. Sombolay (December 3, 1991)

Libya

Waldo Herman Dubberstein (April 30, 1983)

Brian Patrick Regan (August 23, 2001)

Edwin Wilson (April 30, 1983)

North Korea

Giuseppe E. Cascio (September 21, 1951)

John Joungwoong Yai (February 4, 2003)

North Vietnam

Ronald Humphrey (January 31, 1978)

David Truong (January 31, 1978)

Pakistan
Syed Ghulam Nabi Fai (December 6, 2011)

Philippines
Michael Hahn Allen (December 4, 1986)
Virginia Jean Baynes (May 22, 1992; December 27, 1992)
Joseph Garfield Brown (May 22, 1992; December 27, 1992)

Philippines Oppositionists
Leandro Aragoncillo (October 5, 2005)

Saudi Arabia
Michael Stephen Schwartz (October 14, 1995)

South Africa
Stephen Anthony Baba (October 1, 1981)
Thomas Joseph Dolce (April 16, 1988)
Ronald Joshua Hoffman (June 14, 1990)
Donald Charles Lieber (May 1, 1998)
Jonathan P. Pollard (November 21, 1985)
Theresa Marie Squillacote (February 24, 1997)

South Korea
Robert Chaegon Kim (January 24, 1996)

Switzerland
Noshir Sheriarji Gowadia (October 2005)

Syria
Ahmad I. Halabi (September 23, 2003)
Mohamad Anas Haitham Soueid (October 12, 2011)

Taiwan
Donald W. Keyser (September 15, 2004)
Douglas S. Tsou (February 9, 1988)

Venezuela
Franklin Duran (April 23, 2008)
Antonio J. Gomez (April 23, 2008)
Carlos Kauffmann (April 23, 2008)
Moises Maionica (April 23, 2008)

Marjorie Roxby Mascheroni (September 17, 2010)
Pedro Leonardo Mascheroni (September 17, 2010)
Rodolfo Edgardo Wanseele Paciello (April 23, 2008)

Narcotraffickers
Lee Eugene Madsen (August 14, 1979)

Unspecified, or Mishandling of Classified Information
William Cleveland, Jr. (April 9, 2003)
Randall G. Craig, Jr. (April 15, 2008)
David Fleming (October 4, 1988)
Kenneth Wayne Ford, Jr. (January 12, 2004)
Lawrence A. Franklin (May 4, 2005)
Wilfredo Garcia (January 22, 1988)
Ronald Dean Graf (July 6, 1989)
Douglas F. Groat (April 3, 1998)
Stephen Dwayne Hawkins (August 7, 1985)
James F. Hitselberger (November 12, 2012)
Bio Jiant (March 16, 2013)
Geneva Jones (August 3, 1993)
Bruce Leland Kearn (March 1984)
Donald Wayne King (July 6, 1989)
Chelsea née Bradley E. Manning (June 8, 2010)
John Raymond Maynard (August 1983)
William Colton Millay (October 2011)
Samuel Loring Morison (October 1, 1984)
James J. Smith (April 9, 2003)
Edward Snowden (June 6, 2013)
Henry Otto Spade (November 17, 1988)
Jay Clyde Wolff (December 17, 1984)
James J. Yee (September 10, 2003)

For further information on these individuals, see the chronology's entries at the dates that follow their names.

Note: This list does not include individuals who were investigated and later cleared. Many of the individuals listed did not pass classified information to hostile intelligence services, instead falling for federal sting operations.

APPENDIX B:
ALLEGED FOREIGN SPIES

The following is a list of foreign hostile intelligence service officers who were identified, arrested, jailed, declared persona non grata, *traded or released between 1900 and 2014.*

World War I German Services
Dr. Heinrich Albert (July 7, 1914)
Carl Boy-Ed (July 7, 1914)
Kurt Jahnke (March 1917)
Paul Koenig (August 22, 1914)
Count Johann Heinrich von Bernstorff (July 7, 1914)
Captain Rintelen von Kleist (August 1915)
Captain Franz von Papen (July 7, 1914)

Nazi Services
William Joyce (January 3, 1946)
William Lonkowski (March 10, 1938)

KGB and Its Predecessors, Including OGPU, NKVD, NKGB
Roland Abbiate (July 17, 1937)
Rudolph Ivanovich Abel né Vilyam "Willie" Genrikhovich Fisher (May 6, 1957; June 21, 1957; November 20, 2010)
Itzhak Ahkmerov (November 1945)
Aleksandr Bondarenko (September 1968)
Samuel Cahan (1991)
Viktor Cherkashin (February 18, 2001)
Anatoli Alekseyevich Chernyayev (1983)
Alexander Feklisov (July 17, 1950)
Vladimir Galkin (October 8, 1995)
Reino Gikman (February 7, 1990)
Anatoliy Gorsky (November 1945)
Arkadi Vasilyevich Guk (September 16, 1983)
Sergei Illarionov (1992)
Oleg Kalugin (May 20, 1985)
Nikolai Karpekov (April 27, 1963)
Yevgeny P. Karpov (January 7, 1977)

Alexandr Grigoryevich Kopatzky (1949)
Valeri Viktorovich Krepkogorsky (March 1978)
Vladimi Kryuchkov (February 18, 2001)
Anatoli Kuznetsov (August 5, 1981)
Viktor Mechislavovich Lesiovsky (March 1978)
Andrei K. Lugovoi (November 1, 2006)
Maksim Grigorlevich Martynov (February 21, 1955)
Hede Massing (December 20, 1948)
Alice Michelson (October 1, 1984)
Konon Molody (January 7, 1961)
Victor I. Okunev (April 4, 1984)
Nikolai Pavlovich Ostrovsky (July 21, 1955)
Vitaliy Pavlov (August 13, 1948)
Vladimir Putin (December 31, 1999)
Artur Viktorovich Pyatn (January 1980)
Igor Aleksandrovich Sakharovsky (July 5, 1979)
Aleksei Nikolayevich Savin (March 1967)
Violette Seina/Sanni (December 14, 1986)
Leonid Vladimirovich Shebarshin (1983)
Aleksandr Shelepin (October 12, 1957)
Kurt Simon (1989)
Viktor Sokolov (1956)
Boris Solomatin (May 20, 1985)
Bogdan Stashynsky (October 12, 1957)
Alexei Tkachenko (May 20, 1985)
William Weisband (November 1950)
Genrikh Yagoda (March 18, 1937)
Arkadi Yakovlev (July 17, 1950)
Alexi Yefimov (December 14, 1986)
Nikolai Yermakov (2014)
Gennadi Mikhaylovich Yevstafeyev (March 1978)
Nikolai Yezhov (March 18, 1937)

GRU

Boris Bykov (1932)
Sergei Edemski (July 12, 1966)
Vladimir M. Ismaylov (June 19, 1986)
Valery Katula (March 17, 2014)
Yuriy P. Leonov (August 18, 1983)
Stanislav Lunev (1992)
Aleksei R. Malinin (October 24, 1966)
Igor Melekh (October 3, 1960)
Richard Sorge (October 18, 1941; July 7, 2000)
Nikolai Zabotin (September 5, 1945)

Unspecified Soviet Intelligence Service

Rudolf Chernyayev (May 20, 1978)
Victor Chernyshev (July 21, 1973)
Valdik Enger (May 20, 1978)
Valentin Gubitchev (March 4, 1949)
Igor Ivanov (October 29, 1963)
Boris V. Kaprovich (January 7, 1965)
Vladimir I. Olenev (October 29, 1963)
Gleb A. Pavlov (October 29, 1963)
Sergey Viktorovich Petrov (February 14, 1972)
Yuri Pokrovsky (August 20, 1987)
Yuri A. Romashin (October 29, 1963)
Gennadiy F. Zakharov (September 12, 1986)
Vladimir Zinyakin (May 20, 1978)

FSB

Uno Puusepp (2014)

SVR

Anna Chapman née Anya Kushchenko (June 27, 2010)
Tracey Lee Ann Foley (June 27, 2010)
Stanislav Borisovich Gusev (December 9, 1999)
Donald Howard Heathfield (June 27, 2010)
Juan Lazaro (June 27, 2010)
Christopher Metsos (June 27, 2010)
Patricia Mills (June 27, 2010)
Cynthia Murphy (June 27, 2010)
Richard Murphy (June 27, 2010)
Victoria Palaez (June 27, 2010)
Yevgeni Maksimovich Primakov (October 11, 1991)
Mikhael Semenko (June 27, 2010)
Yuri Vlasov (November 16, 1996)
Katia Zatuliveter (December 2, 2010)
Michael Zottoli (June 27, 2010)

Unspecified Soviet or Russian Intelligence Service

Alexey Karetnikov (July 12, 2010)

Anatoloy T. Koreyev (August 25, 1967)
Yuri N. Pakhtusov (March 9, 1989)
Nikolai F. Popov (August 25, 1967)
Arkadi Yakovlev (July 17, 1950)

Cuban DGI

Fernando Gonzalez Llort (January 24, 1998; August 31, 2001)
Rene Gonzalez Sehwerert (January 24, 1998; August 31, 2001)
Antonio Guerrero Rodriguez (January 24, 1998; August 31, 2001)
Ramon Labanino Salazar (August 31, 2001)
Gerardo Hernandez Nordelo (January 24, 1998; August 31, 2001)
Jose Imperatori (February 17, 2000)

Bulgarian Intelligence Service

Penyu B. Kostadinov (December 1983)

Czechoslovakian Stani tajni Bezpecnost (StB)

Erwin van Haarlem (March 3, 1989)
Hana Koecher née Pardamcova (November 27, 1984)
Karl F. Koecher (November 27, 1984)

East German Stasi/HVA (Hauptverwaltung Aufklarung, Main Reconnaissance Administration)

Heinz Gleske (April 1954)
Hans-Jurgen Henze (1985)
Erich Mielke (December 21, 1988)
Karl-Heinz Schneider (1968)
Lothar Ziemer (February 14, 1997)

Polish Intelligence Service

Zdislaw Prychodzien (October 15, 1983)
Marian Zacharski (June 23, 1981)

Chinese Intelligence Services

Gu Chunhui (May 19, 2014)
Hou Desheng (December 21, 1987)
Huang Zhenyu (May 19, 2014)
Sun Kailiang (May 19, 2014)
Wang Dong (May 19, 2014)
Wen Xinyu (May 19, 2014)
Yang Qiming (June 21, 2006)
Yu Zhenghe (June 21, 2006)
Zang Weichu (December 21, 1987)

Ghana

Kojo Tsikata (July 11, 1985)

Israel

Yosef Yagur (November 21, 1985; April 22, 2008)

South African Bureau of State Security (BOSS)

Norman Blackburn (May 27, 1967)

Note: This Appendix lists hostile intelligence service staffers, not recruited assets; public reporting is sometimes unclear regarding their status. "Illegals"—individuals usually reporting to Soviet or Russian services who are not affiliated with diplomatic facilities, and therefor do not have diplomatic immunity—are treated as staffers, not foreign assets, even in cases in which they obtained citizenship of their host countries. A Western near-synonym is "non-official cover." Illegals often "burrow" into their local environments and do not conduct operations for years, sometimes decades, until activated by their handlers.

A GUIDE TO THE LITERATURE
OF COUNTERINTELLIGENCE:
FROM PICKLE THE SPY
TO THE CONFICKER WORM

by Hayden B. Peake

Pickle the Spy was never caught. This agent of Henry Pelham, Secretary of State to King George II, penetrated the entourage of Bonnie Prince Charlie and, inter alia, reported his plan to seize the King—the Elibank Plot—and restore the Catholic Stuarts to power in 1751. The plotters were captured and tried. Though suspected by some, Pickle was trusted by the security conscious Prince and in 1754 retired to become chief of clan Macdonnell of Glengarry.[1] Pickle was finally identified as Alasdair MacDonnell by historian Andrew Lang more than one hundred years later (Lang 1897, 1898).

The case of Pickle the Spy is an example of an English tradition called *espionage civile*, as distinguished from military espionage, intended to "defend the Royal Title and Dignity by preventing ... all plots and conspiracies against the King's Peace" (Richings: 14). In today's vernacular, the functions that accomplish this mission are often called security, counterespionage, or counterintelligence.[2] This essay will first clarify these definitions and then review their application in the historical and contemporary counterintelligence literature, in English, from ancient times to the present. While the scope may be broad and representative, the review is not comprehensive; many other sources could have been included. However, the bibliographies in the major works cited and the section on additional references below combine to cover most of the sources not mentioned.

Readers new to the field of intelligence may wish to consult Lowenthal (2011) before continuing. He provides a sound introductory overview of the intelligence profession in the United States and several other countries, with descriptions of the organizations, missions, functions, problems and terminology involved.

Definitions

The official United States definition of counterintelligence may be found in presidential executive order 12333, as amended on July 31, 2008:

> Para. 3.5a: Counterintelligence means information gathered and activities conducted to identify, deceive, disrupt, or protect against espionage, other intelligence activities, sabotage, or assassinations conducted for or on behalf of foreign powers, organizations or persons or their agents, or international terrorist organizations or activities.

For reasons unclear, this definition has not been widely adopted even in the United States. The National Counterintelligence Executive (NCIX)[3] for example, uses the following variation:

> Counterintelligence is the business of identifying and dealing with foreign intelligence threats to the United States. Its core concern is the intelligence services of foreign states and similar organizations of non-state actors, such

as transnational terrorist groups. Counterintelligence has both a defensive mission—protecting the nation's secrets and assets against foreign intelligence penetration—and an offensive mission—finding out what foreign intelligence organizations are planning to better defeat their aims.

Moreover, authors often create their own definitions as for example: Carl (1996: 124–5); Johnson (2007: 183); West (2005i: 114) and Clark (2007: 69). Most include the basic functions: double agents, defectors, deception operations, communications, and handling moles or penetrations. Johnson (1987: 2–3), Felix (2001), and Watson (1990: 124) include counterespionage—the penetration of foreign intelligence services, as does Wilson (1996: 56), but he only implies penetration. CI liaison with other intelligence services is defined in Johnson (2006: 113, 114–5). Several authors confuse security with CI: Shulsky (2002: 99ff), Holt (1995: 109ff) and Wettering (2008: 324ff), and subordinate personnel, physical, document and cryptologic security responsibilities to CI. While it is true that the military often combines these functions under one staff element, they remain separate offices at the national level, the principal focus of this essay.

Thus identifying a CI operation is a matter of the functions or techniques involved, not compliance with a particular definition. This approach, discussed in Wasemiller (1969), allows comparisons with other countries' CI services, often called security or security-intelligence services.[4] Typical of these is the British Security Service (MI-5) which is responsible for

> protecting the UK against threats to national security from espionage, terrorism and sabotage, from the activities of agents of foreign powers, and from actions intended to overthrow or undermine parliamentary democracy by political, industrial or violent means.[5]

Despite one complication, with this functional concept in mind, the intelligence literature can be examined to determine the evolution of what is now referred to as counterintelligence or security-intelligence. In this context, when Pickle the Spy reported the plans of the pretender to overthrow the reigning government by violent means he was involved in a CI operation.

The complication has to do with the fact that all intelligence operations—collection, analysis, scientific & technological (S&T), clandestine communications, covert action, dissemination—

involve CI and security practices designed to avoid compromise. The practical consequence is that most books, and to a lesser degree articles, deal in some fashion with CI issues. This essay will confine its scope to those works, in part or in full, that are concerned with countering threats to national security as opposed to collecting or analyzing political, military or S&T intelligence—classic espionage.

Counterintelligence in Ancient Civilizations

Antecedent elements of what is today called counterintelligence may be found in various histories of intelligence and warfare. Dvornik (1974: 20–7, 101–07, 129–32, 140–7, 216–224) discusses security services in ancient, Egypt, Assyria, Persia, Greece, Rome, China and Muscovy, with a bibliography but no footnotes. Sheldon (2003a) adds more recent entries that cover much the same ground with the addition of India, and Africa. Russell (1999: 190–225) devotes a well documented chapter to counterintelligence in classical Greece that includes citations from Thucydides and other classical historians. Internal security and deception operations in Biblical times are discussed in Sheldon (2007c: 186, 13 passim) although the principal focus of the study examines the accuracy of the Biblical accounts. Sheldon (2005b), a study of intelligence in ancient Rome, looks at diplomatic and military applications of counterintelligence with emphasis on security. The bibliography is a valuable source of related works.

Sawyer (1998) deals with what he terms spycraft in China throughout the Dynastic periods (2852 BC–1911). While the functions of counterintelligence are prevalent throughout, two chapters are of particular interest. Chapter 5, *Nature and Theory of Agents*, analyzes the contribution of Sun Tzu and his guidance on the necessity for several types of secret agents and the use of deception. Chapter 7, *Secrecy and Countermeasures*, considers the consequences of laxity in applying these concepts. Deacon (1974a) is recommended by Sawyer for a broader view of Chinese intelligence. Two relatively recent biographies make important contributions to the role of counterintelligence in modern China. Wakeman (2003) presents a study of Dai Li, the head of state security under Chiang Kai-shek, and Byron et al. (1992) records the work of Kang Sheng (the Himmler of the orient), the long time head of Mao's security service. These works demonstrate what happens when too much power is invested in a single counterintelligence authority. Examples in the Western services will be discussed below.

Early Security-Intelligence Services in Europe

While counterintelligence functions no doubt persisted in the Middle Ages there are few specifics in the historical record (Sheldon 2003a: 161–2, 167). With the rise of the nation-state, however, rulers gradually created secret political police organizations to safeguard their existence. Deacon (1990b: 1) notes that Charles V (1354–80) "gave France her first intelligence organization ... to promote the security of the state for the happiness of the people." He goes on to outline the development of this capability drawing on the experience of the Catholic Church and the formation of today's services. In Russia, Ivan the Terrible formed the Oprichnina, the earliest predecessor of the KGB, in 1565 to eliminate opposition (Hingley 1970: 1). Monas (1961) examines the early 19th century Russian intelligence service, The Third Section. Zuckerman (1996) looks at Czarist domestic security services from 1880 to 1917. Vassilyev (1930) presents a firsthand account of the pre-revolutionary Russian intelligence service, the Ochrana. Lauchlan (2002) also analyses the Okhrana but from a broader and thoroughly documented perspective.

In 14th century England, Edward III (1327–77) was "the first King who made anything like a regular use of secret intelligence as a political system," though Henry the VII was "the actual founder of secret intelligence as a State policy ... [and] the business of civil espionage." His purpose was to identify deception and "break the knot of conspirators" (Richings 1934: 27, 50, 64). The threat of plots and conspiracies plagued successive monarchs for the next three centuries. Richings provides the only single volume overview of the measures each one implemented to safeguard the crown. Other British historians have documented specific cases, the best known being Elizabeth I's Secretary of State and spymaster, Sir Francis Walsingham. His agents penetrated conspiracies and foreign governments, used ciphers and secret writing to communicate, and intercepted and decrypted enemy letters. In short, he created a security service in all but name, with all the functions of a modern counterintelligence agency (Wilson

2007). Bossy (2001) tells the story of Walsingham's mole in the employ of the French ambassador. Haynes (1994) gives a good overview of Elizabethan espionage, while Alford (2008) takes a broad view of the Elizabethan era. Following the Walsingham precedent, with a notable gap under Charles I (1625–49) who delegated his safety to his "trusty secret agent 'Honest Harry Firebrace'" (Richings 1934: 201), most Secretaries of State found themselves responsible for state security, domestic and foreign (Fraser 1956). John Thurloe, the first to use the post office for counterintelligence purposes—intercepting mail, decrypting messages—served Oliver Cromwell (1649–60) (Hobman: 1961) and initially his successor Charles II (1660–1685). Greaves (1986; 1990; 1992) notes that employing informers and monitoring conversations in taverns was nothing new and gives detailed examples of how plots were exposed and resolved. See Marshall 1994; Ellis 1958: 62ff; Aubrey 1990 for additional particulars.

With the exile of James II (1685–88) Jacobite (supporters of James II) restoration plots threatened the monarchy until the reign of George III; Caulfield (1819; 1820). It was during the early part of this period that the tradition of intelligence memoirs made its debut in four works. In 1694 Matthew Smith offered his services as a Jacobite spy to Secretary of State, the Duke of Shrewsbury, under William and Mary. When Smith found his compensation inadequate, he published *Memoirs of Secret Service* (1699) arguing he had no choice since he was facing penury. Even then, mention of the Secret Service and the naming of those involved was dimly viewed, and the book was confiscated and burned, though copies survived. Historians would judge Smith a mediocre agent (Cruickshanks 1982) and his most notable achievement remains his defiance of Crown security. The second work, *Memoirs of the Secret Services of John Macky, Esq.*, edited by his son (Macky, S. 1733) told of his successful efforts to report on King James the pretender in exile and was favorably received in the then firmly Protestant England. The third work, *A True History of the Several Designs Against His Majesties Sacred Person and Government from 1688 to 1697*, by Richard Kingston (1698), is an unofficial history of Jacobite conspiracies. Kingston was himself a spy exposed by Macky, and he challenged Smith's book in a series of pamphlets (Kingston: 1700). The final work, Kingston (1700b), is his attempt to expose Jacobite conspiracies he discovered as a spy. These volumes, as will be seen, established a pattern by disgruntled former spies that exposed operations about secret service in England.

With the end of the Jacobite movement under George III, the Secret Service, now under William Pitt (Fitzpatrick: 1892), turned its attention to threats—revolution, subversion and terrorism—from Ireland, France, and the colonies. Irish demands for independence, backed by subversion and acts of terror, contributed to the creation of the Metropolitan Police, Special Branch, that would play a role in future CI operations. (Porter 1987: Andrew, 2009: 600ff). Likewise, British counterespionage in was active in France during French Revolutions and Napoleonic era (Sparrow: 1999). Secret intelligence also expanded to "aid the King over the Water" (Richings 1934: 260–78) as the American colonies gradually showed signs of independence. At the same time the colonies realized intelligence needs of their own.

Origins of Counterintelligence in America

In an unusual move for a government intelligence agency, the National Counterintelligence Center—since renamed the National Counterintelligence Executive (NCIX)—published a four-volume counterintelligence reader (Rafalko: c. 1995–2004). While their value is enhanced by chronologies and bibliographies, it is diminished somewhat by lack of an index and spotty sourcing. While Rafalko does not provide a definition of CI, most cases discussed include the operational elements that would eventually be associated with counterintelligence—deception, secret writing, double agents, defectors, and intercepted communications. Though many of the exemplars involve military matters, the first American civilian CI organization—the Committee for Detecting and Defeating Conspiracies—is also mentioned. No source is given though the Committee is well documented in Paltsits (1909). Other works worth consulting on this period include O'Toole (1991); Bakeless (1959); and Van Dorn (1941). For a good treatments of the Franklin mission to Paris and the case of the British penetration agent Edward Bancroft, see Einstein (1933) and Schaeper (2011). The famous Benedict Arnold case of defection and desertion is well told in Palmer (2000).

It was not until the Civil War that there was anything like a domestic counterintelligence agency in the United States and even then it was not a statutory organization. Washington, D.C., was filled with Southerners, all potential spies. Rafalko (c. 1995: Vol. 1, 44ff), relying too heavily on Mogelever (1960), gives far too much credit to Allan Pinkerton, the private detective hired by Gen. George McClellan. And though he had modest success when he caught Rose O'Neal Greenhow (O'Toole 1991: 121–22) his efforts were mostly directed toward collecting military intelligence. His memoirs (Pinkerton 1883) embellished his wartime exploits referring to himself as Chief of the United States Secret Service. No such organization existed during the war. The reality of Pinkerton's meager contribution is spelled out in Fishel (1996: 3, 54, 598).

A second baseless claim to having headed the Union Secret Service was made by Baker (1867), characterized by Fishel (1996: 599) as "having the literary merit and believability of a dime novel." With the exception of the Carrington case that dealt with countering political plots against the North, many of the spy cases Rafalko discusses are just military collection operations, Stringfellow the spy being one example (Rafalko: c. 1996: Vol. 1: 56–8, 62). Milton (1942) presents a well documented treatment of plots against the Union and the efforts to neutralize them. His views on Baker were summed up in Congressional testimony where he stated that "it is doubtful whether he had in any one thing ever told the truth even by accident" (Milton 1942: 76). An unsuccessful Confederate effort to kidnap Lincoln and force the Union to negotiate peace is described in Tidwell (1988). Variations on that theme are presented in Winkler (2003) and Kauffman (2004). In regards to military counterintelligence, Feis (2002), a reliable source, mentions several instances where Grant and his generals dealt with the problem in the field. With the exceptions noted, the Civil War literature dealing with counterintelligence should be viewed with caution.

The post Civil War period saw little counterintelligence activity. O'Toole (1991: 193–2) describes the single CI operation that occurred during the Spanish American War. Since there was no military or civilian CI organization, when the British informed the State Department that a Spanish intelligence station was being formed in Canada that planned to conduct espionage in the United States, Secret Service agents were seconded to the Justice Department to deal with the problem—and they did so effectively. But Justice did not want to depend on Treasury agents again and waged a long bureaucratic battle with Treasury for the investigatory mission. Richard Gid Powers (2004: 80–100) tells how, after the Bureau of Investigation (BI) was created on March 16, 1909, it took another 11 years before Justice emerged victorious. The tipping point came during a series of sabotage attacks during 1914–1916, aimed at denying the allies munitions. Public outrage was high and the Bureau was tasked to investigate. Thanks again to help from British intelligence who unmasked a German double agent, Horst von der Goltz, several of the German saboteurs and spies in America were identified and arrested. Goltz (1917) published his own embellished version of the events but Boghardt (2004: 124–6) gives an accurate account. With the declaration of war on 6 April 1917, 63 suspected German agents were arrested by the BI and the workload grew from there (Powers 2004: 2–3). Thus the Bureau became America's lead agency in domestic security, then called counterespionage, a mission it would never relinquish.

While newspapers were the principal source of news concerning sabotage, several books appeared that alerted the public to the security threat, though they cited no sources. Grant (1915) takes a broad view before concentrating on the intelligence services in Britain, France, Germany and the United States. Graves (1914), though sensationalist in tone, sold more than 100,000 copies in ten printings (Boghardt 2004: 60–3). Journalists Jones (1917) and Jones & Hollister (1918), and Strother (1918) contain a level of detail strongly suggesting government cooperation. In retrospect, it is clear they demonstrated a public appetite for espionage and established a precedent as a means of enlisting popular support for the Bureau which continues to this day.

Military Counterintelligence— Army and Navy—Post–Civil War to End of World War I

Army Captain Arthur Wagner, concerned that not enough attention was paid to military intelligence and security, published a book (Wagner 1893) that became a text in Army training for the next 15 years, with new editions appearing periodically until 1910. He included a chapter on spies, military and civilian, that discussed basic CI topics: recruitment, double agents, giving false information to the enemy, and guarding against hostile spies. In 1895,

British military historian Col. George Furse followed suit with his book *Information in War*, read widely in America. His purpose, inter alia, was to stimulate greater preparedness; intelligence needs to be in place before the war starts, he argued. The book covers much the same ground as Wagner but contains considerably greater historical background (Furse 1895: 237–290). There is little evidence that either book accomplished its goal before World War I. The British called 50 university professors, journalists and businessmen to service in the Intelligence Corps and sent them to France with no training (Gudgin 1989; 29). Gilbert (2005) describes a similar solution to security problems over two years later, when the American Army landed in France.

The establishment of Army military intelligence as an element of the General Staff is covered in Gilbert (2005: 1–21). Naval Counterintelligence has not received as direct a treatment but can be gleaned from Dorwart (1979b: 113–31, passim). O'Toole (1991: 279–300) deals with both services. As war neared, the need for new security measures for the Army and defense plant personnel was obvious. With the press screaming "America Infested with Spies,"[6] and, with certain exceptions, "every German or Austrian ... should be treated as a spy," proposals surfaced in Congress to make the military responsible for counterespionage. The Army had long promoted the idea and, without legislation, created a "Plant Protection Section" to search out spies and saboteurs, putting itself in the domestic security business (Powers 2004: 82–88). This infuriated both the overworked BI and the mission conscious Secret Service still hoping for a slice of the CI pie. Jensen (1968) is a good source for details on how the Army overstepped its authority and was forced to abandon its self-imposed counterespionage mission to the inexperienced BI that, in turn, overreacted in its implementation.

Counterintelligence Literature in Interwar Period

Contemporaneous Accounts

After World War I former intelligence officers, agents, defectors and journalists began publishing accounts of intelligence, counterintelligence and domestic security operations—often in the same book. Some dealt with wartime cases, others with the new Soviet security services, and some, for the first time, with the general

topic of counterespionage. Of those quick out
of the gate Tunney (1919), a former New York
police inspector, wrote of his efforts to "thwart"
German saboteurs. In the journalist category,
Barton (1919) published stories of espionage and
counterespionage cases in Europe and the
United States. British authors Everitt (1920) and
Felsted (1920) both told stories of German espionage that included counterespionage cases.
With one exception, all were anecdotal without
sources or indices. The exception was Landau
(1935), a former SIS officer, who wrote of German sabotage and espionage in America. While
he doesn't include source notes, he does quote
letters and cables in the text and provides photo
copies of documents.

In the first account of a counterespionage case
by a participant, Sir Paul Dukes (1922) told the
story of his mission to overthrow the Bolshevik
regime and his penetration of the Cheka, Russia's new security service. Though Dukes didn't
supply source notes, his story has been documented by Ferguson (2008). The wartime head
of the German secret service published his memoirs and described the counterespionage organization he established (Nicolai 1924: 197–224).
He also mentioned the case of Col. Alfred Redl,
head of the Austrian counterespionage prior to
World War I, recruited by the Russians and
blackmailed because of his homosexuality into
turning over the Kaiser's war plans in 1913. Asprey (1959) adds further detail and sources.
Nicolai was the only source, in English, on German intelligence available before World War II.
Another example of a firsthand account may be
found in Voska (1940). He discusses domestic
security work in America, and his adventures as
an American agent in revolutionary Russia during and after the war. Perhaps the most controversial book in this period is the memoirs of Sidney Reilly (1932) published posthumously. The
details of his exploits and personal life were immediately contested and the accurate story only
emerged in Cook (2004).

Books about the Soviet domestic security
service—the Cheka, forerunner of the KGB—
first reached the English reading public in the
mid–1920s. Deported Russian historian S. Mel-
guonov (1925) described the Red Terror conducted by the Cheka and provides a valuable
bibliography. The memoirs of Soviet defectors
G. Popoff (1925), Brunovsky (1931), G. Agabekov (1931), G. Kitchen (1935) added grue-
some details that Westerners found hard to accept. Two civilians, Finish businessman Boris

Cederholm (1929) and German historian Karl
Kindermann (1933), arrested as spies, published
accounts of their treatment. Despite the absence
of documentation, the overlapping details of
these accounts and subsequent studies as for example Leggett (1986) leave no doubt as to their
general validity. Andrew & Mitrokhin (2000:
55–72) has a chapter on the "great" Soviet illegals
of this era. More recently, Draitser (2010) tells
the story of Dimitri Bystrolyotov, the greatest
of them all. As will be seen, illegals will continue
to play an important role in the CI operations.

An early description in an American book of
how counterespionage functions may be found
in *Spy and Counter-Spy* by Richard Rowan
(1928: 127–228). Five chapters discuss counterespionage which he defines as "organized spying upon spies." His discussion is not confined
to World War I, but rather gives a broad picture
of CE in the major European nations in the 18th
and 19th centuries. Rowan claimed he invented
the term *counter-spy* and was insistent that the
hyphen be included, though common usage
today omits it.[7] A firsthand report on how the
FBI—created in 1935—neutralized the Nazi espionage networks can be found in Turrou (1939).

Historical Accounts of Counterintelligence in the Inter-War Period

With the perspective of time and access to
documentary sources, more detailed accounts of
CI during this period emerged. Rafalko (Vol. 1,
143–173) discusses the search for Japanese spies,
and notes the fact, but not the impact, of the
first defectors from the Soviet intelligence services. Gilbert (17–22) comments more narrowly
on the Army's role. Talbert (1991) examines
Army CI efforts after the war, while adding
background on wartime operations against re-
sisters, unions, and Black Americans. Comments
on Naval CE may be found in Dorwart (1983b).
The biggest and most successful FBI CI case
against German spies is described in Ronnie
(1995) and O'Toole (270–300, 313–83).

In the 1930s the FBI focused mainly on the
subversive activities of the Communist Party in
America. Soviet espionage was largely ignored
even when it was brought to their attention as
happened with the publication of a series of ar-
ticles by Soviet defector Walter Krivitsky in the
Saturday Evening Post (Krivitsky 1939a). In the
May 1939 article, Krivitsky, who served both the
GRU and NKVD, predicted the Hitler-Stalin
Pact and named Soviet agents. He repeated these

charges in his book published in November of that year (Krivitsky 1939b). The FBI declined to interview Krivitsky about the NKVD and the Soviet agents in America that he knew. The full story of the Krivitsky case and the consequences of the Bureau inaction are documented with primary sources in a fine account by Kern (2004). The importance of defectors in the counterintelligence story would become apparent only after World War II. Brook-Shepherd (1977a) provides excellent summaries of several important Soviet cases. Rose and Scott (2009) add an account of a defector and double agent, Jonny De Graff, that only recently came to light.

A number of histories with major portions devoted to counterintelligence services during the interwar period are worth attention. The British activities are examined by Andrew (1985: 174–258, passim; 2009) with emphasis on the Security Service (MI-5); Jeffrey (2010), and Smith (2010) cover the Secret Intelligence Service (MI-6) and its CI responsibilities. Porch (1995: 115–58) and Paillole (2003) deal with the French services, Höhne (1979) describes the German Abwehr. The Japanese services are treated in Matthews (1993), Lamont-Brown (1998) and Deacon (1983). The massive and often undetected CI efforts of the Soviet CI services in Europe, Asia and the United States—illegals, double agents, deception, moles—are recounted in Dallin (1955) and Andrew & Mitrokhin (2000a; 30–161 passim).

The inter-war period also saw several CI developments in Ireland. McMahon (2008; 25ff) describes CI operations during the War of Independence (1919–1921), the Civil War (1922–1923) and the complex internal conflicts that preceded World War II. Additional details may be found in O'Halpin (1999). Dwyer (2005) argues that urban terrorism began during the War of Independence—also known as the Anglo-Irish War—with the assassination squad headed by Michael Collins that penetrated British police forces and intelligence services, and then eliminated the best detectives. J.B.E. Hittle (2011) discusses the same actions—he calls them CI and counterinsurgency operations—from the viewpoint of a professional intelligence officer.

Counterintelligence During World War II and the Early Postwar Era

Accounts Dealing Mainly with Wartime Operations

Rafalko (c. 1995–2004; Vol. 2) gives a good summary of U.S. CI operations during the war including the new CI element of the OSS—X-2. Winks (1987: 322–438) adds more detail about X-2 and one of its key officers, James Angleton, later the controversial Chief of the CI Staff at CIA. Sayer & Botting (1989) write about the Army Counter Intelligence Corps and Batvinis (2007) covers the FBI wartime CI operations. Sibley (2004) looks somewhat too favorably at FBI efforts to counter Soviet espionage in America.

Hinsley (1990) provides a splendid account of British wartime security and counterespionage operations in Britain. Masterman (1995) describes the well known British deception and double agent operations controlled by the Double Cross (XX) committee that he chaired. Elliott (2011) tells the story of Tar Robertson, the counterespionage officer who ran the Double Cross operations. Macintyre (2007, 2010) discusses two double cross operations—MINCEMEAT and ZIGZAG. For a slightly different view of ZIGZAG see Booth (2007) and for another perspective on MINCEMEAT see Smyth (2010); each well documented. West & Pujol (2011) tell the story of GARBO, the most important of the Double Cross Agents. Howard (1990) provides an official historical account of the principal Double Cross operations. *The Liddell Diaries*, West (2005h), add fascinating firsthand insights about ongoing MI-5 cases from a senior manager point of view. Military deception is the subject of Holt (2007), a much more accurate treatment than Brown (1975). While not entirely CI deception, the principles laid out by Holt are the same. Stephan (2004) gives an excellent account of Soviet wartime deception and CI operations against the Germans.

Lamont-Brown (1998) tells how the Japanese counterespionage service operated during the war and Paillole (2003) presents a firsthand account of the French wartime services against the Nazis. Aldrich (1991) deals with the famous *Rote Kapelle* or *Red Orchestra* case and some of its post war consequences. Pratt (1979) is the result of an extensive CIA counterintelligence analysis of the Rote Kapelle and its principal agents based on captured documents, though the latter are not cited. Pringle (2008b) looks at the most notorious Soviet wartime CI organization, SMERSH. Kern (2007b) shows how the FBI reacted to the 1944 Soviet defector and NKGB co-optee, Victor Kravchenko. Trinity College professor O'Halpin (2003) introduces and edits an official British study of wartime "liaison"—a term used to indicate a CI relationship—between MI-5 and Irish intelligence that caused problems with MI-6. Liaison between Poland and Great Britain was also an important factor in World War II. (Stirling et al. 2005) describes field operations of Polish Offensive Counterintelligence Section and gives detailed examples of British-Polish cooperation.

Prelude to Cold War

On September 5, 1945, Soviet code clerk Igor Gouzenko defected to the RCMP with classified documents that revealed multiple ongoing heretofore unknown cases of Soviet espionage in Canada and America and naming Canadian, British and American agents, some working on the atom bomb project. On November 7, 1945, Soviet agent Elizabeth Bentley defected to the FBI and began dictating a 112-page statement naming Soviet agents and members of the Communist Party that had penetrated—some were still active—throughout the government during World War II. Her data confirmed much of what Whittaker Chambers had told the FBI in 1939 about Alger Hiss and other Soviet agents, but which the Bureau ignored—multiple investigations resulted. In 1946 the Army cryptographic unit at Arlington Hall in Virginia began reading NKGB traffic—a project eventually code named VENONA—dealing with Soviet agents that would confirm what Bentley and Chambers provided. By 1950 hundreds of other Soviet agents had been identified including the Rosenberg spy network that passed atomic bomb secrets to the Soviets. Radosh & Milton (1997) is the standard work for the Rosenberg case, while Feklisov (2001), their NKGB handler, ends speculation—except for a dedicated few—as to their guilt. Hornblum (2011) documents the role of Harry Gold, the NKGB agent/courier, without whose confession the Rosenbergs would not have gone to trial.

The first book about these now familiar events was Gouzenko's (1948) memoir. The first American account was Lowenthal (1950). He gave a few details of the FBI investigations including the Judith Coplon case, without knowing she was exposed by VENONA—that source would remain secret until 1995. Mitchell (2002) is the most thorough treatment of the Coplon saga. Two firsthand defector accounts soon followed. Elizabeth Bentley's memoir *Out of Bondage* (1951; 1988), named names and described her activities as a Soviet agent since the late 1930s. One of those she named, Canadian Fred

Rose is examined in Levy (2011). Then Hede Massing (1951) named the State Department agents she had recruited and handled for the Soviets during the 1930s. A recent contribution, Knight (2005), analyses the Gouzenko case and those that became ensnared in it. Rafalko (1995: Vol. 3, 1–75), gives a good overview with short case summaries, a bibliography and a chronology and Dallin (1955) is an equally good source that also includes Soviet operations in the 1930s that impacted the post war era. Weinstein (1997) is the benchmark study of the Alger Hiss-Whittaker Chambers case, while Weinstein & Vassiliev (2000) adds more details based on KGB records.

Studies by Benson & Warner (1996) and Haynes & Klehr (2000) provide additional background on these cases and explain how the FBI CI acquired the evidence to shut down Soviet espionage operations in the U.S. after the war. Lamphere & Shachtman (1986) is a first hand account of the FBI side. West (2000g) describes how the VENONA material was applied to CI cases by Britain, Australia, and Canada. Ball & Horner (1998) examine KGB operations in Australia in detail. Andrew & Mitrokhin (2000a: 180–211) add specifics from the Soviet side.

Turning to the foreign intelligence mission in America, Darling (1990: 94–115, 203), a lethally dull but valuable source, records how, after a battle with the Army Counterintelligence Corps (CIC), the foreign counterespionage mission was assigned to the recently created CIA. Former FBI agent William Harvey was the first chief of the CIA counterintelligence element, Staff-D, and it began active operations in the early 1950s. Stockton (2006: 28ff) covers this period and other CI operations involving Harvey.

Cold War Counterintelligence—1950–1992

The Cambridge 5+

As the United States worked to establish a CI program during the early years of the Cold War, a number of foreign CI cases were exposed in parallel. Some had originated in the 1930s, all were the product of one or more sources—defectors, walk-ins, penetrations, double agents, CI analysis, and VENONA. The so-called "Cambridge 5" case—5 Cambridge graduates, Philby, Maclean, Burgess, Blunt and Cairncross, recruited as NKVD agents in the 1930s—involved all but double-agents and has generated numerous books and articles of varying quality. One critical bibliographic essay on the Philby literature mentions more than 150 volumes (Peake 2003) and more books have appeared since it was published. West and Tsarev (2009) for example, tells of Anthony Blunt's espionage based on KGB documents.

While the basic facts of the Cambridge 5 case are well established, many authors have a problem reporting them accurately. Twigge (2008) and Thomas (2009) provide very unreliable treatments and should be used with great caution. Hamrick (2004) invents a double agents scenario that is not supported by his analysis. The entry on Philby in the *Encyclopaedia Britannica* is filled with errors and has remained unchanged for 20 years. Wikipedia has similar problems calling Philby a double agent—he was not—and getting his recruitment details wrong. Polmar and Allen (2004: 496) write that Philby was recruited at Cambridge rather than in 1934, the year after he graduated. Carlisle (2005: 406) states that Philby defected with Maclean in 1951—Philby defected alone in 1963. Borovik (1994), on the other hand, is a good place to start with the Philby case. His life in Russia is covered in R. Philby (2003).

The Cambridge 5 case is of central importance because its tentacles touched so many other operations and its analysis reveals the strengths and weaknesses of the Western and Soviet intelligence services. The Aleksandr Orlov case makes the point. Orlov, a senior NKVD officer, defected to the United States in 1938 but the FBI didn't learn of it until he published a book attacking Stalin in 1953 (Orlov 1953). When he was finally debriefed, he never revealed his association with three of the Cambridge 5 and kept to himself many other secrets later exposed by Costello and Tsarev (1993). Orlov's memoirs, published posthumously (Orlov 2004), contribute some detail on Sidney Reilly and NKVD European operations in the 1930s, but make no mention of his Cambridge spy links. Gazur (2001), Orlov's last FBI handler, challenges some of Costello and Tsarev's interpretations. Except for Burgess, each of the Cambridge 5 has been the subject of biographies: Blunt (Carter 2001), Maclean (Newton (1991), Cairncross (1997), and Philby (Knightly 1989), the best of many.

The Cambridge 5 were not the only Cambridge students recruited by the Soviets and later the subjects of books. Michael Straight (1983)

was the only American recruited there. Perry (2005b) writes about Straight claiming he served the KGB long after he says he quit, but lacks hard evidence. In an earlier book Perry (1994a) tried and failed to establish that the fifth man in the Cambridge net was Lord Victor Rothschild. McNeish (2007), attempts to persuade readers that New Zealander Paddy Costello was not "the 6th Man"—he is unconvincing. Barros (1987) makes a case that Herbert Norman was Canada's contribution to this group. Bowen (1986) takes a contrarian view. In this case the evidence is not conclusive in either book, but a strict CI analysis would support Barros. The most surprising contribution to the CI history of the Cambridge 5 case came from West & Tsarev (1999) which contained primary source material from the KGB archives, some of which had originally reached the KGB from the agents themselves.

Other Cold War Agents, Defectors, and Illegals

Andrew & Gordievsky (1991: 375–479) present an overview of the CI threat from the KGB during this period. Studies of specific cases that demonstrate how counterespionage functions in the field are also available. At the top of this list is *Mole* (Hood 1993), the story of "walk-in" GRU officer Peter Popov in 1952. Ashley (2004) adds details about the role of Popov's CIA case officer, George Kisevalter. Murphy et al. (1997: 267–81) and Hart (1997) add further details; Hart claims the recruitment was in 1953. Other important defector accounts include KGB officers Peter Deriabin (1959) and Vladimir & Evdokia Petrov (1956) who defected in Australia. A detailed and documented account of the Petrov case from the Australian point of view may be found in Manne (1987). The KGB was not inactive during this period and Bower (1989) tells of its penetration of MI-6 and CIA operations in the Baltic; Bagley (2007) adds further details.

CI cases increased sharply in the 1960s in both Britain and the United States. The principal causes in each instance were defectors and moles. Martin (1980) tells about the Polish intelligence officer and letter writer, Michael Goleniewski, codenamed SNIPER who eventually defected and gave clues that exposed MI-6 officer and KGB agent George Blake, who later published his side of the story (Blake 1990). Bagely (2007: 48ff) adds details to that SNIPER case from a first-hand perspective. KGB defector

Anatoli Golitsyn triggered the 1962 arrest of Admiralty clerk John Vassall, previously recruited in a Moscow homosexual honeytrap and a KGB agent for over ten years (Andrew 2009: 492). His autobiography (Vassall 1975) is important for intelligence officers trying to understand agent motivation, a factor also examined, inter alia, by Taylor & Snow (2007: 302ff). At about the same time GRU officer Oleg Penkovsky "walked-in"—volunteered his services to both the UK and U.S.—and was run jointly as described in a fine book by Schechter & Deriabin (1992). Further details about Kisevalter's role in this case may be found in Ashley (2004). Brook-Shepherd (1989b) gives penetrating assessments of several important Cold War agents and defectors, including the French controlled KGB officer, FAREWELL. A more detailed account of the FAREWELL case may be found in Kostin (2011).

Illegals are a security service's worst nightmare. Conceived by the NKVD in the 1920s and used extensively in throughout the world, they have no contact with the legal residency in the Embassy and are nearly impossible to find. Andrew & Mitrokhin (2000a: 55–72) give a fine account separated into periods. Thanks to defections—Bentley, Massing, et al.—and VENONA, the NKGB recalled their illegals after the war. When things calmed down they began to insert new ones with little success. Andrew & Mitrokhin (2000a: 212–29) discuss post war illegals in North America. A more selective but valuable treatment may be found in West (1993d). Donovan (1964) gives a good account of the Rudolf Abel case including his exchange for U-2 pilot Gary Powers. Barron (1974a) discusses several cases providing detail on KGB illegals training, insertion techniques—often via Canada—and the FBI operations that caught them. Maclean (1978: 278–303) describes the Lonsdale case in Britain, and Andrew & Gordievsky (1991: 447) revealed that Lonsdale was exposed by SNIPER. Lonsdale later told a version of the case in his memoirs, ghosted by Kim Philby (Lonsdale 1965). Lonsdale's principal agent, Harry Houghton, told his story in Houghton (1972). The story of KGB illegal Yuri Loginov is told in Carr (1969) who never realized she was fed the case material as part of the CIA molehunt discussed below (Mangold 1991: 129). Kuzichkin (1990) gives a broad firsthand view of modern KGB illegal training and operations. Wise (200d) reports an unheralded but very successful case involving a GRU sleeper and illegals operating in the United States for more than 20 years. Wise (2011) describes Chinese efforts in this area.

Molehunts

Counterintelligence and security elements are continuously on guard against the threat of operational and organizational penetration by foreign services. The specter of this possibility surfaced in the early 1960s after the defection of KGB officer Anatoli Golitsyn and in 1964 of the late Yuri Nosenko to the CIA. Supported by its CI Chief, James Angleton, Golitsyn was the progenitor of the molehunts and Nosenko became one of his target moles—a putative KGB plant. Golitsyn also found other suspects in the British, Canadian and Australian intelligence services. Beginning with David Martin's (1980) *Wilderness of Mirrors*, an account that lacked source notes, the molehunt at CIA has received periodic literary attention. Epstein (1978, 1989) uses source notes in explaining the Angleton position. He discourses about Golitsyn's fantastic deception game-plan, though he didn't reveal until after Angleton's death that Angleton had also been a key source. Bagley (2007), a participant in the Golitsyn-Nosenko controversy, makes a coherent documented exposition supporting the Angleton view, though he acknowledges some key questions cannot be answered conclusively. Mangold (1991) and Wise (1992b) argue that Nosenko was genuine and that James Angleton blindly accepted Golitsyn's claims that the CIA was penetrated. As a consequence, they point out, some Soviet operations were considered suspect and the careers of several good officers ruined. The *Lygren Affair* mentioned by Riste (1999: 274ff) is an example of the peripheral consequences of the molehunt that led to the unjust arrest of a Norwegian secretary and strained relations with the Norwegian services. A detailed competing hypothesis analysis by Heuer (1995) also concludes Nosenko was genuine. In his recent biography of Angleton, Holzman (2008) gives his views on the formative factors that created this controversial CI figure. And while his bibliography contains some interesting sources, one of the best, Robarge (2003), is missing.

The British molehunt was sparked in part by information Golitsyn supplied during his debriefing by MI-5. West (1989c) provides the detailed treatment of what followed, a complex case that saw both the Director General and his Deputy investigated as possible moles. Pincher (2009; 2011) reviews the latter case based on new material. He also explains the so-called "spy-catcher affair" and the fallout from the book of the same name (Wright 1987) that discussed the molehunt as well as other MI-5 secrets and resulted in a high profile court case in Australia, making the book a bestseller. Fysh (1989) presents a detailed exposition of how open source CI literature was used in the court case.

In the 1970s, after a series of operational failures, the Canadian Security Service began to suspect the head of the counterespionage section, James Bennett, was a KGB agent. Their suspicions coincided with views held by Angleton and Golitsyn, and Bennett was placed under surveillance as part of Operation Gridiron (Sawatsky 1982b: 261ff). Mangold (1991; 284–5 passim) provides further details. Bennett was forced out of the service and years later the true mole was identified; that story has yet to be written.

Other Major Cold War Counterintelligence Cases

In the midst of the CIA molehunt two penetrations of the CIA went undetected. The first, Larry Chin, had been a Chinese agent for over 30 years; his story is told in Hoffman (2008) and Smith (2004: 31–51). The story of the second, Czech/KGB agent Karl Koecher, is told in Kessler (1988a).

Rafalko (c. 1995–2004; Vol. 3 83ff) presents summaries of many other Cold War CI cases including some in Germany. Sheymov (1993), an officer in the KGB equivalent of NSA, tells his own story as a CIA penetration of the KGB and of his exfiltration, with his family, from the Soviet Union in 1980. A number of major cases that became public in the 1980s drew the attention of journalists and historians. Several books were written about the John Walker case; Earley (1988a) is the most comprehensive and the place to start. Hunter (1999) is a valuable first hand account. Kalugin (1994: 83–90) adds important detail from the KGB perspective. Later that same year Jonathan Pollard was arrested as an Israeli agent. Olive (2006) presents the CI perspective from first hand experience pointing out that Pollard could be paroled but he refuses to admit guilt and thus remains in custody. Kessler (1990c) gives a good account of Navy photographer's mate and KGB agent Glen Souther, who escaped arrest and defected to the Soviet Union and died there, a suicide. Stober & Hoffman (2001) tell the story of the Wen Ho Lee, a Chinese agent who penetrated the CIA and was caught after he retired. Rafalko (2011) discusses

MHCHAOS, the illegal CIA CI operation against the radical left.

The 1985 defection to the CIA of KGB Col. Vitali Yurchenko (Kessler 1991d) led to the exposure of a former CIA officer, Edward Howard, who gave up an important CIA agent in Moscow, Adolph Tolkachev. The hallmark study of the Tolkachev case by Royden (2003) is essential to understanding the case. An alternative view may be found in Fischer (2008). Wise (1988a) explains how Howard managed to escape to the Soviet Union where he died in 2002. In his own version of events, Howard (1995) provides a mix of undocumented assertions, fabrication, and chirpy nonsense.

The arrest of CIA officer Aldrich Ames by the FBI in February 1994 led to five books describing a CE case that involved record agent losses. Earley (1998b), the last published, is the most comprehensive and valuable because it contains input from KGB participants. The first published, Adams (1995), is a decent summary of the events then known. Maas (1995) gives the FBI position with no sources. Wise (1995c) and Weiner (1995) are worth attention but lack the depth Earley provides. Each of the books considers deceptive measures the KGB implemented to protect Ames. One example involved leaks to the media about the case of Moscow embassy guard Marine Sgt. Clayton Lonetree, caught in a KGB honeytrap. As portrayed in the book *Moscow Station* (Kessler 1989) the KGB, using Lonetree, gained nocturnal entrée to the Moscow Embassy station and thus access to the files concerning the agents actually given up by Ames. A plausible but completely erroneous explanation that delayed the CIA investigation. Barker (1996) tells Lonetree's side of the story.

There was a similar literary reaction to the arrest of FBI Special Agent Robert Hanssen. Havill (2001) was too quick out of the gate and left substance behind. Vise (2001) has different errors and says much more about FBI Director Freeh's career than about the Hanssen case. Shannon & Blackman (2002) stick to the subject and provide anecdotes on Hanssen's idiosyncratic childhood behavior. Wise (2003e), though without end notes, is the best and most complete account. He is the only one to tell how the FBI persistently ignored contrary evidence and wrongly accused CIA officer Brian Kelley of being the KGB agent responsible for the losses due to Hanssen's espionage. None of the books reveal just how the Bureau obtained the evidence against Hanssen, though Wise comes closest.

Kessler (2011: 134) contains a discussion of the case wherein the FBI case agent is quoted as acknowledging he was wrong about Kelley.

There are also two very valuable books that discuss all three cases—Howard, Ames and Hanssen—from the participants' viewpoint. The first, Bearden & Risen (2003), gives the CIA position. The second, Cherkashin & Feifer (2005), adds detail from the KGB side.

Not to be outdone, the Army's Foreign Counterintelligence Activity solved two major espionage cases during the late 1980s. The first took nearly nine years. In the end, with help from the CIA and the West German security service, Army SFC Clyde Conrad was sent to German prison for life, for passing, inter alia, NATO war plans to the Soviets through a complicated espionage network. The second case took less than two years to conclude, once alerted by an East German walk-in. After a masterful FBI deception operation, Army Warrant Officer James Hall got 40 years. Herrington (1999) provides details on both cases from firsthand experience. Byers (2005) discusses the case of retired Army colonel George Trofimoff who spied for the KGB while on active duty and was caught in a clever FBI sting thanks to Mitrokhin (Andrew & Mitrokhin, 2000a).

Several British books deal with important cold war CI cases in the 1980s. Andrew & Gordievsky (1991) confirmed Cairncross as the 5th man, identified Michael Bettaney's failed attempts to become a KGB walk-in, and revealed Geoffrey Prime's success in doing just that to sell SIGINT GCHQ secrets. Cole (1998) adds curious detail to the Prime case. Gordievsky (1995) tells the story of his MI-6 recruitment, his contributions while run in place, the mystery of how the KGB CI came to suspect him, and his extraordinary exfiltration from the Soviet Union.

Additional cold war cases may be found in Kalugin (1993). A former Chief of the KGB Counterintelligence Directorate, he describes the internal workings of the KGB as well as various operations he supervised, including the Bulgarian Umbrella (Kostov: 1988) and Shadrin kidnapping cases (Hurt: 1981). Wolf (1999) tells how the CI element of the East German foreign intelligence service conducted many successful operations against the Western intelligence services. Pacepa (1987) and Deletant (1995) cover Romanian intelligence and security service operations. Giles (2010) reviews a career in the Canadian counterespionage service.

Post Cold War Counterintelligence Cases and Analyses

Rafalko (c. 1995–2004; Vols. 3 & 4) provides comments on intelligence services and CI cases in Russia, China, Cuba, South Korea, Japan, E. Germany, the Department of Energy, and some Congressional studies. Godson (1995) presents a general analysis of CI with reference to specific cases that is a useful summary. Trulock (2003) gives a good assessment of the Chinese espionage threat in America and Wise (2011) adds several cases.

In Britain, Hollingsworth & Fielding (1999) report on a former MI-5 officer who revealed operational secrets for his own purposes and paid the penalty. More recently in America, Drogin (2007) and Drumheller (2006) discuss the controversial CURVEBALL case, a CI and bureaucratic calamity. Carmichael (2007) is a firsthand account of the DIA analyst Ana Montes, a clever and long term Cuban agent, that unfortunately does not answer all the CI questions; e.g., how she was identified. He does, however, mention other successful penetrations of CIA operations by Cuban CI elements.

In the era where counterintelligence plays a role in counterterrorism—penetrating a foreign intelligence service that performs terrorist acts—Kahlili (2010) is a chilling example of the new threat through the eyes of a CIA agent in Iran. Another perspective is found in Yousef (2010) that describes an Israeli CI recruitment of an agent in Hamas. Berger (2011) and Herridge (2011) deal with the problem of Al Qaeda recruitments in America and the FBI efforts to neutralize them. Prouty (2011) is a case study of an FBI CI investigation gone wrong and then rectified. Summers & Swan (2011) is a lengthy study of the pre and post 9/11 CI efforts of various intelligence agencies to deal with the terrorist threat. Warrick (2011) examines the penetration of the CIA in Afghanistan by a Jordanian triple agent.

Graff (2011) is a compelling account of the FBI response to global terror. Collins & Frantz (2011) offer a case study on the penetration of several foreign intelligence services aimed at preventing nuclear proliferation. Svendsen (2010) studies CI in the relationship between the U.S. and UK in the war on terror.

Several works address the missions and the relationships of the principal organizations involved in the West and the terrorist elements that threaten them. In the former category,

Riebling (2002) is a broad view of the CIA-FBI rivalry that is also discussed in the *WMD Report* (2005; 485–498). The *9/11 Report* (2004) virtually ignores counterintelligence. But since many of its recommendations would, if adopted, influence CI, it should be studied closely. Posner (2007), after insightful analysis, advocates some innovative reforms including a separate CI agency on the MI-5 model for real efficiency.

Intelligence Service Histories

Basic information about a nation's intelligence and security services—organization, mission, personnel, tradecraft—is essential knowledge for all intelligence officers but especially for counterintelligence officers and students of the field—the "know your enemy" principle.

Consider the U.S. intelligence community first. No single source covers the history of the CIA. There are three official scholarly accounts of the early years: Troy (1981), Darling (1990), and Montague (1992) which covers the DCI Smith tenure. Ranelagh (1987) gives the best overview from the early days until the mid 1980s. Valuable background may also be found in biographies of former directors. Allen Dulles is covered in Grose (1994) and Srodes (1999) and Persico (1990) chronicles William Casey. Official biographies of former directors Colby and Helms are available on the CIA web site. Former directors Robert Gates (1996) and George Tenet (1997) have written informative memoirs of their tenures that contain very perceptive comments on the Agency and its missions. Some interesting comments on Agency CI are also found Mahle (2004). Theoharis et al. (2006) give a summary view. Richelson (2008) deals with current intelligence community organization. There are also many contrarian works: Weiner (2007) concentrates on failure and Goodman (2008) does the same but on a wider scope. Trento (2005) is unreliable. Theoharis et al. (1999), Powers (1987; 2004) and Kessler (2002; 2011), provide a good look at the FBI history. The other major U.S. intelligence organization, the National Security Agency (NSA), has received historical attention from Bamford (1982; 2001; 2008) and Aid (2009). These are not conventional histories in the sense that they do not provide all sides of an argument; both authors have an agenda. But for the purposes of this study, they describe the general collection capabilities and dissemination issues that are crucial to CI operations. The most recent American intelligence agency, the Department of Homeland Security (DHS), is a direct product of 9/11 and several sources review its establishment and continued growing pains. Hulnick (2004) and Marks (2010) track the evolution of the agency, the problems encountered, and the question of whether an domestic security service like Britain's MI-5 is desirable here. Jackson (2009) looks at the need for another domestic security agency devoted to counterterrorism. Harris (2010) considers the impact of various American domestic security policies on the nation's body politic.

For the British services see, West (1982a, 1983b) and Dorril (2000). Andrew (2009) and Jeffrey (2010) cover MI-5 and MI-6 respectively and are based on access to official files. Thomas & Thomas (2009, 2010, 2011) are based on the archival records in the British National Archives and cover MI-5 from its inception to the present. They paraphrase the case documents, are densely packed and endnotes are sometimes hard to ascribe to particular facts. Only the first volume has an index. Aldrich (2010) is the first book on Britain's signals intelligence agency, the Government Communications Headquarters (GCHQ). The hardback has too many factual errors; the later paperback editions have some corrections but errors remain.

The KGB history is dealt with by Leggett (1986) and Andrew & Gordievsky (1991) plus the two Andrew & Mitrokhin volumes (200; 2006) that cover many facets of the KGB. Dziak (1988) focuses on what he terms the "counterintelligence state," or domestic security in the Soviet Union with the best treatment of the CI deception operation, *The Trust*. Birstein (2012) provides an in depth treatment of SMERSH (death to spies), the Soviet counterintelligence element concerned with the military services. Preobrazhensky (2008) and Pringle (2006a) describe Russia's contemporary counterintelligence agency, the FSB. Waller (1994) and Knight (1996) examine the first five years of the post KGB Russian foreign intelligence service. The new intelligence services of Central Asia and their links to the Russian services are examined in a fine article by Lefebvre & McDermott (2008). A history of the current Russian foreign intelligence service, the SVR, has yet to be published in English.

Boyadjiev (2006) looks at five intelligence services—Russia/Soviet Union, Bulgaria, Croatia, France and America—through the eyes of former senior intelligence officers. The post–Cold War services in the Czech Republic, Slovakia, and Romania are discussed in Williams & Deletant (2001). There are numerous books on the Stasi; Childs & Popplewell (1996), Koehler (1999), Dennis (2003) and Schmeidel (2008) provide good coverage. DeVore (1999) is a detailed though somewhat dated assessment of the Chinese services. There is a gap to be filled here. Seth (1998) gives a rare account of the Burmese intelligence apparatus.

Sawatsky (1980a) gives a good account of the RCMP Security Service. Its replacement, the Canadian Security Intelligence Service (CSIS), has not received equivalent attention. Barnett (1988) deals with the Australian security intelligence service, while Toohey & Pinwill (1989) do the same for Australia's secret intelligence service. McKay (1993) describes how the neutral Swedish security services dealt with each of the World War II belligerents. Fardust (1999) tells how SAVAK was established and functioned in Iran.

Conboy (2004) gives an account of the Indonesian services and Raman (2002) does the same for India. Dhar (2006) and Farson 2008: 230–46) cover Pakistan. Sanders (2006) discusses the secret services in South Africa. Caroz's (1978) *Arab Secret Services* is the only book on that general topic but is outdated and not detailed; the author is a former Israeli intelligence officer. Farson et al. (2008a, 2008b) provide valuable articles on most of the world's security services. Raviv & Melman (1990) presents a good overview of the Israeli services. Sirrs (2010) provides a history of the Egyptian Intelligence Service. O'Brien (2011) is a fine study of the South African intelligence services. Alem (1980) discusses counterintelligence and counterespionage in India.

Additional Reference Works

There are many so-called encyclopedias and dictionaries of espionage with short summaries of cases, events and organizations that are often useful in getting started or recalling a name. But these vicars of meaning are the weakest links in the intelligence literature. None are comprehensive and most have too many errors and few cite sources. The most recent and the most error plagued is Hastedt (2011). The two volumes of this encyclopedia contain hundreds of factual errors and are unreliable. Bennett (2002) is a strong competitor for the most error filled single volume ever published. Carl (1996) achieves similar status in the dictionary category, while West (2007j) is weak on CI details on CIA, though Kahana (2006) does well on the Israeli

services. Watson et al. (1990) is more of a dictionary than encyclopedia and though out of date, is sound on the basics. Polmar & Allen (2004) is the best in terms of fewest errors and scope of coverage.

Intelligence "readers"—with articles by several experts—offer a collection of articles on a wide range of topics, including CI, by experts that can be of value in the study of counterintelligence. Andrew et al. (2009) and Johnson (2010) are good examples. Johnson & Wirtz (2011) contains a series of articles on all aspects of the intelligence profession. The section on CI is introduced by Paul Redmond, a CIA counterintelligence specialist, and includes several other contributions worthy of close attention.

Bibliographies are also worth the attention of CI officers and students. Constantinides (1983) is a worthwhile annotated bibliography with a section devoted to counterintelligence books. Westerfield (ed.) (1995) has a selection of counterintelligence articles drawn from the journal *Studies in Intelligence*. A much larger list of intelligence articles may be found at https://www.cia.gov/library/center-for-the-study-of-intelligence/index.html. For material on secret inks and other CI tradecraft techniques as applied in cases, consult Wallace & Melton (2008). Calder (1999) is a epic reference work devoted to articles on intelligence with many CI entries and others closely related. Blackstock & Schaf (1978) is out of date but is annotated and can be useful. Likewise, Wolin & Slusser (1957) provide a solid bibliography on the Soviet services. The bibliographies on the British (Davies 1996), French (Cornick & Morris 1993) and Israeli (Clements 1996) services can serve as a starting point.

George & Rishikof (2011) is a unique reference work that examines the organizational cultures of the principal American intelligence agencies—the first book to do so explains why there is so much dysfunction and argues that one must understand the system before reforms can be implemented successfully.

Richard Rowan (1937) has a special place in the intelligence literature. His *Story of Secret Service* is wide in scope, and filled with brief espionage case studies, most sourced. It records cases from antiquity to the mid–1930s. An updated edition, Rowan & Deindorfer (1967) with a Foreword by Allen Dulles, was published after Rowan's death. It deleted some of the older entries while bringing the book up to date. Copies are still available from abebooks.com.

Caveat Lector

As indicated in this study, the number of books and articles dealing with CI is substantial and their quality varies. Thus it is important to keep in mind the dictum that *errors are an enemy no author has defeated* when dealing with the open literature: no fact important to an argument should go unverified. There are a number of authors whose works should be used with great trepidation, in addition to those mentioned above, if one is concerned with accuracy. Ronald Seth, Bernard Newman, Bernard Hutton, E. H. Cookridge, and Kurt Singer are charter members of the fabrication and embellishment club. Singer (1956), for example, invents Banda, Mata Hari's daughter who spied for the CIA and Mao. Books by these authors are not complete fiction, but are poorly documented, if at all, and should be avoided.

Contemporary competition comes from William Stevenson (1956) in his *The Man Called Intrepid* as demonstrated in West (1998f: 90ff); Macdonald (1998) gets it right. Twigge (2008) has too many errors and Thomas (2009) is totally unreliable. Cooper & Redlinger (1988) have earned high marks in this category with their designer counterintelligence terminology that only confuses. But the grand prize for American authors who cannot get it right goes to Trento (2005) for his putative history of the CIA. Only one other book comes close, Corson et al. (1989), and Trento helped write that one, too.

New Approaches to CI in the Post 9/11 Era

CI in this era requires dealing with a new form of threat. Al-Qaeda and other terrorist factions have no KGB or CIA equivalent, but each poses the same problems for its enemies. Counterintelligence and counterterrorism agencies must know how they function and communicate so that they can clandestinely monitor their activities, handle walk-ins, recruit agents, and deal with defectors. Sageman (2008) suggests the Internet is a major factor in this regard; Renfer & Haas (2008) provides examples. Clarke (2010) gives an overall view of the kind of damage that cyber terrorists can inflict. In *Currency Wars*, Richards (2011) discusses the strategic impact of an old technique—currency manipulation—modified by cyber technology and depicts a threat and expertise that CI officers will have to acquire if they are to recruit agents with that specialty or cooperate with others to prevent damage to the global financial system. An equally ominous threat to global security is described by Bowden (2011) in *WORM: The First Digital World War*, the story of the *conficker* worm that has infected millions of government and personal computers. Its originator is unknown and penetrating the organization responsible will require conventional CI techniques coupled with knowledge not formerly part of the CI skill set.

In this era, too, achieving security through sound CI practices while preserving civil liberties can raise operational dilemmas in new forms. In his book, *Securing the State*, David Omand (2010), a former GCHQ director, offers some thoughtful insights that discuss the relationships that need to be created so that the public understands the CI problems and that CI operators meet their requirements while functioning within the law. On the day-to-day operational level, Olson (2006: 116–7) presents some fictional though typical moral dilemmas faced by officers in the field. While he suggests alternative solutions, selecting the "right" one is left up to the reader.

The post–9/11 era has also seen increased attention to the questions of intelligence agency reform. Several books deal with that issue have been cited above, the 9/11 Commission Report (2004) being the most well-known. The need for congressional oversight reform, however, is seldom mentioned and too long neglected. Zegart (2011) presents an astute study that addresses this issue.

Finally, "What is the best book on counterintelligence?" is a question frequently asked. The NCIX web site lists one candidate, *Fundamental Elements of the Counterintelligence Discipline*, but it only lists factors to be considered. Dulles (2004: 120) a reprint of *The Craft of Intelligence*, though out of date in some respects, presents a good introduction to the profession and a chapter on *Counterintelligence* that addresses practical questions like "How does a counterespionage agent penetrate his target?" But the recommendation here is Johnson (2009), *Thwarting Enemies at Home and Abroad: How to be a Counterintelligence Officer*. Written by a professional, it sets out the basics that every intelligence officer should know.

NOTES

1. Douglas, H. (1999). *Jacobite Spy Wars: Moles, Rogues and Treachery*. Gloucestershire, UK: Sutton, 224–27.

2. The U.S. Army first used the term in 1939 (Bidwell, 284).

3. National Counterintelligence Executive, Washington, D.C., http://www.ncix.gov/.

4. For other functional descriptions of counterintelligence missions, see the Canadian Security Intelligence Service (CSIS), http://www.csis-scrs.gc.ca/bts/rlfcss-eng.asp, and the German domestic security service, the Bundesamptes für Verfassungsschutz (BfV), http://www.verfassungsschutz.de/en/en_fields_of_work/espionage/.

5. http://www.mi5.gov.uk/output/Page67.html; http://www.mi6.gov.uk/output/Page79.html.

6. *Literary Digest,* 6 Oct. 1917, p. 9

7. Rowan's claim was made in a letter, in the possession of the author, to a "Mr. Roberts," dated 17 May 1947.

CITATIONS

Adams, J. (1995). *Sellout: Aldrich Ames and the Corruption of the CIA.* New York: Viking.

Agabekov, G. (1931). *OGPU: The Russian Secret Terror.* New York: Brentano's.

Aid, M. (2009). *The Secret Sentry: The Untold Story of the National Security Agency.* New York: Bloomsbury.

Aldrich, R. (2010, 2011). *GCHQ: The Uncensored Story of Britain's Most Secret Intelligence Agency.* London: HarperCollins.

Aldrich, R.J. (1991). Soviet Intelligence, British Security and the End of the Red Orchestra. *Intelligence and National Security,* 6 (1), 196–217.

Alem, J-P. (1980). *Espionage and Counter-Espionage.* New Delhi: S. Chand.

Alford, S. (2008). *Burghley: William Cecil at the Court of Elizabeth I.* New Haven: Yale University Press.

Andrew, C. (1995). *Secret Service: The Making of the British Intelligence Community.* London: Heinemann.

Andrew, C. (2009). *Defend the Realm: The Authorized History of MI5.* New York: Alfred A. Knopf.

Andrew, C., and O. Gordievsky (1991). *KGB: The Inside Story of Its Foreign Operations from Lenin to Gorbachev.* London: Sceptre, with corrections.

Andrew, C., and V. Mitrokhin (2000a). *The Mitrokhin Archive: The KGB in Europe and the West.* London: Penguin.

Andrew, C., and V. Mitrokhin (2006b). *The KGB and the World: The Mitrokhin Archive II.* London: Penguin.

Andrew, C., et al. (2010). *Secret Intelligence: A Reader.* New York: Routledge.

Ashley, C. (2004). *CIA Spymaster.* Gretna, LA: Pelican. Foreword by Leonard McCoy.

Asprey, R. (1959). *The Panther's Feast.* New York: Putnam's. See also Markus, G. (1985). *Der Fall Redl.* Vienna: Amalthea. It has new material not available to Asprey.

Aubrey, P. (1990). *Mr. Secretary Thurloe: Cromwell's Secretary of State 1652–1660.* London: Athlone.

Bagley, T.H. (2007). *Spy Wars: Moles, Mysteries, and Deadly Games.* New Haven: Yale University Press.

Bakeless, J. (1959). *Turncoats, Traitors and Heroes.* Philadelphia: J.B. Lippincott.

Baker, J.E. (2007). *In the Common Defense: National Security Law for Perilous Times.* Cambridge: Cambridge University Press.

Baker, L. (1867). *History of the United States Secret Service.* Philadelphia: L.C. Baker.

Ball, D., and D. Horner (1998). *Breaking the Codes: Australia's KGB Network 1944–50.* St Leonards, NSW: Allen & Unwin.

Bamford, J. (1983). *The Puzzle Palace: Inside the National Security Agency, America's Most Secret Intelligence Organization.* New York: Penguin.

Bamford, J. (2001). *Body of Secrets: Anatomy of the Ultra-Secret National Security Agency from the Cold War through the Dawn of the New Century.* New York: Doubleday.

Bamford, J. (2008). *The Shadow Factory: The Ultra-Secret NSA from 9/11 to the Eavesdropping on America.* New York: Doubleday.

Barker, R. (1996). *Dancing with the Devil: Sex, Espionage, and the U.S. Marines—The Clayton Lonetree Story.* New York: Simon & Schuster.

Barnett, H. (1988). *Tale of the Scorpion.* Winchester, MA: Allen & Unwin.

Barron, J. (1974a). *KGB: The Secret Work of Soviet Secret Agents.* New York: Reader's Digest Press.

Barron, J. (1983b). *KGB Today: The Hidden Hand.* New York: Reader's Digest Press.

Barros, J. (1987). *No Sense of Evil: The Espionage Case of E. Herbert Norman.* New York: Ivy Books.

Barton, G. (1919). *Celebrated Spies and Famous Mysteries of the Great War.* Boston: Page.

Batvinis, R. (2007). *The Origins of FBI Counterintelligence.* Lawrence: University Press of Kansas.

Bearden, M., and J. Risen (2003). *The Main Enemy: The CIA's Battle with the Soviet Union.* New York: Random House.

Bennett, R.M. (2002). *Espionage: An Encyclopedia of Spies and Secrets.* London: Virgin Books.

Benson, R.L., and M. Warner, eds. (1996). *VENONA: Soviet Espionage and the American Response 1939–1957.* Washington, D.C.: NSA & CIA.

Bentley, E. (1951, 1988). *Out of Bondage: KGB Target.* New York: Ivy Books. Second edition, updated with an index and documented Afterword by Hayden B. Peake.

Berger, J. (2011). *Jihad Joe: Americans Who Go to War in the Name of Islam.* Washington, D.C.: Potomac.

Berman, L. (2007). *Perfect Spy: The Incredible Double Life of PHAM XUAN AN—Time Magazine Reporter & Vietnamese Communist Agent.* New York: HarperCollins.

Birstein, V. (2012). *Smersh: Stalin's Secret Weapon, Soviet Military Counterintelligence in World War II.* New York: Dialogue.

Blackstock, P.W., and F.L. Schaf (1978). *Intelligence, Espionage, Counterespionage, and Covert Operations.* Detroit: Bell Tower.

Blake, G. (1990). *No Other Choice: An Autobiography.* New York: Simon & Schuster.

Boghardt, T. (2004). *Spies of the Kaiser: German Covert*

Operations in Great Britain During the First World War Era. New York: Palgrave.

Booth, N. (2007). *ZIGZAG: The Incredible Wartime Exploits of Double Agent Eddie Chapman*. New York: Arcade.

Born, H., and M. Caparini, eds. (2007). *Democratic Control of Intelligence Services: Containing Rogue Elephants*. Burlington: Ashgate.

Borovik, G. (1994). *The Philby Files: The Secret Life of the Master Spy Kim Philby*. Boston: Little, Brown.

Bossy, J. (2001). *Under The Molehill: An Elizabethan Spy Story*. New Haven: Yale University Press.

Bowden, M. (2011). *WORM: The First Digital World War*. New York: Atlantic Monthly Press.

Bowen, R. (1986). *Innocence Is Not Enough: The Life of Herbert Norman*. Vancouver: Douglas & McIntyre.

Boyadjiev, T. et al. (2006). *The Intelligence: Men of Dignity in the Game with No Rules*. Sofia, Bulgaria: Libra Scorp.

Brook-Shepherd, G. (1977a). *The Storm Petrels: The Flight of the First Soviet Defectors*. New York: Harcourt Brace Jovanovich.

Brook-Shepherd, G. (1989). *The Storm Birds: Soviet Postwar Defectors*. New York: Henry Holt.

Brown, A.C. (1975). *Bodyguard of Lies*. New York: Harper & Row.

Brunovsky, V. (1931). *The Methods of the OGPU*. London: Harper.

Burke, D. (2008). *The Spy Who Came in from the CO-OP: Melita Norwood and the Ending of Cold War Espionage*. London: The Boydell Press.

Byers, A.J. (2005). *The Imperfect Spy: The Inside Story of a Convicted Spy*. St. Petersburg: Vandamere Press.

Byron, J., and R. Pack (1992). *The Claws of the Dragon: Kang Sheng, the Evil Genius Behind Mao—and His Legacy of Terror in People's China*. New York: Simon & Schuster.

Cairncross, J. (1997). *The Enigma Spy: The Story of the Man Who Changed the Course of World War II*. London: Century.

Carl, L. (1996). *CIA Insider's Dictionary: U.S. and Foreign Intelligence, Counterintelligence and Tradecraft*. Washington, D.C.: NIBC Press.

Carlisle, R.P., ed. (2005). *Encyclopedia of Intelligence and Counterintelligence, Vols 1 & 2*. Armonk, NY: M.E. Sharpe.

Carmichael, S. (2007). *True Believer: Inside the Investigation and Capture of Ana Montes, Cuba's Master Spy*. Annapolis: Naval Institute Press.

Caroz, Y. (1978). *The Arab Secret Services*. London: Corgi Books.

Carr, B. (1969). *Spy in the Sun: the Story of Yuriy Loginov*. Cape Town: Howard Timmins.

Carter, M. (2001). *Anthony Blunt: His Lives*. New York: Macmillan.

Caulfield, J. (1819, 1820). *Portraits, Memoirs, and Characters of Remarkable Persons from the Revolution in 1688 to the Reign of George the II*. London: Whiteley. In four volumes, 2 in 1819, 2 in 1820. Many entries about those who plotted and spied against the crown, were caught, pardoned, or executed.

Cederholm, B. (1929). *In the Clutches of the Tcheka*. Boston: Houghton Mifflin.

Cherkashin, V., with G. Feifer (2005). *Spy Handler: Memoir of a KGB Officer, the True Story of the Man Who Recruited Robert Hanssen & Aldrich Ames*. New York: Basic Books.

Childs, D., and R. Popplewell. (1996). *The Stasi: The East German Intelligence and Security Service*. London: Macmillan.

Clark, R.J. (2007). *Intelligence and National Security: A Reference Handbook*. Westport, CT: Praeger.

Clarke, R.A. (2008). *Your Government Failed You: Breaking the Cycle of National Security Disasters*. New York: HarperCollins.

Clarke, R.A. (2010). *Cyber War: The Next Threat to National Security and What to Do About It*. New York: HarperColins.

Clements, F.A. (1996). *The Israeli Secret Services*. Oxford: Clio.

Cole, D.J. (1998). *Geoffrey Prime: The Imperfect Spy*. London: Robert Hale.

Cole, J.A. (1984). *Prince of Spies: Henri le Caron*. London: Faber & Faber.

Collins, C., and D. Frantz (2011). *Fallout: The True Story of the CIA's Secret War on Nuclear Trafficking*. New York: Free Press.

Commission on the Intelligence Capabilities of the United States Regarding Weapons of Mass Destruction (WMD Report) (2005). Washington, D.C.: GPO.

Conboy, K. (2004). *INTEL: Inside Indonesia's Intelligence Service*. Jakarta: Equinox.

Constantinides, G.C. (1983). *Intelligence and Espionage: An Analytical Bibliography*. Boulder: Westview.

Cook, A. (2004). *Ace of Spies: The True Story of Sidney Reilly*. Gloucestershire: Tempus.

Cooper, H.H.A., and L.J. Redlinger. (1988). *Catching Spies: Principles and Practices of Counterespionage*. Boulder: Paladin.

Cornick, M., and P. Morris. (1993). *The French Secret Services*. New Brunswick: Transaction.

Corson, W.R., et al. (1989). *WIDOWS*. New York: Crown.

Costello, J., and O. Tsarev. (1993). *Deadly Illusions*. New York: Crown.

Cruickshanks, E., ed. (1982). *Ideology and Conspiracy: Aspects of Jacobitism, 1689–1759*. Edinburgh: John Donald.

Dallin, D.J. (1955). *Soviet Espionage*. New Haven: Yale University Press.

Darling, A.B. (1990). *The Central Intelligence Agency: An Instrument of Government to 1950*. University Park: Pennsylvania State University Press.

Davies, P.H.J. (1996). *The British Secret Services*. Oxford: Clio.

Deacon, R. (1990a). *Kempei Tai: A History of the Japanese Secret Service*. New York: Beaufort Books. Revised and updated.

Deacon, R. (1990b). *The French Secret Service*. London: Grafton.

Deletant, D. (1995). *Ceausescu and the Securitate: Coercion and Dissent in Romania, 1965–1989*. Armonk, NY: M.E. Sharpe.

Dennis, M. (2003). *The Stasi: Myth and Reality*. London: Pearson Education.

Deriabin, P. (1959). *The Secret World*. New York: Doubleday.

DeVore, H.O. (1999). *China's Intelligence and Internal Security Forces*. Alexandria, VA: Jane's Information Group. http://catalog.janes.com/catalog/public/html/intelcentres.html .

Dhar, K. (2006). *Fulcrum of Evil: ISI, CIA, Al Qaeda Nexus*. New Delhi: Manas.

Dobbs, M. (2004). *Saboteurs: The Nazi Raid on America*. New York: Alfred A. Knopf

Donovan, J.B. (1964). *Strangers on a Bridge: The Case of Colonel Abel*. New York: Atheneum House.

Dorwart, J.M. (1979a). *The Office of Naval Intelligence: The Birth of America's First Intelligence Agency, 1865–1918*. Annapolis: Naval Institute Press.

Dorwart. J.M. (1983b). *Conflict of Duty: The U.S. Navy's Intelligence Dilemma, 1919–45*. Annapolis: Naval Institute Press.

Draitser, E. (2010). *Stalin's Romeo Spy: The Remarkable Rise and Fall of the KGB's Most Daring Operative*. Evanston: Northwestern University Press.

Drogin, B. (2007). *Curveball: Spies, Lies, and the Con Man Who Caused a War*. New York: Random House.

Drumheller, T. (2006). *On the Brink: An Insider's Account of How the White House Compromised American Intelligence*. New York: Carroll & Graf.

Dukes, P. (1922). *Red Dusk and the Morrow: Adventures and Investigations in Red Russia*. New York: Doubleday, Page.

Dulles, A. (2006). *The Craft of Intelligence: America's Legendary Spy Master on the Fundamentals of Intelligence Gathering for a Free World*. Guilford, CT: The Lyons Press.

Dvornik, F. (1974). *Origins of Intelligence Services: The Ancient Near East, Persia, Greece, Rome, Byzantium, the Arab Muslim Empires, the Mongol Empire, China, Muscovy*. New Brunswick: Rutgers University Press.

Dwyer, T. (2005). *The Squad and the Intelligence Operations of Michael Collins*. Cork, Ireland: Mercier Press.

Dziak, J.J. (1988). *Chekisty: A History of the KGB*. Lexington, MA: Lexington Books.

Earley, P. (1988a). *Family of Spies: Inside the John Walker Spy Ring*. New York: Bantam.

Earley, P. (1998b). *Confessions of a Spy: The Real Story of Aldrich Ames*. New York: Berkley.

Eftimiades, N. (1994). *Chinese Intelligence Operations*. Annapolis: Naval Institute Press.

Einstein, L. (1933). *Divided Loyalties: Americans in England During the War of Independence*. London: Cobden-Sanderson.

Ellis, K. (1958). *The Post Office in the Eighteenth Century: A Study of Administrative History*. Oxford: Oxford University Press.

Epstein, E. Jay. (1978). *Legend: The Secret World of Lee Harvey Oswald*. New York: Reader's Digest Press.

Epstein, E. Jay. (1989). *Deception: The Invisible War Between the KGB & the CIA*. New York: Simon & Schuster.

Everitt, N (1920). *British Secret Service During the Great War* London: Hutchinson.

Fardust, H. (1999). *The Rise and Fall of the Pahlavi Dynasty: The Memoirs of Former General Hussein Fardust*. New Delhi: Motilal Banarsidass.

Farson, S., et al. (2008a). *PSI Handbook of Global Security and Intelligence, Volume One: The Americas and Asia*. Westport, CT: Praeger.

Farson, S., et al. (2008b). *PSI Handbook of Global Security and Intelligence, Volume Two: Europe, the Middle East, and South Africa*. Westport, CT: Praeger.

Feis, W.B. (2002). *Grant's Secret Service: The Intelligence War from Belmont to Appomattox*. Lincoln: University of Nebraska Press.

Feklisov, A. (2001). *The Man Behind the Rosenbergs*. New York: Enigma Books.

Felix, C. (2001). *A Short Course in the Secret War*. Lanham, MD: Madison Books.

Felsted, S.T. (1920). *German Spies at Bay*. London: Hutchinson.

Ferguson, H. (2008). *Operation Kronstadt: The Greatest True Tale of Espionage to Come Out of the Early Years of MI6*. London: Hutchinson.

Fischer, B. (2008). "The Spy Who Came in for the Gold: A Skeptical View of the GTVANQUISH Case." *Journal of Intelligence History*, 8, 29–54.

Fishel, E.C. (1996). *The Secret War for the Union: The Untold Story of Military Intelligence in the Civil War*. Boston: Houghton Mifflin. Corrected edition.

Fitzpatrick, W.J. (1892). *Secret Service Under Pitt*. London: Longman, Green.

Fraser, P. (1956). *The Intelligence of the Secretaries of State and the Monopoly of Licensed News 1660–1688*. Cambridge: Cambridge University Press.

Furse, Colonel G.A. (1895). *Information in War: Its Acquisition and Transmission*. London: William Clowes.

Fysh, M., ed. (1989). *The Spycatcher Cases*. London: European Law Centre.

Gazur, E. (2001). *Secret Assignment: The FBI's KGB General*. London: St. Ermin's Press.

George, R., and H. Rishikof, eds. (2011). *The National Security Enterprise: Navigating the Labyrinth*. Washington, D.C.: Georgetown University Press.

Gilbert, J.L., et al. (2005). *In the Shadow of the Sphinx: A History of Army Counterintelligence*. Ft. Belvoir, VA: U.S. Army INSCOM.

Giles, L. (2010). *Wearing Red, Tracking Reds: What a Ride!—Policing and Counter-Espionage from Canada to Hong Kong*. Bloomington: Trafford.

Godson, R. (1995). *Dirty Tricks or Trump Cards: U.S. Covert Action and Counterintelligence*. Washington, D.C.: Brassey's.

Golitsyn, A. (1984). *New Lies for Old: The Communist Strategy of Deception and Disinformation*. New York: Dodd, Mead.

Goltz, H. van der (1917). *My Adventures as a German Secret Agent*. New York: Robert M. McBride.

Gordievsky, O. (1995). *Next Stop Execution: The Autobiography of Oleg Gordievsky*. London: Macmillan.

Gouzenko, I. (1948) *The Iron Curtain*. New York: E.P. Dutton.

Graff, G. (2011). *The Threat Matrix: The FBI at War in the Age of Global Terror*. Boston: Little, Brown.

Grant, H. (1915). *Spies and Secret Service: The Story of*

Espionage, Its Main Systems and Chief Exponents. New York: Frederick A. Stokes.

Graves, A.K. (1914). *The Secrets of the German War Office.* New York: McBride, Nast.

Greaves, R.L. (1986). *Deliver Us From Evil: The Radical Underground in Britain, 1660–1663.* New York: Oxford University Press.

Greaves, R.L. (1990). *Enemies Under His Feet: Radicals and Nonconformists in Britain, 1664–1677.* Stanford: Stanford University Press

Greaves, R.L. (1992). *Secret of the Kingdom: British Radicals from the Popish Plot to the Revolution of 1688–89.* Stanford: Stanford University Press.

Grose, P. (1996). *Gentleman Spy: The Life of Allen Dulles.* Amherst: University of Massachusetts Press.

Gudgin, P. (1989). *Military Intelligence: The British Story.* London: Arms & Armour.

Hamrick, S.J. (2004). *Deceiving the Deceivers: Kim Philby, Donald Maclean, and Guy Burgess.* New Haven: Yale University Press.

Harris, S. (2010). *The Watchers: The Rise of America's Surveillance State.* New York: Penguin.

Hart, J.L. (1997). "Pyotr Semyonovich Popov: The Tribulations of Faith." *Intelligence and National Security,* 12 (4), 44–74.

Hastedt, G., ed. (2011). *Spies, Wiretaps, and Secret Operations: An Encyclopedia of American Espionage,* Volume 1 (A–J) & Volume 2 (K–Z). Santa Barbara: ABC-CLIO.

Havill, A. (2001). *The Spy Who Stayed Out in the Cold: The Secret Life of FBI Double Agent Robert Hanssen.* New York: St. Martin's.

Haynes, J.E., and H. Klehr (2000). *Venona: Decoding Soviet Espionage in America.* New Haven: Yale University Press.

Haynes, J.E., H. Klehr, and A. Vassilie (2009). *SPIES: The Rise and Fall of the KGB in America.* New Haven: Yale University Press.

Hennessey, T., and C. Thomas (2009). *Spooks: The Unofficial History of MI5.* Gloucestershire: Amberley.

Herridge, C. (2011). *The Next Wave: On the Hunt for al-Qaeda's American Recruits.* New York: Random House.

Herrington, S.A. (1999). *Traitors Among Us: Inside the Spy Catcher's World.* Novato, CA: Presidio.

Heuer, R. (1995). "Nosenko: Five Paths to Judgment." In H. B. Westerfield. *Inside CIA's Private World: Declassified Articles from the Agency's Internal Journal 1955–1995.* New Haven: Yale University Press, pp. 379–414.

Hilger, A. (2003). "Counterintelligence Soviet Style: The Activities of Soviet Security Services in East Germany, 1945–1955." *The Journal of Intelligence History* 3 (1), 83–105.

Hingley, R. (1970). *The Russian Secret Police: Muscovite, Imperial Russian and Soviet Political Security Operations, 1565–1970.* London: Hutchinson.

Hinsley, F.H., et al. (1990). *British Intelligence in the Second World War, Volume Four: Security and Counter-Intelligence.* London: HMSO.

Hittle, J.E.B. (2011). *Michael Collins and the Anglo-Irish War: Britain's Counterinsurgency Failure.* Washington, D.C.: Potomac.

Hoffman, T. (2008). *The Spy Within: Larry Chin and China's Penetration of the CIA.* Hanover, NH: Steerforth Press.

Höhne, H. (1979). *Canaris: Hitler's Master Spy.* Garden City, NY: Doubleday.

Hollingsworth, M., & N. Fielding. (1999). *Defending the Realm: MI5 and the Shayler Affair.* London: André Deutsch.

Holt, P.M. (1995). *Secret Intelligence and Public Policy: A Dilemma of Democracy.* Washington, D.C.: Q.C. Press.

Holt, T. (2007). *The Deceivers: Allied Military Deception in the Second World War.* New York: Skyhorse.

Holzman, M. (2008). *James Jesus Angleton, the CIA, and the Craft of Counterintelligence.* Amherst: University of Massachusetts Press.

Hood, W. (1993). *MOLE: The True Story of the First Russian Spy to Became an American Counterspy.* Washington, D.C.: Brassey's.

Hornblum, A. (2010). *The Invisible Harry Gold: The Man Who Gave the Soviets the Atom Bomb.* New Haven: Yale University Press.

Houghton, H. (1972). *Operation Portland: The Autobiography of a Spy.* London: Rupert Hart-Davis.

Howard, E. (1995). *Safe House: The Compelling Memoirs of the Only CIA Spy to Seek Asylum in Russia.* Bethesda: National Press Books.

Howard, M. (1990). *British Intelligence in the Second World War: Volume Five: Strategic Deception.* (London: HMSO.

Hulnick, A. (2004). *Keeping Us Safe: Secret Intelligence and Homeland Security.* Westport, CT: Praeger.

Hunter, R.W. (1999). *Spy Hunter: Inside the FBI Investigation of the Walker Espionage Case.* Annapolis: Naval Institute Press.

Hurt, H. (1981). *Shadrin: The Spy Who Never Came Back.* New York: Reader's Digest Press.

Jackson, B., ed. (2009). *The Challenge of Domestic Intelligence in a Free Society: A Multidisciplinary Look the Creation of a U.S. Domestic Counterterrorism Agency.* Arlington: Rand.

Jeffrey, K. (2010). *MI6: The History of the Secret Intelligence Service 1909–1949.* London: Bloomsbury.

Jensen, J.M. (1968). *The Price of Vigilance.* Chicago: Rand McNally.

Johnson, L. (2006). "The Liaison Arrangements of the Central Intelligence Agency." In A. Theoharis et al., eds., *The Central Intelligence Agency: Security Under Scrutiny.* Westport, CT: Greenwood.

Johnson, L., ed. (2007). *Strategic Intelligence, Volume 4: Counterintelligence and Counterterrorism.* Westport, CT: Praeger.

Johnson, L. (2010). *The Oxford Handbook of National Security Intelligence.* New York: Oxford University Press.

Johnson, L., and J. Wirtz (2011). *Intelligence: The Secret World of Spies.* New York: Oxford University Press.

Johnson, W. R. (2009). *Thwarting Enemies at Home and Abroad: How to Be a Counterintelligence Officer.* Washington, D.C.: Georgetown University Press.

Jones, J.P. (1917). *The German Spy in America: The Secret Plotting of German Spies in the United States and the Inside Story of the Sinking of the Lusitania*. London: Hutchinson.

Jones, J.P., and P.M. Hollister. (1918). *The German Secret Service in America*. Boston: Small, Maynard.

Kahana, E. (2006). *Historical Dictionary of Israeli Intelligence*. Lanham, MD: Scarecrow Press.

Kahlili, R. (2010). *A Time to Betray: The Astonishing Double Life of a CIA Agent Inside the Revolutionary Guards of Iran*. New York: Simon & Schuster.

Kalugin, O. (2009). *SPYMASTER: My 32 Years in Intelligence and Espionage Against the West*. New York: Basic Books. Second revised edition, originally *The First Directorate* (1994).

Kauffman, Michael W. (2004) *American Brutus: John Wilkes Booth and the Lincoln Conspiracies*. New York: Random House.

Kern, G. (2004). *A Death in Washington: Walter G. Krivitsky and the Stalin Terror*. New York: Enigma Books. Revised.

Kern, G. (2007). *The Kravchenko Case: One Man's War on Stalin*. New York: Enigma Books.

Kessler, R. (1988). *Spy vs. Spy: Stalking Soviet Spies in America*. New York: Scribner's.

Kessler, R. (1989). *Moscow Station: How the KGB Penetrated the American Embassy*. New York: Macmillan.

Kessler, R. (1990). *The Spy in the Russian Club: How Glen Souther Stole America's Nuclear War Plans and Escaped to Moscow*. New York: Scribner's.

Kessler, R. (1991). *Escape from the CIA: How the CIA Won and Lost the Most Important KGB Spy Ever to Defect to the U.S.* New York: Pocket Books.

Kessler, R. (2002). *The Bureau: The Secret History of the FBI*. New York: St. Martin's Press.

Kessler, R. (2011). *The Secrets of the FBI*. New York: Crown.

Kindermann, Dr. K. (1933). *In the Toils of the O.G.P.U.* London: Hurst & Blackett.

Kingston, Richard. (1698). *A True History of the Several Designs Against His Majesties Sacred Person and Government from 1688 to 1697*. London: Richard Kingston.

Kingston, R. (1700a). *Modest Answer to Captain Smith's Immodest Memorial of Secret Service*. London: Richard Kingston.

Kingston, R. (1700b). *Tyranny Detected and the Late Revolution Justy'd, by the Law of God, the Law of Nature, and the Practices of All Nations: A History of the Late King James's Reign, and a Discovery of His Arts, and Actions, for Introducing Popery and Arbitrary Powers, and the Intended Subversion of the Protestant Interest in Three Kingdoms*. London: John Nutt.

Kitchen, G. (1935). *Prisoner of the OGPU*. London: Longmans, Green.

Klehr, H., and R. Radosh (1996). *The Amerasia Case: Prelude to McCarthyism*. Chapel Hill: University Press of North Carolina.

Knight, A. (2006). *How the Cold War Began: The Igor Gouzenko Affair and the Hunt for Soviet Spies*. New York: Carroll & Graf.

Knight, A. (1996). *Spies Without Cloaks: The KGB's Successors*. Princeton: Princeton University Press.

Knightley, P. (1989). *The Master Spy: the Story of Kim Philby*. New York: Alfred A. Knopf.

Koehler, J.O. (1999). *STASI: The Untold Story of the East German Secret Police*. Boulder: Westview.

Kostin, S., and E. Raynaud. *FAREWELL: The Greatest Spy Story of the Twentieth Century*. Las Vegas: AmazonCrossing.

Kostov, V. (1988). *The Bulgarian Umbrella: The Soviet Direction and Operations of the Bulgarian Secret Service in Europe*. New York: St. Martin's.

Krivitsky, W.G. (1939a). *Saturday Evening Post*, an 8-part series starting 15 April 1939.

Krivitsky, W.G. (1939b). *In Stalin's Secret Service: An Exposé of Russia's Secret Policies by the Former Chief of the Soviet Intelligence in Western Europe*. New York: Harper. The Enigma Books edition (2000) adds an index.

Kuzichkin, V. (1990). *Inside the KGB: Myth & Reality*. London: André Deutsch.

Lamont-Brown, R. (1998). *Kempeitai: Japan's Dreaded Military Police*. Gloucestershire: Sutton.

Lamphere, R.J., and T. Shachtman (1986). *The FBI-KGB War: A Special Agent's Story*. New York: Random House.

Landau, H. *The Enemy Within: The Inside Story of German Sabotage in America*. New York: Putnam's.

Lang, A. (1897). *Pickle The Spy: or The Incognito of Prince Charles*. London: Longmans, Green.

Lang, A. (1898). *The Companions of Pickle: Being a Sequel to "Pickle the Spy."* London: Longmans, Green.

Lefebvre, S., and R.N. McDermott (2008). "Russia and the Intelligence Services of Central Asia." *International Journal of Intelligence and Counterintelligence*, 21 (2), 251–301.

Leggett. G. (1986). *The Cheka: Lenin's Political Police*. New York: Oxford University Press.

Levy, D. (2011). *Stalin's Man in Canada: Fred Rose and Soviet Espionage*. New York: Enigma Books.

Lonsdale, G. (1965). *SPY: Twenty Years in Soviet Secret Service—The Memoirs of Gordon Lonsdale*. New York: Hawthorne Books.

Lowenthal, Mark (2011). *Intelligence: From Secrets to Policy*, 5th ed. Washington, D.C.: Sage.

Lowenthal, Max (1950). *The Federal Bureau of Investigation*. New York: William Sloane.

Maas, P. (1995). *Killer Spy: The Inside Story of the FBI's Pursuit and Capture of Aldrich Ames, America's Deadliest Spy*. New York: Warner Books.

Macdonald, B. (1998). *The True "Intrepid": Sir William Stephenson and the Unknown Agents*. Surrey, BC: Timberholme Books.

Macintyre, B. (2007). *Agent ZIGZAG: The True Wartime Story of Eddie Chapman: Lover, Betrayer, Hero, Spy*. London: Bloomsbury.

Macintyre, B. (2010). *Operation Mincemeat: The True Story That Changed the Course of World War II*. London: Bloomsbury.

Maclean, F. (1978). *Take Nine Spies*. New York: Atheneum.

Macky, S. (ed.) (1733). *Memoirs of the Secret Services of*

John Macky, Esq; During the Reigns of King William, Queen Anne, and King George I. London: S. Macky.

Macrakis, K. (2008). *Seduced by Secrets: Inside the Stasi's Spy-Tech World.* Cambridge: Cambridge University Press.

Mangold, T. (1991). *Cold Warrior: James Jesus Angleton, the CIA's Master Spy Hunter.* New York: Simon & Schuster.

Manne, R. (1987). *The Petrov Affair: Politics and Espionage.* Sydney: Permagon.

Marshall. A. (1994). *Intelligence and Espionage in the Reign of Charles II, 1660–1685.* Cambridge: Cambridge University Press.

Martin, D. (1980). *Wilderness of Mirrors.* New York: Harper & Row.

Massing, H. (1951). *This Deception: The Story of a Woman Agent.* New York: Duell, Sloan & Pearce.

Masterman, J.C. (1995). *The Double-Cross System: In the War of 1939 to 1945.* New Haven: Yale University Press. Revised; important introduction by N. West that adds new agent names and explains Masterman's prepublication problems.

Matthews, T. (1993). *Shadows Dancing: Japanese Espionage Against the West 1939–45.* London: Robert Hale.

McKay, C.G. (1993). *From Information to Intrigue: Studies in Secret Service Based on the Swedish Experience.* London: Frank Cass.

McMahon, P. (2008). *British Spies & Irish Rebels.* Woodbridge: *The Boydell Press.*

McNeish, J. (2007). *The Sixth Man: The Extraordinary Life of Paddy Costello.* London: Random House.

Melgounov, S.P. (1926). *The Red Terror in Russia.* London: J.M. Dent.

Milton, G.F. (1942). *Abraham Lincoln and the Fifth Column.* New York: Vanguard Press.

Mitchell, M., and T. Mitchell (2002). *The Spy Who Seduced America: Lies & Betrayal in the Heat of the Cold War—The Judith Coplon Story.* Montpelier: Invisible Cities Press.

Mogelever, J. (1960). *Death to Traitors: The Story of General Lafayette C. Baker Lincoln's Forgotten Secret Service Chief.* New York: Doubleday.

Monas, S. (1961). *The Third Section: Police and Society in Russia under Nicholas I.* Cambridge, MA: Harvard University Press.

Murphy, D.E., et al. (1997). *Battleground Berlin: CIA vs KGB in the Cold War.* New Haven: Yale University Press.

Newton, V.W. (1991). *The Cambridge Spies: The Untold Story of Maclean, Philby and Burgess in America.* Lanham, MD: Madison Books.

Nicolai, W. (1924) *The German Secret Service.* London: Stanley, Paul.

9/11 Commission Report (2004). *Final Report of the National Commission on Terrorist Attacks Upon the United States.* New York: Barnes & Noble. Indexed.

O'Brien, K. (2011). *The South African Intelligence Services: From Apartheid to Democracy.* New York: Routledge.

O'Halpin, E. (1999). *Defending Ireland: The Irish State and Its Enemies Since 1922.* Oxford: Oxford University Press.

O'Halpin, E., ed. (2003). *MI5 and Ireland, 1939–1945: The Official History.* Portland: Irish Academic Press.

Olive, R.J. (2006). *Capturing Jonathan Pollard: How One of the Most Notorious Spies in American History Was Brought to Justice.* Annapolis: Naval Institute Press.

Olson, J. (2006). *Fair Play: The Moral Dilemmas of Spying.* Washington, D.C.: Potomac.

Omand, D. (2010). *Securing the State.* New York: Columbia University Press.

Orlov, A. (1953). *The Secret History of Stalin's Crimes.* New York: Random House.

Orlov, A. (2004). *Alexander Orlov: The March of Time.* London: St. Ermin's Press.

O'Toole, G. (1991). *Honorable Treachery: A History of U.S. Intelligence, Espionage, and Covert Action from the American Revolution to the CIA.* New York: Atlantic Monthly Press.

Pacepa, I. (1987). *Red Horizons: Chronicles of a Communist Spy Chief.* Washington, D.C.: Regnery.

Paillole, Col. P. (2003). *Fighting the Nazis: French Military Intelligence and Counterintelligence 1935–1945.* New York: Enigma Books.

Palmer, D.R. (2006). *George Washington and Benedict Arnold: A Tale of Two Patriots.* Washington, D.C.: Regnery.

Paltsits, V.H., ed. (1909). *Minutes of the Commissioners for Detecting and Defeating Conspiracies in the State of New York: Albany Country Sessions, 1778–1781, 3 Volumes.* Albany: State of New York.

Peake, H.B. (2003). *The Philby Literature.* In R. Philby, *The Private Life of Kim Philby: The Moscow Years.* London: St. Ermin's Press, pp. 297–400.

Pedahzur, A. (2009). *The Israeli Secret Services & the Struggle Against Terrorism.* New York: Columbia University Press.

Perry, R. (1994). *The Fifth Man.* London: Sidgwick & Jackson.

Perry, R. (2005). *Last of the Cold War Spies: The Life of Michael Straight the Only American in Britain's Cambridge Spy Ring.* Cambridge, MA: Da Capo Press.

Persico, J. (1990). *Casey: The Lives and Secrets of William J. Casey: From the OSS to the CIA.* New York: Viking.

Petrov, V., and E. Petrov. (1956). *Empire of Fear.* New York: Praeger.

Philby, K. (1968). *My Silent War.* New York: Grove Press.

Philby, R., et al. (2003). *The Private Life of Kim Philby: The Moscow Years.* London: St. Ermin's Press.

Pincher, C. (2009). *Treachery: Betrayals, Blunders and Cover-Ups: Six Decades of Espionage Against America and Britain.* New York: Random House.

Pincher, C. (2011). *Treachery: Betrayals, Blunders and Cover-ups: Six Decades of Espionage Against America and Britain.* London: Mainstream. This edition adds news material not included in the 2009 edition.

Pinkerton, A. (1885). *The Spy of the Rebellion; Being a True History of the Spy System of the United States Army During the Late Rebellion.* New York: G.W. Carleton. Reprinted 1989, Lincoln: University of Nebraska Press.

Polmar, N., and T.B. Allen (2004). *SPY BOOK: The Encyclopedia of Espionage,* 3d ed. New York: Random House.

Popoff, G. (1925). *The Cheka: The Red Inquisition.* London: A.M. Philpot.

Porch, D. (1995). *The French Secret Services: From the Dreyfus Affair to the Gulf War.* New York: Farrar, Straus and Giroux.

Porter, B. (1987). *The Origins of the Vigilant State: the London Metropolitan Police Special Branch Before the First World War.* London: Weidenfeld & Nicolson.

Posner, R.A. (2007). *Countering Terrorism: Blurred Focus, Halting Steps.* Lanham, MD: Rowman & Littlefield.

Powers, R.G. (1987). *Secrecy and Power: The Life of J. Edgar Hoover.* New York: Free Press.

Powers, R.G. (2004). *Broken: The Troubled Past and Uncertain Future of the FBI.* New York: Free Press.

Pratt, Donovan (1979). *The Rote Kapelle: The CIA's History of Soviet Intelligence and Espionage Networks in Western Europe, 1936–1945.* Frederick, MD: University Press of America. The author is not listed on most printings of this book and it is often cited as the CIA study of the Red Orchestra or Rote Kapelle.

Pringle, R.A. (2006). *Historical Dictionary of Russian and Soviet Intelligence.* Lanham, MD: Scarecrow Press.

Pringle, R. (2008b) "SMERSH: Military Counterintelligence and Stalin's Control of the USSR." *International Journal and Counterintelligence,* 21 (2008).

Prouty, N. (2011). *Uncompromised: The Rise, Fall, and Redemption of an Arab American Patriot in the CIA.* New York: Palgrave Macmillan.

Radosh, R., and J. Milton (1997). *The Rosenberg File,* 2d ed. New Haven: Yale University Press.

Rafalko, F.G. (c. 1995–2004). *A Counterintelligence Reader—The American Revolution to WWII—Volume 1; Counterintelligence in World War II—Volume 2; Post World War II to Closing the 20th Century—Volume 3; American Revolution into the New Millennium—Volume 4.* Washington, D.C.: National Counterintelligence Executive (NCIX). The fourth volume was only published online. All four are available at http://ftp.fas.org/irp/ops/ci/docs/index.html. Volume 4, *American Revolution into the New Millennium,* does not mention the American revolution.

Rafalko, F.G. (2011). *MH/CHAOS: The CIA's Campaign Against the Radical New Left and the Black Panthers.* Annapolis: Naval Institute Press.

Raman, B. (2002). *Intelligence: Past, Present & Future.* New Delhi: Lancer.

Raviv, D., and Y. Melman (1990). *Every Spy A Prince: The Complete History of Israel's Intelligence Community.* Boston: Houghton Mifflin.

Reilly, S. (1932). *Britain's Master Spy: The Adventures of Sidney Reilly, A Narrative Written by Himself Edited and Completed by His Wife.* New York: Harper.

Renfer, M.A., and H.S. Haas. (2008). "Systematic Analysis in Counterterrorism: Messages on an Islamist Internet Forum." *International Journal of Intelligence and Counterintelligence,* 21 (2), 314–36.

Richards, J. (2011). *Currency Wars: The Making of the Next Global Crisis.* New York: Penguin.

Richings, M.G. (1934). *ESPIONAGE: The Story of the Secret Service of the English Crown.* London: Hutchinson.

Riste, O. (1999). *The Norwegian Intelligence Service 1945–1970.* London: Frank Cass.

Robarge, D.K. (2003). "Moles, Defectors, and Deceptions: James Angleton and CIA Counterintelligence." *The Journal of Intelligence History,* 3 (2), 21–49.

Robertson, T. (2011). *Gentleman Spymaster: How Lt. Col. Tommy Robertson Double-Crossed the Nazis.* London: Methuen.

Ronnie, A. (1995). *Counterfeit Hero: Fritz Duquesne, Adventurer, & Spy.* Annapolis: Naval Institute Press.

Rose, R.S., and G.D. Scott. (2009). *Johnny: A Spy's Life.* University Park: Pennsylvania State University Press.

Rout, L.B., Jr., and J. Bratzel (1986). *The Shadow War: German Espionage & United States Counterespionage in Latin America During World War II.* Frederick, MD: University Publications of America.

Rowan, R.W. (1929). *Spy and Counter Spy: The Development of Modern Espionage.* New York: Viking.

Rowan R.W. (1937). *The Story of Secret Service.* Garden City, NY: Doubleday.

Rowan, R.W., and R.G. Deindorfer (1967). *Secret Service: 33 Centuries of Espionage.* New York: Hawthorne.

Royden, B. (2003). "A Worthy Successor to Penkovsky: An Exceptional Espionage Operation." *Studies in Intelligence* 43/3.

Russell, F.S. (1999). *Information Gathering in Classical Greece.* Ann Arbor: University of Michigan Press.

Sageman, M. (2008). *Leaderless Jihad: Terror Networking in the Twenty-First Century.* Philadelphia: University of Pennsylvania Press.

Sakmyster, T. (2011). *RED Conspirator: J. Peters and the American Communist Underground.* Urbana: University of Illinois Press.

Sanders, J. (2006). *Apartheid's Friends: The Rise and Fall of South Africa's Secret Service.* London: John Murray.

Sawatsky, J. (1980). *Men in the Shadows: The RCMP Security Service.* Toronto: Doubleday.

Sawatsky, J. (1982). *For Services Rendered: Leslie James Bennett and the RCMP Security Service.* Toronto: Doubleday.

Sawyer, R.D. (1998). *The TAO of SPYCRAFT: Intelligence Theory and Practice in Traditional China.* Boulder: Westview.

Sayer, I., and D. Botting. (1989). *America's Secret Army: The Untold Story of the Counter Intelligence Corps.* New York: London: Grafton.

Schaeper, T. (2011). *Edward Bancroft: Scientist, Author, Spy.* New Haven: Yale University Press.

Schecter, J.L., and P. Deriabin (1992). *The Spy Who Saved the World: How a Soviet Colonel Changed the Course of the Cold War.* New York: Scribner's.

Schmeidel, J. (2008). *Stasi: Shield and Sword of the Party.* New York: Routledge.

Seth, A. (1998). "Burma's Intelligence Apparatus." *Intelligence and National Security,* 13 (4), 33–70.

Shannon, E., and A. Blackman. (2002). *The Spy Next Door: The Extraordinary Secret Life of Robert Philip Hanssen, The Most Damaging FBI Agent in U.S. History*. Boston: Little, Brown.

Sheldon, R.M. (2003). *Espionage in the Ancient World: An Annotated Bibliography of Books and Articles in Western Languages*. Jefferson, NC: McFarland.

Sheldon, R.M. (2005). *Intelligence Activities in Ancient Rome*. London: Frank Cass.

Sheldon, R.M. (2007). *Spies of the Bible: Espionage in Israel from the Exodus to the Bar Kokhba Revolt*. St. Paul: MBI.

Sheymov, V. (1993). *Tower of Secrets: A Real Life Spy Thriller*. Annapolis: Naval Institute Press.

Shulsky, A.N., and G.J. Schmitt. (2002). *Silent Warfare: Understanding the World of Intelligence*, 3d ed. Washington, D.C.: Brassey's.

Sibley, K.A.S. (2004). *Red Spies in America: Stolen Secrets and the Dawn of the Cold War*. Lawrence: University Press of Kansas.

Sims, Jennifer E., and B. Gerber, eds. (2009). *Vaults, Mirrors & Masks: Rediscovering U.S. Counterintelligence*. Washington, D.C.: Georgetown University Press.

Singer, K. (1956). *Spies Over Asia*. London: W.H. Allen.

Sirrs, O. (2010). *A History of the Egyptian Intelligence Service: A History of the Mukhabarat*. New York: Routledge.

Smith, I.C. (2004). *Inside: A Top G-Man Exposes Spies, Lies, and Bureaucratic Bungling Inside the FBI*. Nashville: Nelson Current.

Smith, Matthew (1699). *Memoirs of Secret Service*. London: A. Baldwin.

Smith, Michael (2010). *MI6: The Real James Bonds 1909–1939*. London: Dialogue.

Smyth, D. (2010). *Deathly Deception: The Real Story of Operation Mincemeat*. New York: Oxford University Press.

Sparrow, E. (1999). *Secret Service: British Agents in France, 1792–1815*. Woodbridge: Boydell Press.

Srodes, J. (1999). *Allen Dulles: Master of Spies*. Washington, D.C.: Regnery.

Stephan, R. (2004). *Stalin's Secret War: Soviet Counterintelligence Against the Nazis. 1941–1946*. Lawrence: University Press of Kansas.

Stevenson, W. (1976). *The Man Called Intrepid: The Secret War*. New York: Harcourt Brace Javonovich.

Stirling, T., et al. (2005). *Intelligence Co-Operation Between Poland and Great Britain During World War II: Report of the Anglo-Polish Historical Committee*. London: Vallentine Mitchell.

Stober, D., and I. Hoffman (2001). *A Convenient Spy: Wen Ho Lee and the Politics of Espionage*. New York: Simon & Schuster.

Stockton, B. (2006). *Flawed Patriot: The Rise and Fall of CIA Legend Bill Harvey*. Washington, D.C.: Potomac.

Straight, M. (1983). *After Long Silence* New York: W.W. Norton.

Strother, F. (1918). *Fighting Germany's Spies*. New York: Doubleday.

Svendsen, A. (2010). *Intelligence Cooperation and the War on Terror: Anglo-American Security Relations After 9/11*. New York: Routledge.

Talbert, R. (1991). *Negative Intelligence: The Army and the American Left, 1917–1941*. Jackson: University Press of Mississippi.

Taylor, S.A., and D. Snow (2007). "Cold War Spies: Why They Spied and How They Got Caught." In Johnson, L., and J. Wirtz, eds. *Intelligence and National Security: The Secret World of Spies*. New York: Oxford University Press, pp. 302–11.

Tenet, G. (2008). *At the Center of the Storm: The CIA During America's Time of Crisis*. New York: Harper.

Thomas, G. (2009). *Secret Wars: One Hundred Years of British Intelligence Inside MI5 and MI6*. New York: St. Martin's Press.

Tidwell, W.A., et al. (1988). *Come Retribution: The Confederate Secret Service and the Assassination of Lincoln*. Jackson: University Press of Mississippi.

Toohey, B., and W. Pinwill (1989). *OYSTER: The Story of the Australian Secret Intelligence Service*. Port Melbourne: Heinemann Australia.

Trento, J.P. (2005). *The Secret History of the CIA*. New York: Carroll & Graff. New Introduction.

Treverton, G. (2009). *Intelligence for an Age of Terror*. Cambridge: Cambridge University Press.

Trulock, N. (2003). *Code Name Kindred Spirit: Inside the Chinese Nuclear Espionage Scandal*. San Francisco: Encounter Books.

Tunney, T.J. (1919). *Throttled: The Detection of the German and Anarchist Bomb Plotters in the United States*. Boston: Small, Maynard.

Turrou, L.G. (1939). *Nazi Spies in America*. New York: Random House.

Twigge, S., et al. (2008) *British Intelligence: Secrets, Spies & Sources*. London: National Archives.

Van Dorn, C. (1941). *Secret History of the American Revolution*. New York: Viking.

Vassall, J. (1975). *VASSALL: The Autobiography of a Spy*. London: Sidgwick & Jackson.

Vassilyev, A.T. (1930). *The Ochrana: The Russian Secret Police*. Philadelphia: J.B. Lippincott.

Vise, D. (2002). *The Bureau and the Mole: The Unmasking of Robert Philip Hanssen, the Most Dangerous Double Agent in FBI History*. New York: Atlantic Monthly.

Voska, V., and W. Irwin (1940). *Spy and Counterspy*. New York: Doubleday, Doran.

Wagner, A. (1893). *The Service of Security and Information*. Washington, D.C.: James W. Chapman.

Wakeman, F. (2003). *Spymaster: Dai Li and the Chinese Secret Service*. Berkeley: University of California Press.

Walker, J.A., Jr. (2008). *My Life as a Spy*. Amherst: Prometheus.

Wallace, R., and H.K. Melton (2008). *Spycraft: The Secret History of the CIA's Spytechs from Communism to Al-Qaeda*. News York: Dutton.

Waller, M. (1994). *The Secret Empire: The KGB in Russia Today*. Boulder: Westview Press.

Wasemiller, A.C. (1969). "The Anatomy of Counterintelligence." *Studies in Intelligence* Winter, pp. 9–24. Available on the CIA Internet site.

Watson, B., et al. (1990). *United States Intelligence: An Encyclopedia*. New York: Garland.

Weiner, T., et al. (1995). *Betrayal: The Story of Aldrich Ames, an American Spy*. New York: Random House.

Weinstein, A., and A. Vassiliev. (2000). *The Haunted Wood: Soviet Espionage in America—the Stalin Era*. New York: Modern Library.

Weinstein, Allen (1997). *Perjury: The Hiss-Chambers Case*. New York: Random House. Second edition, revised.

West, N. (1982). *MI5: British Security Service Operations 1909–1945*. London: Bodley Head; *The Circus: MI5 Operations 1945–1972*. New York: Stein & Day.

West, N. (1989). *Molehunt: Searching for Soviet Spies in MI5*. New York: William Morrow. A much updated version of the 1987 edition, same title. London: Weidenfeld & Nicolson.

West, N. (1993). *The Illegals: The Double Lives of the Cold War's Most Secret Agents*. London: Hodder & Stoughton.

West, N. (1998). *Counterfeit Spies: Genuine or Bogus? An Astonishing Investigation into Secret Agents of the Second World War*. London: St. Ermin's Press

West, N. (2000). *Venona: The Greatest Secret of the Cold War*. London: HarperCollins. Paperback edition, corrections.

West, N., ed. (2005a). *The Guy Liddell Diaries: MI5's Director of Counter-Espionage in World War II, Vols. I & II*. London: Routledge.

West, N. (2005b). *Historical Dictionary of British Intelligence*. Lanham, MD: Scarecrow Press.

West, N. (2007). *Historical Dictionary or Cold War Counterintelligence*. Lanham, MD: Scarecrow Press.

West, N., and O. Tsarev. (1999). *The Crown Jewels: The British Secrets Exposed by the KGB Archives*. London: HarperCollins.

Westerfield, H.B., ed. (1995). *Inside CIA's Private World: Declassified Articles from the Agency's Internal Journal 1955–1995*. New Haven: Yale University Press.

Wettering, F.L. (2008). "Counterintelligence: The Broken Triad." In Johnson, L.K., and J.J. Wirtz, eds. *Intelligence and National Security: The Secret World of Spies*, 2d edn. New York: Oxford University Press.

Whitaker, R., and G. Marcuse. (1994). *Cold War Canada: The Making of a National Insecurity State, 1945–1957*. Toronto: University of Toronto Press.

Whymant, R. (1996). *Stalin's Spy: Richard Sorge and the Tokyo Espionage Ring*. New York: St. Martin's Press.

Williams, K., and D. Deletant. (2001). *Security Intelligence Services in the New Democracies: The Czech Republic, Slovakia, Romania*. New York: Palgrave.

Wilson, D. (2007). *Sir Francis Walsingham: A Courtier in an Age of Terror*. New York: Carroll & Graf.

Wilson, W. (1996). *Dictionary of the United States Intelligence Services*. Jefferson, NC: McFarland.

Winkler, H.D. (2003) *Lincoln and Booth: More Light on the Conspiracy*. Nashville: Cumberland House.

Winks, R.W. (1987). *Cloak & Gown: Scholars in the Secret War, 1939–1945*. New York: William Morrow.

Wise, D. (1988). *The Spy Who Got Away: The Inside Story of Edward Howard, the CIA Agent Who Betrayed His Country's Secrets and Escaped to Moscow*. New York: Random House.

Wise, D. (1992). *MOLEHUNT: The Secret Search for Traitors That Shattered the CIA*. New York: Random House.

Wise, D. (1995). *Nightmover: How Aldrich Ames Sold the CIA to the KGB for $3.6 Million*. New York: Random House.

Wise, D. (2000). *Cassidy's Run: The Secret Spy War Over Nerve Gas*. New York: Random House.

Wise, D. (2003). *SPY: The Inside Story of How the FBI's Robert Hanssen Betrayed America*. New York: Random House. New Afterword.

Wise, D. (2011). *Tiger Trap: America's Secret Spy War with China*. Boston: Houghton Mifflin.

Witcover, J. (1989). *Sabotage at Black Tom: Imperial Germany's Secret War in America—1914–1917*. Chapel Hill: Algonquin.

Wolf, M., with A. McElvoy (1999). *Man Without a Face: The Autobiography of Communism's Greatest Spymaster*. New York: Public Affairs.

Wolin, S., and R. Slusser (1957). *The Soviet Secret Police*. New York: Praeger.

Wright, P., with P. Greengrass (1987). *SPYCATCHER: The Candid Autobiography of a Senior Intelligence Officer*. New York: Viking Penguin.

Yousef, M. (2010). *Son of Hamas: A Gripping Account of Terror, Betrayal, Political Intrigue, and Unthinkable Choices*. Carol Stream, IL: Tyndale House.

Zegart, A. (2011). *Eyes on Spies: Congress and the United States Intelligence Community*. Stanford, CA: Hoover Institution Press.

Zuckerman, F.S. (1996). *The Tsarist Secret Police: in Russian Society, 1880–1917*. London: Macmillan.

FURTHER READING

Those seeking further information on the cases described in the chronology can start where I did, with the books and websites in this listing. As mentioned in the introduction, I found the websites of federal agencies with counterintelligence roles—the FBI, USMC, NACIC, and CIA—most helpful and authoritative. Also useful was *The Sword and the Shield: The Mitrokhin Archive and the Secret History of the KGB*, based on material spirited out of the KGB files. This bibliography notes many human source (humint) operations throughout the world, not just against American interests, as well as key counterintelligence/counterespionage cases. Also included are memoirs of case officers, defectors, and traitors.

Print

Abbott, Karen. *Liar, Temptress, Soldier, Spy: Four Women Undercover in the Civil War*. New York: Harper, 2014, 368 pp.

Adams, James. *The New Spies: Exploring the Frontiers of Espionage*. London: Hutchinson, 1994, 380 pp.

Adams, James. *Sellout: Aldrich Ames and the Corruption of the CIA*. New York: Viking, 1995, 322 pp.

Adams, William R. *St. Augustine and St. Johns County: A Historical Guide*. Sarasota: Pineapple Press, 2009, 111 pp.

Agee, Philip. *Inside the Company: CIA Diary*. New York: Stonehill, 1975, 640 pp.

Agrell, W., and R. Huldt, eds. *Clio Goes Spying: Eight Essays on the History of Intelligence*. Lund: University of Lund, 1983, 213 pp.

Aid, Matthew M., and Cees Wiebes, eds. *Secrets of Signals Intelligence During the Cold War and Beyond*. London: Frank Cass, 2001, 348 pp.

Akhmedov, Ismail Gusseynovich. *In and Out of Stalin's GRU: A Tatar's Escape from Red Army Intelligence*. Frederick, MD: University Publications of America, 1984, 222 pp.

Albats, Yevgenia. *The State Within a State: The KGB and Its Hold on Russia: Past, Present, and Future*. New York: Farrar, Straus and Giroux, 1994, 401 pp.

Albright, Joseph, and Marcia Kunstel. *Bombshell: The Secret Story of America's Unknown Atomic Spy Conspiracy*. New York: Time Books, 1997, 399 pp.

Aldrich, Richard J. *Espionage, Security and Intelligence in Britain 1945–1970*. Manchester: Manchester University Press, 1998, 262 pp.

Aldrich, Richard J., and Michael F. Hopkins, eds. *Intelligence, Defence and Diplomacy: British Policy in the Post-War World*. London: Frank Cass, 1994, 273 pp.

Allen, Thomas, and Norman Polmar. *Merchants of Treason: America's Secrets for Sale from the Pueblo to the Present*. New York: Delacorte, 1988, 378 pp.

Allen, Thomas B. *50 Top Secret Documents That Changed History*. Washington, D.C.: National Geographic, 2008, 320 pp.

Alsop, Stewart, and Thomas Braden. *Sub Rosa: The OSS and American Espionage*. New York: Reynal Hitchcock, 1948.

Alvarez, David. *Secret Messages: Codebreaking and American Diplomacy 1930–1945*. Lawrence: University Press of Kansas, 2000, 292 pp.

Alvarez, David. *Spies in the Vatican: Espionage and Intrigue from Napoleon to the Holocaust*. Lawrence: University Press of Kansas, 2002, 341 pp.

Anders, Karl. *Murder to Order*. New York: Devin-Adair, 1967, 127 pp.

Andrew, Christopher. *Defend the Realm: The Authorized History of MI5*. New York: Knopf, 2009, 994 pp.

Andrew, Christopher. *For the President's Eyes Only: Secret Intelligence and the American Presidency from Washington to Bush*. New York: HarperCollins, 1995, 660 pp.

Andrew, Christopher. *Her Majesty's Secret Service: The Making of the British Intelligence Community*. New York: Penguin, 1987, 619 pp.

Andrew, Christopher, and Oleg Gordievsky. *Instructions from the Centre: Top Secret Files on KGB Foreign Operations 1975–1985*. London: Hodder and Stoughton, 1991, 238 pp.

Andrew, Christopher, and Oleg Gordievsky. *KGB: The Inside Story of Its Foreign Operations from Lenin to Gorbachev*. New York: HarperCollins, 1990, 776 pp.

Andrew, Christopher, and Vasili Mitrokhin. *The Sword and the Shield: The Mitrokhin Archive and the Secret History of the KGB*. New York: Basic Books, 1999, 700 pp.

Andrew, Christopher, and Vasili Mitrokhin. *The World Was Going Our Way: The KGB and the Battle for the Third World, Newly Revealed Secrets from the Mitrokhin Archive*. New York: Basic Books, 2005, 677 pp.

Andrew, Christopher, and David Dilks, eds. *The Missing Dimension: Governments and Intelligence Communities in the Twentieth Century*. London: Macmillan, 1984, 300 pp.

Andrew, Christopher, and Jeremy Noakes, eds. *Intelligence and International Relations, 1900–1945*. Exeter: Exeter University Publications, 1987, 314 pp.

Ashby, Timothy. *The Bear in the Backyard: Moscow's Caribbean Strategy*. Lexington, MA: Lexinton Books, 1987, 240 pp.

Augur, Helen. *The Secret War of Independence*. New York: Duell, Sloan and Pearce, 1955, 381 pp.

August, Frantisek, and David Rees. *Red Star Over Prague*. London: Sherwood, 1984, 176 pp.

Avni, Zeev. *False Flag: The Inside Story of the Spy Who Worked for Moscow and the Israelis*. London: St. Ermin's Press, 1999, 225 pp.

Axelrod, Alan. *The War Between the Spies: A History of Espionage During the American Civil War*. New York: Atlantic Monthly Press, 1992, 308 pp.

Baer, Robert. *See No Evil: The True Story of a Ground Soldier in the CIA's War on Terrorism*. New York: Crown, 2002, 284 pp.

Bagley, Tennent H. *Spymaster: Startling Cold War Revelations of a Soviet KGB Chief*. New York: Skyhorse, 2013, 302 pp.

Bailey, Geoffrey. *The Conspirators*. New York: Harper, 1960, 306 pp.

Bakeless, John. *Spies of the Confederacy*. Mineola: Dover, 1970, 456 pp.

Bakeless, John. *Turncoats, Traitors and Heroes*. Philadelphia: J.B. Lippincott, 1959, 406 pp.

Ball, Desmond. *Soviet Signals Intelligence*. Canberra: Australian National University, 1989, 147 pp.

Ball, Desmond, and David Horner. *Breaking the Codes: Australia's KGB Network 1944–1950*. St. Leonards, NSW: Allen and Unwin, 1998, 468 pp.

Bamford, James. *Body of Secrets: Anatomy of the Ultra-Secret National Security Agency from the Cold War through the Dawn of a New Century*. New York: Doubleday, 2001, 721 pp.

Barcousky, Len. "Eyewitness 1863: Female Teen Is Accused of Being Southern Spy." *Pittsburgh Post-Gazette*, April 28, 2013.

Barker, Rodney. *Dancing with the Devil: Sex, Espionage, and the U.S. Marines—The Clayton Lonetree Story*. New York: Simon & Schuster, 1996, 336 pp.

Barron, John. *Breaking the Ring: The Rise and Fall of the Walker Family Spy Network*. New York: Avon, 1988, 250 pp.

Barron, John. *KGB: The Hidden Hand*. New York: Reader's Digest, 1983, 489 pp.

Barron, John. *KGB: The Secret Work of Soviet Agents*. New York: Reader's Digest, 1974, 462 pp.

Barron, John. *Operation Solo: The FBI's Man in the Kremlin*. Washington, D.C.: Regnery, 1996, 368 pp.

Barros, James. *No Sense of Evil: The Espionage Case of E. Herbert Norman*. New York: Ivy Books, 1987, 303 pp.

Batvinis, Raymond J. *Hoover's Secret War Against Axis Spies: FBI Counterespionage During World War II*. Lawrence: University Press of Kansas, 2014, 334 pp.

Bearden, Milton, and James Risen. *The Main Enemy: The Inside Story of the CIA's Final Showdown with the KGB*. New York: Random House, 2003, 506 pp.

Bearse, Ray, and Anthony Read. *Conspirator: The Untold Story of Tyler Kent*. New York: Doubleday, 1991, 332 pp.

Benson, Robert Louis, and Michael Warner, eds. *VENONA: Soviet Espionage and the American Response 1939–1957*. Washington, D.C.: CIA and NSA, 1996, 450 pp.

Bentley, Elizabeth T., with afterword by Hayden B. Peake. *Out of Bondage: The Story of Elizabeth Bentley*. New York: Ivy Books, 1988, 339 pp.

Bereanu, Vladimir, and Kalin Todorov. *The Umbrella Murder*. Bury St. Edmunds, Suffolk: TEL, 1994, 103 pp.

Berkeley, Roy. *A Spy's London*. London: Leo Cooper, 1994, 363 pp.

Berkowitz, Bruce D., and Allan E. Goodman. *Best Truth: Intelligence in the Information Age*. New Haven: Yale University Press, 2000, 203 pp.

Berkowitz, Bruce D., and Allan E. Goodman. *Strategic Intelligence for American National Security*. Princeton: Princeton University Press, 1989, 232 pp.

Bernikow, Louise. *Abel*. New York: Trident Press, 1970, 347 pp.

Betts, Richard K., and Thomas G. Manhken, eds. *Paradoxes of Strategic Intelligence; Essays in Honor of Michael I. Handel*. London: Frank Cass, 2003, 210 pp.

Bhattacharjee, Yudhijit. "My Father and Me: A Spy Story of Nathan and Harold Nicholson." *The Intelligencer: Journal of U.S. Intelligence Studies* 19, no. 2 (Summer–Fall 2012), pp. 21–25.

Bidwell, Bruce W. *History of the Military Intelligence Division, Department of the Army General Staff: 1775–1941.* Frederick, MD: University Publications of America, 1986, 625 pp.

Binney, Marcus. *The Women Who Lived for Danger: The Women Agents of SOE in the Second World War.* London: Hodder and Stoughton, 2002, 380 pp.

Bissell, Richard M., Jr., with Jonathan E. Lewis and Frances T. Pudlo. *Reflections of a Cold Warrior: From Yalta to the Bay of Pigs.* New Haven: Yale University Press, 1996, 268 pp.

Bittman, Ladislav. *The KGB and Soviet Disinformation: An Insider's View.* McLean, VA: Pergamon-Brassey's, 1985, 226 pp.

Bittman, Ladislav. *New Image Makers: Soviet Propaganda and Disinformation Today.* London: Pergamon-Brassey's, 1988, 262 pp.

Bittman, Ladislav, ed. *The Deception Game: Czechoslovak Intelligence in Soviet Political Warfare.* Syracuse: Syracuse University Research Corporation, 1972, 246 pp.

Blair, William A. *With Malice Toward Some: Treason and Loyalty in the Civil War Era.* Chapel Hill: University of North Carolina Press, 2014, 432 pp.

Blake, George. *No Other Choice: An Autobiography.* London: Jonathan Cape, 190, 288 pp.

Blitzer, Wolf. *Territory of Lies: The Exclusive Story of Jonathan Jay Pollard, the American Who Spied on His Country for Israel and How He Was Betrayed.* New York: Harper and Row, 1989, 336 pp.

Blum, Howard. *Dark Invasion 1915: Germany's Secret War and the Hunt for the First Terrorist Cell in America* New York: HarperCollins, 2014, 475 pp.

Blum, Howard. *I Pledge Allegiance: The True Story of the Walkers, an American Spy Family.* New York: Simon & Schuster, 1987, 438 pp.

Borovik, Genrikh. *The Philby Files: The Secret Life of Master Spy Kim Philby.* Boston: Little, Brown, 1994, 320 pp.

Boucard, Robert. *The Secret Services of Europe.* London: Stanley and Paul, 1940, 260 pp.

Bowen, Roger. *Innocence Is Not Enough: The Life and Death of Herbert Norman.* Vancouver: Douglas and McIntyre, 1986, 409 pp.

Bower, Tom. *The Perfect English Spy: Sir Dick White and the Secret War, 1935–1990.* London: Heinemann, 1995.

Bower, Tom. *The Red Web: MI6 and the KGB Master Coup.* London: Aurum, 1989, 214 pp.

Boyle, Andrew. *The Fourth Man: The Definitive Account of Kim Philby, Guy Burgess, and Donald Maclean and Who Recruited Them for Russia.* New York: Dial, 1979, 504 pp.

Bradley, Mark A. *A Very Principled Boy: The Life of Duncan Lee, Red Spy and Cold Warrior.* New York: Basic Books, 2014, 343 pp.

Breckinridge, Scott D. *The CIA and the U.S. Intelligence System.* Boulder: Westview, 1986, 364 p.

Brenner, Joel. "Strategic Counterintelligence." Speech given to the American Bar Association Standing Committee on Law and National Security, March 29, 2007, available at www.ncix.gov/publications/speeches/ABAspeech.pdf.

Bristow, Desmond. *A Game of Moles: The Deceptions of an MI6 Officer.* Boston: Little, Brown, 1993, 292 pp.

Broda, Paul. *Scientist Spies: A Memoir of My Three Parents and the Atom Bomb.* Leicester: Matador, 2011, 344 pp.

Brook-Shepherd, Gordon. *The Storm Birds: Soviet Post-War Defectors.* London: Weidenfeld and Nicolson, 1988, 303 pp.

Brook-Shepherd, Gordon. *The Storm Petrels: The Flight of the First Soviet Defectors.* New York: Harcourt Brace Jovanovich, 1977, 241 pp.

Brown, Anthony Cave. *C: The Secret Life of Sir Stewart Menzies, Spymaster to Winston Churchill.* New York: Macmillan, 1987, 830 pp.

Brown, Anthony Cave. *The Last Hero: Wild Bill Donovan.* New York: Times Books, 1982, 891 pp.

Brown, Anthony Cave. *Treason in the Blood: H. St. John Philby, Kim Philby, and the Spy Case of the Century.* Boston: Houghton Mifflin, 1994, 677 pp.

Bryden, John. *Best Kept Secret: Canadian Secret Intelligence in the Second World War.* Toronto: Lester, 1993, 390 pp.

Buranelli, Vincent, and Nan Buranelli. *Spy/Counterspy: An Encyclopedia of Espionage.* New York: McGraw-Hill, 1982, 361 pp.

Burn, Michael. *The Debatable Land: A Story of the Motives of Spies in Two Ages.* London: Hamish Hamilton, 1970, 285 pp.

Cairncross, John. *The Enigma Spy: An Autobiography.* London: Century Random House, UK Limited, 1997, 203 pp.

Calder, James D. *Intelligence, Espionage and Related Topics: An Annotated Bibliography of Serial Journal and Magazine Scholarship—1844–1998.* Westport, CT: Greenwood Press, 1999, 1330 pp.

Canadian Royal Commission. *The Report of the Royal Commission to Investigate the Facts Relating to and the Circumstances Surrounding the Communication, by Public Officials and Other Persons in Postings of Trust, of Secret and Confidential Information to Agents of a Foreign Power.* Ottawa: Cloutier, 1946, 733 pp.

Carr, Barbara. *Spy in the Sun: The Story of Yuriy Loginov.* Cape Town: Howard Timmins, 1969, 224 pp.

Carter, Miranda. *Anthony Blunt: His Lives.* New York: Farrar, Straus and Giroux, 594 pp.

Castro-Hidalgo, Orlando. *Spy for Fidel.* Miami: E.A. Seeman, 1971, 110 pp.

Cecil, Robert. *Divided Life: A Biography of Donald Maclean.* London: Bodley Head, 1988, 212 pp.

Central Intelligence Agency. *The Rote Kapelle: The CIA's History of Soviet Intelligence and Espionage Networks in Western Europe, 1936–1945.* Washington, D.C.: University Publications of America, 1979, 390 pp.

Chalou, George, ed. *The Secrets War: The Office of Strategic Service in World War II.* Washington, D.C.: National Archives, 1991, 392 pp.

Chambers, Whittaker. *Witness.* 1952. New York: Regnery, 1987, 808 pp.

Charney, David L. "True Psychology of the Insider Spy." *The Intelligencer: Journal of U.S. Intelligence Studies* 18, no. 1 (Fall–Winter 2010), pp. 47–54.

Charters, David, and Maurice A.J. Tugwell, eds. *Deception Operations: Studies in the East-West Context.* London: Brassey's, 1990, 447 pp.

Cherkashin, Victor, with Gregory Feifer. *Spy Handler: Memoirs of a KGB Officer: The True Story of the Man Who Recruited Robert Hanssen and Aldrich Ames.* New York: Basic Books, 2005, 368 pp.

Chester, Lewis, Stephan Fay, and Hugo Young. *The Zinoviev Letter: A Political Intrigue.* Philadelphia: J.B. Lippincott, 1967, 219 pp.

Childs, David, and Richard Popplewell. *The Stasi: The East German Intelligence and Security Service.* London: Macmillan, 1996, 253 pp.

Clarridge, Duane R. *A Spy for All Seasons: My Life in the CIA.* New York: Scribner's, 1997, 430 pp.

Clayton, Anthony. *Forearmed: A History of the Intelligence Corps.* London: Brassey's, 1993, 318 pp.

Clift, A. Denis. *Clift Notes: Intelligence and the Nation's Security,* 2d ed. Washington, D.C.: Joint Military Intelligence College, 2002, 244 pp.

Cline, Marjorie, Carla E. Christiansen, and Judith M. Fontaine. *Scholar's Guide to Intelligence Literature: Bibliography of the Russell J. Bowen Collection in the Joseph Mark Lauinger Memorial Library Georgetown University.* Frederick, MD: University Publications of America, published for the National Intelligence Study Center, 1983, 236 pp.

Cline, Ray. *The CIA Reality Vs. Myth.* Washington, D.C.: Acropolis, 1982, 351 pp.

Cline, Ray. *The CIA Under Reagan, Bush and Casey: The Evolution of the Agency from Roosevelt to Reagan.* Washington, D.C.: Acropolis, 1981, 351 pp.

Cobban, Alfred. *Ambassadors and Secret Agents: The Diplomacy of the First Earl of Malmesbury at the Hague.* London: Jonathan Cape, 1954, 255 pp.

Colby, William, and Peter Forbath. *Honorable Men: My Life in the CIA.* New York: Simon & Schuster, 1978, 493 pp.

Cole, D.J. *Geoffrey Prime: The Imperfect Spy.* London: Robert Hale, 1998, 191 pp.

Cole, Eric. *Hiding in Plain Sight: Steganography and the Art of Covert Communication.* Indianapolis: Wiley, 2003, 335 pp.

Cole, J.A. *Prince of Spies: Henri Le Caron.* London: Faber and Faber, 1984, 221 pp.

Colitt, Leslie. *Spy Master: The Real-Life Karla, His Moles, and the East German Secret Police.* Reading, MA: Addison-Wesley, 1995, 302 pp.

Conant, Jennet. *The Irregulars: Roald Dahl and the British Spy Ring in Wartime Washington.* New York: Simon & Schuster, 2009, 393 pp.

Conquest, Robert. *Inside Stalin's Secret Police; NKVD Politics, 1936–1939.* Stanford, CA: Hoover Institution Press, 1985, 222 pp.

Constantinides, George. *Intelligence and Espionage: An Analytical Bibliography.* Boulder: Westview, 1983, 559 pp.

Cookridge, E.H. *Secrets of the British Secret Service: Behind the Scenes of the World of British Counter-Espionage During the War.* London: Sampson Low, Marston, 1948, 216 pp.

Corson, William R., and Robert T. Crowley. *The New KGB: Engine of Soviet Power.* New York: Morrow-Quill, 1986, 582 pp.

Costello, John. *Mask of Treachery: Spies, Lies, Buggery and Betrayal.* New York: Morrow, 1988, 765 pp.

Costello, John, and Oleg Tsarev. *Deadly Illusions: The First Book from the KGB Archives.* London: Century, 193, 538 pp.

Cowell, Alan S. *The Terminal Spy: A True Story of Espionage, Betrayal and Murder.* New York: Doubleday, 2008, 432 pp.

Craig, R. Bruce. *Treasonable Doubt: The Harry Dexter White Spy Case.* Lawrence: University Press of Kansas, 2004, 436 pp.

Cram, Cleveland. *Of Moles and Molehunters: A Review of Counterintelligence Literature: 1977–1992.* Washington, D.C.: CIA, Center for the Study of Intelligence, 1993.

Crawford, David J. *Volunteers: The Betrayal of National Defense Secrets by Air Force Traitors.* Washington, D.C.: U.S. Government Printing Office, 1988, 217 pp.

Critchfield, James H. *Partners at the Creation: The Men Behind Postwar Germany's Defense and Intelligence Establishments.* Annapolis: Naval Institute Press, 2003, 243 pp.

Crosswell, D.K.R. *Beetle: The Life of General Walter Bedell Smith.* Lexington: University Press of Kentucky, 2010, 1070 pp.

Crozier, Brian. *Free Agent: The Unseen War, 1941–1991.* London: HarperCollins, 1993, 314 pp.

Crumpton, Henry A. *The Art of Intelligence: Lessons from a Life in the CIA's Clandestine Service.* New York: Penguin, 2012, 338 pp.

Cull, Nicholas John. *Selling War: The British Propaganda Campaign Against American "Neutrality" in World War II.* New York: Oxford University Press, 1995, 276 pp.

Cunningham, Cyril. *Beaulieu: The Finishing School for Secret Agents.* London: Leo Cooper, 1998, 62 pp.

Currey, Cecil B. *Code Number 72: Ben Franklin, Patriot or Spy?* Englewood Cliffs, MJ: Prentice-Hall, 1972, 331 pp.

Curry, John. *The Security Service 1908–1945: The Official History.* Kew: Public Records Office, 1999, 442 pp.

Cutler, Richard W. *I Came, I Saw, I Wrote: A Risk-Taker's Life in Law, Espionage, Community Service, Start-Ups and Writing.* Brookfield, WI: Burton and Mayer, 2010, 183 pp.

Daigler, Kenneth A. *Spies, Patriots, and Traitors: American Intelligence in the Revolutionary War* Washington, D.C.: Georgetown University Press, 2014, 318 pp.

Dailey, Brian D., and Patrick J. Parker, eds. *Soviet Strategic Deception.* Lexington, MA: Lexington Books, 1987, 538 pp.

Dallin, David. *Soviet Espionage.* New Haven: Yale University Press, 1955, 558 pp.

Daniel, Donald C., and Katherine L. Herbig. *Strategic Military Deception.* New York: Pergamon, 1982, 378 pp.

Darling, Arthur C. *The Central Intelligence Agency: An Instrument of Government, to 1950.* University Park: Pennsylvania State University Press, 1990, 509 pp.

Dasch, George J. *Eight Spies Against America.* New York: Robert M. McBride, 1959, 241 pp.

Davies, Philip H.J. *The British Secret Services.* Oxford: Clio press, 1996, 147 pp.

Dawidoff, Nicholas. *The Catcher Was a Spy: The Mysterious Life of Moe Berg.* New York: Pantheon, 1994, 453 pp.

Deacon, Richard. *The British Connection: Russia's Manipulation of British Individuals and Institutions.* London: Hamish Hamilton, 1979, 291 pp.

Deacon, Richard. *The Greatest Treason: The Bizarre Story of Hollis, Liddell and Mountbatten.* London: Century Hutchinson, 1989, 212 pp.

Deacon, Richard. *A History of the Russian Secret Service.* London: Grafton, 1987, 512 pp.

Deacon, Richard. *Spyclopaedia: The Comprehensive Handbook of Espionage.* London: Macdonald, 1988, 416 pp.

Deacon, Richard, with Nigel West. *Spy! Six Stories of Modern Espionage.* London: British Broadcasting, 1980, 190 pp.

Deakin, F.W., and G.R. Storry. *The Case of Richard Sorge.* New York: Harper and Row, 1966, 373 pp.

Dear, Ian. *Sabotage and Subversion: Stories from the Files of the SOE and OSS.* London: Arms and Armour Books, 1996, 224 pp.

Dear, Ian. *Spy and Counterspy: A History of Secret Agents and Double Agents from the Second World War to the Cold War.* Stroud: History Press, 2013, 256 pp.

Dear, Ian. *Ten Commando: 1942–1945.* New York: St. Martin's Press, 1987, 208 pp.

Dearing, Judge Peter J., and C. Douglas Jones. "The Helmich Case." Presentation to the FBI retirees association, Jacksonville, Florida, January 9, 2015.

Dennis, Mike. *The Stasi: Myth and Reality.* London: Pearson Education, 2003, 269 pp.

Deriabin, Peter, and T.H. Bagley. *The KGB: Masters of the Soviet Union.* New York: Hippocrene, 1990, 466 pp.

Deriabin, Peter, and Frank Gibney. *The Secret World.* New York: Ballantine, 1988.

De Silva, Peer. *Sub Rosa: The CIA and the Uses of Intelligence.* New York: New York Times Book, 1978, 308 pp.

Devine, Jack, and Vernon Loeb. *Good Hunting: An American Spymaster's Story.* London and New York: Farrar, Straus and Giroux/Sarah Crichton Books, 2014, 336 pp.

Dillard, James E., and Walter T. Hitchcock, eds. *The Intelligence Revolution and Modern Warfare.* Chicago: Imprint, 1996, 202 pp.

Dobbs, Michael. *Saboteurs: The Nazi Raid on America.* New York: Knopf, 2004, 316 pp.

Dobson, Christopher, and Ronald Payne. *The Dictionary of Espionage.* London: Harrap, 1984, 234 pp.

Doerries, Reinhard. *Imperial Challenge: Ambassador Count Bernstorff and German-American Relations, 1908–1917* Chapel Hill: University of North Carolina Press, 1989.

Donovan, James B. *Strangers on a Bridge: The Case of Colonel Abel.* New York: Atheneum, 1964, 432 pp.

Dorwart, Jeffrey M. *The Office of Naval Intelligence: The Birth of America's First Intelligence Agency, 1885–1918.* Annapolis: Naval Institute Press, 1979, 173 pp.

Dorwart, Jeffrey M. *Conflict of Duty: The U.S. Navy's Intelligence Dilemma, 1919–1945.* Annapolis: Naval Institute Press, 1983, 262 pp.

Downton, Eric. *Wars Without End.* Toronto: Stoddart, 1987, 350 pp.

Doyle, David. *Inside Espionage: A Memoir of True Men and Traitors.* London: St. Ermin's, 2000, 280 pp.

Duff, William E. *A Time for Spies: Theodore Stephanovich Mally and the Era of the Great Illegals.* Nashville: Vanderbilt University Press, 1999, 249 pp.

Duffy, Peter. *Double Agent: The First Hero of World War II and How the FBI Outwitted and Destroyed a Nazi Spy Ring.* New York: Scribner's, 2014, 384 pp.

Dulles, Allen. *The Craft of Intelligence.* New York: Harper and Row, 1963, 277 pp.

Dulles, Allen. *Great True Spy Stories.* New York: Harper and Row, 1968, 393 pp.

Dvornik, Francis. *Origins of Intelligence Services: The Ancient Near East, Persia, Greece, Rome, Byzantium, the Arab Muslim Empires, the Mongol Empire, China, Muscovy.* New Brunswick: Rutgers University Press, 1974, 334 pp.

Dzhirkvelov, Ilya. *Secret Servant: My Life with the KGB and the Soviet Elite.* London: Collins, 1987, 398 pp.

Dziak, John J. *Chekisty: A History of the KGB.* New York: Ivy Books, 1988, 295 pp.

Earley, Peter. *Comrade J: The Untold Secrets of Russia's Master Spy in America After the End of the Cold War.* New York: Putnam, 2007, 352 pp.

Earley, Peter. *Confessions of a Spy: The Real Story of Aldrich Ames.* New York: Putnam's, 1997, 364 pp.

Earley, Peter. *Family of Spies: Inside the John Walker Spy Ring.* New York: Bantam, 1989, 385 pp.

Edwards, Duval. *Spy Catchers of the U.S. Army: In the War with Japan.* Tucson: Red Apple, 1994, 299 pp.

Eftimiades, Nicholas. *Chinese Intelligence Operations.* Annapolis: Naval Institute Press, 1994, 169 pp.

Elliff, John T. *The Reform of FBI Intelligence Operations.* Princeton: Princeton University Press, 1979, 248 pp.

Elliot, S.R. *Scarlet to Green: A History of Intelligence in the Canadian Army 1903–1963.* Toronto: Canadian Intelligence and Security Association, 1981, 769 pp.

Elliott, Geoffrey. *I Spy: The Secret Life of a British Agent.* London: St. Ermin's, 1998, 283 pp.

Elliott, Nicholas. *Never Judge a Man by His Umbrella.* Chantry Wilton: Michel Russell, 1991, 201 pp.

Elliott, Nicholas. *With My Little Eye.* London: Michael Russell, 1993, 111 pp.

Epstein, Edward Jay. *Deception: The Invisible War Between the KGB and the CIA.* New York: Simon & Schuster, 1989, 335 pp.

Epstein, Edward Jay. *Dossier: The Secret History of Armand Hammer.* New York: Random House, 1996, 418 pp.

Fahey, John A. *Licensed to Spy: With the Top Secret Military Liaison Mission in East Germany.* Annapolis: Naval Institute Press, 2002, 209 pp.

Faligot, Roger, and Reme Kauffer. *The Chinese Secret Service.* London: Headline, 1989, 524 pp.

Faligot, Roger, and Pascal Krop. *La Piscine: The French Secret Service Since 1944.* Oxford: Basil Blackwell, 1989, 344 pp.

Farago, Ladislas. *The Game of the Foxes: The Untold Story of German Espionage in the United States and Great Britain During World War II.* New York: David McKay, 1971, 696 pp.

Farson, A. Stuart, David Stafford and Wesley Wark, eds. *Security and Intelligence in a Changing World: New Perspectives for the 1990s.* London: Frank Cass, 1991, 202 pp.

Feis, William B. *Grant's Secret Service: The Intelligence War from Belmont to Appomattox.* Lincoln: University of Nebraska Press, 2002, 330 pp.

Feklisov, Alexander, and Sergei Kostin. *The Man Behind the Rosenbergs.* New York: Enigma, 2001, 431 pp.

Felix, Christopher. *A Short Course in the Secret War.* Lanham, MD: Madison Books, 2001, 301 pp.

Fergusson, Thomas G. *British Military Intelligence, 1870–1914: The Development of a Modern Intelligence Organization.* Frederick, MD: University Publications of America, 1984, 280 pp.

Finnegan, John Patrick, and Romana Danysh. *Military Intelligence.* Washington, D.C.: U.S. Army Center for Military History, 1998, 437 pp.

Fishel, Edwin C. *The Secret War for the Union: The Untold Story of Military Intelligence in the Civil War.* Boston: Houghton Mifflin, 1996, 734 pp.

Fisher, John. *Gentleman Spies: Intelligence Agents in the British Empire and Beyond.* Phoenix Mill: Sutton, 2002, 209 pp.

Flexner, James Thomas. *The Traitor and the Spy: Benedict Arnold and John Andre*, 2d ed. Boston: Little, Brown, 1975, 453 pp.

Foot, M.R.D. *Secret Lives: Lifting the Lid on Worlds of Secret Intelligence.* Oxford: Oxford University Press, 2002, 302 pp.

Foote, Alexander. *Handbook for Spies.* Garden City, NY: Doubleday, 1949, 273 pp.

Foster, Jane. *An Un-American Lady.* London: Sidgwick and Jackson, 1980, 253 pp.

Frolik, Josef. *The Frolik Defection: The Memoirs of an Intelligence Agent.* London: Leo Cooper, 1975, 184 pp.

Funder, Anna. *Stasiland.* London: Granta, 2003, 288 pp.

Fysh, Michael Q.C., ed. *The Spycatcher Cases.* London: European Law Center, 1989, 749 pp.

Garbler, Florence Fitzsimmons. *CIA Wife: One Woman's Life Inside the CIA.* Santa Barbara: Fifthian Press, 1994, 163 pp.

Garlinski, Jozef. *The Swiss Corridor: Espionage Networks in Switzerland During World War II.* London: J.M. Dent, 1981, 222 pp.

Gates, Robert Michael. *From the Shadows: The Ultimate Insider's Story of Five Presidents and How They Won the Cold War.* New York: Simon & Schuster, 2000, 608 pp.

Gazur, Edward P. *Secret Assignment: The FBI's KGB General.* London: St. Ermin's, 2001.

Gentry, Curt. *J. Edgar Hoover: The Man and the Secrets.* New York: W.W. Norton, 1991, 846 pp.

George, Willis. *Surreptitious Entry.* New York: D. Appleton-Century, 1946, 214 pp.

Geraghty, Tony. *Beyond the Front Line: The Untold*

Exploits of Britain's Most Daring Cold War Spy Mission. London: HarperCollins, 1996, 355 pp.

Gerolymatos, Andre. *Espionage and Treason: A Study of the Proxenia in Political and Military Intelligence Gathering in Classical Greece.* Amsterdam: J.C. Gieben, 1986, 140 pp.

Gilligan, Tom. *CIA Life: 10,000 Days with the Agency.* Guilford, CT: Foreign Intelligence Press, 1991, 285 pp.

Giskes, H.J. *London Calling North Pole.* London: William Kimber, 1953, 208 pp.

Glees, Anthony. *The Secrets of the Service: British Intelligence and Communist Subversion 1939–1951.* London: Jonathan Cape, 1987, 447 pp.

Glees, Anthony. *The Stasi Files: East Germany's Secret Operations Against Britain.* London: Free Press, 2003, 461 pp.

Glinsky, Albert. *Theremin: Ether Music and Espionage.* Urbana: University of Illinois Press, 2000, 403 pp.

Godson, Roy. *Dirty Tricks or Trump Cards: U.S. Covert Action and Counterintelligence.* New Brunswick: Transaction, 1995, 337 pp.

Godson, Roy, ed. *Intelligence Requirements for the 1980s: Volume One, Elements of Intelligence,* rev. ed. New York: National Strategy Information Center, Consortium for the Study of Intelligence, 1983, 148 pp.

Godson, Roy, ed. *Intelligence Requirements for the 1980s: Volume Three, Counter-Intelligence,* rev. ed. Washington, D.C.: National Strategy Information Center, 1980, 337 pp.

Godson, Roy, ed. *Intelligence Requirements for the 1990s: Collection, Analysis, Counterintelligence, and Covert Action.* Lexington, MA: Lexington Books, 1989, 269 pp.

Godson, Roy, Ernest R. May, and Gary Schmitt, eds. *U.S. Intelligence at the Crossroads; Agendas for Reform.* Washington, D.C.: Brassey's, 1995, 315 pp.

Golitsyn, Anatoliy. *New Lies for Old: The Communist Strategy of Deception and Disinformation.* London: The Bodley Head, 1984, 412 pp.

Goodrich, Austin. *Born to Spy: Recollections of a CIA Case Officer.* New York: iUniverse, 2004, 159 pp.

Gordievsky, Oleg. *Next Stop Execution: The Autobiography of Oleg Gordievsky.* London: Macmillan, 1995, 396 pp.

Gouzenko, Igor. *The Iron Curtain.* New York: E.P. Dutton, 1948, 280 pp.

Granovsky, Anatoli. *I Was an NKVD Agent.* New York: Devin-Adair, 1962, 343 pp.

Greenwald, Glenn. *No Place to Hide: Edward Snowden, the NSA, and the U.S. Surveillance State.* New York: Metropolitan Books/Henry Holt, 2014, 259 pp.

Grimes, David, and Tom Becnel. "The Nazi Invasion of Florida." *Florida Curiosities.* Guilford, CT: Globe Pequot Press, 2011, pp. 68–69.

Grimes, Sandra, and Jeanne Vertefeuille. *Circle of Treason: A CIA Account of Traitor Aldrich Ames and the Men He Betrayed.* Annapolis: Naval Institute Press, 2012, 228 pp.

Grose, Peter. *Gentleman Spy: The Life of Allen Dulles.* Amherst: University of Massachusetts Press, 1994, 641 pp.

Gross, Felix. *I Knew These Spies.* London: Hurst and Blackett, 1940, 255 pp.

Gup, Ted. *The Book of Honor: Covert Lives and Classified Deaths at the CIA.* New York: Doubleday, 2000, 390 pp.

Haldane, R.A. *The Hidden War: The Exciting Behind-the-Scenes Story of Counterintelligence in World War II.* London: Robert Hale Limited, 1978, 224 pp.

Hall, Richard. *Patriots in Disguise: Women Warriors of the Civil War.* New York: Paragon House, 1993, 224 pp.

Hall, Richard. *The Rhodes Scholar Spy.* Milsons Point, NSW: Random House Australia, 1991, 214 pp.

Hall, Roger. *You're Stepping on My Cloak and Dagger.* New York: W.W. Norton, 1957, 219 pp.

Hamilton, Norman R. *Accused: R. Craig Smith—The Spy Left Out in the Cold.* Bountiful, UT: Horizon, 1979, 232 pp.

Handel, Michael I., ed. *Intelligence and Military Operations.* London: Frank Cass, 1990, 464 pp.

Hannas, William C., James C. Mulvenon, and Anna B. Puglisi. *Chinese Industrial Espionage: Technology Acquisition and Military Modernisation.* New York: Routledge, 2013.

Harding, Luke. *The Snowden Files: The Inside Story of the World's Most Wanted Man.* London: Guardian Farber, 2014, 352 pp.

Harris, Charles H., III, and Louis R. Sadler. *The Archaeologist Was a Spy: Sylvannus G. Morley and the Office of Naval Intelligence.* Albuquerque: University of New Mexico Press, 2003, 450 pp.

Harris, Tomas. *Garbo: The Spy Who Saved D-Day.* London: PRO, 2000, 410 pp.

Hart, Jennifer. *Ask Me No More.* London: Peter Halban, 1998, 230 pp.

Hart, John Limond. *The CIA's Russians.* Annapolis: Naval Institute Press, 2003, 224 pp.

Hastedt, Glenn P., ed. *Controlling Intelligence.* London: Frank Cass 1991, 190 pp.

Haswell, Jock. *Spies and Spymasters: A Concise History of Intelligence.* London: Thames and Hudson, 1997, 176 pp.

Hatch, Robert McConnell. *Major John Andre: A Gallant in Spy's Clothing.* Boston: Houghton Mifflin, 1986, 333 pp.

Havill, Adrian. *The Spy Who Stayed Out in the Cold: The Secret Life of FBI Double Agent Robert Hanssen.* New York: St. Martin's, 2002, 262 pp.

Haynes, John Earl, and Harvey Klehr. *Early Cold*

War Spies: The Espionage Trials That Shaped American Politics. Cambridge: Cambridge University Press, 2006.

Haynes, John Earl, and Harvey Klehr. *Spies: The Rise and Fall of the KGB in America.* New Haven: Yale University Press, 2010, 704 pp.

Haynes, John Earl, and Harvey Klehr. *VENONA: Decoding Soviet Espionage in America.* New Haven: Yale University Press, 1999, 487 pp.

Headley, Lake, William Hoffman, and William Kuntsler. *The Court Martial of Clayton Lonetree.* New York: Henry Holt, 1989, 240 pp.

Heaps, Leo. *Thirty Years with the KGB: The Double Life of Hugh Hambleton.* London: Methuen, 1984, 158 pp.

Helms, Cynthia, with Chris Black. *An Intriguing Life: A Memoir of War, Washington, and Marriage to an American Spymaster.* Lanham, MD: Rowman & Littlefield, 2013, 199 pp.

Helms, Richard, with William Hood. *A Look Over My Shoulder: A Life in the Central Intelligence Agency.* New York: Random House, 2003.

Henderson, Bernard R. *Pollard: The Spy's Story.* New York: Alpha Books, 1988, 202 pp.

Hennessy, Peter. *The Secret State: Whitehall and the Cold War.* London: Allen Lane, 2002, 234 pp.

Herken, Gregg. *Brotherhood of the Bomb: The Tangled Lives and Loyalties of Robert Oppenheimer, Ernest Lawrence, and Edward Teller.* New York: Henry Holt, 2002, 448 pp.

Herrington, Stuart A. *Traitors Among Us: Inside the Spy Catcher's World.* Novato, CA: Presidio Press, 1999, 408 pp.

Hilton, Stanley E. *Hitler's Secret War in South America: German Military Espionage and Allied Counterespionage in Brazil, 1939–1945.* Baton Rouge: Louisiana State University Press, 1981, 353 pp.

Hinsley, F.H., and C.A.G. Simkins *British Intelligence in the Second World War, Volume 4: Security and Counter-Intelligence.* London: Her Majesty's Stationery Office, 190, 408 pp.

Hirsch, Richard. *The Soviet Spies: The Story of Russian Espionage in North America.* London: Nicholas Kaye, 1947, 164 pp.

Hitz, Frederick P. *The Great Game: The Myth and Reality of Espionage.* New York: Knopf, 2004.

Hoffman, Tod. *The Spy Within: Larry Chin and China's Penetration of the CIA.* Hanover, NH: Steerforth, 2008, 320 pp. Reviewed in *AFIO Weekly Intelligence Notes* #43–08, November 10, 2008.

Hohne, Heinz. *Codeword: "Director": The Story of the Red Orchestra.* New York: Coward, McCann and Geoghegan, 1971, 310 pp.

Holm, Richard. *The American Agent: My Life in the CIA.* London: St. Ermin's, 2003, 462 pp. An updated version was released as *The Craft We Chose: My Life in the CIA.* Mountain Lake Park, MD: Mountain Lake Press, 2011, 568 pp.

Holzman, Michael. *Guy Burgess: Revolutionary in an Old School Tie.* London: Chelmsford, 2012, 386 pp.

Holzman, Michael Howard. *James Jesus Angleton, The CIA, and the Craft of Counterintelligence.* Amherst: University of Massachusetts Press, 2008, 398 pp.

Hood, William. *Mole: The True Story of the First Russian Spy to Become an American Counterspy.* Washington, D.C.: Brassey's, 1993, 288 pp.

Hornblum, Allen M. *The Invisible Harry Gold: The Man Who Gave the Soviets the Atom Bomb.* New Haven: Yale University, 2010, 480 pp.

Houghton, Harry. *Operation Portland: The Autobiography of a Spy.* London: Rupet Hart-Davis, 1972, 164 pp.

House, Jonathan M. *Military Intelligence, 1870–1991: A Research Guide.* Westport, CT: Greenwood, 1993, 165 pp.

Howard, Edward Lee. *Safe House: The Compelling Memoirs of the Only CIA Spy to Seek Asylum in Russia.* Bethesda: National Press Books, 1995, 299 pp.

Howe, Russell Warren. *Mata Hari: The True Story.* New York: Dodd, Mead, 1986, 292 pp.

Howe, Russell Warren. *Sleeping with the FBI: Sex, Booze, Russians and the Saga of an American Counterspy Who Couldn't.* Washington, D.C.: National Press Books, 1993, 394 pp.

Hristov, Hristo. *Kill Vagabond.* Bulgaria, 2005.

Huminik, John. *Double Agent.* New York: New American Library, 1967, 181 pp.

Hunter, Robert W. *Spy Hunter: Inside the FBI Investigation of the Walker Espionage Case.* Annapolis: Naval Institute Press, 1999, 250 pp.

Hurt, Henry. *Shadrin: The Spy Who Never Came Back.* New York: Reader's Digest, 1981, 301 pp.

Huss, Pierre J., and George Carpozi, Jr. *Red Spies in the UN.* New York: Coward-McCann, 1965, 287 pp.

Hyde, H. Montgomery. *The Atom Bomb Spies.* New York: Athenaeum, 1980, 339 pp.

Hyde, H. Montgomery. *Secret Intelligence Agent.* London: Constable, 1982, 281 pp.

Hynd, Alan. *Betrayal from the East: The Inside Story of Japanese Spies in America.* New York: National Travel Cub, 1943, 287 pp.

Hynd, Alan. *Passport to Treason: The Inside Story of Spies in America.* New York: Robert M. McBridge, 1943, 306 pp.

Intelligence in the Civil War. Washington, D.C.: U.S. Central Intelligence Agency, 2007, 50 pp., available on www.cia.gov.

Intelligence in the War of Independence. Washington, D.C.: U.S. Central Intelligence Agency, 2007, available on www.cia.gov

Irwin, Richard. *KH601: And Ye Shall Know the Truth and the Truth Shall Make You Free.* Adducent/Fortis, 2010, 436 pp.

Jacoby, Susan. *Alger Hiss and the Battle for History.* New Haven: Yale University Press, 2009, 256 pp.

James, William. *The Code Breakers of Room 40: The Story of Admiral Sir William Hall, Genius of British Counterintelligence.* New York: St. Martin's, 1956, 212 pp.

Jeffery, Keith. *MI6: The History of the Secret Intelligence Service 1909–1949.* London: Penguin, 2010.

Johnson, Chalmers. *An Instance of Treason: Ozaki Hotsumi and the Sorge Spy Ring,* expanded ed. Stanford, California: Stanford University Press, 1990, 324 pp.

Johnson, Loch, ed. *The Oxford Handbook of National Security Intelligence.* New York: Oxford University Press, 2010, 886 pp.

Johnson, William R. *Thwarting Enemies at Home and Abroad: How to be a Counterintelligence Officer.* Bethesda: Stone Trail Press, 1987, 174 pp.

Jones, John Price. *The German Spy in America: The Secret Plotting of German Spies in the United States and the Inside Story of the Sinking of the Lusitania.* London: Hutchinson, 1917, 256 pp.

Jones, John Price, and Paul Merrick Hollister. *The German Secret Service in America.* Boston: Small, Maynard, 1918, 340 pp.

Jones, R.V. *Reflections on Intelligence.* London: Heinemann, 1989, 386 pp.

Jones, R.V. *The Wizard War: British Scientific Intelligence 1939–1945.* New York: Coward, McCann and Geoghegan, 1978, 556 pp.

Judd, Alan. *The Quest for C: Mansfield Cumming and the Founding of the Secret Intelligence Service.* London: HarperCollins, 1999, 501 pp.

Kahn, David. *Hitler's Spies: German Military Intelligence in World War II.* New York: Macmillan, 1978, 552 pp.

Kaiser, Frederick M., and Sherry B. Shapiro. *The U.S. Intelligence Community: A Selective Bibliography.* Washington, D.C.: Congressional Research Service, Report #79-273, October 31, 1979, 86 pp.

Kalugin, Oleg. *The First Directorate: My 32 Years in Intelligence and Espionage Against the West.* New York: St. Martin's, 1994, 375 pp.

Kashmeri, Zuhair, and Brian McAndrew. *Soft Target: How the Indian Intelligence Service Penetrated Canada.* Toronto: James Lorimer, 1989, 162 pp.

Kates, Gary. *Monsieur d'Eon Is a Woman: A Tale of Political Intrigue and Sexual Masquerade.* New York: Basic Books, 1995, 368 pp.

Katz, Samuel M. *Soldier Spies: Israeli Military Intelligence.* Novato, CA: Presidio, 1992, 389 pp.

Kaufman, Louis, and Tom Sewell. *Moe Berg: Athlete, Scholar, Spy.* Boston: Little, Brown, 1974, 265 pp.

Kaznacheev, Aleksandr I. *Inside a Soviet Embassy: Experiences of a Russian Diplomat in Burma.* Philadelphia: J.B. Lippincott, 1962, 250 pp.

Keegan, John. *Intelligence in War: Knowledge of the Enemy from Napoleon to al-Qaeda.* New York: Knopf, 2003, 387 pp.

Kelso, Nicholas. *Errors of Judgment: SOE's Disaster in the Netherlands, 1941–44.* London: Robert Hale, 1988, 266 pp.

Kern, Gary. *A Death in Washington: Walter Krivitsky and the Stalin Terror.* New York: Enigma, 2003, 491 pp.

Kessler, Lauren. *Clever Girl: Elizabeth Bentley and the Dawn of the McCarthy Era.* New York: HarperCollins, 2003, 384 pp.

Kessler, Ronald. *Escape from the CIA: How the CIA Won and Lost the Most Important KGB Spy Ever to Defect to the U.S.* New York: Pocket Books, 1991, 210 pp.

Kessler, Ronald. *Inside the CIA: Revealing the Secrets of the World's Most Powerful Spy Agency.* New York: Pocket Books, 1992, 283 pp.

Kessler, Ronald. *Moscow Station: How the KGB Penetrated the American Embassy.* New York: Scribner's, 1989, 305 pp.

Kessler, Ronald. *The Spy in the Russian Club: How Glenn Souther Stole America's Nuclear War Plans and Escaped to Moscow.* New York: Pocket Books, 1992, 275 pp.

Kessler, Ronald. *Spy vs. Spy: Stalking Soviet Spies in America.* New York: Scribner's, 1988, 308 pp.

Khokhlov, Nikolai, and Emily Kingsbury. *In the Name of Conscience: The Testament of a Soviet Secret Agent.* New York: D. McKay, 1959, 365 pp.

Kimche, Jon. *Spying for Peace: General Guisan and Swiss Neutrality.* New York: Roy, 1961, 169 pp.

Kimura, Hisao, as told to Scott Berry. *Japanese Agent in Tibet: My Ten Years of Travel in Disguise.* London: Serindia, 1990, 232 pp.

Kirschner, Don S. *Cold War Exile: The Unclosed Case of Maurice Halperin.* Columbia: University of Missouri Press, 1995, 332 pp.

Klehr, Harvey, John Earl Haynes, and Fridrikh Igorevich Firsov. *The Secret World of American Communism.* New Haven: Yale University Press, 1995, 348 pp.

Klehr, Harvey, and Ronald Radosh. *The Amerasia Spy Case: Prelude to McCarthyism.* Chapel Hill: University of North Carolina Press, 1996, 266 pp.

Klein, Alexander. *The Counterfeit Traitor.* New York: Henry Holt, 1958, 301 pp.

Klimov, Gregory Petrovich. *The Terror Machine: The Inside Story of the Soviet Administration in Germany.* London: Faber and Faber, 1953, 400 pp.

Kneece, Jack. *Family Treason: The Walker Spy Case.* New York: Briar Cliff Manor, 1986, 234 pp.

Knight, Amy. *Beria: Stalin's First Lieutenant.* Princeton: Princeton University Press, 1993, 312 pp.

Knight, Amy *The KGB: Police and Politics in the Soviet Union*. Boston: Unwin Hyman, 1988, 348 pp.

Knightley, Phillip. *The Master Spy: The Story of Kim Philby*. New York: Knopf, 1989, 292 pp.

Koehler, John. *Spies in the Vatican: The Soviet Union's Cold War Against the Catholic Church*. New York: Pegasus, 2009, 296 pp.

Koehler, John O. *STASI: The Untold Story of the East German Secret Police*. Boulder: Westview, 1999, 460 pp.

Kostin, Sergei, and Eric Raynaud, translated by Catherine Cauvin-Higgins. *Farewell: The Greatest Spy Story of the Twentieth Century*. AmazonCrossing, 2011.

Kostov, Vladimir. *The Bulgarian Umbrella: The Soviet Direction and Operations of the Bulgarian Secret Service in Europe*. London: Harvester Wheatsheaf, 1988, 204 pp.

Koudelka, Edward F. *Counter Intelligence: The Conflict and the Conquest—Recollections of a World War II Agent in Europe*. Guilderland, NY: Ranger Associates, 1986, 149 pp.

Krasnov, Vladislav. *Soviet Defectors: The KGB Wanted List*. Stanford, CA: Hoover Institution, 1986, 264 pp.

Krivitsky, Walter. *I Was Stalin's Agent*. London, 1940, reprinted by Sutton, 1992, 320 pp.

Kuzichkin, Vladimir. *Inside the KGB: Myth and Reality*. New York: Pantheon, 1990, 406 pp.

Lamphere, Robert J., and Tom Schachtman. *The FBI-KGB War: A Special Agent's Story*. New York: Random House, 1986.

Lanoir, Paul. *The German Spy System in France*. London: Mills and Boon, 1910, 264 pp.

Laqueur, Walter. *A World of Secrets: The Uses and Limits of Intelligence*. New York: Basic Books, 1985, 404 pp.

Latell, Brian. *After Fidel: The Inside Story of Castro's Regime and Cuba's Next Leader*. New York: Palgrave Macmillan, 2002, 273 pp.

Lathrop, Charles E. *The Literary Spy: The Ultimate Source for Quotations on Espionage and Intelligence*. New Haven: Yale University Press, 2004, 477 pp.

Lee, Wen Ho. *My Country Versus Me*. New York: Hyperion, 2001.

Levchenko, Stanislav. *On the Wrong Side: My Life in the KGB*. New York: Pergamon-Brassey's, 1988, 244 pp.

Linklater, Andro. *An Artist in Treason: The Extraordinary Double Life of General James Wilkinson, Commander in Chief of the U.S. Army and Agent 13 in the Spanish Secret Service*. New York: Walker, 2010, 400 pp.

Lonsdale, Gordon. *Spy: Twenty Years in Soviet Secret Service*. London: Neville Spearman, 1965, 220 pp.

Lowenthal, Mark M. *Intelligence: From Secrets to Policy*, 6th ed. Washington, D.C.: CQ Press, 2014, 560 pp.

Lucas, Edward. *Deception: The Untold Story of East-West Espionage Today*. New York: Walker, 2012, 372 pp.

Lucas, Norman. *The Great Spy Ring*. London: Arthur Baker, 1966, 284 pp.

Lunev, Stanislav, with Ira Winkler. *Through the Eyes of the Enemy: Russia's Highest Ranking Military Defector Reveals Why Russia Is More Dangerous Than Ever*. Washington, D.C.: Regnery, 1998, 177 pp.

Maas, Peter. *Killer Spy: The Inside Story of the FBI's Pursuit and Capture of Aldrich Ames, America's Deadliest Spy*. New York: Warner, 1995, 243 pp.

Macintyre, Ben. *Operation Mincemeat: The True Spy Story That Changed the Course of World War II*. London: Bloomsbury, 2010, 400 pp.

Macintyre, Ben. *A Spy Among Friends: Kim Philby and the Great Betrayal*. New York: Crown, 2014, 368 pp.

Mackenzie, Compton. *Aegean Memories*. London: Chatto and Windus, 1940, 419 pp.

Mackenzie, Compton. *First Athenian Memories*. London: Cassell, 1931, 402 pp.

Mackenzie, Compton. *Gallipoli Memories*. London: Cassell, 1929, 406 pp.

Mackenzie, Compton. *Greek Memories*. London: Cassell, 1932, 588 pp.

Mahoney, Henry Thayer. *Women in Espionage: A Biographical Dictionary*. Santa Barbara: ABC-CLIO, 1993, 253 pp.

Mahoney, Henry Thayer, and Marjorie Locke Mahoney. *American Prisoners of the Bolsheviks: The Genesis of Modern American Intelligence*. Bethesda: Academica Press, 2001, 470 pp.

Mahoney, Henry Thayer, and Marjorie Locke Mahoney. *Biographic Dictionary of Espionage*. San Francisco: Austin and Winfield, 1998, 622 pp.

Mahoney, Henry Thayer, and Marjorie Locke Mahoney. *Espionage in Mexico: The 20th Century*. San Francisco: Austin and Winfield, 1997, 290 pp.

Mahoney, Henry Thayer, and Marjorie Locke Mahoney. *Gallantry in Action: A Biographic Dictionary of Espionage in the American Revolutionary War*. Lanham, MD: University Press of America, 1999, 445 pp.

Mahoney, Henry Thayer, and Marjorie Locke Mahoney. *Ireland Defined: Espionage Through the Ages*. Bethesda: Maunsel, 2001, 349 pp.

Mains, A.A. *Field Security: Very Ordinary Intelligence*. Chippenham: Picton, 1992, 200 pp.

Mandiant Corporation. *APT1*. Mandiant, 2013, 74 pp.

Mangold, Tom. *Cold Warrior: James Jesus Angleton, The CIA's Master Spy Hunter*. New York: Simon & Schuster, 1991, 462 pp.

Mann, Wilfred Basil. *Was There a Fifth Man? Quintessential Recollections.* Oxford: Pergamon, 1982, 170 pp.

Manne, Robert. *The Petrov Affair: Politics and Espionage.* Elmsford, NY: Pergamon, 1987, 310 pp.

Markle, Donald E. *The Fox and the Hound: The Birth of American Spying* New York: Hippocrene, 2013, 300 pp.

Markle, Donald E. *Spies and Spymasters of the Civil War.* New York: Hippocrene, 1994, 244 pp.

Marshall, Allan. *Intelligence and Espionage in the Reign of Charles II, 1660–1685.* Cambridge: Cambridge University Press, 1994, 334 pp.

Marshall, Robert. *All the King's Men.* London: Collins, 1988, 314 pp.

Martin, David C. *Wilderness of Mirrors.* New York: Harper and Row, 1980, 236 pp.

Masetti, Jorge. *In the Pirate's Den: My Life as a Secret Agent for Castro.* San Francisco: Encounter Books, 2002, 164 pp.

Massing, Hede. *This Deception: KGB Target America.* New York: Ivy, 1987, 289 pp.

Masterman, J.C. *The Double-Cross System: In the War of 1939 to 1945.* New Haven: Yale University Press, 1972, 203 pp.

Masters, Anthony. *The Man Who Was M: The Life of Maxwell Knight.* Oxford: Basil Blackwell, 1984, 212 pp.

Matthews, Tony. *Shadows Dancing: Japanese Espionage Against the West 1939–1945.* Oxford: Oxford University Press, 1993, 240 pp.

May, Gary. *Un-American Activities: The Trials of William Remington.* New York: Oxford University Press, 1994, 393 p.

McCaslin, Leland C. *Secrets of the Cold War: U.S. Army Europe's Intelligence and Counterintelligence Activities Against the Soviets During the Cold War.* Solihull: Helion, 2010, 248 pp.

McIntosh, Elizabeth P. *Sisterhood of Spies: The Women of the OSS.* Annapolis: Naval Institute Press, 1998, 282 pp.

McKay, C.G. *From Information to Intrigue: Studies in Secret Service Based on the Swedish Experience 1939–1945.* London: Frank Cass, 1993, 306 pp.

Meissner, Hans Otto. *The Man with Three Faces: The Story of Russia's Master Spy.* New York: Rinehart, 1956, 243 pp.

Melchior, Ib. *Case by Case: A U.S. Army Counterintelligence Agent in World War II.* Novata, CA: Presidio, 1993, 352 pp.

Melman, Yossi, and Dan Raviv. *The Imperfect Spies: The History of Israeli Intelligence.* London: Sidgwick and Jackson, 1989, 469 pp.

Melton, H. Keith. *The Ultimate Spy Book.* New York: Dorling Kindersly, 1996, 176 pp., 2d ed., 2002, 208 pp.

Melton, H. Keith, and Robert Wallace with Henry R. Schlesinger. *Spy Sites of New York City: Two Centuries of Espionage in Gotham.* Boca Raton: Foreign Excellent Trenchcoat Society, 2012, 160 pp.

Mendelsohn, John, ed. *Covert Warfare: The History of the Counter Intelligence Corps (CIC).* New York: Garland, 1989.

Mendez, Antonio J., and Jonna Mendez with Bruce Henderson. *Spy Dust: Two Masters of Disguise Reveal the Tools and Operations That Helped Win the Cold War.* New York: Atria, 2003, 298.

Mendez, Antonio J., with Malcolm McConnell. *The Master of Disguise: My Secret Life in the CIA.* New York: Morrow, 1999, 351 pp.

Mercado, Stephen. *The Shadow Warriors of Nakano: A History of the Imperial Japanese Army's Elite Intelligence School.* Washington, D.C.: Brassey's, 2002, 331 pp.

Meyer, Cord. *Facing Reality: From World Federalism to the CIA.* New York: Harper and Row, 1980, 433 pp.

Mickolus, Edward. *The Secret Book of CIA Humor.* Gretna, LA: Pelican, 2011, 240 pp.

Mickolus, Edward. *Stories from Langley: A Glimpse Inside the CIA.* Washington, D.C.: Potomac, 2014, 288 pp.; Volume 2, forthcoming.

Mikes, George. *A Study in Infamy: The Hungarian Secret Police (AVO).* London: Andre Deutsch, 1959, 175 pp.

Milano, James U., and Patrick Brogan. *Soldiers, Spies, and the Rat Line: America's Undeclared War Against the Soviets.* Washington, D.C.: Brassey's, 1995, 242 pp.

Miles, Jonathan. *The Dangerous Otto Katz: The Many Lives of a Soviet Spy.* New York: Bloomsbury, 2010, 384 pp.

Miller, Nathan. *Spying for America: The Hidden History of U.S. Intelligence,* 2d ed. New York: Marlowe, 1997, 491 pp.

Minnick, Wendell L. *Spies and Provocateurs: A Worldwide Encyclopedia of Persons Conducting Espionage and Covert Action, 1946–1991.* Jefferson, NC: McFarland, 1992, 310 pp.

Mitchell, Marcia, and Thomas Mitchell. *The Spy Who Seduced America: Lies and Betrayal in the Heat of the Cold War—The Judith Coplon Story.* Montpelier: Invisible Cities Press, 2002, 359 pp.

Modin, Yuri. *My Five Cambridge Friends.* London: Headline, 1994, 282 pp.

Montague, Ludwell Lee. *General Walter Bedell Smith as Director of Central Intelligence: October 1950–February 1953.* University Park: Pennsylvania State University Press, 1992, 308 pp.

Moravec, Frantisek. *Master of Spies: The Memoirs of General Frantisek Moravec.* Garden City, NY: Doubleday, 1975, 240 pp.

Morgan, Ted. *A Covert Life—Jay Lovestone: Communist, Anti-Communist, and Spymaster.* New York: Random House, 1999, 402 pp.

Moyzisch, L.C. *Operation Cicero.* London: Allan Wingate, 1952, 208 pp.

Mulley, Clare. *The Spy Who Loved: The Secrets and Lives of Christine Granville, Britain's First Female Special Agent of World War II.* New York: Macmillan, 2012, 426 pp.

Murphy, Brendan M. *Turncoat: The Strange Case of British Traitor Sergeant Harold Cole, "The Worst Traitor of the War."* New York: Harcourt Brace Jovanovich, 1987, 301 pp.

Murphy, David E., Sergei A. Kondrashev, and George Bailey. *Battleground Berlin: CIA vs. KGB in the Cold War.* New Haven: Yale University Press, 1997, 530 pp.

Myagkov, Aleksei. *Inside the KGB: An Expose by an Officer of the Third Directorate.* Richmond, Surrey: Foreign Affairs, 1977, 131 pp.

Nagy, John A. *Dr. Benjamin Church, Spy: A Case of Espionage on the Eve of the American Revolution.* Yardley, PA: Westholme, 2014, 211 pp.

Nagy, John. *Invisible Ink: Spycraft of the American Revolution.* Yardley, PA: Westholme, 2010, 385 pp.

Nagy, John A. *Spies in the Continental Capital: Espionage Across Pennsylvania During the American Revolution.* Yardley, PA: Westholme, 2011, 273 pp.

Nash, Jay Robert. *Spies: A Narrative Encyclopedia of Dirty Deeds and Double Dealing from Biblical Times to Today.* New York: M. Evans, 1997, 624 pp.

Neilson, Keith, and B.J.C. McKercher. *Go Spy the Land: Military Intelligence in History.* Westport, CT: Praeger, 1993, 205 pp.

Nelson, Kay Shaw. *The Cloak and Dagger Cook: A CIA Memoir.* Gretna, LA: Pelican, 2009.

Nelson, Wayne. *A Spy's Diary of World War II: Inside the OSS with an American Agent in Europe.* Jefferson, NC: McFarland, 2009, 204 pp.

Newton, Verne W. *The Cambridge Spies: The Untold Story of Maclean, Philby, and Burgess in America.* Lanham, MD: Madison Books, 1991, 448 pp.

Nicholson, Samuel. "A Most Unlikely Agent: Robert S. Allen." *The Intelligencer: Journal of U.S. Intelligence Studies* 18, no. 1 (Fall–Winter 2010), pp. 35–41.

Nicolai, W. *The German Secret Service.* London: Stanley Paul, 1924, 299 pp.

Occleshaw, Michael. *Armour Against Fate: British Military Intelligence in the First World War.* London: Columbus Books, 1989, 423 pp.

O'Donnell, Patrick K. *They Dared Return: The True Story of Jewish Spies Behind the Lines in Nazi Germany.* Cambridge, MA: Da Capo Press, 2009, 239 pp.

Olive, Ron. *Capturing Jonathan Pollard: How One of the Most Notorious Spies in American History Was Brought to Justice.* Annapolis: U.S. Naval Institute Press, 2006, 299 pp.

Olmsted, Kathryn S. *Red Spy Queen: A Biography of Elizabeth Bentley.* Chapel Hill: University of North Carolina Press, 2002, 268 pp.

Olson, James M. *Fair Play: The Moral Dilemmas of Spying.* Washington, D.C.: Potomac, 2007, 306 pp.

Orlov, Alexander. *Handbook of Intelligence and Guerrilla Warfare.* Ann Arbor: University of Michigan Press, 1965.

Orlov, Alexander. *The March of Time: Reminiscences.* London: St. Ermin's, 2004, 438 pp.

Orlov, Alexander. *The Secret History of Stalin's Crimes.* New York: Random House, 1953, 366 pp.

O'Toole, George. *Encyclopedia of American Intelligence and Espionage.* New York: Facts on File, 1988, 539 pp.

O'Toole, George. *Honorable Treachery: A History of U.S. Intelligence, Espionage, and Covert Action from the American Revolution to the CIA.* New York: Atlantic Monthly, 1991, 591 pp.

Owen, David. *Hidden Secrets: A Complete History of Espionage and the Technology Used to Support It.* Toronto: Firefly Books, 2002, 224 pp.

Pacepa, Ion Mihai. *Red Horizons: Chronicles of a Communist Spy Chief.* Washington, D.C.: Regnery Gateway, 1987, 446 pp.

Page, Bruce, David Leitch, and Phillip Knightley. *The Philby Conspiracy.* New York: Doubleday, 1968, 300 pp.

Paillole, Paul. *Fighting the Nazis: French Intelligence and Counterintelligence 1935–1945.* New York: Enigma, 2003, 492 pp.

Parrish, Michael. *Soviet Security and Intelligence Organizations 1917–1990: A Biographical Dictionary and Review of Literature in English.* Westport, CT: Greenwood, 1992, 669 pp.

Parritt, B.A.H. *The Intelligencers: The Story of British Military Intelligence Up to 1914.* Ashford, Kent: Intelligence Corps Association, 1983, 237 pp.

Paseman, Floyd L. *A Spy's Journey: A CIA Memoir.* St. Paul: Zenith Press, 2004.

Pattinson, Juliette. *Secret War: A Pictorial Record of the Special Operations Executive.* London: Caxton, 2001.

Peake, Hayden B. *The Reader's Guide to Intelligence Periodicals.* Washington, D.C.: NIBC Press, 1992, 250 pp.

Peake, Hayden B., and Samuel Halpern. *In the Name of Intelligence: Essays in Honor of Walter Pforzheimer.* Washington, D.C.: NIBC Press, 1994, 640 pp.

Penkovsky, Oleg. *The Penkovsky Papers.* New York: Ballantine, 1982, 381 pp.

Penrose, Barrie, and Simon Freeman. *Conspiracy of Silence: The Secret Life of Anthony Blunt.* New York: Farrar, Straus and Giroux, 1987, 616 pp.

Perrault, Gilles. *The Red Orchestra: The Anatomy of*

the Most Successful Spy Ring of World War II. New York: Simon & Schuster, 1969, 512 pp.

Perry, Roland. *The Exile Burchett: Reporter of Conflict.* Richmond, Victoria: William Heinemann Australia, 1988, 258 pp.

Perry, Roland. *The Fifth Man.* London: Sidgwick and Jackson, 1994, 486 pp.

Perry, Shirley H. *My Life as a Spy and Other Grand Adventures.* Ashland, OR: Hellgate Press, 2011.

Persico, Joseph E. *Casey: The Lives and Secrets of William J. Casey: From the OSS to the CIA.* New York: Penguin, 1991, 601 pp.

Persico, Joseph E. *Roosevelt's Secret War: FDR and World War II Espionage.* New York: Random House, 2001, 564 pp.

Persico, Joseph E. *Piercing the Reich: The Penetration of Nazi Germany by American Secret Agents During World War II.* New York: Viking, 1979, 376 pp.

Petersen, Neal H. *American Intelligence, 1775–1990: A Bibliographic Guide.* Claremont, CA: Regina Books, 1992, 406 pp.

Petersen, Neal H., ed. *From Hitler's Doorstep: The Wartime Intelligence Reports of Allen Dulles, 1942–1945.* University Park: Pennsylvania State University Press, 1996, 684 pp.

Peterson, Edward N. *The Secret Police and the Revolution: The Fall of the German Democratic Republic.* Westport, CT: Praeger, 2002, 286 pp.

Petrov, Vladimir and Evdokia Petrov. *Empire of Fear.* New York: Praeger, 1956, 351 pp.

Pforzheimer, Walter, ed. *Bibliography of Intelligence Literature.* Washington, D.C.: Defense Intelligence College, 1985, 90 pp.

Philby, Eleanor. *Kim Philby: The Spy I Loved.* London: Hamilton, 1968, 175 pp.

Philby, Kim. *My Silent War.* New York: Grove, 1968, 262 pp.

Philby, Rufina, with Hayden Peake and Mikhail Lyubimov. *The Private Life of Kim Philby: The Moscow Years.* London: St. Ermin, 1999, 449 pp.

Phillips, David Atlee. *The Night Watch.* New York: Atheneum, 1977, 309 pp.

Phillips, David Atlee. *Secret Wars Diary: My Adventures in Combat, Espionage Operations and Covert Action.* Bethesda: Stone Trail Press, 1989, 343 pp.

The Photographic History of the Civil War: Soldier Life and Secret Service. Secaucus: Blue and Grey Press, 1987, 383 pp.

Pincher, Chapman. *Spycatcher Affair.* New York: St. Martin's, 1988.

Pincher, Chapman. *Their Trade Is Treachery.* London: Sidgwick and Jackson, 1981, 240 pp.

Pincher, Chapman. *Too Secret Too Long.* New York: St. Martin's, 1984, 638 pp.

Pinck, Dan C., Geoffrey M.T. Jones, and Charles T. Pinck. *Stalking the History of the Office of Strategic Services: An OSS Bibliography.* Boston: OSS/Donovan Press, 2000, 143 pp.

Pinkerton, Allan. *The Spy of the Rebellion: Being a True History of the Spy System of the United States Army During the Late Rebellion, Revealing Many Secrets of the War Hitherto Not Made Public.* New York: G.W. Carleton, 1883, 688 pp.

Polgar, Thomas. *The KGB: An Instrument of Soviet Power.* McLean, VA: Association of Former Intelligence Officers, 1986, 25 pp.

Polmar, Norman, and Thomas B. Allen. *Spy Book: The Encyclopedia of Espionage.* New York: Random House, 1998, 645 pp.

Popov, Dusko. *Spy CounterSpy: The Autobiography of Dusko Popov.* New York: Grosset and Dunlap, 1974, 339 pp.

Porch, Douglas. *The French Secret Services: From the Dreyfus Affair to the Gulf War.* New York: Farrar, Straus and Giroux, 1995, 623 pp.

Poretsky, Elizabeth K. *Our Own People: A Memoir of "Ignace Reiss" and His Friends.* Ann Arbor: University of Michigan Press, 1969, 278 pp.

Powe, Marc B., and Edward E. Wilson. *The Evolution of American Military Intelligence.* Fort Huachuca, AZ: U.S. Army Intelligence Center and School, 1973, 148 pp.

Powell, Bill. *Treason: How a Russian Spy Led an American Journalist to a U.S. Double Agent.* New York: Simon & Schuster, 2002, 208 pp.

Powers, Thomas. *The Man Who Kept the Secrets: Richard Helms and the CIA.* New York: Knopf, 1979, 393 pp.

Prange, Gordon W., with Donald M. Goldstein and Katherine V. Dillon. *Target Tokyo: The Story of the Sorge Spy Ring.* New York: McGraw-Hill, 1984, 595 pp.

Proctor, Tammy M. *Female Intelligence: Women and Espionage in the First World War.* New York: New York University Press, 2003, 204 pp.

Prunckun, Hank. *Counterintelligence Theory and Practice.* Lanham, MD: Rowman & Littlefield, 2012, 216 pp.

Prunckun, Henry W. *Special Access Required: A Practitioner's Guide to Law Enforcement Intelligence Literature.* Lanham, MD: Scarecrow Press, 1990, 200 pp.

Pujol, Juan, with Nigel West. *Garbo: The Personal Story of the Most Successful Double Agent Ever.* London: Weidenfeld and Nicolson, 1985, 178 pp.

Quigley, Martin. *A U.S. Spy in Ireland: The Truth Behind Irish "Neutrality" During World War II.* Lanham, MD: Roberts Reinhart, 202, 218 pp.

Rado, Sandor. *Codename Dora: The Memoirs of a Russian Spy.* London: Abelard-Schuman, 1977, 298 pp.

Rafalko, Frank J., ed. *A CounterIntelligence Reader: American Revolution to World War II,* vol. I. Washington, D.C.: National Counterintelligence Center, 1998, 202 pp.

Rafalko, Frank J., ed. *A CounterIntelligence Reader:*

Counterintelligence in World War II, vol. II. Washington, D.C.: National Counterintelligence Center, 1998, 243 pp.

Rafalko, Frank J., ed. *A CounterIntelligence Reader: Post World War II, to Closing the 20th Century*, vol. III. Washington, D.C.: National Counterintelligence Center, 1998, 435 pp.

Ranelagh, John. *The Agency*. New York: Simon & Schuster, 1986, 847 pp.

Reinsch, Richard M. *Whittaker Chambers: The Spirit of a Counterrevolutionary*. Wilmington, DE: ISI Books, 2010, 190 pp.

Rennie, James. *The Operators: On The Streets with 14 Company—The Army's Top Secret Elite*. London: Century, 1996, 234 pp.

Reppeto, Thomas A. *Battleground New York City: Countering Spies, Saboteurs, and Terrorists Since 1861*. Washington, D.C.: Potomac , 2012.

Richelson, Jeffrey T. *American Espionage and the Soviet Target*. New York: William Morrow, 1987.

Richelson, Jeffrey T. *A Century of Spies: Intelligence in the Twentieth Century*. New York: Oxford University Press, 1995, 534 pp.

Richelson, Jeffrey T. *Foreign Intelligence Organizations*. Cambridge, MA: Ballinger, 1988, 330 pp.

Richelson, Jeffrey T. *Sword and Shield: Soviet Intelligence and Security Apparatus*. Cambridge, MA: Ballinger, 1986, 279 pp.

Richelson, Jeffrey T. *The U.S. Intelligence Community*. Boulder: Westview, 1999, 526 pp.

Riebling, Mark. *Wedge: The Secret War Between the FBI and CIA*. New York: Knopf, 1994, 563 pp.

Rizzo, John. *Company Man: Thirty Years of Controversy and Crisis in the CIA*. New York: Scribner, 2014, 320 pp.

Robenalt, James David. *The Harding Affair: Love and Espionage During the Great War*. New York: Palgrave Macmillan, 2009, 396 pp.

Roberts, Sam. *The Brother: The Untold Story of Atomic Spy David Greenglass and How He Sent His Sister, Ethel Rosenberg, to the Electric Chair*. New York: Random House, 2001, 543 pp.

Rocca, Raymond G., and John J. Dziak. *Bibliography on Soviet Intelligence and Security Services*. Boulder: Westview, 1985, 203 pp.

Rodriquez, Jose A., and Bill Harlow. *Hard Measures: How Aggressive CIA Actions After 9/11 Saved American Lives*. New York: Threshold Editions, 2012, 368 pp.

Rogers, Leigh Platt. *Sticky Situations: Stories of Childhood Adventures Abroad*. Haverford, PA, 2004, 184 pp.

Romanov, A.I. *The Nights Are Longest There: A Memoir of the Soviet Security Services*. Boston: Little, Brown, 1972, 256 pp.

Romerstein, Herbert, and Eric Breindel. *The Venona Secrets: Exposing Soviet Espionage and America's Traitors*. Washington, D.C.: Regnery, 2001, 400 pp.

Romerstein, Herbert, and Stanislav Levchenko. *The KGB Against the "Main Enemy": How the Soviet Intelligence Service Operates Against the United States*. Lexington, MA: Lexington Books, 1989, 369 pp.

Rose, R.S., and Gordon D. Scott. *Johnny: A Spy's Life*. University Park: Pennsylvania State University Press, 2010, 462 pp.

Rout, Leslie B., Jr., and John F. Bratzel. *The Shadow War: German Espionage and United States Counterespionage in Latin America During World War II*. Frederick, MS: University Publications of America, 1986, 496 pp.

Rowan, Richard Wilmer. *The Story of Secret Service*. Garden City, NY: Doubleday, Doran, 1937, 732 pp.

Rubin, Barry. *Istanbul Intrigues*. New York: McGraw-Hill, 1989, 301 pp.

Sakharov, Vladimir, with Umberto Tosi. *High Treason: Revelations of a Double Agent*. New York: Putnam, 1980, 318 pp.

Sawatsky, John. *For Services Rendered: Leslie James Bennett and the RCMP Security Service*. Toronto: Doubleday Canada, 1982, 339 pp.

Sawatsky, John. *Men in the Shadows: The RCMP Security Service*. Toronto: Doubleday Canada, 1980, 302 pp.

Sayer, Ian, and Douglas Botting. *America's Secret Army: The Untold Story of the Counter Intelligence Corps*. London: Grafton Books, 1989, 400 pp.

Schecter, Jerold L., and Peter S. Deriabin. *The Spy Who Saved the World: How a Soviet Colonel Changed the Course of the Cold War*. New York: Scribner's, 1992, 488 pp.

Schecter, Jerold L., and Leona Schecter. *Sacred Secrets: How Soviet Intelligence Operations Changed American History*. Washington, D.C.: Brassey's, 2002, 402 p.

Schiller, Lawrence. *Into the Mirror: The Life of Master Spy Robert P. Hanssen*. New York: HarperCollins, 2002, 317 pp.

Schwarzwalder, John. *We Caught Spies*. New York: Duell, Sloan and Pearce, 1945, 296 pp.

Seale, Patrick, and Maureen McConville. *Philby: The Long Road to Moscow*. New York: Simon & Schuster, 1973, 282 pp.

Shackley, Theodore. *The Third Option: An American View of Counterinsurgency Operations*. New York: McGraw-Hill, 1981, 185 pp.

Shackley, Theodore, and Richard A. Finney. *Spymaster: My Life in the CIA*. Washington, D.C.: Potomac, 2005, 336 pp.

Shannon, Elaine, and Ann Blackman. *The Spy Next Door: The Extraordinary Secret Life of Robert Philip Hanssen, the Most Damaging FBI Agent in U.S. History*. Boston: Little, Brown, 2002, 247 pp.

Shedlock, Jerzy. "Former JBER Soldier Pleads Guilty

to Attempted Espionage." *Alaska Dispatch,* April 11, 2013.

Sheldon, R.M. *Espionage in the Ancient World: An Annotated Bibliography.* Jefferson, NC: McFarland, 2003, 232 pp.

Shelton, Christina. *Alger Hiss: Why He Chose Treason.* New York: Threshold Editions, 2012, 330 pp.

Sheymov, Victor. *Tower of Secrets: The Inside Story of the Intelligence Coup of the Cold War.* Annapolis: Naval Institute Press, 1993, 416 pp.

Shipley, Peter. *Hostile Action: The KGB and Secret Soviet Operations in Britain.* London: Pinter, 1989, 224 pp.

Shultz, Richard H., and Roy Godson. *Dezinformatsia: Active Measures in Soviet Strategy.* Washington, D.C.: Pergamon-Brassey's, 1984, 210 pp.

Shvets, Yuri B. *Washington Station: My Life as a KGB Spy in America.* New York: Simon & Schuster, 1994, 298 pp.

Smith, Joseph B. *Portrait of a Cold Warrior: Second Thoughts of a Top CIA Agent.* New York: Putnam, 1976.

Smith, Michael. *New Cloak, Old Dagger.* London: Victor Gollancz, 1996, 338 pp.

Smith, Michael. *The Spying Game: The Secret History of British Espionage.* London: Politico's, 2003, 502 pp.

Smith, Myron J., Jr. *The Secret Wars: Volume I, Intelligence, Propaganda and Psychological Warfare, Resistance Movements and Secret Operations, 1939–1945.* Santa Barbara: ABC-CLIO, 1980, 256 pp.

Smith, Myron J., Jr. *The Secret Wars: Volume II, Intelligence, Propaganda and Psychological Warfare, Covert Operations, 1945–1980.* Santa Barbara: ABC-CLIO, 1981, 389 pp.

Smith, Richard Harris. *OSS: The Secret History of America's First Central Intelligence Agency.* New York: Lyons, 2005, 456 pp.

Soldatov, Andrei, and Irina Borogan. *The New Nobility: The Restoration of Russia's Security State and the Enduring Legacy of the KGB.* New York: Public Affairs, 2010.

Srodes, James. *Allen Dulles: Master of Spies.* Washington, D.C.: Regnery, 1999, 624 pp.

Stafford, David. *Camp X: Canada's School for Secret Agents 1941–1945.* Toronto: Lester and Orpen Dennys, 1986, 327 pp.

Stafford, David. *Spies Beneath Berlin.* London: John Murray, 2002, 211 pp.

Stead, Philip John. *Second Bureau.* London: Evans, 1959, 212 pp.

Stephens, R.W.G. *Camp 020: MI5 and the Nazi Spies.* Kew: Public Records Office, 2000, 376 pp.

Stiller, Werner, with Jefferson Adams. *Beyond the Wall: Memoirs of an East and West German Spy.* Washington, D.C.: Brassey's, 1992, 240 pp.

Stober, Dan, and Ian Hoffman. *A Convenient Spy:*

Wen Ho Lee and the Politics of Nuclear Espionage. New York: Simon & Schuster, 2001, 384 pp.

Stout, Mark. "Guide to the Study of Intelligence: Intelligence in World War I: 1914–1918." *Intelligencer: Journal of U.S. Intelligence Studies* 20, no. 3 (Spring–Summer 2014), pp. 35–38.

Straight, Michael. *After Long Silence.* New York: W.W. Norton, 1983, 351 pp.

Sudoplatov, Pavel, and Anatoli Sudoplatov, with Jerrold L. Schecter and Leona P. Schecter. *Special Tasks: The Memoirs of an Unwanted Witness—A Soviet Spymaster.* Boston: Little, Brown, 1994, 509 pp.

Sulick, Michael J. *American Spies: Espionage Against the United States from the Cold War to the Present.* Washington, D.C.: Georgetown University Press, 2013, 384 pp.

Sulick, Michael J. *Spying in America: Espionage from the Revolutionary War to the Dawn of the Cold War.* Washington, D.C.: Georgetown University Press, 2013, 320 pp.

Sullivan, John F. *Of Spies and Lies: A CIA Lie Detector Remembers Vietnam.* Lawrence: University Press of Kansas, 2002, 250 pp.

Summers, Anthony, and Stephen Dorril. *Honeytrap: The Secret Worlds of Stephen Ward.* London: Weidenfeld and Nicolson, 1987, 264 pp.

Suvorov, Viktor. *Inside Soviet Military Intelligence.* New York: Macmillan, 1984, 193 pp.

Tanenhaus, Sam. *Whittaker Chambers: A Biography.* New York: Modern Library, 1998, 656 pp.

Tenet, George J., with William Harlow. *At the Center of the Storm: My Years at the CIA.* New York: Harper, 2007, 576 pp.

Thamm, Gerhardt B. *The Making of a Spy: Memoir of a German Boy Soldier Turned American Army Intelligence Agent.* Jefferson, NC: McFarland, 2010, 223 pp.

Tidwell, William A. *April 65: Confederate Covert Action in the American Civil War.* Kent: Kent State University Press, 1995, 264 pp.

Tidwell, William A. *Come Retribution: The Confederate Secret Service and the Assassination of Lincoln.* Jackson: University Press of Mississippi, 1988, 510 pp.

Tokaev, G.A. *Betrayal of an Ideal.* London: Harvill, 1954, 298 pp.

Tokaev, G.A. *Comrade X.* London: Harvill, 1956, 370 pp.

Trahair, Richard C.S., and Robert L. Miller. *Encyclopedia of Cold War Espionage, Spies, and Secret Operations,* 3d ed. New York: Enigma, 2012, 687 pp.

Troy, Thomas F. *Donovan and the CIA: A History of the Establishment of the Central Intelligence Agency.* Frederick, MD: University Publications of America, 1981, 589 pp.

Trulock, Notra. *Kindred Spirit: Inside the Chinese*

Nuclear Espionage Scandal. San Francisco: Encounter Books, 2003.

Tumanov, Oleg. *Tumanov: Confessions of a KGB Agent.* Chicago: edition q, 1993, 187 pp.

Turner, Stansfield. *Secrecy and Democracy: The CIA in Transition.* Boston: Houghton Mifflin, 1985, 304 pp.

Turrou, Leon G. *Nazi Spies in America.* New York: Random House, 1939, 299 pp.

U.S. Department of Justice, Office of Public Affairs. "U.S. Charges Five Chinese Military Hackers for Cyber Espionage Against U.S. Corporations and a Labor Organization for Commercial Advantage." Press release. Monday, May 19, 2014, http://www.justice.gov/opa/pr/2014/May/14-ag-528.html.

Van Der Rhoer, Edward. *The Shadow Network: Espionage as an Instrument of Soviet Policy.* New York: Scribner, 1983, 359 pp.

Varon, Elizabeth R. *Southern Lady, Yankee Spy: The True Story of Elizabeth Van Lew, a Union Agent in the Heart of the Confederacy.* New York: Oxford University Press, 2003, 336 pp.

Vespa, Amleto. *Secret Agent of Japan.* Boston: Little, Brown, 1938, 301 pp.

Vise, David A. *The Bureau and the Mole: The Unmasking of Robert Philip Hanssen, the Most Dangerous Double Agent in FBI History.* New York: Atlantic Monthly Press, 2002, 272 pp.

Volodarsky, Boris. *The KGB's Poison Factory: From Lenin to Litvinenko.* Minneapolis: Zenith, 2010, 288 pp.

de Vosjoli, Philippe L. Thyraud. *Lamia.* Boston: Little, Brown, 170, 344 pp.

Voska, Victor Emanuel, and Will Irwin. *Spy and CounterSpy.* New York: Doubleday, 1940, 322 pp.

Waagenaar, Sam. *Mata Hari: A Biography.* New York: Appelton-Century, 1965, 305 pp.

Wade, A.G. *Counterspy.* London: Stanley Paul, 1938, 288 pp.

Wakeman, Frederick. *Spymaster: Dai Li and the Chinese Secret Service.* Berkeley: University of California Press, 2003, 650 pp.

Walker, John A., Jr. *My Life as a Spy.* New York: Prometheus, 2008, 350 pp.

Walker, Laura. *Daughter of Deceit: The Human Drama Behind the Walker Spy Case.* Dallas: Word, 1988, 239 pp.

Wallace, Robert, and H. Keith Melton. with Henry Robert Schlesinger. *Spycraft: The Secret History of the CIA's Spytechs from Communism to al-Qaeda.* New York: Dutton, 2008, 549 pp.

Waller, Douglas. *Wild Bill Donovan: The Spymaster Who Created the OSS and Modern American Espionage.* New York: Free Press, 2011, 480 pp.

Waller, John H. *The Unseen War in Europe: Espionage and Conspiracy in the Second World War.* New York: Random House, 1996, 475 pp.

Waller, Michael. *Secret Empire: The KGB in Russia Today.* Boulder: Westview, 1994, 371 pp.

Waste, James. *Don't Shoot the Ice Cream Man: A Cold War Spy in the New World Disorder.* Alta, CA: Ringwalt Press, 2010, 456 pp.

Waters, T. J. *Class 11: My Story Inside the CIA's First Post–9/11 Spy Class.* New York: Plume, 2007, 320 pp.

Watson, Bruce W., Susan M. Watson, and Gerald W. Hopple, eds. *United States Intelligence: An Encyclopedia.* New York: Garland, 1990, 792 pp.

Weber, Ralph. *Spymasters: Ten CIA Officers in Their Own Words.* Wilmington, DE: Scholarly Resources, 1999, 355 pp.

Weiner, Tim, David Johnston, and Neil A. Lewis. *Betrayal: The Story of Aldrich Ames, an American Spy.* New York: Random House, 308 pp.

Weinstein, Allen, and Alexander Vassiliev. *The Haunted Wood: Soviet Espionage in America—The Stalin Era.* New York: Random House, 1999, 402 pp.

Weiser, Benjamin. *A Secret Life: The Polish Officer, His Covert Mission, and the Price He Paid to Save His Country.* New York: Public Affairs, 2004.

Werner, Ruth. *Sonja's Report.* London: Chatto and Windus, 1991, 318 pp.

West, Nigel. *The Circus: MI5 Operations 1945–1972.* New York: Stein and Day, 1983, 196 pp.

West, Nigel. *Counterfeit Spies: Genuine or Bogus? An Astonishing Investigation into Secret Agents of the Secret World War.* London: St. Ermin's, 1998, 308 pp.

West, Nigel. *The Faber Book of Espionage.* London: Faber and Faber, 1993, 610 pp.

West, Nigel. *The Faber Book of Treachery.* London: Faber and Faber, 1995, 442 pp.

West, Nigel. *The Friends: Britain's Post-War Secret Intelligence Operations.* London: Weidenfeld and Nicolson, 1988, 189 pp.

West, Nigel. *Games of Intelligence: The Classified Conflict of International Espionage.* New York: Crown, 1989, 248 pp.

West, Nigel. *Historical Dictionary of Ian Fleming's World of Intelligence: Fact and Fiction.* Lanham, MD: Scarecrow Press, 2010, 272 pp.

West, Nigel. *The Illegals: The Double Lives of the Cold War's Most Secret Agents.* London: Hodder and Stoughton, 1993, 254 pp.

West, Nigel. *MI5: The True Story of the Most Secret Counterespionage Organization in the World.* New York: Stein and Day, 1982, 366 pp.

West, Nigel. *MI6: British Secret Intelligence Service Operations 1909–1945.* New York: Random House, 1983, 266 pp.

West, Nigel. *Molehunt: Searching for Soviet Spies.* New York: Morrow, 1989, 254 pp.

West, Nigel. *Mortal Crimes: The Greatest Theft in*

History: Soviet Penetration of the Manhattan Project. New York: Enigma, 2004, 275 pp.

West, Nigel. *Seven Spies Who Changed the World.* London: Secker and Warburg, 1991, 241 pp.

West, Nigel. *A Thread of Deceit: Espionage Myths of World War II.* New York: Random House, 1985, 166 pp.

West, Nigel. *Venona: The Great Secret of the Cold War.* London: HarperCollins, 1999, 384 pp.

West, Nigel, and Madoc Roberts. *Snow: The Double Life of a World War II Spy.* New York: Biteback, 2011, 272 pp.

West, Nigel, and Oleg Tsarev. *The Crown Jewels: The British Secrets at the Heart of the KGB Archives.* London: HarperCollins, 1998, 366 pp.

West, Rebecca. *The New Meaning of Treason.* New York: Viking, 1964, 374 pp.

West, W.J. *Truth Betrayed.* London: Duckworth, 1987, 262 pp.

Westerfield, H. Bradford, ed. *Inside CIA's Private World: Declassified Articles from the Agency's Internal Journal, 1955–1992.* New Haven: Yale University Press, 1995, 489 pp.

Wheelwright, Julie. *The Fatal Lover: Mata Hari and the Myth of Women in Intelligence.* London: Collins and Brown, 1992.

Whitaker, Reg, and Gary Marcuse. *Cold War Canada: The Making of a National Insecurity State, 1945–1957.* Toronto: University of Toronto Press, 1994, 511 pp.

White, G. Edward. *Alger Hiss's Looking-Glass Wars: The Covert Life of a Soviet Spy.* New York: Oxford University Press, 2004, 320 pp.

Whitehead, Don. *An Agent in Place: The Winnerstrom Affair.* New York: Viking, 1966, 150 pp.

Whiteside, John W., III. *Fool's Mate: A True Story of Espionage at the National Security Agency.* CreateSpace, 2014, 271 pp.

Whitney, Craig R. *Spy Trade: The Darkest Secrets of the Cold War.* New York: Times Books, 1993, 375 pp.

Whittell, Giles. *Bridge of Spies: A True Story of the Cold War.* New York: Broadway, 2010, 274 pp.

Whitwell, John. *British Agent.* London: William Kimber, 1966, 224 pp.

Whymant, Robert. *Stalin's Spy: Richard Sorge and the Tokyo Espionage Ring.* London: I.B. Tauris, 1996, 368 pp.

Winkler, H. Donald. *Stealing Secrets: How a Few Daring Women Deceived Generals, Impacted Battles, and Altered the Course of the Civil War.* Naperville, IL: Cumberland House, 2010, 352 pp.

Wise, David. *Nightmover: How Aldrich Ames Sold the CIA to the KGB for $4.6 Million.* New York: HarperCollins, 1995, 356 pp.

Wise, David. *Molehunt: The Secret Search for Traitors That Shattered the CIA.* New York: Random House, 1992, 309 pp.

Wise, David. *Spy: The Inside Story of How the FBI's Robert Hanssen Betrayed America.* New York: Random House, 2002.

Wise, David. *The Spy Who Got Away: The Inside Story of Edward Lee Howard, the CIA Agent Who Betrayed His Country's Secrets and Escaped to Moscow.* New York: Random House, 1988, 288 pp.

Wise, David. *Tiger Trap: America's Secret Spy War with China.* New York: Houghton Mifflin Harcourt, 2011, 304 pp.

Witcover, Jules. *Sabotage at Black Tom: Imperial Germany's Secret War in America 1914–1917.* Chapel Hill: Algonquin, 1989, 339 pp.

Wolf, Markus, with Anne McElvoy. *Man Without a Face: The Autobiography of Communism's Greatest Spymaster.* New York: Times Books, 1997, 367 pp.

Wolin, Simon, and Robert M. Slusser, eds. *The Soviet Secret Police.* New York: Praeger, 1957, 407 pp.

Womack, Helen. *Undercover Lives: Soviet Spies in the Cities of the World.* London: Weidenfeld and Nicolson, 1998, 307 pp.

Worthington, Peter. *Looking for Trouble: A Journalist's Life … and Then Some.* Toronto: Key Porter Books, 1984, 470 pp.

Wright, E. Lynne. "John Wilkes Booth's Florida Conspirator." Chapter 2, *Speaking Ill of the Dead: Jerks in Florida History.* Guilford, CT: Globe Pequot Press and Morris, 2013, pp. 11–21.

X, Mr., with Bruce Henderson and C.C. Cyr. *Double Eagle: The Autobiography of a Polish Spy Who Defected to the West.* Indianapolis: Bobbs-Merrill, 1979, 227 pp.

Yu, Maochun. *OSS in China: Prelude to Cold War.* New Haven: Yale University Press, 1996, 340 pp.

Zegart, Amy. *Eyes on Spies: Congress and the U.S. Intelligence Community.* Stanford, CA: Hoover Institution Press, 2011, 134 pp.

Web

http://cases.justia.com/us-court-of-appeals/F2/384/554/392676/

http://cicentre.com/Documents/

http://www.dhra.mil/perserec/reports/tr08-05.pdf

http://www.docstoc.com/docs/5794901/A-Counterintelligence-Reader-Volume-3-Table-of-Contents

http://www.eyespymag.com/spylistmain3.htm

http://www.fbi.gov/about-us/investigate/counterintelligence/cases

http://www.hqmc.usmc.mil/PP&O/PS/pss/Espionage_Cases_75-04.pdf

intellit.muskingum.edu/spycases_folder/usother_folder/

www.nacic.gov

http://www.nationalmuseum.af.mil/factsheets/

http://www.ncix.gov/issues/CI_Reader/

www.spymuseum.com/pages/

www.spyschool.com

INDEX

The plethora of references to the Air Force, Army, and Navy in the book would swamp the index. Instead, I have listed the military ranks of individuals mentioned in the index. The index does not cover Appendices A and B, which lists individuals otherwise mentioned herein, nor authors cited in the lists of readings, except for individuals mentioned as topics of the readings. If an organization is more popularly known by its acronym than its complete name, the acronym is listed first.

223